Power, Politics, and the Decline of the Civil Rights Movement

Power, Politics, and the Decline of the Civil Rights Movement

A Fragile Coalition, 1967–1973

CHRISTOPHER P. LEHMAN

PRAEGER

AN IMPRINT OF ABC-CLIO, LLC
Santa Barbara, California • Denver, Colorado • Oxford, England

Library of Congress Cataloging-in-Publication Data

Lehman, Christopher P.
   Power, politics, and the decline of the civil rights movement: a fragile coalition, 1967–1973/Christopher P. Lehman.
        pages cm
   Includes bibliographical references and index.
   ISBN 978-1-4408-3265-9 (acid-free paper)—ISBN 978-1-4408-3266-6 (ebook) 1. Civil rights movements—United States—History—20th century. 2. African Americans—Civil rights—History—20th century. 3. United States—Race relations—History—20th century. I. Title.
E185.61.L512 2014
323.1196′0730904—dc23   2014010447

ISBN: 978-1-4408-3265-9
EISBN: 978-1-4408-3266-6

18 17 16 15 14   1 2 3 4 5

This book is also available on the World Wide Web as an eBook.
Visit www.abc-clio.com for details.

Praeger
An Imprint of ABC-CLIO, LLC

ABC-CLIO, LLC
130 Cremona Drive, P.O. Box 1911
Santa Barbara, California 93116-1911

This book is printed on acid-free paper ∞
Manufactured in the United States of America

Contents

Acknowledgments

I have several people to thank for this writing. For granting interviews and correspondence to me, I thank Juanita Abernathy, Ralph Abernathy III, Beckie Aiken, Jamil Al-Amin, Karma Al-Amin, Fran Beal, Julian Bond, former U.S. representative Bill Clay, Mae Jackson, Christopher Jenks, Wayne Kempton, Lonnie King, Martin Oppenheimer, Gwen Patton, Carlos Richardson, Mario Salas, and Bob Zellner.

Several of my colleagues at St. Cloud State University helped me through the research and writing process. I am grateful to Phil Godding, Jeanne Lacourt, Sharon Cogdill, Judith Kilborn, Lalita Subrahmanyan, and Carol Mohrbacher. I thank my personal friend Sean P. Trende for reading an earlier proposal for the book.

While at the National Endowment for the Humanities Summer Institute at Harvard University's W. E. B. Du Bois Institute in 2011, I received invaluable support and help. I thank the facilitators Henry Louis Gates Jr., Waldo Martin, and Patricia Sullivan; institute lecturers Eric Foner, Martha P. Noonan, Raymond Gavins, Kimberley Phillips, Peniel Joseph, and Gerald Early; and my institute colleagues Karchiek Sims-Alvorado, Chris Bonastia, Mark Burford, Kyle Day, Kwame Dixon, Kathy Forde, Gregory Mixon, Sheila Lloyd, David Lucander, Melissa Stuckey, Carlos Rodriguez, and Alicia Rodriquez.

I extend my thanks to several staffers of libraries. From Harvard, I am grateful to Pam Matz and Gabrielle Lochard of Lamont Library. I thank Kerrie Cotton Williams of the Auburn Avenue Research Library, the staff of Emory University, and Sean Heyliger of the University of Texas at San Antonio.

I am grateful to Sha-Shana Crichton, my literary agent, for her faith in my project.

I thank my family for their support and sacrifice as I worked on my book. And most of all, I thank my wife, Sam.

Introduction: Old and New Movements

The African American struggle for freedom and civil rights has been steadfast since the end of slavery in 1865—through Reconstruction, the advent of Jim Crow, the Harlem Renaissance, World War II, and other events. African Americans had effectively organized and fought for those rights long before the Supreme Court's *Brown v. Board of Education* outlawed public school segregation in 1954 and before the Montgomery bus boycott began in 1955. From the mid-1950s to the mid-1960s, several national civil rights groups—including the National Association for the Advancement of Colored People (NAACP), the National Urban League (NUL), the Congress of Racial Equality (CORE), the Southern Christian Leadership Conference (SCLC), and the Student Nonviolent Coordinating Committee (SNCC)—acted collectively to pursue federal legislation to end segregation and disenfranchisement. Congress legally ended both practices when it passed the Civil Rights Act of 1964 and the Voting Rights Act of 1965, largely because of the efforts of the civil rights coalition.

The Supreme Court reignited a long-dormant public national discourse about African American civil rights on June 25, 2013, when its 5–4 decision rendered unconstitutional Section 4 of the Voting Rights Act of 1965. The section consisted of standards that the federal government used to determine which states required federal oversight of their elections, but the Court's removal of the section also took away that supervision. The Court based its ruling on the section's guidelines having remained unchanged for four decades. "Our country has changed," said Chief Justice John Roberts, "and while any racial discrimination in voting is too much, Congress must ensure that the legislation it passes to remedy that problem speaks to current conditions." In her blistering dissent, Justice Ruth Bader Ginsburg determined that the Court "err[ed] egregiously" in its decision. "Throwing out preclearance when it has worked and is continuing to work to stop discriminatory changes is like throwing away your umbrella in a rainstorm because you are not getting wet," she quipped.[1]

African American political activists John Lewis and Al Sharpton suggested that the civil rights coalition had disappeared after the 1960s, because they called for a new movement that summer. Lewis, who marched in Alabama in the spring of 1965 to dramatize the need for federal oversight of Southern states to prevent segregation at the polls, predicted that the Court's decision would motivate masses of people to demonstrate. "The vote is precious," he reasoned. In July 2013, Sharpton called Florida the "battleground of a new civil rights movement," because a court there had just acquitted George Zimmerman of any crimes for killing unarmed African American teenage boy Trayvon Martin.[2]

At what point between the act's passage and the Court's decision had the civil rights movement disappeared? Almost all of the major national civil rights groups in existence in 1965—the NAACP, SCLC, CORE, and the Urban League—remain in operation as of 2014; only SNCC had disbanded. In addition, the organizations continued to work collectively for several years after Johnson signed the act. In the late 1960s and early 1970s, they resolved initial differences over Black Power and opposition to the Vietnam War. The NAACP, the Urban League, and SCLC quarreled with SNCC chairman Rap Brown's declaration of violence as "necessary" for African Americans in July 1967, but by the 1970s they were publicly questioning if he was right.

The movement increasingly embraced radical and militant positions and people. It denounced the killings of Black Panthers and African American college students by police officers, and it opposed the Nixon White House before the president's first term was halfway over. Civil rights groups also nurtured alliances with Black Power activists such as the Black Panthers and Angela Davis. SCLC championed Davis, and the NAACP led an investigation of a shooting death of a Panther.

In the meantime, the groups divided over the issues of feminism, African American separatism, and political careers for civil rights activists—and the movement could not overcome these differences and its repression by the federal government. Women strengthened their roles in the civil rights struggle while quarreling with the male-dominated movement groups. Women in SNCC caucused among themselves by supporting Angela Davis and prison rights. Coretta Scott King's public popularity rendered her indispensable to

SCLC after her husband's death, much to the chagrin of some SCLC men. As the civil rights coalition unraveled, African Americans' success in electoral politics delivered the death blow to the movement. In the early 1970s, politics was considered "the movement of the seventies," as Atlanta mayor Maynard Jackson put it, and civil rights veterans campaigned for and won public office. By the end of 1973, the movement was no more.[3]

The end of the civil rights movement was a gradual process that extended well beyond the late 1960s. The civil rights groups' individual and collective activities between 1967 and 1973 are part of the story of the country's social, political, and cultural transition from the sixties to the seventies, not unlike the moon landings after Apollo 11 and the war in Vietnam under President Nixon. SCLC's Ralph Abernathy made major news when he attended the Apollo 11 launch, shared a stage with hippie characters from the Broadway musical *Hair*, supported the Black Panthers and Angela Davis, and met with Shirley Chisholm. Figures from the NAACP, the Urban League, and SNCC joined a choir to sing *Hair*'s "Let the Sunshine In" for a national television commercial promoting nonviolence. Civil rights organizations remained socially relevant by lending their activists and resources to more popular causes like Black Power, feminism, and opposition to the Vietnam War. This book—*Power, Politics, and the Decline of the Civil Rights Movement: A Fragile Coalition, 1967–1973*—examines the movement's activities in its waning years.

CHAPTER 1

Violence Is Necessary

Nineteen sixty-seven marked Roy Wilkins's forty-fifth year in the NAACP. During his membership he remained a steadfast devotee of the organization's practices and beliefs. In 1955, upon becoming the executive director, he retained the group's lawyers, who had just successfully convinced the Supreme Court to call segregated public schools unconstitutional the previous year. Wilkins also continued the NAACP's longtime publicizing of vigilante killings of African Americans when he condemned the lynching of Emmett Till. "They had to prove they were superior," Wilkins noted with sarcasm in one of his first public addresses as executive director. "They had to prove it by taking away a fourteen-year-old boy. You know it's in the virus, it's in the blood of the Mississippian. He can't help it."[1]

Most importantly, Wilkins maintained the organization's opposition to separatism according to skin color. Ever since its founding in 1909, the NAACP had been an integrated organization that worked to integrate African Americans into American society. To the group, separatism endangered African American progress. As a result, the NAACP fought segregation by European Americans and disapproved of any efforts to convince African Americans to isolate themselves from European Americans and their institutions. The NAACP had rebuked all separatists, whether the Ku Klux Klan worked to organize European Americans or Marcus Garvey mobilized African Americans.

During Wilkins's tenure as executive director, one of his officials committed two grave sins against the NAACP. In 1959, Robert F. Williams led a branch of the group in Monroe, North Carolina—a city thoroughly segregated and rife with violence against African Americans. He advocated that African Americans separate themselves *and* lynch European Americans. Wilkins confronted Williams about the remarks, and the latter stood by what he had said. The director then suspended Williams because the NAACP could not fight against the lynching of one ethnic group while appearing to endorse the lynching of another. The organization had to remain lawful, at least where lynching was concerned.

On the other hand, Wilkins had no qualms about the civil disobedience that African American college students nationwide were practicing in the winter and spring of 1960. After all, the adolescents and young adults conducting sit-ins at lunch counters did exactly what student members of the NAACP had done since the 1940s. Wilkins could not understand why these students in 1960 managed to spark a nationwide trend, but he welcomed it just the same. He credited the young activists for giving ethnic relations "a fresh and dynamic turn." On behalf of older generations, he expressed solidarity with and empathy to the newcomers. "These Negro young people are right," he declared. "They know about going to the back door, using the freight elevator, riding in the rear of the bus, living on dirt streets, forgetting about election day, being thankful for food and shelter on a farm—and no cash. They know about the insults, the beatings, the whippings, the killings." He claimed that they held the fate of the country in their hands, patriotically predicting, "As these young Negro students recover their freedom, they will be recovering America's also." He then offered gratitude: "We owe them and their white student cooperators a debt for rearming our spirits and renewing our strength."[2]

Wilkins felt such a strong kinship toward the students that he was insulted when he perceived that Martin Luther King Jr., of the SCLC discouraged the young activists from associating with the NAACP. The SCLC called sit-in students to a conference at Shaw University in North Carolina in April, and King congratulated them for "moving away from tactics which are suitable merely for gradual and long-term change." Although Wilkins admired the SCLC leader's approach of overwhelming segregationists with love, he advocated self-defense for African Americans. He took no offense at King's preaching of nonviolence to the students, but he bristled at the suggestion that the NAACP preferred slow progress and told King so.[3]

During the conference, the students followed the advice of longtime civil rights activist Ella Baker, who told them not to become a youth faction of either the NAACP or the SCLC. She wanted them to form their own organization and to give each member equal power in the group, so that it would not give one person a monopoly of power. Moreover, such a democratic organization would reduce the chances of sexism restricting its female participants—a fate Baker had suffered in both the NAACP and SCLC. The new group christened itself the SNCC, but the other organizations still offered support to SNCC in its formative years. The NAACP's lawyers lent their services to students who were jailed for sit-ins, and SCLC members joined the students for some of the sit-ins.[4]

The protests from the civil rights groups displeased the federal government. The White House pleaded with activists to adopt a "go slow" approach and to refrain from asking for too much at too rapid a pace. The activists often countered that they wanted the protection of rights that the government had promised to African Americans through the Fourteenth and Fifteenth Amendments back in the 1860s. To them, over 90 years of waiting was slow enough. The movement and elected officials frequently arrived at this impasse for the next few years. The federal government eventually yielded on illegalizing Jim Crow through the Civil Rights Act of 1964 and voter discrimination through the Voting Rights Act of 1965.

Suddenly, in 1966, SNCC's introduction of Black Power into the civil rights movement shook the tenuous consensus the organizations had maintained over the years. SNCC associates like Stokely Carmichael argued for African Americans to hold public offices in places where they comprised the majority of the population, such as counties and cities in the South. The CORE, an integrated and pacifist civil rights group, endorsed the phrase. King said in a press conference that he opposed the words but supported their underlying message. "I believe we cannot abandon militancy in the effort to disassociate ourselves from riot," he advised. Whitney Young, director of the NUL since 1961, similarly dismissed the slogan as vague and not worth discussing while violent, impoverished cities needed more tangible help than two mere words.[5]

Wilkins, meanwhile, condemned Black Power full stop. To him, it was the latest manifestation of the skin-color separatism he had long opposed. Pulling no punches, he called Black Power "a reverse Mississippi, a reverse Hitler, a reverse Ku Klux Klan." He removed the NAACP from a planned joint march in Mississippi with SCLC, SNCC, and CORE when Carmichael revealed his plans to launch the slogan at the demonstration. Speaking against Black Power became Wilkins's major cause for the remainder of the year. Every issue of the NAACP's monthly magazine *The Crisis* criticized either the slogan or Stokely Carmichael from June to December 1966. The June issue called the phrase a "polarizing" concept like "white supremacy," and in December the periodical reported NAACP–Iowa's denouncing of racism, "whether it was 'black power or white.'"[6]

The Vietnam War further split the movement. Wilkins and Young chose to focus on domestic concerns and not criticize President Lyndon Johnson's policy on the war. They applied their concerns of integration and equality to the African Americans fighting overseas. *The Crisis* beamed in December 1966, "Integration in the Armed Forces—a longtime goal of the NAACP—has come to fruition in the war in Vietnam." When Young visited South Vietnam in 1966 and 1967, he reported almost exclusively on the treatment of African American servicemen by the military. His findings resembled the NAACP's assessment about the integration of troops abroad but acknowledged segregation among high-ranked positions and during the soldiers' leisure time.[7]

In contrast, SNCC and SCLC publicly opposed the conflict—the former officially condemning it in January 1966 and the latter in April 1967. Civil rights leaders then confronted each other about the war throughout the spring of 1967. King told Young to take a stand, but Young warned King about jeopardizing the movement's access to the White House. The NUL leader professed faith in Johnson's ability to afford to fight the Vietnamese abroad and address poverty at home. Meanwhile, in the April 1967 issue of *The Crisis*, the NAACP issued its statement of neutrality. "We are not a peace organization, nor a foreign policy association," the group stated. "We are a civil rights organization." The NAACP decided to let "dedicated organizations whose No. 1 task is to work for peace" address the war.[8]

The civil rights coalition also unraveled over its basic principles. Young militant activists stopped practicing nonviolence due to its failure to help bring African American poverty and repression to an end. They also questioned the movement's goal of integration, and SNCC became an exclusively African American organization by the spring of 1967. Meanwhile, the federal government lost its tolerance of civil rights activism and failed to produce new civil rights laws. But public officials could not ignore civil rights demonstrations forever. Something had to give.[9]

Maryland was an unlikely state to break the stalemate. The state had rarely captured the nation's attention on civil rights throughout the 1960s, hiding in newspapers' back pages behind front-page stories of demonstrations in "Deep South" states like Alabama and Mississippi. Yet ethnic tension was alive and well there, and Cambridge, Maryland, became a national civil rights flashpoint in 1963. SNCC students had come into the city to help organize residents, especially in the largely African American Second Ward, to conduct sit-in demonstrations against the segregated conditions there. Cambridge was so segregated that even the very street that divided the residents was called Race Street. Tensions escalated when police officers beat teenaged demonstrators they had arrested. When a woman went door-to-door to tell African American residents about the violence, they swarmed to the jail with their weapons. The mayor called in the National Guard to monitor the African Americans.

An African American local activist in her forties named Gloria Dandridge worked hard to keep the city from erupting into a riot. Cambridge remained quiet that summer, but persistent inequality led activists to resume protests in early 1964. Two-thirds of the Second Ward households had incomes below $3,000, and three-fifths of them lacked hot water. Almost one-third of the residents were unemployed, but one-third of the employed worked for barely half a year. Demonstrators picketed the offices of the Welfare Board and the State Unemployment Security Commission in February, and by June the federal government was ready to provide on-the-job training for up to 200 African Americans there. Dandridge did not know if the solution provided sufficient relief for them. "You have a segment of Negroes who are getting tired of nonviolence," she warned, "and they are beginning to break out."[10]

Dandridge left the city that year and later married, but she remained deeply concerned about the Second Ward and wanted someone prominent in the movement to go there and speak to the residents. Three years later she reacquainted herself with a civil rights worker who, at 19 years old, had worked for her in Cambridge in 1963 in the organization she had cofounded—the Cambridge Nonviolent Action Committee. He had since relocated to New York, but she invited him to return to Cambridge on July 24, 1967, to speak in the Second Ward. Her former protégé—a man named Hubert Gerold Brown—accepted.[11]

Brown was part of a generation of Americans who lived through several wars before the age of 30. He was born in 1943, during World War II. In his first years at elementary school, the Korean conflict took place. He spent his entire childhood in the segregated South—a region where European Americans had waged a violent sociopolitical conflict against African Americans like himself. The threat of the military draft loomed over Brown's young adulthood as President Lyndon Johnson escalated the number of military forces in South Vietnam. Although many Americans saw the first two decades after the end of World War II as "peacetime," the threat and reality of lynching in several communities across the United States for disobeying Jim Crow's rules kept many African Americans like Brown in a never-ending state of war.

In the summer of 1967, however, he was less concerned about those wars than about how to address the urban uprisings by his fellow African Americans across the country. With four years of experience in political activism, Brown at age 23 was now well equipped to mobilize masses of people to demonstrate for changes they sought in their communities. Sporting an

Afro and a droopy mustache and often wearing sunglasses, his appearance ran counter to the standard close-cut hairstyles and clean-shaven look that middle-class and upper-class African American men had adopted by the end of World War II. His look, however, reflected that the United States had long rejected him as a citizen and that, as a result, he now considered himself in opposition to mainstream America.

On the other hand, Brown had been, in some respects, an all-American boy from Baton Rouge, Louisiana. He lived in a middle-class neighborhood with other members of his ethnic group. He joined the Cub Scouts in elementary school and played fourth-string quarterback for his high school football team. An excellent student, he graduated one year ahead of his class and entered Southern University at age 15. While there he studied sociology, philosophy, and chemistry.

Like other Southern boys of that era, Brown was familiar with guns. His father, a laborer at an Esso Standard Oil refinery, enjoyed hunting in his spare time. Brown learned about firearms in a more formal manner—through his membership in the Reserve Officers' Training Corps (ROTC) of Southern University. He eventually became a member of the Pershing Rifle drill team. On a university campus and among his peers, his training for gun usage was not unusual.[12]

Nevertheless, Brown was African American, and in those days mainstream America did not publicly discuss African Americans arming themselves for domestic self-defense. Newspaper readers and television viewers across the country had become conditioned to see African Americans as people willing to take blows and shots to their bodies and firebombs to their houses without armed retaliation in order to be free. Martin Luther King Jr., who had first come to national prominence while leading the Montgomery bus boycott in 1955 and 1956, was the nation's most visible apostle of nonviolence by the 1960s. His famous "I Have a Dream" speech at the March on Washington in 1963 and his Nobel Peace Prize the following year enhanced his celebrity. If the SNCC students wanted to march with King and benefit from the publicity he fostered, they had to support nonviolence, and they did. The other civil rights groups also tolerated it—at least, for a while.

Meanwhile, SNCC's new ideas slowly gained momentum. In the summer of 1967, 400 people attended a Black Power conference in Newark, New Jersey. During the four-day gathering from July 20 to July 23, the facilitators banned European Americans from attending, which allowed African American activists to discuss social, political, and economic issues among themselves. The participants collectively displayed a wide array of opinions on Black Power. Some of the attendees were movement activists trying to apply the concept to integrationist struggle, but others were nationalists wanting nothing of integration and advocating that only African Americans fight for their own rights. Whatever their disagreements, the attendees sat together and formed a collective body when addressing European American reporters outside the proceedings. At this meeting, Dandridge caught up with Brown and invited him to Cambridge.[13]

Not everyone welcomed his homecoming. To the Maryland State Police, Brown's impending arrival was bad news. After learning on July 21 about the invitation, the force took action as if readying the state for a foreign invasion. State officers began meeting over the next three days with the National Guard and the Cambridge Police to prepare for his speech. The city police ordered the removal and locking away of all guns and ammunition in local stores. On the day of the speech, the city's police chief, Brice Kinnamon, bought a 45-70 caliber rifle and ammunition and kept it in his office. By 7:45 p.m., city-level and state-level officers and the National Guard had arrived to the office, too. If they could help it, the destructive and deadly urban insurrections by young African Americans earlier that week in both Newark and Detroit would not come to Cambridge, too.[14]

Still, no one had any reason to expect any bombast from the SNCC activist himself. He had just started serving as chairman of the organization two months earlier. His debut press conference had been uneventful. His predecessor in the position, Stokely Carmichael, had joined him at the conference and stolen some of the spotlight by egging on the reporters. However, Brown had not provided inflammatory comments for the press as he spoke, thus leaving some journalists to conclude that perhaps the new leader would be more sedate than Carmichael. Only those who worked with him in SNCC knew of his talent for humorous, clever wordplay in his rhetoric, and they nicknamed him "Rap" because of it. They approved of his chairmanship as much for his calm demeanor as for his long, consistent commitment to civil rights work, and they hoped that he would keep the press from reporting inflammatory rhetoric from SNCC.[15]

In Cambridge's Second Ward, about 350 people gathered to hear Brown speak. He inadvertently kept the audience waiting for over an hour because he missed his bus. Still, they waited patiently for him. Meanwhile, Chief Kinnamon dispatched the five African American officers of his police force into the crowd, and a reporter was at the ready to record the speech for the officers gathered back at the city's police headquarters. Finally, at 9:00 p.m. Brown climbed atop a car, stood up, and addressed the crowd. The spectators circled around him. Was he going to speak about Black Power? After all, Carmichael talked about that constantly. Was Brown going to call European Americans "honkies" like Carmichael did? Was he going to shout? Was he going to raise his fist? If the onlookers were expecting a militant speech, Brown did not disappoint them. However, his rhetoric was of a different kind of militancy than his predecessor's.[16]

Brown used the occasion to rally the Second Ward to armed rebellion on the basis of skin color. He started by reminding the spectators of the recent disturbances in Detroit, Newark, and Harlem. Then he announced, "It's time for Cambridge to explode, baby," explaining that European Americans were out to get African Americans. "When the Klan gets together to kill a nigger, they just kill anyone they see walking down the street," he reasoned. "And the Klan thinks like white folk in America, brother."[17] His remarks reflected SNCC's new state as an exclusively African American organization. Only seven months earlier, African American participants had requested that their European American colleagues leave SNCC to organize with people of their own skin color. When the organization had been integrated, Brown's public conflating of European Americans with the Ku Klux Klan would have been unthinkable and would have undermined SNCC's previous goal of changing the nation into an integrated "beloved community." Now, speaking to an African American audience, Brown had no inclination to temper his references to European Americans.[18]

The SNCC leader also assured the crowd that they could accomplish an uprising in Cambridge. As someone who had served in ROTC and on a drill team, the SNCC chairman knew of what he was speaking when it came to tactically using firearms. "I know who my enemy is, and I know how to kill him," he bantered. "No one has to tell me when or how to kill my enemy." He told them that the city had enough people to conduct a successful rebellion. "You don't have to have a big group to do it, brothers. In a town this size, three men can burn it down. That's what they call guerilla warfare," he explained.[19]

Brown expressed surprise that Cambridge was not one of the cities that had already gone up in smoke over the past few hot urban summers. After scolding his listeners for not having burned it down earlier, he offered the collective history of slavery and segregation as the rationale for African Americans to torch the city. "This ain't no riot, brother," he clarified. "This is a rebellion, and we got 400 years of reason to tear this town apart." Moreover, Brown saw no likely help toward ending oppression in Cambridge from the city's African American police officers. "They ain't nothing but niggers," he sneered. "All you got is 5 nigger cops [out of 21 officers], and they ain't even working for you." He then vowed historical vengeance: "When I get mad, I'm going out and look for a honky, and I'm going to take out 400 years' worth of dues on him."[20]

After 45 minutes he was finished. Nothing happened in Cambridge right away, but the reporter who had recorded the speech rushed to Chief Kinnamon's office to play it for the officers gathered there. Meanwhile, Brown went to a local movement office, where people were milling about and chatting. After a few minutes, he left to walk home an African American girl who was intimidated by the police officers who flanked Race Street. A crowd followed the girl and Brown, but he was annoyed because he did not want to draw further attention to himself. The followers were peaceful, content to trail behind their charismatic guest and head to wherever he was going.

The police, in contrast, reacted violently upon seeing Brown in front of a large African American mass appearing to approach the "white" side of Cambridge. When the crowd was halfway down the city's color line, a deputy sheriff stationed fired a shotgun twice—hitting Brown in the neck. The firing by the officers continued for the next five minutes, and the crowd fled to nearby Pine Street. Four European American adolescents drove up and down that street in a compact car, either shooting guns or throwing firecrackers from the car windows. The crowd begged the African American officers to stop the car, but they responded that they could not. The people in the car were European American, and Cambridge Police allowed its African American officers to arrest only those of their own ethnic group.[21]

Then the city became quiet again. A resident took Brown into his house, kept the SNCC leader's neck from bleeding any further, and escorted him to a nearby doctor. After receiving a shot from the physician, the SNCC chairman returned to the streets and told some African American men not to fire at each other. Then, he left the Second Ward. Despite the disturbance caused by the police, the residents of the ward still did not appear to be taking Brown's remarks to heart. After all, the firing of gunshots and a police officer's shooting could have happened in any city, and sporadic sounds of gunfire hardly constituted anything near a "rebellion."[22]

Shortly after midnight, new events developed that worsened the city's interethnic tensions. A police officer responding to a call at a vandalized laundry was hit by pellets to the face, arms, and hand. The young African Americans who shot him had thought that the police car was about to open fire on them. At that, police city and state officials decided to seal off the Second Ward in order to contain the violence there. That decision, in turn, sealed the fate of an abandoned building that had once served as an important community resource. Around 2:00 a.m., the ward's Pine Street Elementary School was afire. Ninety minutes later firefighters arrived but did not immediately confront the blaze. Chief Kinnamon did not initially allow the firemen to go into the Second Ward. He feared for their safety because one of his officers had already been shot. His caution, however, let the fire spread beyond the school. Sixteen other buildings had burned down before dawn, when the firefighters extinguished the inferno. The casualties were minimal; Brown and four others were injured, and the SNCC chairman felt well enough to leave the city. In the meantime, at least 600 National Guardsmen arrived to occupy Cambridge.[23]

Local citizens were outraged by the initial lack of response to their pleas for help. Regardless of how they had initially received Brown's remarks, they now seemed to agree with his comments about the government's lack of interest in protecting African Americans, especially in the context of the fire. Moreover, some residents were convinced that city officials had enjoyed witnessing the ward's destruction. "One little lousy truck could have easily put it out," lamented a resident. "That was their way of getting revenge. They just let the place burn down," said another. Chief Kinnamon had reportedly told one community leader at the scene, "You goddam niggers started this fire, now you goddam niggers watch it burn."[24]

Compared to uprisings in other cities earlier that month, Cambridge arguably experienced the least traumatic of them. During the previous week, the insurrection in Newark had lasted for five days and killed 26 people. Two days before the disturbance in Cambridge, Detroit's uprising had begun and did not end until four days after Cambridge's fires were extinguished. Forty-three people died in the Motor City's rebellion. Remarkably, nobody died as a result of the violence and arson of July 24 and 25 in Cambridge. As a result, newspapers gave the events there considerably less coverage than in Detroit.

Republican Maryland governor Spiro Agnew, however, was not happy. A "race riot" had taken place on his watch, and his placing of 600 guardsmen in Cambridge to calm the African Americans compromised his reputation as a "moderate" on civil rights. He was also livid that someone from out of state had come into his state, made incendiary comments, and then left the state as listeners violently acted upon the comments. For the next few weeks, the governor played to office visitors a recording of Brown's speech, agitatedly pacing the floor and complaining, "Listen to that. Isn't that incitement? Isn't it?" When playing the tape for local African American activists visiting his office, he expected them to share his frustration at the destruction of not only the buildings but also his administration's progress on civil rights. Instead, to Agnew's surprise and dismay, they respected Brown's good intentions while disagreeing with his rhetoric. The governor never forgot the permissiveness of the local leaders but decided to wait until another time to publicly address it.[25]

Agnew believed in the sanctity of the laws of the United States. As the Baltimore County executive, he enforced the law on a county level from

1963 to 1967, which included working to desegregate public facilities in the county. In July 1963, he conducted negotiations by telephone between the owners of a segregated amusement park in Towson and local civil rights leaders to open the park to African Americans. In this regard, he took "All men are created equal" to include African Americans. On the other hand, he did not tolerate disobedience of the law, even as a means of addressing inequality. When he became Maryland's governor in January 1967 at age 48, he brought his ideas about equality under the law with him to that office.[26]

While touring the ruins of Cambridge on July 25, Agnew decided to make Brown an antagonist in the media's civil rights narrative. As reporters followed him, he stated that he found the chairman's words "entirely reprehensible and criminal" and considered him "guilty of breaking the law." Blaming the SNCC leader's "inflammatory statements" for the violence at Cambridge, the governor snarled, "I hope they pick him up soon, put him away, and throw away the key. Such a person cannot be permitted to enter a state with the intention to destroy and then sneak away leaving these poor people with the results of his evil scheme." Agnew also called him a "rabble-rouser" and a "professional agitator."[27]

Agnew's remarks at this point constituted a radical departure from earlier condemnations of civil rights activists by public officials. In public addresses and press conferences over the past few years, governors and sheriffs had blamed King and SNCC for coming into communities and arousing the anger of European Americans. To the officials, the movement's outside agitators did not understand the ethnic relations of the communities they invaded. The officials' harangues against the demonstrators rarely included entreaties for the European Americans to stop being violent, but then again the point of their comments was to present a movement figure as an antagonist offensively attacking the South's "way of life." Agnew, on the other hand, portrayed Brown as a different kind of outside agitator. The SNCC chairman was coming into communities and arousing African American anger instead of European American ire. That development made Brown more dangerous than both the nonviolent King and even the African American rioters themselves.

More importantly, Agnew used Brown to tie the civil rights movement to the urban uprisings and, by extension, to violence. Until then, politicians and the media had treated urban disturbances as a separate phenomenon from the movement. Reporters often asked movement leaders for advice about why people were rebelling and what could be done about it. But they had not blamed the leaders for the unrest. In contrast, Agnew identified a movement figure as the cause of a "riot." As the appeal of nonviolent confrontation lessened among young African Americans and insurrections continued, the governor's connection of the movement to violence proved tough for the activists to sever.

In addition, Agnew's personal image turned SNCC's old media narrative strategy of visual contrasts on its head. When the organization's students had conducted its first sit-ins in 1960, they had dressed formally to play against the usually unkempt mobs of people who attacked them at the places where they demonstrated. They had won the sympathy of liberals and conservatives alike by fostering an appearance of calm and respectable collective protagonists with their suits and ties and Sunday dresses. But as members of the group later decided to go into rural areas for voter registration drives, they wore denim clothing in order to better relate to the African American local peasantry they encountered. By 1967 they were also wearing Afro hairstyles and sunglasses, and Brown often had a toothpick jutting from his mouth. The governor, on the other hand, dressed in the conservative manner that SNCC had originally embraced, but painstakingly so. Now it was his turn to play the well-dressed protagonist facing the unkempt "rabble-rousers," and he played it to the hilt. He exemplified what *Time* magazine called the "strained perfectionism" of "the corporation lawyer look—three-piece Yale-gray suits, white shirts and club ties." An image consultant once remarked of him, "Every hair is in place on that man." Agnew indeed left no stone unturned, according to the consultant: "He always buttons his buttons."[28]

Completely neglecting to discuss the people who had done the actual violence of the previous night, Governor Agnew zeroed in on Brown when he announced that he had directed the authorities to find Brown and bring him to trial. In the process of painting the activist as an antagonist, the governor flirted dangerously with vigilantism. His comments implied Brown's guilt, thus making Agnew look as much like a judge or jury as a governor. As a result, he jeopardized the leader's chances of receiving a fair and impartial trial. In addition, the governor's accusations were ironic, considering that he had made his living as a practicing lawyer before entering politics. Whether he knew the law and did not care about the possibility of prejudicing the State of Maryland with his remarks, or whether he honestly thought Brown's guilt was a fait accompli simply because Agnew had said so as governor, his pursuit of the SNCC chairman now started to take on an extralegal quality.

Local African Americans disapproved of Agnew's handling of the Cambridge uprising. Some people did not like that he had sent 600 guardsmen to the city, especially considering the minimal damage and violence. Other people considered his campaign against Brown excessive. At least one person thought the Republican official's response was a long-term political ploy. Baltimore activist Walter Lively accused Agnew of using the amount of force he had because of his interest in "seeking a national position in the Republican Party and pushing for the vice presidency" in the next year's election. At the time the idea was not widely circulated, because Agnew was only in office for half a year; his anti-Brown comments came six months to the day after his inauguration. As a result, a shot at a national office so early in his gubernatorial tenure was highly unlikely.[29]

Even after the Federal Bureau of Investigation (FBI) arrested the activist in Virginia on July 26, the governor continued to exaggerate Brown's criminality. At a news conference that same day, he did admit that his "lock him up and throw away the key" remark was a "visceral reaction," and he proceeded to discuss Brown's rights as if shocked at having to do so. Even then, however, his retraction sounded extralegal. "Obviously, I think anybody who's accused of a crime is entitled to the full protection of the law, a fair trial, and a fair punishment," he said while omitting that someone accused had to first be found guilty before receiving any punishment. He then proceeded to publicly condemn Brown anyway for the second day in a row, thus negating his acknowledgment of the SNCC leader's rights. "Well, we are going to prosecute him," the governor proclaimed, using first-person plural pronouns when speaking on behalf of the state of Maryland. "Obviously he is in our opinion guilty of breaking the law, and he has to be prosecuted and he should be punished."[30]

Agnew then discussed the activist's lack of self-control. He made a point of saying that some participants in the movement were "lenient," "intelligent," and "very well motivated," and that they acted "with restraint." To him, Brown did not fit that categorization. The SNCC chairman, for example, was not fair in his analysis of prominent national figures, according to the governor. Brown called George Washington a slaveholder, which he was, and opined that Abraham Lincoln really did not care about African Americans. Agnew also referred to Brown's "characterization of the President of the United States as some honky" as evidence of the activist's lack of both objectivity and restraint. By doing so, the governor conflated rhetoric of incitement with rhetoric of antipatriotism, as if calling presidents "slaveholders" and "honkies" caused African Americans to burn and vandalize buildings as much as saying, "It's time for Cambridge to explode" did. Agnew was charting new territory among public officials by making this claim about a movement figure and by mentioning the word "honky" in a gubernatorial news conference.[31]

Authorities arrested Brown in Virginia that same day for avoiding prosecution in Maryland for inciting a riot. However, the governor's tough talk against the SNCC leader only inspired the "irresponsible militant" to talk tougher. Upon his release from jail on July 27 on a $10,000 bond, he held a press conference and proceeded to denigrate the positions and rhetoric of his fellow civil rights leaders. Dressed in the usual SNCC denim and sporting a bandage on his forehead, he repudiated nonviolence and called King, Wilkins, and Young "morally wrong" for encouraging it. "You can't be nonviolent with a wild mad dog," Brown observed. "You'd better get rid of them." He also deviated from standard movement protocol with an ad-hominem attack on the president. "Lyndon Johnson is a wild mad dog," he said, suggesting that Johnson was the dog to "get rid of."[32]

"I say violence is necessary," Brown announced. Then, the rationale he gave for this observation became his most famous—or infamous—quote and shaped the next six years of public discussion about American social upheaval: "Violence is part of America's culture and is as American as cherry pie."[33]

The flavor he identified was certainly unusual. By then the phrase "as American as apple pie" was part of the national lexicon. Still, Brown had his reasons for choosing the cherry. To him that particular fruit symbolized the United States because of an old tale involving the first U.S. president. In the story a boy named George Washington had chopped down a cherry tree and, when confronted about the incident, declared, "I cannot tell a lie." If Washington made the cherry a part of Americana, then cherry pie was American by extension. Thus, Brown identified both cherry pie and violence as national symbols and connected them to each other, because he figured that no one would ever denounce George Washington.[34]

At least one person disagreed, however. For the governor, this statement was just too much. Agnew evolved from condemning to unforgiving towards Brown after those remarks. Speaking at Friendship International Airport three days later, he considered the SNCC chairman as much of a national threat as the Viet Cong. "Our country is as much threatened by the lawless rioting in our streets as it is by our enemies abroad," he observed. However, he empathized with the rioters themselves by relating to their frustration. He acknowledged that persistent discrimination, poor conditions in ghettoes, and unequal opportunities in education and employment and housing provided enough frustration for African Americans to revolt. He also noted that recent progress that African Americans had made did not sufficiently address the problems. Curiously, the act of rioting elicited more sympathy from the governor than the act of telling people to riot.[35]

Agnew then introduced the concept of the "responsible militant"—a "divide-and-conquer" attempt to distinguish constructive civil rights activists from destructive ones. "I believe that responsible militants within the Negro leadership should use every means available to place legitimate pressure on those in authority to break the senseless and artificial barriers of racial discrimination," he said. Listing specifically whom he would accept as "responsible," he continued, "The problem-solving must be done by constructive militants such as the [Roy] Wilkinses, [Martin Luther] Kings, [Whitney] Youngs, and [A. Philip] Randolphs—not by the [Stokely] Carmichaels, [LeRoi] Joneses and [H. Rap] Browns." In case anyone construed that he only wanted middle-aged activists, he promised to welcome contributions from "younger responsible leadership." However, he stressed, "Responsibility is the yardstick."[36]

After reminding people somewhat condescendingly that "there are proper ways to protest, and they must be used," the governor announced Maryland's new policy "to immediately arrest any person inciting to riot and to not allow that person to finish his vicious speech." He promised a strong and quick prosecution of anyone accused of violating that law, and he banned the accused from ever discussing problems with him concerning African Americans. "The violent cannot be allowed to sneak unnoticed from the war dance to the problem-solving meeting," he explained. He would only listen to "those who shun lawlessness, who win their places at the conference table by leadership that builds rather than destroys"—in other words, "responsible militants."[37]

In the White House—only 90 miles from Cambridge—President Lyndon Johnson publicly responded to the summer's uprisings through statements. On July 27, he signed a proclamation declaring July 30 a National Day of Prayer and Reconciliation. He wrote of the need for U.S. citizens to "pray for peace in the land we love." He also indirectly referred to the SNCC chairman's rhetoric by saying, "We deplore the few who rely upon words and works of terror." The statement was a new direction for Johnson, who had never, in all of his previous years in office during civil rights demonstrations and summers of burning cities, paid attention to "words of terror."[38]

That same day he orally repeated his point in an address to the nation. "The apostles of violence, with their ugly drumbeat of hatred, must know that they are now heading for ruin and disaster," he warned. Still, he did not merely condemn Brown but also wanted to understand why the uprisings he blamed on "apostles" like Brown were taking place. In that same speech, he announced the creation of the National Advisory Commission on Civil Disorders. Among the African American members he appointed to it included Roy Wilkins of the NAACP and Massachusetts Senator Edward Brooke.[39]

Reporters immediately seized upon the absence of spokespeople with militant rhetoric like Brown and Carmichael from the president's commission.

They asked Johnson why the "more militant Negro point of view" had no representatives on it. He gave the diplomatic response of having chosen "the people who we think will be best on the commission." He elaborated on the criteria, "We tried to select men and women of experience, ability, and judgment whom we felt could consider all the evidence and make a judicious finding." Then, coining a new word, he continued, "We didn't consider them from the standpoint of militancy or *antimilitancy*." He was not as abrasive as Agnew when addressing Brown, but he did follow Agnew's precedent in keeping the SNCC leader and his ilk from the discussion table on civil rights. Although not a national figure, the governor had already started to influence national politics.[40]

Privately, the president shared Agnew's anger and sense of being let down by African Americans after having established positive relations with them. For Johnson, it was the second time that year that the movement disappointed him. When King had spoken out against the Johnson administration's Vietnam War policies, the president was incensed and ordered the FBI to follow SCLC more vigorously. Still, he conceded that the organization still had constructive activism to offer in relation to civil rights. He echoed Agnew in preferring King's nonviolent approach to Brown's rhetoric and in wanting the SNCC chairman prosecuted. Attorney General Ramsey Clark reminded Johnson that the administration lacked proof that Brown had broken any federal statutes. The president then reluctantly retreated from his call for the activist's prosecution. Lacking the benefit of Clark's counsel, Agnew made no such retreat.[41]

Neither did the FBI. Exactly one month after Agnew's initial response to the Cambridge uprising, FBI director J. Edgar Hoover launched the "Black Nationalist/Hate Groups" campaign of the bureau's counterintelligence program (COINTELPRO). In this new campaign, the FBI targeted SNCC, SCLC, the Revolutionary Action Movement, the CORE, and the Nation of Islam (NOI). The bureau sought to "neutralize" the organizations' activities, expose their danger to the nation, exploit each group's internal conflicts, and generate conflicts between groups. As a result, Governor Agnew's divide-and-conquer approach to the movement had quickly risen from the state level to the federal level in one of the nation's most dangerous activities against its own citizens. As part of this new campaign, COINTELPRO sent letters and made telephone calls to members of one organization, saying that another organization was trying to kill them. Also, the agency began recruiting African Americans to serve as "ghetto informants" who would penetrate an organization and typically tell one member that another was out to harm him. COINTELPRO had the potential to weaken the movement by leading activist groups to argue with each other. If the argument were serious enough, perhaps militants would kill each other.[42]

Meanwhile, members of Congress were just as quick as the president and the FBI to pick up on the governor's remarks. Several weeks earlier William Cramer, a Republican from Florida, had drafted an antiriot bill to make a federal crime of traveling across state lines to incite a riot. By the middle of August, legislators were using deliberations on the proposal as an excuse to denigrate the movement. Elmer Holland, a Democrat from Pennsylvania, called for Brown's condemnation. He said that no antiriot bill could be discussed without mentioning the SNCC leader. On the other hand, other representatives claimed that the bill was tailor-made to put down King. The SCLC president had recently called for nationwide nonviolent civil disobedience in Northern cities, so that the movement could gain momentum there as it had in the South. Cramer responded to his colleagues, "Now, that is insurrection." Democrat Roman Pucinski of Illinois agreed, warning that King was bent on destroying the United States from within and by any means necessary.[43]

Fellow Republican governor Claude Kirk of Florida shared his Maryland colleague's distaste for Brown, but Kirk did not believe in cutting off dialogue with people whose politics he disputed. On August 9, Brown was in Jacksonville to speak at a Black Power rally at a stadium—the Durkerville Ball Field. Governor Kirk was in Tallahassee when he learned that the event was to take place later that day. He immediately took a flight to Jacksonville and made his way to the stadium. Like Agnew, Kirk was a new governor, having won the previous year's election with the slogan "A Man's Home Is His Castle." Florida was his home, and he wanted to personally receive his "militant" houseguest.

At the rally, Kirk was the only European American present to receive Brown. About 2,000 African Americans had made their way to the stadium. As the SNCC leader was driven to the field, people cried, "Yeah, Rap" and "Black Power." When he left the car and raised his fists, the crowd rose and cheered. While Brown made his way to a microphone, the audience also applauded Governor Kirk as he waded through the crowd. They suddenly began to boo intensely when he approached a microphone on the stage, but undaunted, he began to speak. "Quiet, quiet," he started. "May I have your attention?" Brown interrupted, "They don't want to hear you. They want to hear me." Indeed, the crowd shouted down the governor at every turn. At one point the spectators cheered, "We want H. Rap Brown!" Another time they yelled, "We don't want you, honky!"[44]

Kirk then made a series of friendly gestures toward Brown. Any physical connection between the two would have made a significant photo opportunity.

Brown, however, did not respond to the outreach. The governor tried to put his arm around the speaker, but Brown kept dodging it. Kirk extended his hand, but the SNCC leader refused to shake it. Kirk then made his boldest move. He greeted, "Welcome to Florida," while placing his hand on Brown's shoulder. The activist, in turn, brushed off Kirk's hand and brusquely rebuked him, "Honky, you better get your hands off of me, and keep them off."[45]

Brown considered Kirk's actions and demeanor nothing more than a political stunt of some sort, and he accordingly told the crowd, "If this honky wants to campaign, let him pay for it." Kirk retreated from the stage to let his houseguest address the crowd. However, in the friendliest gesture of all, he then went into the stands, sat down, and listened to his visitor's remarks.

Later that evening Governor Kirk further deviated from Agnew's approach to Brown. Speaking on television next to an African American member of Florida's National Guard, Kirk disputed the claim that the SNCC chairman actually posed any real danger to anyone. "Brown is incapable of inciting a riot," he declared. He was, instead, a publicity seeker full of uninspiring rhetoric. "The thing to do with him," he said, "is to put him on national television for three hours, let everybody see him, and that will be that." Some of his fellow Florida statesmen were horrified that he had "welcomed" a militant. However, the great majority of the state's newspapers gave his actions favorable coverage. They said that his presence at the rally had caught Brown off guard and had cooled the heads of the audience. Local reporters even credited him for keeping Jacksonville from erupting into an urban uprising.[46]

Kirk's confrontation with Brown soon became national news. Federal government officials shared Agnew's belief in Brown's danger and criminality, but national news magazines and newspapers across the country publicized Kirk's dismissive response to the activist's militant rhetoric. Meanwhile, Agnew's remarks from July remained a local story in Maryland during the summer of 1967. He would have to wait for the rest of the country to catch on to his way of thinking.

CHAPTER 2

Open Season

Two days after Rap Brown's Cambridge address, civil rights leaders Martin Luther King Jr., A. Philip Randolph, Roy Wilkins, and Whitney Young issued a joint statement. In it they expressed solidarity with President Johnson's appeal for law and order in the cities, thus distancing themselves from the SNCC chairman and trying to remain in the White House's good graces. More importantly, the movement reprimanded Brown without naming him, saying, "We call upon Negro citizens throughout the nation to forego the temptation to disregard the law." For King and Wilkins, the request was ironic, considering their support of SNCC's first sit-ins and King's own practicing of nonviolent civil disobedience throughout his activist career. On the other hand, the statement addressed Brown's call for *violent* civil disobedience. "Killing, arson, looting are criminal acts and should be dealt with as such," read the statement. "Equally guilty are those who incite, provoke and call specifically for such action."[1]

The leaders could agree on little else, however, and failed to collectively respond to Brown in an effective manner after releasing their joint statement. Part of the disagreement lay in whether to call attention to the SNCC chairman at all. Some activists were busy with major programs and considered the controversy over Brown a very unwanted distraction, while others wanted to exploit Brown's celebrity to their advantage but did not know how to direct the energy his words unleashed among young people. The leaders merely concurred that urban, poor conditions were dire; they reached no consensus as to whether integrated struggle or separatist insurrection would improve those conditions.

Brown appealed to many young African Americans in a way that the other major civil rights figures did not. His call for violence seemed cathartic to people who had long disagreed with nonviolent civil disobedience as an effective tool for protest. "He's kinda crazy," an 18-year-old girl in Harlem admitted of Brown, "but it's a feel-good crazy."[2] In addition, SNCC received encouragement from people after Brown's speech in Cambridge, even from European American organizations. Columbia University's Students for a Democratic Society (SDS) sent a simple telegram to SNCC's national office in Atlanta: "CONDEMN RACIST IMPERIALIST ARREST OF H. RAPP [sic] BROWN. WITH YOU ALL THE WAY FOR GUNS AND FREEDOM."[3]

Civil rights groups understood the generation gap and privately bridged it, thus avoiding President Johnson's anger. Brown received qualified support from civil rights leaders except for Roy Wilkins, who offered no support. The NAACP leader chose instead to avoid discussing Brown at all, issuing no public statement about the Cambridge incident. The silence marked a sharp reversal from the organization's constant critiques of either Black Power or Stokely Carmichael the previous year. Wilkins had helped yield media attention to the phrase and been its champion by speaking so much about it, however negatively. Rap Brown, on the other hand—as someone who called for African Americans to arbitrarily shoot European Americans—represented a more dangerous threat. He was Robert F. Williams all over again, and Wilkins chose not to give the SNCC chairman any more publicity than he had to.

The only time *The Crisis* mentioned Brown in late 1967 was to stress his irrelevance. The magazine reported the results of a poll by the weekly periodical *The Carolina Times* in which people nationwide ranked nine civil rights leaders. Wilkins came out on top with 1.2 million votes, closely followed by Martin Luther King Jr. Whitney Young came in fourth place behind Thurgood Marshall, a former NAACP lawyer recently elevated to the Supreme Court. Then, after longtime activist A. Philip Randolph, African American freshman senator Edward Brooke of Massachusetts, and former baseball player Jackie Robinson, SNCC leaders rounded out the list. Stokely Carmichael came in at eighth place with one-fifth the number of Wilkins's votes, and Brown finished last with one-tenth of the winner's total.[4]

Whitney Young was under tremendous pressure from his European American supporters to denounce the SNCC chairman. Like Agnew, they thought of the NUL leader as a "responsible" activist and told him that speaking against Brown constituted responsible behavior. At the risk of offending European Americans who thought they knew best about African American leadership, Young defended Brown's right to an opinion. Speaking at a gathering in July 1967, Young diverted attention from the rioting and the rhetoric to focus on the causes of urban poverty. "The Negro has as much right to have his extremists as anybody else," he declared. Then, sounding like a preacher, he repeated a theme: "Rap Brown did not cause unemployment in the country. Rap Brown did not put Negroes in ghettos. Rap Brown did not perpetrate upon Negroes inferior education." Rather, "other people" caused those problems, and "it is to the other people that we must look." He eventually placed the blame on "white racism" and called for it to be cured.[5]

Now that the nation's attention focused on poverty, Young's group became a more valuable partner in the movement. Former SNCC member Julian Bond considered the NUL a social welfare organization instead of a civil rights organization in the strictest sense. To him, the NAACP, SNCC, SCLC, and CORE performed the traditional civil rights labor of challenging white supremacy through protests, lawsuits, and agitation. Meanwhile, the league worked to help African Americans improve their economic status through education, counseling, and convincing employers to hire more African Americans. By blaming "white racism" for the uprisings of the impoverished, Young linked his "social welfare" work of economic improvement with the "civil rights" work of "fighting white supremacy."[6]

Young's statements that summer were bold, but because he did not reprimand anyone specifically for the problems—especially federal officials—he remained in the good graces of the federal government that month. Hoover, for example, did not include him or his organization on the list of COINTELPRO's militant targets. Also, Young won an audience in Congress. In his testimony there, he suggested that time had run out for nonviolence and warned that adolescents and young adults "no longer hear" the moderate message, "Turn the other cheek." Moreover, he validated the anger that African Americans expressed through their destructiveness but sought to "channel that anger into effective ways." However, he did not go to Congress to complain about nonviolence's unpopularity but rather to urge the federal government to make a "dramatic new national commitment" to improve urban conditions that lay at the root of riots. Seeing no middle ground for urban African Americans, he starkly warned legislators, "It comes right down to liberate or exterminate the Negro."[7]

Martin Luther King Jr., indirectly responded to the fuss over Brown by issuing a call for massive civil disobedience on the issue of poverty. Marian Wright—a personal friend and an antipoverty activist—had proposed the idea to him. She had just testified to Congress about poverty, and Senator Robert Kennedy of New York told her that Congress would not address poverty unless it was made uncomfortable enough to do so. Thus, a demonstration similar to the Bonus Army of World War I was in order, she reasoned. King agreed and told the press to expect a massive encampment of the nation's poorest in Washington, D.C., until the federal government responded to the problem of poverty. One columnist, familiar with the competitiveness among civil rights organizations, surmised that King had announced such a bold idea because he had been "overshadowed for months by the more bizarre antics of Brown and Carmichael."[8]

A constant compromiser, King's answer to Brown's remarks lay somewhere in the middle between Wilkins's silence and Young's vociferousness. Like Wilkins, the SCLC leader issued no statement about the SNCC chairman, but privately King supported Brown. On January 9, 1968, King sent the SNCC chairman a telegram of encouragement. "We strongly protest the continued restrictions of your freedom of movement and basic constitutional rights," King sympathized. Then, after calling for the immediate return of Brown's "free speech and movement throughout the United States," the minister made a promise to the young militant: "We will support and undertake all possible measures to insure these rights."[9]

SNCC let its civil rights colleagues and the press fight among themselves about Brown's comments, offering no official statements in support of or opposition to its chairman. The organization was too busy trying to survive. Its funds had declined sharply over the past year, during which the group had made both its public antiwar statement and its request for European Americans to work among themselves. By September 22, 1967, the public fallout over Brown's remarks cast a pall over the organization. Its Central Committee met that fall day to discuss how SNCC should move forward. The group was at a crossroads, as far as some members were concerned. It had lost focus, distracted by the celebrity of not only Brown and his predecessor Carmichael but also, by extension, of the group itself. How could SNCC become a strong organization again? How should it respond to what reporters and journalists were saying about it?

Ralph Featherstone spoke first. One of the senior members of the organization, he had served on several projects for years, and he was a member of the group's small delegation to the recent "Black Power" conference in Newark. His fellow SNCC associates highly valued his opinions. Although they considered him quiet and reserved, he was also brilliant. Whenever the organization held a meeting, the attendees turned to him for the final word.

He gave an unplanned oral report in which he admitted that "we really don't have any projects." He noted that members Johnny Jackson and John Buffington had resigned from SNCC "because of what Stokely and Rap were saying." He also felt that the group devoted too many of their resources to foreign affairs. In 1967 alone, SNCC organizers—especially Carmichael— traveled to Algeria, Cuba, China, Guinea, North Vietnam, and the Soviet Union. On SNCC's International Program, Featherstone complained,

"I think it has run away with the organization so to speak. . . . [I]n relationship to what we have going on inside the country, I just think it is too much.
The priority of the resources that we do have should be inside the country."[10]

Stanley Wise expressed concern for the nuts and bolts of the organization. On financial matters he proclaimed that "the organization is in a dire
financial crisis. We are surviving from month to month." Most of SNCC's
associates held part-time jobs outside of the organization, because it could
not afford to pay full-time salaries to its members. Seconding Featherstone's
point about the absence of programs, Wise complained that instead of organizing among the masses, "[t]he organization at this time just seems to be
primarily an organization of leaders. We in Atlanta live from press conference
to press conference. We used to live from activity to activity." Despite his
complaints about low funds and too much leadership, he then noted that he
and Featherstone wanted SNCC to create a defense fund for either Brown or
SNCC. Returning to the problem of proliferating leadership, he said that he
did not even know who some of the leaders were. SNCC offices emerged in
places where Wise did not know had started branches, and he did not want
SNCC resources to go to just anyone or for just anyone to be able to arbitrarily identify themselves as part of SNCC. "I just want to ask what the fuck
goes on," he said.[11]

Julius Lester did not have an answer for Wise, but he did focus on the
complicity of SNCC itself in the media's portrayal of the group. He said that
125 insurrections had happened since January. He observed that the organization welcomed the publicity the group received by extension of the press
coverage of Brown. "We have been letting some cats up in a newsroom put
our name or Rap's name to something and we are being made the scape-
goats for very basic problems inside this country," he stated. "Yet we have
not addressed ourselves to this problem at all," he complained. SNCC had
tapped into the energy of urban demonstrators but had yet to organize it. As
a result, to Lester, "In a *real* sense we have become a reactionary organization. . . . We call ourselves revolutionary without having any idea of what that
means." Before the meeting ended, SNCC did not come to an agreement as
to what it meant.[12]

Brown and Carmichael—the most prominent participants in the organization—did not help matters. They disagreed as to how to organize for
revolution. Some SNCC associates supported Brown's view that the group
needed to align itself with other ethnic minorities, but others agreed with
Carmichael's organizing on a Pan-African basis. Instead of coming to a
consensus, each person decided to let the group's factions remain and to
allow each associate in SNCC to join one of them. Although the strategy

allowed the organization a wider range of activism, the problem of ideology remained.[13]

The group tried to present a brave face whenever it met the media spotlight, but SNCC repudiated its own history in the process. When speaking and writing publicly about SNCC's lack of ideology, the organization did not mention it as a problem but rather as a benefit. "One of the saving graces of 'the movement' and of SNCC, in particular, has been its unwillingness to dogmatically align itself with any doctrine," Lester wrote in 1968. "Each individual in SNCC is like a separate political party and any attempt by others to force rigid doctrine on the organization is firmly resisted." In addition, SNCC refused to engage in what veteran nonviolent activist Bayard Rustin called the "buy and sell" or compromise in politics—"that's why we're not in politics and want no power of the American way." Only four years earlier, SNCC had helped organize the Mississippi Freedom Democratic Party, not only participating politically in the "American way" but also aligning itself with a political party and, by extension, an ideology. In the following year the group assisted in the organizing of the Lowndes County Freedom Organization—an independent political party in Alabama. As the year 1967 drew to a close, however, SNCC was not actively facilitating the development of any domestic political parties, and its participants had lost interest in organizing among the rural poor.[14]

The media started to portray the organization as weak and in decline, especially as the phrase "Black Power" lost much of its shock value. Much to Rap Brown's dismay, Whitney Young of the NUL associated the phrase with African American capitalism. Other people simply began using the slogan as a comic punch line. An advertisement for the "Pink Panther" animated cartoons of the 1967–1968 season featured the phrase "Pink Power," and Snoopy ran for president as a "Paw Power" candidate in the comic strip *Peanuts*. Even SNCC's calls for revolution received some ribbing by February 1968. An episode of the new series *Rowan & Martin's Laugh-In* predicted that in 20 years, "President Stokely Carmichael" would lead the United States from "his office in Hanoi."[15]

Some media figures expressed more wistfulness than humor, wondering what had happened to the SNCC of the early 1960s. Dwight Macdonald proclaimed in the November 1967 issue of *Esquire* that the organization was rapidly deteriorating, moving from "dedication and idealism" to "racial hatred, a neurotic delight in violence, corny melodrama, [and] ignorant fanaticism." The article was hardly objective, however. The author observed SNCC's changes with personal disdain because of his own involvement with the group. He huffed, "To think I gave them $25 once!" and demanded of them, "This honky wants a refund, blackey."[16]

In response, Lester predictably told the writer, "[T]ake your money and shove it, if taking your money means taking your orders." He had a point in noting that donating to the group did not mean owning it. Also, his retort continued the organization's long history of maintaining its independence from people, especially other civil rights groups, who wanted to use the young activists' energy and organizational talents for their own purposes. Movement veteran Ella Baker had first advised SNCC to be its own group back in its first national meeting in 1960, and the students had done so ever since.[17]

Still, Lester missed Macdonald's point that SNCC was now losing control of its media narrative. By eliminating its defining characteristics, the group was letting others define it. SNCC argued that it was no longer "cuddly" because of the shift to "Black Power" among other reasons. On the other hand, by talking about how much power African Americans had and how potential revolution was, the organization forfeited its media role as a non-violent protagonist underdog. Governor Agnew's subsequent condemnation of Brown as violent further lessened the likelihood that journalists would portray SNCC as revolutionary protagonists. As "irresponsible militants," they were antagonists.[18]

Some SNCC activists decided to try new approaches to activism to revitalize the group. Women intensified their efforts to retain a significant voice in the organization. Ethel Minor was the only woman to hold a national administrative position in the group as of the summer of 1967. Meanwhile, former stalwarts like Mississippi Delta resident Fannie Lou Hamer—a tireless worker with SNCC on the creation of the Freedom Democratic Party—left the group, but some of the younger urban associates did not find her relevant to the struggle anyway. They had also stopped consulting with Ella Baker for advice by then. Women in SNCC suffered a further severe blow when Ruby Doris Robinson became ill early in 1967 and died before the year ended. She had been in the group since 1960 and involved herself in its most prominent programs, press conferences, and internal discussions over the years. Despite these losses, women in SNCC managed to blaze new trails for the organization. In January 1968, Angela Davis, an instructor at the University of California, helped start a branch of the organization in Los Angeles.[19]

The national group's internal squabbling affected how activists outside of the movement organized for struggle. Starting in 1967, SNCC developed alliances with several groups and, as a result, involved them in its factionalism. Some of these organizations consisted of different ethnic groups of color, which related to Brown's preference for activism. Other organizations were exclusively African American in membership, which appealed to Carmichael.

The groups were relatively new, compared to the seven-year-old SNCC, and appreciated both the publicity that the SNCC name carried and the wisdom and advice its members had to give. In turn, SNCC was able to remain an active organization despite its lack of programs because it became involved in the activities of other groups. By developing as many alliances as it eventually did, the organization seemed to try to develop an ideology through osmosis.

SNCC fostered one of its more fruitful associations that year with the Southwestern Hispano Land Grant (SHLG). The relationship reflected Brown's concern for dispossessed people of various skin colors. During his chairmanship, SNCC invited the SHLG's leader, Reies Lopez Tijerina, to the New Politics Conference in Chicago. Julian Bond of SNCC asked fellow member Maria Varela to accompany Tijerina during the event in order for the guest to feel more at ease with another Latino at the conference.

Tijerina returned the favor that fall by inviting a SNCC delegation to a "treaty-signing" summit in Albuquerque, New Mexico—the *Convención Nacionál de la Alianza Federal de los Pueblos Libres*. SNCC accepted and sent a few of its associates to the convention, which met on October 21 and 22. Reflecting the open-mindedness of SNCC, delegation members included some of the group's highest-profile supporters of "Black Power," such as Willie Ricks, who had helped introduce the slogan in 1966 in a march in Mississippi, and Ralph Featherstone, who had attended the "Black Power" conference in Newark in July 1967. They were among very few African Americans who attended the mostly Latino-populated convention of around 400 participants. Varela was there, too, and she helped with arrangements for the convention.[20]

Through their shared opposition to oppression on the basis of color, SNCC and SHLG were kindred spirits. When Tijerina sought Varela's support in particular for the Albuquerque meeting, he framed his proposal around the violent history of Mexico's relationship with the United States; he recalled that the United States had "invaded and seized control" of Mexico in 1846 and had refused to protect Mexicans despite promises made in the Treaty of Guadalupe Hidalgo two years later. At times appearing to speak on behalf of Mexicans, he declared that "many of our people soon learned to hate and mistrust the Anglo—to hate with a passion that has transcended and effected [sic] generations of La Raza." Then, very much in concert with Brown's rhetoric of combat against European Americans, Tijerina declared, "We have been and are at war with the Gringo for a hundred years; and there doesn't look like any peace in sight." After calling for all minorities to band together and fight "against the Anglo," he ended his letter by attempting to appeal to Varela on the basis of their shared ethnicity. "I would like to say that it would be very nice if you could come to Albuquerque and spend some time with your people," he remarked.[21]

By attending the convention, SNCC began to spread Black Power beyond color and the urban North to the indigenous of the rural Southwest, and the organization was able to continue the rural organizing activity that had made the group's presence so strong in Mississippi only three years earlier. Featherstone reflected the organization's new apolitical stance and the leaders' militant rhetoric in his remarks to the convention. He said that the participants should not collectively form a political party, nor should they restrict themselves to peaceful means for change. Not every aspect of the convention concerned politics. The SNCC delegation also met with various Native American and Mexican American freedom fighters, toured the Tierra Amarilla Land Grant, and posed for pictures while holding guns on horseback.[22]

By the start of 1968, SNCC had also begun associating with the two-year-old Black Panther Party (BPP) for Self-Defense. Both groups were attracted to one another, but each organization expressed concern for how the other operated. SNCC marveled at how well the BPP connected with young African Americans in ghettos. On the other hand, the BPP's refusal to disavow assistance from European Americans disturbed SNCC. Meanwhile, BPP officer Bobby Seale believed that an alliance with SNCC would yield alliances with other organizations because of the prominence of the group. Seale observed, however, that SNCC was in a fragile state with Brown and Forman controlling one faction of the group and Carmichael leading another. Nevertheless, SNCC members started attending and speaking at BPP rallies, and some SNCC members joined the BPP.[23]

Forman, who had joined SNCC in 1961, was responsible for bringing his organization to the West Coast. When he traveled to Los Angeles for a speaking engagement in early 1968, he met Angela Davis, who told him that her organization was in trouble. It was called the "Black Panther Political Party," but a member of the BPP had demanded that her group change its name. Forman suggested that her group become SNCC's Los Angeles branch. The organization lacked a presence in the West at the time, and it already had a working relationship with the BPP. While still in SNCC, its national spokesmen served in BPP positions: Carmichael as prime minister, Brown as minister of justice, and Forman as minister of international affairs. The members of Davis's group agreed to the name change. Davis especially approved, because she respected the contributions SNCC had made to the movement.[24]

The SNCC-BPP relationship peaked soon afterward. Both groups jointly held a rally in California to call attention to the imprisonment of BPP chairman Huey P. Newton. In addition to Carmichael, Brown, and Forman, speakers included BPP figure Bobby Seale and SHLG leader Reies Tijerina. Both Forman and Carmichael applied Brown's standard rhetoric of violent retribution to specific people. The former called for the crowd of 5,000 people to kill Southern officials if any of the SNCC leaders present were assassinated, and in the event of Newton's death, "the sky's the limit." The latter vaguely threatened, "Brother Huey will be set free—or else." Despite the size of the audience, not everyone in both groups agreed with the speeches, especially Carmichael's. The BPP welcomed European American support, and as a result, did not care for his suggestion that African Americans only organize among themselves. Davis, on the other hand, was a Communist and disagreed with his rejection of communism and socialism solely on the basis of their European American roots. Still, the SNCC-BPP partnership continued.[25]

Alliances, however, could not substitute for the leadership vacuum in SNCC. Complicating matters, Brown continued to face legal troubles on other charges, and his time in and out of jail and in and out of court compromised his ability to serve as chairman. In September 1967, he was arrested for carrying firearms across state lines while under federal indictment for his comments from the previous July. When he was released, the court restricted him to the Southern District of New York. On January 11, 1968, Brown was charged with intimidating/assaulting a New York City police officer as he and another SNCC worker were leaving the lobby of the Cuban Mission. The incident occurred after the officer inquired about a package the SNCC worker was carrying. Brown remained in the embassy for hours while his attorneys held conversations with the NYPD. The charge finally was dropped the following month.

Then on February 18, Brown left the Southern District of New York. He traveled to California in order to talk with his attorneys. While in California, Brown was invited to speak at the SNCC-BPP rally with his attorneys present. Brown returned to New York on February 20, and was arrested approximately seven hours later. He was charged with violating the terms of his bond from the previous September. His attorneys argued that the trips to talk with his attorneys were allowed by the court. Brown was released in New York the same day and required to appear in New Orleans the following day.

A fair trial was not in the cards for Brown in the Crescent City. Before proceedings began, Judge Lansing Mitchell had privately vowed to "get that nigger." After the trial commenced, Mitchell set the SNCC chairman's bail at $50,000. During the court recess, Brown was charged with threatening an FBI agent in the court hallway; the agent said that Brown had vowed to kill him. Brown maintained that he had merely called the African American agent an "Uncle Tom," and other witnesses testified on the defendant's behalf. Their efforts did not help, because Mitchell himself was a former FBI agent and did not take kindly to the offense against a fellow G-man. The judge added another $50,000 to Brown's bail and then jailed him.[26]

SNCC–Los Angeles immediately went into action. The branch started a fundraising drive for Brown's bail money. Associates drafted and distributed a petition that demanded the lowering of his fine. Participants went door-to-door and approached churches, community centers, and shopping areas to promote the "Let Rap Rap" campaign. SNCC–Los Angeles followed in its Mississippi counterpart's footsteps by developing plans for a "liberation school." The branch also set up office space. At the end of each workweek at the university, Angela Davis lived as a commuting activist, hopping into her old Buick and speeding from La Jolla to the City of Angels to conduct organizational business.[27]

For at least one year, SNCC had been fostering a similar reputation to that of SCLC as a leader-driven civil rights organization. Brown himself reinforced the group's transformation by borrowing a tactic directly from King. Just as the SCLC president had written the "Letter from Birmingham Jail," the SNCC chairman wrote a letter while incarcerated in New Orleans on the day of his sentencing. But there the similarities ended. Whereas King had asked clergymen to take a public stand against segregation, Brown theorized that any killing of an African American at the hands of European Americans necessitated reciprocal European American killings in greater numbers by African Americans. King wrote about wanting African Americans no longer segregated, but Brown said, "To desire freedom isn't enough. We must move from resistance to aggression, from revolt to revolution." Moreover, Brown commented at length about himself as a political prisoner and mentioned his hunger strike while incarcerated to demonstrate his willingness for martyrdom. He wrote what became his most often quoted written passage:

> America, if it takes my death to organize my people to revolt against you,
> And to organize your jails to revolt against you,
> And to organize your troops to revolt against you,
> And to organize your children to revolt against you,
> And to organize your God to revolt against you,
> And to organize your poor to revolt against you,
> And to organize your country to revolt against you,
> And to organize Mankind to rejoice in your destruction and ruin,
> Then, here is my Life![28]

Brown's strike and letter did little to lead people to his cause. No "Free Rap" rallies on the scale of "Free Huey" rallies for the imprisoned BPP leader Huey Newton were forthcoming. Brown had neglected in his letter to explain why or how his death would lead people to revolt against the nation. Especially because SNCC had no programs and had performed little organizing that year, the organization had no masses to organize for the revolution. All SNCC had was the rhetoric. But for now, due to Brown's new prominence, rhetoric was barely enough for the organization to survive just a little while longer.

Meanwhile, as late as mid-January 1968, King still had trouble convincing his organization that the Poor People's Campaign (PPC) would work. Hosea Williams did not want to do it at all. Jesse Jackson, on the other hand, wanted SCLC to have a local victory before trying something so ambitious on a national scale. Jackson had a point, because the March on Washington in August 1963 had taken place three months after SCLC's victorious demonstrations for desegregation in Birmingham, Alabama. Still, King did not let the idea drop. He pleaded with aide Bernard Lafayette to relocate to Atlanta to devote all his time to planning the poverty march. "This may be my last campaign," he reasoned, "and we're going for broke."[29]

SCLC's publicity director Andrew Young sided with King in that he believed something had to be done to stop poverty. On the other hand, his reasoning resembled Rap Brown's comparison of Nazi Germany to the current American urban situation. He said, "We're at the point now where the Jews were when Hitler took power. Either we're going to wait and be put in concentration camps, or we're going to organize and fight." He then endorsed Whitney Young's "liberate or exterminate" notion. "I'm not going to sit around," the SCLC official vowed. "I'm going to fight."[30]

On February 7, King met with SNCC's Brown and Carmichael in Washington, D.C., to build support within the movement for his strategy on poverty. The minister asked the young activists not to jeopardize what he called his "Poor People's Campaign" by coming there and using violent rhetoric. SNCC complied, for the group had no reason to oppose or thwart a project that resembled what its members had done a few years earlier. Carmichael saw the PPC as a similar project to SNCC's earlier work with poor people in Mississippi. In 1964, during the group's "Freedom Summer" project, students from across the country had come to the poorest, most remote African American communities of the state to build schools and train residents on voting rights. Four years later SCLC met poor people throughout the nation but wanted to bring them all to Washington, D.C., and build a makeshift city for them while waiting for the federal government to help them. Because the students had developed their antipoverty project before SCLC had, King once again seemed dry on his own ideas and imitative of SNCC.[31]

On the other hand, one of the few advantages SCLC had over SNCC was money. The willingness of Brown and Carmichael to acquiesce to King partly resulted from SCLC's active support of SNCC with money and employment. Some SNCC activists in Atlanta had recently contacted King because of their group's dire financial straits. They asked him for money in order for SNCC to become more financially stable. In response, he presented a compromise to them, offering to assist SNCC with funding if the organization adopted a more nonviolent stance concerning civil rights activism. SNCC agreed, and SCLC began funding the group. Well into the spring of 1968, SNCC associates remained on SCLC's payroll, having no other source of income. SCLC benefited as well because the organization needed additional personnel. Executive Director William Rutherford, for example, chose to employ three SNCC activists in SCLC's department of information.[32]

Despite having bought SNCC's toned-down rhetoric, King continued to worry about the organization's prominence at his expense. On at least one occasion, King shared his concern about SNCC's media attention with a member of the fourth estate. On the same day of the SCLC–SNCC meeting in Washington, D.C., the minister held a press conference there. After it ended reporter Daniel Schorr commented on the leader's sad demeanor. King immediately unleashed his frustration on Schorr by blaming "you people in television." He held television journalists responsible for "driving people like me, who are nonviolent, into saying more and more militant things." He rationalized that "if we don't say things militantly enough for you, we don't get on the evening news. And who does? Stokely Carmichael and H. Rap Brown." He claimed that the media had the power to define the movement and that they were "selecting the more militant black leaders to be civil rights leaders, because everybody sees your television programs."[33]

King's pleas for Schorr and other reporters to still find him newsworthy fell on deaf ears, especially as the SCLC leader did not appear to take responsibility for failing to make his nonviolent demonstrations more attractive to television news programs. Moreover, the reporter and the minister operated with different motives. Whereas networks focused on Brown primarily to generate high ratings in order to defeat competition and stay in business, the minister expressed the televising of nonviolence instead of violence as purely a moral issue. He lamented that network coverage of SNCC was "putting a premium on violence."[34]

King found nonviolence preferable to violence. However, despite his neglect in mentioning financial concerns to Schorr, the civil rights leader and his group stood to benefit monetarily from any possible increase in exposure by television reporters. More positive publicity for nonviolent civil disobedience provided potential for an increase from television viewers in donations to SCLC. By early 1968, the group desperately needed such a windfall. Besides failing to recruit the supporters at the higher levels of earlier years, financial contributions to the organization also plummeted. Some people stopped supporting it because they felt it had become too radical by protesting housing segregation in the North (Chicago) and condemning the Vietnam War. In contrast, other donors decided that SCLC was not militant enough and sent their money to more militant groups. King also worried himself over the potential for young African Americans to follow SNCC personnel like Carmichael and Brown, and the minister predicted that the militant leaders would lead their young followers to their doom.[35]

Nonviolent protest, however, suffered a fatal setback only one day after King's press conference and yielded a now-familiar pattern of responses. A two-day nonviolent protest by approximately 50 African American college students to desegregate a bowling alley ended in gunfire. Armed officers shot and killed 3 unarmed students and wounded dozens more in Orangeburg, South Carolina. Governor Robert McNair took a cue from fellow governor Agnew and blamed the incident on SNCC member Cleveland Sellers, alleging that Sellers had led people to riot when he had advised demonstrators days earlier. McNair, like Agnew and Kirk, had just been elected to his first full gubernatorial term in the fall of 1966. These new governors apparently thought that attacking individual participants in SNCC was the way to stop African American unrest.

Civil rights leaders were unified in the disgust they expressed. Roy Wilkins issued a protest against Orangeburg's police, noting that the students had not conducted themselves in a disorderly manner. His defense of the students reflected well upon Sellers by extension, because Wilkins was indirectly saying that Sellers had not led anyone to engage in an uprising. The NAACP leader's response, therefore, was one of his most supportive toward anyone in SNCC since the Black Power controversy of two years earlier.[36]

SNCC was, predictably, more direct in its statement about Orangeburg. On the night of the shooting, Brown called the incident the "Orangeburg Massacre." The group's leader used the incident as an opportunity to once again publicly disavow nonviolence. In New York, Chairman Brown stated, "The lesson for us is very clear and evident." He fatalistically observed the bitter fruits of nonviolence: "If we seek redress of our grievances through peaceful and so-called legal means, we will be shot down and murdered." There was no reason for him to support nonviolent protest, because the intensity of the police brutality against peaceful demonstrators that night in Orangeburg defied reasoning. "Three dead and fifty injured is too high a price to pay for a goddam bowling alley," he lamented.[37]

Brown had never spoken more eloquently in favor of violence, with the possible exception of the "cherry pie" quip. In the rush of crafting a statement, the leader impressively managed to make a historical literary connection to his call for self-defense. Evoking Claude McKay's poem of the Harlem Renaissance period, Brown announced, "If we must die, let us die with the enemy's blood on our hands. . . . Let us die like men, fighting back." The poem not only reflected Brown's militancy but also connected the Orangeburg deaths to the frequent lynching of African Americans in McKay's era. After all, the officers had executed the students without arrest, trial, or judgment. Then, leaving no doubt about whom he wanted African Americans to fight, Brown concluded, "If we are going to be murdered for acting peacefully, we might as well be murdered while trying to kill a few honkies."[38]

Neither King nor SCLC offered any immediate public commentary on the incident, thus ceding the media spotlight to Brown. Despite SNCC's inflammatory condemnation of nonviolence, SCLC did not respond to defend the tactic. Doing so would have been an uphill battle, because the fact of the police killing nonviolent demonstrators spoke for itself in SNCC's favor. The incident's timing of having followed SCLC's public call for nonviolence comprised one of the deadliest direct repudiations of King's philosophy since the bombing of a church that had killed four African American girls in Birmingham only two weeks after the March on Washington in 1963. More recently, two European Americans had been murdered after SCLC's march in Selma, Alabama, in 1965.

Instead of trying to reassure the public about nonviolence's relevance, King requested that the federal government address the incident in Orangeburg. It was a novel tactic, given that SCLC rarely counted on federal protection during demonstrations and hardly sought federal justice for killings carried out by state and county officials. The movement largely took for granted that members put their lives at risk through their activism. The violence in Orangeburg, however, seemed so lawless to King that he took drastic measures to keep what had happened in South Carolina from spreading to other states. On Valentine's Day 1968, reports surfaced of a telegram King had sent to Attorney General Ramsey Clark, ordering him to "act now to bring to justice the perpetrators of the largest armed assault undertaken under cover of law in recent Southern history." King said the state troopers committed an "immense overreaction" and that the killings and wounding there "must not go unpunished."[39]

In recent years the SCLC leader had communicated bluntly with the federal government about the Vietnam War and the War on Poverty. Now his correspondence with the Johnson administration returned specifically to the topic of civil rights. Moreover, the telegram marked one of the few times that King communicated with the Johnson administration after SCLC had angered the president with its opposition to the Vietnam War—another indication of how strongly the Nobel Peace Prize winner felt about Orangeburg. Still, King's message failed to interest the press. The daily newspapers tucked reports about the telegram in their back pages.

Weeks later, on leap year day, King received a reprieve of sorts from the federal government and his fellow civil rights leader. President Johnson's Commission on Civil Disorders—and by extension, commission member Roy Wilkins—validated the feelings King had begun to express about the country dividing itself by skin color. Ever since 1966, the SCLC leader had spoken about the split. That year he had firsthand witnessed both the embrace by young people of Black Power and the hostility of European Americans in Chicago toward open housing. He started talking about the violence of "white America" and differentiating it from African Americans. "It was not a black society which produced a Mr. Oswald in Texas," he reminded an audience in Alabama that year. "It was not a black society which killed four little girls in Birmingham." Nearly two years later Johnson's commission echoed King's sentiment, warning of the country's approaching split into "two societies, one black, one white—separate and unequal."[40]

The commission shared several ideas with the movement. The group espoused King's faith in the country to redeem itself, claiming that the division was reversible. It listed social conditions as causes of the recent urban disturbances, just as activists like King had claimed all along. "Almost invariably the incident that ignites disorder arises from police action," the commission concluded. Although "pervasive discrimination and segregation," "black migration and white exodus," and "black ghettos" collectively comprised "the most bitter fruits of white racial attitudes," the report named the police as the embodiment of "white power, white racism, and white oppression" among African Americans. As a result of the findings, the commission became the first federal government entity to blame someone else besides civil rights leaders for riots.[41]

For activists more pessimistic than King, on the other hand, the commission reinforced their frustration about the country. They tended to focus on the group's warning of "two societies," and they saw no reversal in sight. "Even if he lives in the ghetto, white America must not think the middle class Negro is the solution to the race problem," argued the African American scholar Vincent Harding. The failure of legislators since 1966 to pass civil rights bills made Congress a target of African American hostility. "Congress is in a nasty and a very ugly mood, reflecting the nasty mood of white America," lamented a former aide to an African American U.S. representative. "We are entering the first phase of open season on niggers."[42]

Despite King's feelings about his decline in public stature, COINTELPRO still considered the leader enough of a threat to try to discredit him. On March 8, 1968, Baltimore's special agent in charge (SAC) informed Hoover by letter that SCLC's new branch in that city provided copies of the NOI's newspaper *Muhammad Speaks* and that a poster of Muhammad Ali was on one of the office walls. The agent also said that a Nation member had been in contact with an SCLC member there. The FBI director responded six days later, telling the Baltimore SAC to contact a local newspaper with that same information. "If a newspaper publicized the apparent alliance between King and the NOI, a militant, black nationalist group, it might prove embarrassing to King," Hoover reasoned. He warned against talking to an African American newspaper, believing that such a periodical would give SCLC's PPC positive press coverage. As it turned out, COINTELPRO did not need to use the NOI against SCLC, because King soon unwittingly gave the press an unprecedented opportunity to discredit him in a way Hoover had not imagined.[43]

That same month King decided to use a labor dispute in Memphis, Tennessee, as a dry run for his march of poor people to Washington, D.C. Ever since he had announced the march the previous summer, his colleagues in the movement refused to publicly support the idea. In Memphis, African American sanitation strikers—picketing since February 12—wanted strike leaders to bring in SNCC's Carmichael or Brown. However, longtime civil rights activist and nonviolence advocate Jim Lawson convinced the strikers to ask the SCLC president to lead the strikers in a nonviolent marching demonstration, and King accepted Lawson's invitation.

King was asked on short notice, and his staff did not have the usual amount of time to go into the community and speak to the locals on nonviolent participation in demonstrations. Still, SCLC went into Memphis and hoped for the best. On March 28, King arrived late to lead the march to Clayborne Temple. Five thousand participants, half of whom were schoolchildren, lined up, and SCLC and the sanitation workers started out in front at 11:00 a.m. A group of adolescents and young adults suddenly charged up from behind, tearing signs from poles, breaking store windows, looting, and calling others to arson. Police officers then swarmed into the streets and used their clubs, mace, and tear gas to disperse the crowd. They arrested 300 people and shot

4—1 of them to death. King's staff commandeered a passing motorist's car to remove him from the demonstration, and by 11:15 a.m., he was out of the march. The young vandals ruined SCLC's otherwise perfect record of leading marchers who never turned to violence.[44]

King's status as a nonviolent alternative to Rap Brown immediately disintegrated, because both civil rights leaders were now tied to urban insurrection. Several reporters described King in the same way that Governor Agnew had portrayed Brown eight months earlier. Just as the governor had harped on Brown's leaving of Cambridge when its disturbance happened, reporters made a point of noting that when the marchers King had led in Memphis started to become violent, he fled the scene. Southern newspapers were especially brusque, as if relishing the opportunity to herald the failure of the region's longtime "outside agitator." The *Memphis Commercial Appeal* called him "Chicken à la King." Most damningly, an editorial cartoon in the *St. Louis Globe-Democrat* featured King holding a gun, implying that he was to blame for the deadly uprising. The caption depicted him as saying, "I'm not firing it—I'm only pulling the trigger."[45]

As much as President Johnson had already disliked King for publicly opposing the Vietnam War, he showed considerable restraint when addressing the violence in Memphis during a speech in Washington, D.C., to the AFL-CIO on March 29. He offered King more mercy than Governor Agnew had given to Brown. While promising federal help to the city if needed, he proclaimed that "we will not let violence and lawlessness take over this country." Perhaps his most direct swipe at King and his civil disobedience was Johnson's call for all U.S. citizens to "strive to prevent violence, to obey the law and to preserve conditions of social stability which are essential to progress." In other words, the president wanted the minister and all other activists to stop demonstrating in ways that led to social unrest. Like Agnew, Johnson did not specifically outline what those methods were. But unlike the governor's vitriol against Brown, the president did not call for the Nobel Peace Prize winner's arrest for inciting to riot or specifically name him as the cause of the disturbance in Memphis.[46]

King was full of self-pity as he bunkered down with SCLC staffers in a hotel room and kept a television set on all evening long. He listened solemnly and quietly to each news bulletin about the Memphis march, almost as if torturing himself by subjecting himself repeatedly to the details of the catastrophe. He considered withdrawing from activism—a "sabbatical," as he told staffer Dorothy Cotton—and allowing Brown and Carmichael to have media access alone. He reasoned that they did not know what they were doing and that their time in the spotlight would consequently be brief. The nation would then learn that violence was wrong and give nonviolence another chance.

The SCLC leader's main problem lay in his failure to see himself as part of the civil rights backlash. By claiming that the media would eventually tire of Brown and Carmichael and return to him, he refused to acknowledge that much of the public now considered him as violent as the SNCC associates. Thus, a turn of the public away from Brown and Carmichael did not guarantee a turn toward King, especially if his "sabbatical" from activism kept him from rehabilitating his image. Moreover, he not only differentiated himself from the young militants but even sounded like such foes as Governor Agnew in private conversations about them. King complained, "The Stokely Carmichaels and Rap Browns are famous for coming into a community and leaving it in turmoil."[47]

SCLC colleague Ralph Abernathy tried to pull King out of his funk. He had been King's closest partner in activism over the past 12 years of civil rights campaigns. They confided in each other and were often arrested and jailed together at demonstrations. At mass meetings, the rural Abernathy gave funny, folksy sermons to either warm up the congregation for King's philosophical, erudite messages or to follow his friend with explanations of what was just said. At age 42, Abernathy was 3 years King's senior, but he was content to defer to and support King's role as SCLC president. To Abernathy, the violence of the Memphis march did not take away from the need for his friend to draw the nation's attention to the problem of poverty. Appealing to King's high prioritization of both nonviolence and dependability, Abernathy told him that the organization needed to honor its commitment to go to Washington and launch the PPC.

All through the evening, Abernathy and SCLC aide Bernard Lee continued trying to talk King out of giving up on the PPC. SCLC's president eventually agreed, saying that he had a duty to publicly support nonviolence. Despite his worries of the growing influence of SNCC's main spokespeople, he scheduled another march in Memphis for April 8, determined to prove one more time that nonviolent demonstrations could still work. The other civil rights groups and the federal government held their breath to see if it actually would.[48]

CHAPTER 3

Shocked and Saddened

In early 1968, very little of American rhythm-and-blues music reflected the sensibilities of civil rights organizations, and the members of the Chicago-based singing group the Impressions were not likely candidates to become icons of the more militant phase of the movement. When the group formed in the late 1950s, its members adopted an ordinary visual style. They did not dance while they performed their ballads on stage. They wore suits and ties, reflecting the establishment instead of the denim look of activist organizations like SNCC. Lead vocalist Curtis Mayfield offered a falsetto that, although melodic, rarely connoted a position of strength or authority.

In the mid-1960s, the Impressions gravitated toward pro-social songs and co-opted the movement's tendency to apply Christianity to current struggle. "People Get Ready," for example, contained gospel references. Comparing social change to boarding a train, the lyrics promised that people only had to thank the Lord to become passengers. Other songs, like "Amen," were simply rhythm-and-blues renditions of hymns. Such religious music, however, did not appeal to civil rights workers who had grown disenchanted with ministers like Martin Luther King Jr.

By the spring of 1968, however, the Impressions adapted their music to the rising popularity of militant speakers. The lyrics to the group's new song "We're a Winner"—a chart-topper in rhythm and blues that March—contained some of the usual gospel references. However, "We're a Winner" also had lyrics that were optimistic, assertive, and political. "People Get Ready" had told listeners to prepare for change in the future, but *now* was the arrival of the "blessed day" of achievement in "We're a Winner." The new song declared that the time for crying was over; instead, it was time to "show . . . no fear." Also, joining the group was a crowd of young people cheering during the recording. Their vocal enthusiasm—one person shouted the current popular catchphrase, "Sock it to me"—demonstrated that the group sought a hit with the youth market. More importantly, the Impressions implored their listeners to continue struggling according to the directives of "your leaders." By mentioning more than one leader, the song suggested that King's dominance in the movement had disappeared and that leaders like Rap Brown were now just as capable as the Nobel Peace Prize winner of drawing people to struggle. "We're a Winner" was an unofficial theme of the phase of the movement in which Brown overshadowed King.

"We're a Winner" struck a chord with civil rights workers that spring. The Impressions musically immortalized a moment in American culture in which African Americans, especially young adults, began to experiment with combining nonviolent activism and both oral and visual bravado. Students conducting a takeover of the administration building of the African American institution Howard University blasted the song loudly through on-campus speakers. SNCC began playing it at rallies. Brown and Carmichael watched the Impressions perform it at a "Free Huey" rally in San Francisco. Tellingly, when the *New York Times* reported on the song's resonance with the movement, the article did not mention any quotes about it from the SCLC. Whether the reporter had failed to contact anyone in the group, or the organization had declined to comment on the song, the omission was a bad sign for a group that struggled to regain media attention. Instead, in the report the CORE, another movement group and fellow promoter of the song, called the new hit "folk involvement in freedom music," as opposed to "folk music." Because "We're a Winner" was more militant, according to CORE, it was "more akin to the spirit of the times."[1]

On April 4, 1968, the FBI also seemed to be in a relatively lighthearted mood. The riots of the previous summer were eight months in the past. Legal troubles kept Brown out of the limelight. The agency was still very serious about keeping "militant" African American sentiments and leaders suppressed. However, in this more relaxed atmosphere, a special agent for COINTELPRO thought of an uncharacteristically fun way for the program to discredit the SNCC chairman. The agent proposed the idea of a coloring book to Hoover. It would be distributed to "the youth of the ghetto," in order to convince them not to become black nationalists later in life. The agent reasoned that a humorous coloring book would reach a wider audience than a documentary or a serious publication. COINTELPRO would call it *Culla Me (H. Rap Brown)*. It would have the speaker's biographical information, speaking fees, and nationalist views. It would also present various scenes of Brown speaking to crowds and then ditching them by plane, in order to show him as cowardly. Moreover, exaggeration was fine. "Factual data is not necessary," wrote the agent. "The only goal is effect." The jingle that the agent composed about Brown for the book summarized the caricatured image the government wanted to promote about the militant:

Ole Rap Brown
Came to town
With his shades
Hanging down

He hollored [*sic*] fight
Take what's right
Then he flew, man
In the night.[2]

SCLC staffers were also in good spirits. The group was still aglow from the sermon King had given in Memphis on April 3. He had foreshadowed "difficult days ahead" for the sanitation workers' strike, but then he roused the crowd by promising, "I may not get there with you, but I want you to know tonight that we as a people will get to the Promised Land!" The next day the organization successfully petitioned a court to have an injunction against a second march in Memphis eliminated. The staff celebrated in the Lorraine Motel by playfully tackling each other and engaging in a pillow fight. Then they gathered outside on the balcony and in the parking lot to discuss dinner plans and the upcoming Sunday church service. Standing on the balcony, King requested one of his favorite songs—"Precious Lord, Take My Hand"—for the service, and he directed musician Ben Branch, "Play it real pretty."

Suddenly, shortly after 6:00 p.m., a shot rang out. King slumped to the floor of the balcony. Abernathy rushed over to him, cradling the leader's head with one hand and patting his cheek with the other. Struggling to keep King conscious, Ralph Abernathy told him repeatedly, "This is Ralph. It will be all right." As King's life slipped away, Abernathy remained in the role of the SCLC president's comforter, offering reassurances to the very end.

Although King was not dead, SCLC members began to dispute the ultimate meaning of his shooting. Running quickly to Abernathy and King, Andrew Young saw the bloodied Nobel Prize winner and, assuming King had died, came to a premature conclusion. "Ralph," he cried, "it is over!"

Young did not clarify what "it" was. "It" could have been the upcoming PPC. Perhaps "it" was SCLC. Or was "it" the movement itself? Somehow at that moment Abernathy knew what Young meant. As Abernathy nursed King's wound, he adamantly responded that "it" would never be over. This conversation was one of the first public disagreements that Abernathy had with another SCLC staffer about the direction of the organization. It would not be the last.

Medical help soon arrived at the hotel. SCLC staffers accompanied King in the ambulance to St. Joseph's Hospital in Memphis. Abernathy and Bernard Lee kept vigil with him in the emergency room. They stood by helplessly while doctors worked frantically to save him. About an hour later, Lee and Abernathy emerged from the room and solemnly approached Young in a waiting room. Lee said softly, "He's gone."[3]

Upon King's death, the cultural moment that had inspired the militant pride of "We're a Winner" and the government's frivolous *Culla Me (H. Rap Brown)* suddenly vanished that evening, too. Prime-time television programming had barely begun that evening before news coverage of the assassination completely took over the networks that night. Television viewers had just settled in at 8:00 p.m. to such escapist fare as the western *Cimarron Strip*, the frontier drama *Daniel Boone*, and the sitcom *The Flying Nun*. Any of those choices would have taken audiences away from the nation's contemporary social concerns. However, at 8:19 p.m., a news bulletin of King's death aired on television networks. The networks would not return to their regular programming for the remainder of the evening.

When responding to King's death, civil rights organizations had to face their individual and collective shortcomings. As a movement, the groups unilaterally grieved King's loss. However, as when responding to Brown, they still could not collectively agree on whether to plea for integrated peace and nonviolence or embrace separatist insurrection. Some activists claimed that King still had relevance, but others wondered if Rap Brown, Stokely Carmichael, or Ralph Abernathy carried more weight. The press and the federal government magnified these splits, waiting to see who would pass down the stricken leader's ideas.

At 9:07 p.m. on April 4, President Johnson interrupted the television news bulletins with an impromptu speech. He called for his fellow citizens to grieve out of a sense of patriotism, claiming that "America is shocked and saddened by the brutal slaying tonight of Dr. Martin Luther King." He continued, "I ask every citizen to reject the blind violence that has struck Dr. King, who lived by nonviolence." He disclosed that he and his wife had paid condolences to King's widow. Then he returned to his theme of patriotic grief: "I know that every American of good will join me in mourning the death of this outstanding leader and in praying for peace and understanding throughout this land." He carried himself as if hoping that by saying the country agreed with his views of King's life and the meaning of King's death, it would be so. He had rarely looked or sounded less confident on camera.[4]

Afterward, all he could offer were platitudes about uniting lawfully as a nation. "We can achieve nothing by lawlessness and divisiveness among the American people," he stated. "It is only by joining together and only by working together that we can continue to move toward equality and fulfillment for all of our people. I hope that all Americans tonight will search their hearts as they ponder this most tragic incident."[5] Even as he then announced the cancellation of his plans for the evening and the postponing of his trip to Hawaii until the next day, he neglected to reveal what he would do with his time instead. Finally, he concluded with thanks to his media audience for listening. Then he went off the air, never having told his fellow Americans how exactly to join together and work together or precisely what to seek in their hearts.

Some people searched their hearts but then concluded that King had caused his own death. A couple of first-term governors placed his assassination in the context of the movement's perceived lawlessness. Lester Maddox of Georgia argued that King had reaped what he had sown through his illegal protests. Ronald Reagan of California similarly condemned civil disobedience, claiming that the leader's death was precipitated by "our first acceptance of compromise with the law."[6]

One of the country's most powerful anti-movement groups—the Citizens' Council—shared the sentiments of the governors. Although expressing regret for King's death, an editorial in the segregationist organization's journal *The Citizen* agreed that the minister had it coming: "We also regret the efforts of his life's work and the white Liberal sickness that made it possible. For the wages of integration and 'black power' are violence, anarchy and death."[7] In addition, the editor did not understand all the fuss about the fallen civil rights leader. The writer lamented the constant television coverage of King's assassination. The *Citizen* took offense with the visible emotion shown by NBC newsman Chet Huntley and *Tonight Show* host Johnny Carson, who dared to wear a black suit to host that night's episode. "Everybody who was anybody in the hierarchy of Liberalism rushed before the cameras," the author complained. "The nation wallowed in a sea of negritude."[8]

SNCC associates rallied in their grief. At about 8:30 p.m. on the night of April 4, Lester McKinnie and Stokely Carmichael of the organization led marchers through Washington, D.C., streets, requesting that businesses close in memory of King. Businessmen complied, but marchers still turned violent in spite of pleas from McKinnie and Carmichael not to do so. Carmichael witnessed the crowd's shock and grief transforming into anger. He felt powerless to calm them down. Then again, he felt little need to do so, because he himself was enraged. Local SCLC leader Walter Fauntroy tried unsuccessfully to get Carmichael off the streets. Meanwhile, African American youths grabbed rocks and bottles to hurl, saying that they preferred Stokely's way now that King was gone. Thirty minutes later, rage poured into the streets. SNCC organizer Cleveland Sellers and fellow members tried to stop the rebels and prepare them for police confrontation. But by 11:00 p.m. rebellion was irreversible.[9]

The next day, SNCC addressed reporters in a less chaotic but just as dramatic setting. Joining Sellers, McKinnie, and Carmichael in Washington, D.C., for a press conference was Winkie Hall of the organization's local branch. McKinnie introduced his colleagues to the press and then announced that the conference would not last longer than five minutes. He added a rule about housekeeping, telling the journalists not to leave a mess. "Your films, your cigarette butts, you take them with you. You waste any water, you will have to clean it up."[10] Carmichael noted that SNCC was not exploiting King's death for the sake of media exposure, and he pointedly observed that SNCC had originally called the conference before King's killing in order to address Brown's current jail sentence and Governor Agnew's "nonsensical charges" against the chairman. But because of the previous night's events, a change in subject was unavoidable.

In the process of eulogizing King, Carmichael discussed the Kerner Commission's prediction of a color-based split as a foregone conclusion. "I think white America made the biggest mistake when she killed Dr. Martin Luther King last Thursday," he warned. "When she killed Dr. King, she killed the one man of our race in this country, in the generation, who is non-militant and a revolutionist in the masses of colored people, who has been sincere even though sometimes they did not agree with him," he mourned.[11] His reference to the late SCLC founder as "non-militant" absolved King of the accusations of violence that he had first received from the media and the government just eight days earlier, after the abortive march in Memphis.

To state the ramifications of King's death, Carmichael distorted the recent history of nonviolence and the appeal of urban violence. He claimed that King was the only African American who had "tried to teach our people to have love, compassion and mercy for what white people have done," but both CORE and SNCC had tried to love people out of their violence in countless sit-ins and marches. Echoing Rap Brown, Carmichael promised, "The rebellions that have been occurring in cities of this country has [sic] been light stuff to what is about to happen. We are going to retaliate." Elaborating on his theme of vigilantism, he predicted that revenge would not be in court or talks. "It will be in the streets of America." He then returned to his theme of the country's now-irreversible division by skin color. "White America will live to regret that she killed Dr. King," he predicted.[12]

SNCC then offered itself as a more appropriate alternative for martyrdom than King. "It would have been better if she killed Rap Brown and/or Stokely Carmichael. But when she killed Dr. King, she lost it." The fallen leader, after all, had believed in the redeeming power of nonviolence to save the United States. Assassinating a true believer in the country was worse than killing someone who had already considered himself in a revolution against the country. McKinnie then elaborated that white Americans shot down a symbol of nonviolence, just as the nonviolent demonstrators in Orangeburg were shot. King's killing was merely the latest "lesson which white America has taught us many times before"—the lesson of "day-to-day torture of black people by white people in America and throughout the world."[13]

Carmichael assured the press that King's death did not negate SNCC's agreement with SCLC regarding the PPC. The former SNCC chairman repeated the group's promise from two months earlier to support SCLC's upcoming demonstration in Washington, D.C. Having originally made the vow out of deference to King, the group now chose to keep that last promise to him as a memorial. "Whatever the Southern Christian Leadership Conference asks for today, we will give to them," Carmichael declared, "except our tears." He stated that no one would cry from that point onward "for any black man killed." African Americans did nothing but constantly die anyway and for naught—"cutting and fighting each other inside our own communities" and dying "in Vietnam for the honkies."[14]

He then wavered between embracing survival and embracing death, as if he did not want to fully believe that murder by European Americans was the only option for African Americans. At first the only useful activity he could see for African Americans was to "die in the streets for the people." But he also said that the nation had entered a "final showdown" and that "black people are going to have to find ways to survive." Still, even survival had violent connotations to him because "[t]he only way to survive is to get some guns." He saw his own chances for survival as very slim. "The Hell with my life," he proclaimed. "You should fear for yours. I know I'm going to die. I know I'm leaving."[15]

Remarkably, for all of Carmichael's talk of supporting SCLC and defending himself, the press saw *him* as violent. A reporter asked if he was declaring war. However, Carmichael responded by shifting the focus of violence:

"White America has declared war on black people." The movement had previously portrayed itself as an antagonist against a specific oppressive local-level individual and then relied on sympathetic media coverage to pressure the federal government to intervene on behalf of the activists. With Carmichael's statement, however, sympathetic coverage of the civil rights coalition was not forthcoming. Making "white America" the antagonist also included the mostly European American journalists, television networks, and federal officials. In addition, their ownership of these institutions meant that they were not likely to promote themselves or even "white America" as the nation's enemy.[16]

If anyone had doubts whether SNCC supported nonviolence in its press conference, the staging of Carmichael's remarks said it all. Members of the organization stood in front of large photographs of the late Malcolm X and the incarcerated Rap Brown. SNCC chose to visualize its remarks with images of two of the highest-profile people who disagreed with nonviolent civil disobedience. The organization's participants did not mention either person once, but the group placed the faces of the two on stage with it in order to imply solidarity with them. The staging indirectly validated SNCC's concern last September of constantly prioritizing its media image over substantive programming. In addition, the pairing of Brown with Malcolm X demonstrated that SNCC considered Brown an icon worthy of the same level of respect and esteem that many people had begun to give to Malcolm X. Moreover, although Malcolm X had been dead for three years, the presence of his image showed that his ideas still had relevance to the organization. Despite SNCC's multiple references to King in the press conference, the SCLC leader's photograph was noticeably absent there. Then again, in 125 cities across the country that day, so was nonviolence. After the press conference Carmichael drove from Washington, D.C., to Atlanta to attend King's upcoming funeral. From his car on the interstate, he could see smoke clouds rising from cities after every 100 miles.[17]

The other civil rights organizations were more subdued but no less grief-stricken than SNCC. As with Carmichael, Wilkins witnessed the post-assassination uprising in Washington, D.C., firsthand. The NAACP leader expressed more concern about the mood of the rioters there than about the uprising itself. Both he and entertainer Sammy Davis Jr. observed that the young people in the streets did not appear to be mourning. Rather, the rioters carried on happily as if at a carnival. Wilkins cynically concluded that they had been itching to engage in destruction and that King's death provided a convenient excuse to do so.[18]

Whitney Young focused not on rioters but on his feelings when commenting on King's death. The NUL director's comments significantly evolved in the week following the shooting. On the night King died, Young called his colleague's passing a "mortal blow" to devotees of nonviolence. Four days later, however, he validated whatever anger African Americans felt about the killing, just as he had supported Rap Brown's right to express himself the previous July. Moreover, Young couched his anger over King's passing in the context of Brown's angry image—an irony, considering that Brown was imprisoned at the time and offered no public statement from behind bars. "If you think that I am not as angry as Rap Brown, then you misread me," Young revealed. "I'm just no fool. I'm not going to give them an excuse to kill all Negroes with all the new weapons and practice they have." His remarks were another variation of Brown's Nazis-Jews connection and his own "liberate or exterminate" theory. King had been exterminated, and Young saw rioting in response as a means to secure his own extermination. He instead wanted to work constructively to be liberated.[19]

Meanwhile, SCLC tackled the difficult issue of the funeral and other aspects of the public presentation of the organization's transition period. Nearly all of the members wanted a stately funeral for King. He was, after all, a refined and urbane person as well as a Nobel Peace Prize winner who had conferred with U.S. presidents. On the other hand, SCLC official Hosea Williams insisted on having the pallbearers wear denim and for a mule train to pull the coffin through the streets of Atlanta. It would mark the launching point of SCLC's PPC. It would visibly represent the group's commitment to the poor and to King's vision of the PPC. The rest of the organization capitulated to Williams.

The members also discussed how to handle the announcement of Abernathy's ascension to the SCLC presidency. For years the organization had understood the contingency plan: in the event of King's death, Abernathy was to succeed him. The officials agreed, however, that Abernathy was not to announce his own rise to the position. Instead, Coretta Scott King agreed to make the announcement, and on April 6 she did. Because Abernathy had the public blessing of the King family for succession, the public reserved judgment about him.

Most of the mail that SCLC received immediately after King's death failed to mention Abernathy. People offering their condolences tended to address their letters to "sirs," "gentlemen," "SCLC staff," or "whom it may concern." On the other hand, the mail that Abernathy specifically received was overwhelmingly positive. Ray Hartsough of the American Friends Service Committee pledged the group's "sympathy and vote of confidence." Assuming that SCLC would conduct business as usual, he wished, "May your witness to the power of love and nonviolence continue strong and clear." Charles S.

Spivey was more specific about SCLC's upcoming business when encouraging Abernathy. "We stand ready to support your leadership in Memphis and for the Poor People's Campaign in Washington, DC," he promised.[20]

News commentators did not know what to make of SCLC's decision to name Abernathy the new president. They largely talked about how little they knew of the man—a sign that he had performed his "lieutenant" job well. They inevitably drew contrasts of preaching styles and professional backgrounds. King was the "city slicker," Abernathy the "country preacher." Most of the editorials had in common the notion of Abernathy as an unknown quantity. But because his predecessor was such a large public figure and SCLC was a world-famous movement group, Abernathy's anonymity vanished with King's last breath.

Abernathy did not help matters; in the first days of his presidency, he publicly drew comparisons between himself and his predecessor in inconsistent ways. At one gathering he claimed that he and King had the same dream. At another event, Abernathy distinguished between King's "dream" and his own "vision." In one instance he contradicted himself in the same speech. "I don't have to tell you that I am the leader. Baby, I am going to show you," he boasted. His next sentence, however, contained references to his presidency and to King's last speech: "We will get to the Promised Land. It will happen in *my* time and under *my* leadership." Even his attempts to reassure people of his self-confidence faltered. Longtime SCLC supporter Harry Belafonte did not like that Abernathy felt the need to tell audiences how good he felt about himself, as when he declared, "I've been Ralph David Abernathy for 42 years, and each time I look in the mirror in the morning I look better and better."[21]

A more fundamental problem remained, and it required more attention than SCLC could give to it because of King's upcoming funeral and the PPC. In the time between the organization's succession agreement and King's death, neither King nor SCLC had groomed Abernathy for the possibility of someday leading the group. No one had worked to build up Abernathy's image as a leader in the organization, as he had done for King. Abernathy had no "lieutenant" of his own. In addition, his role in SCLC largely concerned supporting King's vision, and King's directive that Abernathy was to always publicly agree with him prohibited Abernathy from developing leadership skills and experience within the group. As long as King had been alive, Abernathy had not been central in policy-making decisions. Now he was not only a policymaker but the public face of all of SCLC's policies during his presidency.[22]

The first task he and the organization performed upon King's death was to publicly commit to nonviolent civil disobedience. The death of the "dreamer" did not mean the demise of his dreams. The group vowed to each other on the night of King's death to continue the PPC. As reporters repeatedly asked what was to become of the fallen leader's plans and his organization, SCLC responded immediately. The group was still a viable entity. The second Memphis march, which King had scheduled for April 8, would take place as scheduled. King's PPC would go forward as planned.[23]

That message was not what Attorney General Ramsey Clark wanted to hear. Appearing on *Meet the Press* on April 7, he advised against the PPC. He warned, "Civil disobedience could be very risky at this time." Whereas his boss had asked people to pray and search their hearts, Clark offered rational reasons why the nation should calm down. He assured viewers that the authorities were working hard to find King's killer. Clark also tried to allay people's fears of conspiracies or organized efforts toward the post-assassination urban disturbances, saying that "the conduct in these cities was of the most random, the most disorganized type that could be imagined. It was purely capricious." Most unfortunate, however, was that a reporter felt the need to ask about rumors among African Americans about concentration camps to be constructed for them. Moreover, the attorney general was compelled to dignify the inquiry. Clark answered, as if hoping to settle the matter definitively, "There are no concentration camps in this country. There have been no concentration camps in this country. There will be no concentration camps in this country."[24]

SCLC chose to ignore Clark's advice against demonstrations. The organization carried out King's commitment to have a nonviolent march in Memphis. It took place on April 8—only 11 days after the violent march King had led. Twenty thousand people marched, and no violence from the marchers, the police, or anyone else marred the event. Abernathy spoke at the demonstration. Just as King had said the night before his death, his successor announced that he too had been to the mountaintop. He promised, "If God will lead me, I am going to lead my people into the Promised Land."[25]

Droves of various politicians and entertainers associated themselves with SCLC during the first week after King's death. Condolence calls and telegrams from Vice President Hubert Humphrey, former vice president Richard Nixon, and others poured into the King home and SCLC offices. New York governor Nelson Rockefeller offered his plane to fly King's remains from Memphis to Atlanta. Stokely Carmichael and New York senator Robert Kennedy worshiped at SCLC member Walter Fauntroy's church in Washington, D.C., on Sunday, April 7. After the service Fauntroy gave the senator a walking tour of the destruction in the nation's capital.

That same day, Nixon flew to Atlanta to visit Mrs. King at her home for about an hour. Meeting her in her room, he was struck by her poise and calmness. It was hardly a private gathering; photographers clicked their cameras as she thanked him for seeing her, and he told her how he had met King in 1957 and how he had admired her late husband. For the ex-vice president, the visit allowed him to make amends for a major mistake he had made with the King family eight years earlier. When King had been arrested during a sit-in in October 1960, Mrs. King appealed to Nixon, who was running for the presidency that year, for help. The Eisenhower administration did nothing. The Kennedy family, however, arranged for the minister's release and used the event to score political points with potential African American voters. The Kennedys funded pamphlets with the message "No Comment Nixon" and distributed them to African American churches nationwide. King's father, who had earlier supported Nixon, publicly switched his support to Kennedy. Now that Nixon was running for the presidency again, he made sure not to repeat the mistake of mishandling the King family.[26]

The funeral in Atlanta on April 9 marked the peak of the massive rallying around SCLC. Television networks covered the event live. Four members of SNCC attended the service, marched with SCLC to the gravesite, and saw King interred. Jackie Kennedy and Betty Shabazz, widows of other martyrs of the 1960s, paid their respects. Most of the celebrities merely attended the funeral, but the list of luminaries was impressive, considering the loss of support and publicity the organization had suffered in recent months. Sports figures Floyd Patterson and Jackie Robinson were there, as were actors Marlon Brando, Sammy Davis Jr., Eartha Kitt, and Paul Newman. Singers in attendance were Aretha Franklin and Motown personalities Stevie Wonder and the Supremes. Politicians included presidential candidates of both parties—Hubert Humphrey, Eugene McCarthy, Richard Nixon, George Romney, Nelson Rockefeller, and Robert Kennedy. The only missing presidential candidate was former Alabama governor George Wallace, who showed solidarity with his fellow Deep South politicians in avoiding the funeral. He was a segregationist, after all, and had famously stood at the door of the University of Alabama in 1963 to prevent the integration of the school. Despite his absence he echoed his presidential competitors in showing unqualified sympathy, calling King's death "a senseless, regrettable and tragic act" and demanding the immediate capture of the killer.[27]

Of all the presidential hopefuls at the funeral, Kennedy made the biggest impression on SCLC that day. He was the only presidential candidate who, like SNCC, went to the funeral, the march, and the burial. He marched yards away from Abernathy, who saw himself as a potential target for assassination.

When Kennedy met with SCLC later that day, however, the activists laid out their suspicions of him. They accused him of coming to Atlanta merely to win African American votes. He reassured SCLC that he had a program to bring the poor into the American economy and, by extension, into American society. Abernathy ended the meeting by embracing him. From that point onward, SCLC saw Kennedy as someone who could continue King's work in helping the poor and disadvantaged. As a result, the organization began giving some of its hope and loyalty to him.[28]

Meanwhile, Hoover kept tabs on SCLC's transfer of leadership. He told President Johnson that at the group's executive board meeting to confirm Abernathy's presidency that week, Jesse Jackson could possibly facilitate a "power struggle for leadership." No such conflict took place. On the other hand, the group's acceptance of Abernathy as the new president did not signify that he had become the new leader of the movement as a whole. SCLC's transferring of its aspirations and trust to Kennedy spoke to his impressive winning over of the organization in the few weeks since his campaign had begun. It also, however, spoke to how SCLC did not see its own president, who had been in the group from the beginning and had taken many of the same arrests and risks to life as King, as the same kind of leader. To SCLC officials, Kennedy was King's heir apparent as the national spokesman for civil rights, but Abernathy's role was to lead only SCLC. Hoover demonstrated an awareness of Abernathy's standing in SCLC when writing to Johnson that an internal takeover could happen.[29]

April 11 turned out to be a busy day for the critics of the movement. Now that Hoover knew that the unofficial position of national movement leader was up for grabs, he wanted to monitor the succession process. Consequently, COINTELPRO was soon contemplating ways of preventing Brown from gaining a larger following in the wake of King's death. The ideas in the week since King's death were more serious than before; no one proposed coloring books anymore. One new proposal concerned fostering distrust and suspicion among SNCC leaders toward each other. Such a tactic stood a great chance of success because the organization was rife with factionalism by then. However, Hoover turned down his New York–based special agent's idea of sending the following phony letter to Brown:

Dear Rap,

Dig this man. I got it from inside. Stokely and Forman sent you to the West Coast so that the man would get you. They are a little too cool for you Rap Baby. With you out of the way, they can have the whole pie.

Soul Brother[30]

Elsewhere on the East Coast that same day, Maryland governor Spiro Agnew decided to process the events of the past week by addressing the "responsible militants" of the state. Speaking to a collection of local civil rights activists at a conference room in Baltimore, his opening sentence—"Hard on the heels of tragedy come the assignment of blame and the excuses"—was hardly encouraging. He had come to them to bring not peace in the aftermath of King's death, but a sword dividing the movement, as he had first done last July. He proceeded to congratulate the invited leaders for earning their leadership, noting that "each leader present has *worked* his way to the top." And in a dig at Brown and his ilk, Agnew noted the absence of "the ready-mix, instantaneous type of leader," "the circuit-riding, Hanoi-visiting type of leader," and "the caterwauling, riot-inciting, burn-America-down type of leader" from the gathering.

The governor then blamed his audience for allowing the uprisings in Maryland to take place because of their refusal to speak out publicly against Carmichael, who had appeared in Baltimore the day before King's death. The city did indeed go up in flames on April 4, but Agnew's claim that Carmichael had agitated local African Americans on April 3 implied that somehow the organizer had known in advance that someone would shoot King the next day. Regardless, Agnew tried to show his audience that he understood why they did not condemn Carmichael, saying that people like the SNCC leader embraced a "perverted concept of race loyalty" that made any African American who criticized another of his or her ethnic group an ethnic traitor. "You were stung by insinuations that you were Mr. Charlie's boy, by epithets like 'Uncle Tom,'" he surmised. "God knows I cannot fault you who spoke out for breaking and running in the face of what appeared to be overwhelming opinion in the Negro community," he patronizingly consoled.[31] He then reassured them that only the irresponsible militants embraced these views, which is why his audience did not need to be hesitant to publicly criticize them. His words of comfort fell on deaf ears as African Americans began to walk out of the address in disgust.

Undeterred, the governor decided to present himself as an example of responsible African American leadership, despite his Greek American ethnicity. "I publicly repudiate, condemn and reject all white racists," he announced, failing to mention that he was not sacrificing anything by doing so. Indeed, he did not need to fear anyone calling him "Mr. Charlie's Boy" or "Uncle Tom" for his stance. Nevertheless, he continued, "I call upon you to publicly repudiate, condemn and reject all black racists. This, so far, you have not been willing to do." In case the audience was ignorant as to who were the "black racists," Agnew became more specific: "I call upon you as Americans to speak out now against the treason and hate of Stokely Carmichael and Rap Brown." To him, race relations had become a zero-sum game in the wake of the Kerner Commission's findings of the nation as two distinct societies of "white" and "black." If Agnew as "white" had to condemn racists of his group, then by his logic, "you have an obligation, too."[32]

The governor's challenge incensed his audience. Local NAACP lawyer Juanita Jackson Mitchell, however, attempted to explain to Agnew her view that the uprising grew out of slow to nonexistent progress through civil disobedience. Without offering specific examples, she reasoned that many protesters felt that violence succeeded where nonviolence had failed. She disliked that it was so, but "this city, this government have made our children what they are . . . have made our children burners and looters." Her remarks were nearly identical to those Agnew himself had given back in July, when he had claimed that he could understand what drove people to insurrection despite its illegality.

Agnew, however, seemed unable to recognize his own words from her. He yelled at her in response and demanded, "Are you willing, as I am, to repudiate the Carmichaels and the Browns? Answer me! Answer me!" He continued, "Do you repudiate Rap Brown and Stokely Carmichael? Do you? Do you?" Mitchell was shaken but refused to repudiate them as people. Shortly afterward, the governor adjourned the meeting and left the room, having failed to rally the civil rights leaders to his cause through condescension and goading.[33]

Nevertheless, he had finally said what he had wanted to say to the activists for months. He had been angered by them ever since they had refused to condemn Brown back the previous July for his remarks in Cambridge. The Baltimore uprising simply provided the occasion for him to justify calling them all to a meeting for him to vent his frustration at them. In addition, by gathering them, he avoided condemning anyone on an individual basis; he was able to lash out against the movement as a whole. In a sense, he capitalized on the trend he had started. Ever since his response to Cambridge the previous July, some politicians had begun blaming various individual militants for uprisings, which led to other officials placing the movement at fault. Only Agnew, however, had been able to blame the movement en masse in the presence of the movement itself.

Although Governor Agnew did not admit as much to the activists, the movement genuinely perplexed him. He was firm in his belief that agitators caused riots, but Baltimore's implosion in the wake of King's killing left Agnew unable to grasp the rationale behind the destruction the vandals and arsonists had caused. Because King's death had led people to violently demonstrate, he no longer was a "responsible militant," as far as the governor was concerned. "I never did think that Martin Luther King was a good American, anyhow," he groused to an aide.[34]

African American leaders responded to the governor's harangue with tempered outrage. Evoking antebellum times, state senator Clarence Mitchell claimed that Agnew had tried to identify the attendees as house servants to be held in higher esteem than the uninvited militant field servants. Others called him "sick" and a "bigot." When they tried to explain his behavior, however, most of the activists gave the governor the benefit of the doubt out of respect for his office. They figured that he was tired from having dealt with the uprising in Baltimore earlier that week. Perhaps he had lost sleep while handling the crisis. Even as some leaders walked out in a huff, they interspersed encouraging statements like "We love you" with demands of respect: "We'll come back when you talk to us like ladies and gentlemen."[35]

Other local African Americans responded more dramatically. Shortly after Agnew's meeting with the leaders, a group of college students draped a white sheet and a bullwhip over the fence of the governor's mansion. By choosing symbols evoking the Ku Klux Klan instead of using mere words, the students specifically sought the visual media coverage of periodicals and television. In addition, by associating the governor with the Klan, the students challenged his moderate reputation. Also, by tying him to an organization known for its hostility toward the movement, the students were among the first African Americans to receive media coverage for giving him the antagonist role in the civil rights narrative. They were certainly not the last to do so.[36]

Because the governor addressed only local leaders at the meeting, the proceedings escaped national media coverage. Agnew was not a nationally known figure, and the activists he attacked did not campaign beyond the local level. However, in nearby Washington, D.C., a young man named Pat Buchanan saw a story about the conference, clipped it out of the periodical, and showed it to his employee—Republican presidential candidate Richard Nixon. The former vice president was greatly impressed by the governor's conduct toward his audience.[37]

As Agnew grew agitated in Baltimore, President Johnson somberly signed the Civil Rights Act of 1968 in Washington, D.C., that day. On the heels of King's assassination, Congress had quickly passed a law providing strengthened federal enforcement of open housing. It represented a legislative memorial of sorts to the fallen SCLC leader. However, it did not come without compromise. It also included a provision attached by a conservative Senate coalition led by South Carolina's Dixiecrat senator Strom Thurmond. The provision stated that the "intent" to incite to riot constituted a criminal offense. The law prescribed a fine of $10,000 or five years in prison—or both—for anyone who "travels in interstate commerce or uses any facility of interstate or foreign commerce, including but not limited to the mail, telegraph, telephone, radio or television, with intent to incite riot."[38]

Just as Johnson was currently trying to balance funding America's "guns" in Vietnam and "butter" for the hungry, Congress wanted its new act to please both the "civil rights" and "law and order" crowds. Although the nation's courts had often judged a defendant's intent, such as the offense of assault with intent to kill, the antiriot provision introduced the controversial possibility for the government to determine a person's frame of mind regarding civil disorders. As a result the new law threatened to spark overwhelming and broad questions concerning the distinction between lawful dissent and an unlawful intent to create disorder. *Time* magazine wondered if the new law was unconstitutional, considering that "a host of local, state and federal laws already cover acts of incitement to riot." Regardless, Senator Thurmond's provision served as a federal reprimand of Brown's actions in Cambridge, and the antiriot provision of King's memorial law was soon nicknamed "The H. Rap Brown Act." Even in death, King remained tied to Brown.[39]

Upon signing the legislation, Johnson addressed Congress by shaming the legislators, eulogizing King, and calling for national unity. He referred to the history of the new law, first introduced in Congress two years earlier, as "a long and strange trip." He reminded the legislators of their previous rejections of the act and referred to their resistance as an absence of justice. He then declared, "Now, with this bill, the voice of justice speaks again." He assumed that the country shared his respect for King, claiming, "Of course, all America is outraged at the assassination of an outstanding Negro leader who was at that meeting that afternoon in the White House in 1966." On the other hand, he spoke as if the nation disagreed with Brown's call for revolutionary arson, even as the last of the urban fires had just been extinguished hours ago. "America is also outraged at the looting and burning that defiles our democracy," he observed. "We just must put our shoulders together and put a stop to both." He ended with a plea for people to have faith in the nation's legal system, professing that "the only real road to progress for free people is through the process of law, and that is the road that America will travel."[40]

His speech was mismatched at best, but its structure and clashing themes perfectly fit the current post-King national discord. Within days, Chicago mayor Richard Daley ordered his police force to "shoot to kill" rioters. People argued over whether King was a martyr for freedom or a victim of the violence his demonstrations fostered. President Johnson's address also reflected the current instability of the movement as it frantically struggled to redefine itself immediately after King's assassination.

CHAPTER 4

Facing Annihilation

Immediately after King's funeral, SCLC went to work on the PPC. Andrew Young worked hard to arrange for the African American press to publicize the journey to Resurrection City. Abernathy appeared on the cover of *Jet* magazine's May 30 issue, wearing denim and driving a wagon pulled by mules. Before then, Abernathy had rarely been photographed without King at his side. Now he not only was in a photograph alone, but he was also imaged as holding the reins, taking charge. The mules represented the rest of SCLC, putting forth a public show of support of Abernathy's leadership. However, the nagging question from the press about whether the "mules" would remain compliant or begin to stubbornly resist him followed the mule train all the way to Resurrection City.[1]

The denim and the mules were not the only parts of SCLC's new look. At Resurrection City people wore armbands with the letters "MGD." They stood for "Mississippi God Damn"—a reference to a song Nina Simone had written in response to the deaths in 1963 of NAACP member Medgar Evers by gunfire and four girls in a church bombing. Just as Simone had musically expressed frustration with the slow pace of civil rights progress, SCLC said the armband was the organization's warning that God would damn the state unless it corrected itself. Simone, however, cursed Mississippi in the song because of the repression that it inflicted on its citizens. Regardless of how Abernathy interpreted the song, he wore the armband, too—a clear stylistic break from King that the media immediately noted.[2]

SCLC also launched a new slogan to blend its integrationist vision with the appeal of power to young people. Anyone could chant "Soul Power"; it was not just for African Americans to attain. Also, no one could argue—as critics of Black Power had done—that calling for Soul Power took away from the power of European Americans. Jesse Jackson led chants of the slogan to rally the residents of Resurrection City on various occasions. However, as with Black Power, no one could easily define the new phrase.

Nevertheless, the slogan symbolized the fragile solidarity among the major civil rights organizations after King's funeral. They offered support to Resurrection City more to honor King's last wish than to rally around his successor Ralph Abernathy. Meanwhile, SCLC tried to balance its commitments to nonviolence and integrationism with its drive to appeal to young, increasingly militant people. Disagreements about Black Power, the Vietnam War, and Rap Brown's rhetoric did not go away, but civil rights workers set them aside for a few weeks to make King's PPC as successful as possible.

Thousands of poor people encamped at West Potomac Park in Washington, D.C., that May. A-frame houses made of plywood filled the area. Many of the houses remained sparse, but some people planted gardens around their plywood homes. Some of the campers had brought nothing with them, making their new houses their only possessions. People put signs on some of the new buildings to designate "city" offices or social organizations. The PPC made a city hall, schools, and a health care facility, among other institutions.

As a memorial to King, Resurrection City transcended political viewpoint. In May, SNCC's Stokely Carmichael and Lester McKinnie visited Resurrection City as a gesture of goodwill. Keeping their promise to King, no one from SNCC publicly said anything to detract from SCLC's efforts. Also, Democrat and Republican presidential candidates considered a stop by the encampment to be good politics. Vice President Hubert Humphrey, New York mayor John Lindsay, and Senator Charles Percy of Illinois made appearances, and Eugene McCarthy sent a telegram of encouragement.[3]

Some of the political blurring did harm to Resurrection City. Reies Tijerina led a delegation of the PPC, showing his willingness to cooperate with SCLC as well as with SNCC. His was an unlikely participation, especially because his demonstrations with the SHLG were purposely not nonviolent. He and his fellow members occupied lands and facilities while carrying firearms—an image considerably more similar to that of the BPP than to SCLC. His involvement provided a means for him to publicize issues concerning Mexican Americans. He quarreled with SCLC officials, however, as to the extent of the involvement of Mexican Americans in the facilitating of Resurrection City. The dispute fractured the image of multiethnic solidarity that the PPC had tried to promote to the public.[4]

Senator Robert Kennedy was the PPC's closest political kindred spirit in expressing concern for the poor. By aligning with African Americans, he was swimming against an increasingly strong tide in the aftermath of King's death. People stopped asking him what he was going to do about the problems facing African Americans. Instead, they asked him what he was going to do to address the urban uprisings. Some of the people he defended criticized him, too. In California he met with young members of the NAACP, the BPP, and SNCC. They proceeded to harangue him for two hours. During that time they often refused to let him fully answer their questions. And when they allowed him to respond, they dismissively accused him of lying. However, when he decided to take two additional questions after the moderator—an African American assemblyman named Willie Brown—had ended the proceedings, the senator earned the assemblyman's respect.

Kennedy's steadfastness to the concerns of the poor and of minority ethnic groups won him a multiethnic array of supporters, not unlike the population of Resurrection City. Moreover, he embraced the SCLC project as part of the culture of his campaign. When he traveled to Los Angeles to greet people, a mass of African Americans and Mexican Americans came to see him. They yelled his name, begged for his autograph, and touched whatever part of his hand they could when he extended it to the crowd. Kennedy, in turn, relished the turnout and the energy of the attendees. He exuberantly called them his "Resurrection City"—a reference not only to the makeshift city in Washington, D.C., but also to his hopes that California's minority voters would resurrect his presidential campaign after a recent loss in the Oregon primary.[5]

California indeed came through for him. He won the state's primary on June 4. At his state's campaign headquarters at the Ambassador Hotel, he took the stage. "My thanks to all of you," he cheered, "and now it's on to Chicago, and let's win there!"[6] Among those joining him on stage during his victory speech was Marian Wright, who had come up with the idea of Resurrection City.

When Kennedy was shot in that hotel shortly after midnight on June 5 and died the next day, the PPC's fragile multiethnic coalition at Resurrection City crumbled. Once again, violence seemed to be the answer to people's nonviolent efforts in bringing about change for minority groups. Almost immediately, the various ethnic groups at West Potomac Park were at each other's throats. Tijerina and SCLC had a final falling-out over a demonstration he had assumed SCLC had approved. Although the organization did not endorse his idea to lead a march at the State Department, he did it anyway. Elsewhere in the city, one ethnic group blamed Latinos for taking away jobs, while another chided the indigenous people for not defeating the cowboys. The one display of solidarity among the minorities was the curses they shouted at the nuns who came daily to feed the campers, just because the nuns were European American. Anger now permeated Resurrection City.[7]

Meanwhile, SCLC members grieved Kennedy's death in their own way. The organization had worked hard on Resurrection City for the past two months in order to show that King's death had not paralyzed the organization. However, the group did not allow itself to grieve King's loss until Kennedy died. When Stoney Cooks heard of the senator's assassination, he said to himself, "My God, again." In a final show of support for the PPC, the train carrying the late senator's remains stopped at Resurrection City. Then, the next day SCLC carried on its work without yet another leader.[8]

COINTELPRO remained busy, as well, laboring to discredit the PPC. And after months of trying to figure out how to undermine SCLC's efforts, the FBI finally found something that gained traction. Agents learned that two people associated with the PPC were staying at the lavish Pitts Motel in Washington, D.C., while the impoverished wallowed in the mud on West Potomac Park. The agents wanted to confidentially send the information to cooperative news outlets. They tailored the revelation to contrast the PPC workers' exquisite lodgings with the squalor of Resurrection City.

Consequently, over the course of the campaign, more and more detractors paid attention to who in SCLC was settled among the poor and who was not. The organization had lost control of the dialogue about its event; journalists and politicians stopped focusing on the issue of poverty itself. By June, Governor Agnew had returned to national prominence by regularly criticizing the project, calling SCLC members hypocrites and "lobbyists for opportunism" for both living in the mud and flying cross-county for speeches. He also harped on "the Cadillacs parked around Resurrection City."[9]

Agnew had a nationally televised forum to express his disdain for the PPC as well as for the movement later that month. On June 16, he appeared with three other Republican governors on *Meet the Press* and fielded several questions about his views on civil rights. He claimed to be "more liberal today than I was when I took office" in relation to championing equality for all. He disliked, however, that the movement concerned itself with issues having little to do with civil rights. Singling out SCLC's new president for criticism, Agnew complained, "It concerns me when I read in the paper that a leader who is consistently before the media, such as Mr. Abernathy, is advocating turning a city upside-down." Next, attacking SCLC and President Johnson at the same time, he remarked, "I said that I was not at all in sympathy with the Poor People's March and that I couldn't visualize any President giving any group of people having a special interest the right to camp out on that public land." He then restated his accusation that the PPC was pulling a hoax. "I question the identification of these people as the poor people," he said. "No one has ever proved to me that these people are poor, and there are a lot of Cadillacs parked over there."[10]

At times the public criticized Resurrection City, too. Some people sent postcards to the residents at large, trying to persuade them to leave the encampment. One person blamed the demonstrators for their own laziness. The postcard's only words were, "You want help? Get a job. *Work!* Then ask for welfare." Another person tried to foster distrust toward Abernathy, especially in the context of the reports about his indoor lodgings. "He is having a ball while y'all suffer," the writer announced. "You better watch him."[11]

With Kennedy's death, SCLC intensified its efforts to convince the public that Resurrection City represented an alternative to violence. People had to support the PPC if they wanted nonviolence to remain a relevant, viable option of protest. Within the organization, however, differences arose over how to predict the ramifications of the failure of the PPC. Abernathy noted that African Americans would turn violent and conduct another summer of urban insurrections—a prediction King himself had made months earlier. In contrast, James Bevel warned that European Americans would be the violent ones, following Andrew Young's lead in co-opting Rap Brown's references to Nazi Germany. "When fear becomes sufficient in a Hitler's Germany, they will murder off Jews in an attempt to eliminate their own anxiety," he lectured. "We're sittin' around playin' dead, duckin', pretending like we're into somethin', and we're facing annihilation."[12]

Nothing that the White House offered to the poor seemed to help. The PPC sent its demands to President Johnson's cabinet members shortly after Resurrection City's residents arrived. The heads of Agriculture, Health, Education and Welfare, Housing and Urban Development, the Interior, Labor, the Office of Economic Opportunity, and State sent multipage responses to the PPC between May 25 and June 5. However, in the space of only three days—June 12, 13, and 14—the PPC responded negatively to each department. Each official addressed the demands inadequately, as far as the PPC was concerned. In its responses the group noted where departments tried to solve problems and where departments simply ignored the demands. The Johnson administration gave no further rebuttal to the campaign, thus severing itself—once and for all—from SCLC.[13]

Solidarity Day—June 19—marked not only the high point of the PPC but also its turning point. As with King's funeral, politicians and entertainers attended. It was an all-day affair at the Washington Monument, not unlike the

1963 March on Washington. Presidential candidates used their attendance there as a photo opportunity and a way to demonstrate concern for African Americans. Campaigning for the Democratic nomination, Eugene McCarthy drew cheers while there, but Vice President Humphrey received boos. Meanwhile, on the Republican side, Steven Rockefeller represented his father, New York governor Nelson Rockefeller. Actors included Eartha Kitt and costars Bill Cosby and Robert Culp of the recently cancelled television series *I Spy*; and among the singers were Jerry Butler, Pete Seeger, and the folk trio Peter, Paul, and Mary. Even the leaders of the more conservative African American groups, like Whitney Young of the NUL and Roy Wilkins of the NAACP, came to speak. The mood, however, was somber. Young raised the possibility of the event becoming the last nonviolent demonstration of the movement, and among the signs were the militant "Red Power" from indigenous attendees and "Up Against the Wall Motherfuck*r" from antiwar activists who slightly censored their own sign. Actor Ossie Davis set the tone for the day as master of ceremonies by declaring, "We didn't come down here to sing and dance. We mean business."[14]

The addresses people gave repulsed the audience instead of inspiring it. The spectators were struggling to hear the speakers over the loud jets that flew overhead throughout the event, and they were sweltering from the oppressive heat of the day. They did not appreciate hearing repetitive antigovernment speeches from one orator after another. Placing the concerns of SCLC in the context of her own personal politics, Coretta Scott King provided one of the more uplifting messages. But even hers had started with condemnations of indomitable social problems. After leading the crowd to sing, "Come by Here," she reinforced SCLC's commitment to nonviolence by warning the spectators that poverty routinely produced violence. She gave a list of several items that constituted violence: "starving a child . . . suppressing a culture . . . neglecting schoolchildren . . . punishing a mother and her child . . . discrimination against a workingman . . . ghetto housing . . . . ignoring medical needs . . . contempt for equality . . . even a lack of will power to help humanity."[15] She then made a feminist reference—a rarity for movement groups such as the male-dominated SCLC—by calling for women to fulfill their particular "moral obligation" to stop the Vietnam War. Next, when moving to SCLC's tendency to compare the war to domestic issues, she offered examples of how the federal government could help the impoverished by ending the conflict and dispersing money for new housing and job creation. She concluded by powerfully delivering words that were not her own—Langston Hughes's poem "Mother to Son" and her late husband's "I Have a Dream" speech. The latter was so familiar to the listeners that they joined in the recitation at the end. A teary Mrs. King left the stage to a rousing standing ovation.[16]

Mrs. King's address may have been the highlight of Solidarity Day, but it was not the keynote speech. The delivery of that message fell to Abernathy. His was an unenviable task in multiple ways. He not only competed with screaming planes and the hot sun, but now he had to follow Mrs. King's successful remarks. On the one hand, it was ironic that he was the follow-up to a King instead of the warm-up speaker. On the other hand, his position on the Solidarity Day agenda reflected his current position as SCLC president—taking his turn after a dazzling performance by a King. He responded to the challenge with a mixture of pessimism and anti-government bravado. "The promise of a Great Society was burned to ashes by the napalm in Vietnam," Abernathy bemoaned, "and we watched the Johnson administration perform as the unwitting midwife at the birth of the sick society."[17] Holding out hope that the country could still save itself, he recited a list of demands in order for the government to accomplish that goal. He finished by defiantly vowing not to vacate Resurrection City if its permit for occupation lapsed. He claimed that his personal permit came not from the government, not from the Constitution, but "from God almighty." He greeted his company on stage with a raised-fist "Soul Power" salute as he left the microphone.[18]

No speech could save Solidarity Day, however. People had started filling the Washington Monument area since the morning hours, but Mrs. King did not deliver her speech until 5:00 p.m.—30 minutes after the event had been scheduled to end. Abernathy's address began an hour later. The initial crowd of 50,000 people gradually dwindled to 10,000—half the number of the Memphis marchers of April 8—before Solidarity Day ended at 7:00. Even Andrew Young considered the event long and full of boring speeches.[19]

After having spent weeks leading the PPC to directly confront government agencies without much success, Abernathy decided to go it alone for the biggest target. On Sunday, June 23, he saw an opportunity for a face-to-face meeting with President Johnson at a house of worship. The SCLC president tried to attend the church that Johnson usually attended. The president's security detail was one step ahead of Abernathy, however, and relocated Johnson to another church. The two leaders never saw each other that day.[20]

The next morning Abernathy resumed his work on the PPC with yet another march. He led over 200 marchers to the Capitol. Or at least, he attempted to do so. The demonstrators were intimidated by the massive lines of gray-clothed police officers along the way, and Abernathy struggled to keep the protesters focused on him. The police would not let the marchers onto the Capitol grounds. Abernathy tried for an hour to appeal to them. He tried with sympathy: "People are dying of starvation." He tried with citizenship: "This is our Capitol. We pay taxes. . . . These are our Senators and our Congressmen."[21] Nothing worked. The permit had expired, and the PPC had to either leave or face arrest. Directing his demonstrators to sit down, Abernathy chose the latter.

The police chief then set up his own office in the street. He and his officers began processing the marchers for detainment and arrested them. Abernathy smiled as officers walked him to their vehicle. It was his first arrest after King's death. For the first time in years, his best friend would not be joining him in jail. As the jailed leader of his predecessor's campaign that had fallen apart on his watch, Abernathy had a truly solitary confinement.

The marchers experienced a peaceful expulsion, compared to what happened to the other citizens of Resurrection City that morning. Police officers overdressed with protective apparel and weapons as if storming North Vietnam instead of a nonviolent domestic encampment. They knocked on the A-frames, ordering the occupants to remove themselves. They sprayed residents with tear gas and dragged them through the streets, out of the makeshift city.

In a matter of hours, the police disestablished Resurrection City. All that remained after the arrests were the visible reminders of the presence of the nation's poorest. Officers dismantled all of the wooden frames. Bulldozers came and razed King's final project. After nearly two months, West Potomac Park was once again vacant.[22]

With SCLC's president detained, the task of keeping the evicted from rioting fell to Jesse Jackson later that evening. Indigenous and Latino settlers like Tijerina deserted the city, leaving Jackson with mostly African Americans in his midst. Instead of giving a speech, he thought of a "call and response" to involve and perhaps distract the dispossessed. He started leading a chant of "I am somebody." He told them, "If you are somebody, you don't riot." The crowd did not turn to uprising that night. Soul Power saved the day.[23]

After the city disintegrated, SCLC officials still showed their detachment from the former campers. They spoke less about the displaced than about the running of Resurrection City. In contrast to the despair of the evicted, the leaders of the defunct municipality expressed relief. Hosea Williams had not liked the idea of the Resurrection City campaign in the first place. He looked forward to having SCLC redirecting its attention to Congress instead of managing a city. Although not as opposed to the former city, Andrew Young mused more bluntly that "whoever ran us out maybe did us a favor."[24]

Meanwhile, the organization and the media rallied around Abernathy as he remained incarcerated. In early July, SCLC board chair Joseph Lowery asked the members and allies who were not currently in Washington, D.C., to "wire words of encouragement to our president, and encourage your constituents to do the same." Also, a television interview Abernathy had taped before his arrest happened to broadcast that week. He appeared on *The Merv Griffin Show*, telling the host about the problems of poor Southerners. As he sat in his cell, he told a radio reporter a simple message he had for his supporters: "Please write to me."[25]

As a result of all these efforts, the SCLC president received several cards and letters of prayer and pleas for him to stay strong while in jail. Longtime civil rights activist Esau Jenkins saluted him, "We join with thousands and thousands of your admires on the tremendous sacrifice you are making for the Poor People of this country." Lillie Hunter wrote a letter of encouragement but also expressed concern to Abernathy about not having King incarcerated with him now. "Try not to miss him too deeply," she advised.[26]

SCLC historian L. D. Reddick used his letter to help Abernathy learn from Resurrection City and plan the organization's future steps. He praised the group leader for having scored "touchdowns" early in his tenure by helping the Memphis sanitation workers settle with the city and by holding a successful Solidarity Day. Then he assessed SCLC's condition, observing that "we are now so exhausted from the months-long Poor People's march that we ought to 'cool it' for a while, take stock, re-group and re-tool before we move on." He saw harmful media exposure as a major problem for the organization, but he partly blamed SCLC officials for the negative publicity. "Your staff does not seem to be able to resist the mikes and the cameras," he noted. Comments such as Young's "did us a favor" remark fed into rumors that the group planned the city's shutdown, Reddick observed. He wanted SCLC to refrain from such public comments in order for activists to be able to fully trust the organization's integrity. He even called Abernathy to task: "In retrospect, was it wise for you not to live for a while in Resurrection City?"[27]

Even with the dismantling of Resurrection City, SCLC remained defiant and was far from ready to "cool it." On July 5, Hosea Williams sent telegrams to SCLC's female members, asking them to meet in Washington, D.C., in five days to "set up a National Steering Committee to mobilize women throughout America for a 'Women's Go to Jail Day.'" Days later, Abernathy—newly freed from jail—and Young told the press that the city's closure did not end the PPC but rather just the first phase of it. They announced SCLC's intent to maintain a presence in Washington, D.C., on behalf of the poor. They intended to lobby in Congress, conduct boycotts against companies that ignored poverty issues, and demonstrate at political conventions. SCLC, however, had already tried and failed to arouse the attention of Congress, and the PPC did not attract African Americans who were residents of the nation's capital. The organization's rhetoric of a second phase merely constituted an attempt to save face.[28]

On July 7, Charles Evers of the NAACP in Mississippi offered his opinion of the PPC on *Face the Nation*. "I don't think Resurrection City failed," he began. To him, the United States was to blame for not noticing problems facing poor people of all ethnic groups. "We haven't failed," he restated. "We have proved our point." As far as poverty was concerned, SCLC had done all that it could do to show the issue to the nation. Evers placed the onus on the United States to "do what is right or suffer the consequences." His was a message that activists from the conservative King to the militant BPP had been preaching for over a year now, and like the others Evers presented no details as to how the United States could do right by the poor, what exactly was "what is right," what were "the consequences," and how the consequences would manifest themselves. Moreover, the absence of consistent, unifying leadership in the movement made the possibility for concrete specifics infinitely remote.[29]

Although Senator Kennedy had aligned himself with SCLC, his killing in June led journalist Ronald G. Cohen to talk about Rap Brown later that week. The reporter saw the senator's death as validation of Brown's declaration of violence as "American as cherry pie." To prove his point, Cohen collected quotes from several well-respected academicians who agreed with the SNCC speaker. "We are a violent people with a violent history," began the historian Arthur Schlesinger Jr., "and the instinct for violence has seeped into the bloodstream of our national life." David Abrahamson of Brandeis University asserted that Americans condoned violence and that "we love to fight." To him, competition among Americans for achievement was central to the fighting spirit. "We're not a melting pot, we're a damned pressure cooker," he lamented. "Our society is not built on the restraints of family or class, it's built on success. If you don't have it you're frustrated." And that frustration, in turn, was "the wet nurse of violence."[30]

The article was unique for its exclusive focus on Brown. At the time the press and elected officials often illustrated Brown and Carmichael as if they spoke as a pair, and public figures frequently mentioned the two leaders' names together when discussing current domestic unrest. Both men were now ex-chairmen of SNCC, and they had developed ties to the Black Panthers. On the other hand, the two speakers only rhetorically shared dissatisfaction with nonviolence as a demonstration tool. Still, the media rarely differentiated Carmichael as a Pan-Africanist or Brown for his concern for various ethnic minority groups.

SNCC's decision that month to deemphasize the prominence of its chair position symbolized a tacit agreement with Brown about the country's violent tendencies. Near the end of June, the organization resolved at a staff meeting to restructure its leadership from one chairman to several deputy chairmen. They were James Forman and Johnny Wilson of New York, Bob Smith and Donald Stone of Atlanta, Ronald "Brother Crook" Wilkins of Los Angeles, George Ware of Tuskegee, and Stanley Wise of North Carolina. It was a drastic measure to stop encouraging the media's portrayal of the chairman as leader at the expense of the organizing efforts of the remainder of the organization. Also, in the aftermath of King's death, SNCC's continued use of only one chairman put the official at great risk as a target for assassination. Especially with Brown having been wounded in Cambridge last July while serving as chairman, SNCC's concern was not at all farfetched.[31]

Brown took himself out of the running for reelection to the chairman position, having only been released from prison two months earlier. He did not serve as a cochairman or in any other administrative role after SNCC's reorganization, but he remained active in the group. He kept his organizational office in New York. He spent most of that time writing his autobiography, and his colleague Julius Lester helped him prepare it for publication. Meanwhile, SNCC took pains to assure the public that the former chairman was still a member of the organization. The New York branch publicly demanded justice for him, noting that "H. Rap Brown was not tried by a jury of his peers" but by people with "middle-class values and absolutely no concept of Rap's work in the black liberation struggle."[32]

Although Brown had condemned other civil rights leaders for promoting nonviolence, SNCC–New York had no qualms about exploiting the doctrine's late apostle. The group claimed in a document from May 24 that "Dr. Martin Luther King, Jr.'s last official public act was to sign a petition . . . demanding that Rap be set free by the Federal Government. [He] understood that Rap was a political prisoner jailed in violation of his right to freedom of speech." This reference to King solidified a shift in how civil rights activists promoted him to serve their causes. With the slain leader now buried, the time for berating "white America" for killing him had passed. Now it was time for civil rights groups to publicize how he had pushed toward the same goals that they still wanted. SCLC had masterfully done so by promoting Resurrection City as King's last campaign, and the other organizations started drawing their own parallels to him. Perhaps their exploitation of his name would attract celebrities and presidential candidates, too.[33]

Brown's adjustment to domestic life also contributed to his vacating of the SNCC chairmanship. On May 3, he had married a local schoolteacher named Lynne Doswell. She was a child of the movement; her mother had worked for Thurgood Marshall's Legal Defense Fund for the NAACP. As an adult, Doswell worked with SNCC but did not officially join the organization. By 1966, she had started a chapter of Friends of SNCC—an offshoot organization based outside the South, collecting funds and other resources for SNCC—at the State University of New York at Oswego.

Brown and Doswell had met exactly one week after his remarks in Cambridge. They immediately started regularly dating. Meanwhile, Doswell started organizing for SNCC–New York to help out her new beau. Their courtship survived the next nine months of arrests, court dates, and speeches. Brown's lawyer William Kunstler, in fact, arranged the wedding and hosted the ceremony at his house. After the ceremony, Brown went on trial in New Orleans, and Doswell flew there to sit at the hearing.

The newlyweds sought privacy in their relationship. As Brown stepped down from SNCC's chairman position, Doswell curtailed her public activism. The household already had one well-known infamous public figure, and Doswell saw that her husband carried a heavy burden with his infamy. As a result, the couple rarely conducted public activities together, and they kept a peaceful home. He took seriously his role of her protector and was also careful to keep the household secure. The couple initially kept their marriage a secret, at the insistence of Doswell's mother—but it remained private knowledge for only two weeks. On the day Doswell returned to work, a newspaper headline revealed, "Black Power Advocate Got Married in White Lawyer's House." As she was teaching in her classroom, a colleague yelled out to her, "Congratulations!"[34]

Carmichael did not enjoy as good a standing in SNCC as his successor did, and the organization's care to keep Brown a part of the group did not extend to Carmichael. The latter did not attend SNCC meetings after Brown had replaced him as chairman the previous year, and his colleagues cringed whenever reporters attributed his personal comments to the group—which frequently happened. When he missed the reorganization meeting, his associates fired him in his absence. They drafted a letter and listed the reasons for his removal, alleging that he was in a "power struggle" against James Forman, claiming that Carmichael had not informed them of the trips he took, and disagreeing with his reported intention to purchase a $70,000 home in Washington, D.C.[35]

SNCC had so little active programming that Carmichael would not have had much to do for the organization. To justify its inactivity the group engaged in revisionist history about its own past, taking the credit for the urban unrest of the past few years. In a report about the June 1968 meeting, the group said that people who had not even been organized by SNCC were carrying out the organization's work through their insurrections. Grasping at straws, the report tied the group's popular but nonviolent direct action activities of the early 1960s to the urban uprisings of the late 1960s. On the four original 1960 sit-in students of Greensboro, SNCC said, "They were engaged in a new wave of rebellious activity by black college students that has mounted and raised the consciousness of our people to new heights of resistance in the streets of Watts, Newark, Detroit and many other cities throughout the United States." The claim distorted the truth, because none of the initial members of SNCC in 1960 led the recent insurrections. Also, the practices by African Americans of armed self-defense and violent responses to urban conditions did not begin in the 1960s and certainly not with SNCC. The organization's report more convincingly declared, "The armed rebellions of black people in the so-called ghettoes are just another manifestation of the resistance spirit of our people."[36]

SNCC also attempted to give itself a higher global profile by assessing the international significance of its most famous slogan. In so doing it again took liberty with its own institutional history and presented empty rhetoric. The report argued, "Black Power is a revolutionary force that seeks the elimination of capitalism and the industrial-military complex which undergirds it."[37] However, the phrase had originally to do with the election of African Americans to offices in counties where the ethnic group was the majority of the population. SNCC, by redefining Black Power, was reestablishing the slogan's relevance to African Americans in the context of its recent disavowal of involvement in American politics. Full of platitudes, the report asked people to "intensify the revolutionary consciousness among our people to unite in the fight against racism, capitalism and imperialism," but offered no suggestions as to how to intensify the consciousness; nor did SNCC say how to unite or how to fight. Nevertheless, the group promised, "It is through our unity and an unrelenting struggle by whatever means necessary that we will help in the liberation of oppressed people throughout the world." The report then ended with a curious, cryptic poem that symbolized the vagueness of the organization.[38]

Despite SNCC's best efforts at keeping the media and the government from latching onto one specific person and dubbing him a leader, the organization still suffered that fate but not through any of the eight deputy chairmen. Rather, the program secretary received the attention, because he was in the most contact with the press. On June 21, Hoover told President Johnson that Phil Hutchings had recently become SNCC's spokesman and that Hutchings was 26 years old, from Cleveland, a former student of Howard

University and a friend and classmate of Carmichael there. Hoover also noted that Howard had dropped Hutchings due to "poor scholarship" and that the spokesman had previously served as regional coordinator of SNCC–New Jersey and, in 1965, with SDS–New Jersey.[39]

It fell to the new program secretary to finally, albeit indirectly, inform Carmichael of his removal from SNCC. Hutchings told the press that the group had made the decision "with regret and no pleasure." He praised "Brother Carmichael" for making "tremendous strides in the fight for black liberation" during his former chairman's eight-year tenure in SNCC. On the other hand, "for some time . . . SNCC and Stokely Carmichael were moving in different directions," Hutchings lamented. Even then, however, Carmichael remained unaware of his firing. While in Washington, D.C., he finally learned of his dismissal when a reporter had asked for his response to a press release from Atlanta that had announced his firing. He admitted to "political differences" with SNCC but refused to reveal them to the press. A short time after his gracious response, SNCC sent him the letter of termination that itemized his associates' grievances with him. He was not pleased to have received such treatment from the group.[40]

Overall, SNCC's reorganization succeeded in placing the group at a low profile. The media covered it less often without the fiery speeches of Brown and Carmichael, and neither the deputy chairmen nor the program secretary made themselves as accessible to the press as the ex-chairmen had. In addition, the media and the federal government paid more attention to the BPP. COINTELPRO did not stop its surveillance of SNCC and SCLC, but agents devoted nearly all of their attention at neutralizing the BPP after SNCC restructured itself and after Resurrection City closed.

At the June meeting, SNCC decided to help develop the BPP. The Panthers had a very similar start to SNCC's early years: intense publicity and criticism of their aggressive response to oppression. As a result, some SNCC associates saw themselves as mentors to an even younger group of activists. "This means that we must use our resources, our contacts, our experiences, our minds, our revolutionary zeal to further expand the Black Panther Party," SNCC explained in a statement.

The relationship soon fell apart, however. On July 22, the BPP failed to attend a joint press conference the two groups had called. SNCC immediately called for "complete disassociation" from the Panthers, and James Forman promptly quit the BPP. He cited its lack of discipline and "collectivism," but Hoover told President Johnson that Forman had feared for his safety. The FBI director reported that Panthers had threatened to harm Forman and that the SNCC associate had gone to Beth Israel Hospital in New York for exhaustion. Meanwhile, Rap Brown also resigned from the BPP, and by the following month the working relationship between two organizations had ended.[41]

Nevertheless, the FBI wanted to ensure against any possibility of reconciliation between SNCC and the BPP. As a result, that summer COINTELPRO developed new ideas of exacerbating tension between the groups. Agents proposed having someone pretend to be with the NOI, calling New York's SNCC office and warning the group in "a Negro dialect and ghetto language" that the BPP was "out to get them." The agents there also developed the flyer "Strangle Black Panther" to portray movement associates as establishment pawns and traitors to African Americans. COINTELPRO–New York planned to have "local Negro boys" distribute copies of the document at the "busy street corners" of Harlem and Bedford-Stuyvesant. "BROTHERS—WE HAVE BEEN TAKEN," the circular proclaimed. "SNCC and Black Panther is the game the Man is running on us." As proof that the groups were actually tools of "the Man," the document noted the marriages of SNCC members James Forman and Julius Lester to European American women. "Don't be fooled," it concluded.[42]

One immediate consequence of the SNCC-BPP split was the dissolution of SNCC's Los Angeles branch. The local group became autonomous, because the national group's separation from the California-based BPP also extended by default to SNCC–Los Angeles. The West Coast associates operated a youth organization and a liberation school, but the organization suffered devastating effects of sexism and factionalism. Angela Davis and other female participants managed the headquarters and the organization itself. However, when they involved themselves in programs, male colleagues complained of the women taking over the group. Meanwhile, national leaders sympathetic to Davis's plight did not visit Los Angeles to address the branch's sexism. In addition, SNCC–Los Angeles purged itself of its Communist members, one of which was Davis. The associates claimed that national policy dictated a Communist free organization, but again no national figure weighed in on the terminations. Shortly thereafter, further dismissals slashed the group's local membership from 200 to 10. As the summer of 1968 began, the branch lost its office space, too.[43]

SNCC carried on without the Black Panthers but diminished itself through its reorganization. COINTELPRO reported soon after the June meeting that SNCC's Atlanta office was "practically closed down" and had only five staff members, who comprised the "Inner Circle" there. In addition, the personnel of the office there consisted almost entirely of newcomers, who replaced older members shortly after the meeting. As for SNCC's usually high-profile ex-chairman, COINTELPRO reported, "H. Rap Brown has had little if any influence on the operation of SNCC recently. His presence in Atlanta has been extremely limited and his exact status with the organization is somewhat hazy." Still, the organization had branches in several cities throughout the country, and a new branch developed in San Antonio that summer.[44]

As SNCC regrouped, SCLC seemed to be on the mend, as well. On July 9, Andrew Young appeared on NBC's *Today* show in an interview that won him several positive notices from viewers. One contributor to the organization was offended that the activist had said that Nixon was "playing games." Still, most people who contacted Young complimented him for his mild manner and his calmness as he had spoken. Despite the emotion in his voice, he delivered a sense of urgency in a demeanor of gentleness. The *Today* show staff apparently were impressed, too, because they invited him back for further appearances. He did not appear on television as often as Abernathy did, but he carved his niche in SCLC and in the movement as a mellow, thoughtfully speaking advocate for nonviolent direct action with mainstream appeal.

He also distinguished himself in another manner. One of his new fans, Mrs. Jay B. Davis from Arlington, Virginia, told him in her letter that her family had seen him on *Today* and found his responses compelling, informative, and—most importantly—credible. "From this we are of the opinion," she declared, "that rather than being *anyone's* assistant, you would be much more helpful to your people in politics." She reasoned that he possessed "the unique attributes necessary for politics, which few have." It was certainly a bold suggestion for her to make, considering that no African American had held electoral office in Congress from the South since the end of Reconstruction nine decades earlier. Legal voter discrimination by color was only three years in the past, as well. Nevertheless, for whatever reason, Mrs. Davis believed that Young had the ability to overcome whatever obstacles remained for African Americans seeking office and become a successful politician.[45]

Like SNCC, SCLC members did not seek political office. During his lifetime, Martin Luther King Jr. had objected to having members of his organization run for office. Their involvement in "the system" threatened to compromise their objectivity in relation to it, as far as he was concerned. Because SCLC was still concerned with governing itself in a way that its murdered founder would have, none of its members—including Young— launched political campaigns in the electoral year of 1968. Young took Mrs. Davis's letter, had it placed in an administrative correspondence file, and carried on with his organizational work.[46]

The movement's nonviolent civil disobedience survived one of its most trying periods during the spring and summer of 1968, as Brown's rhetoric about violence appeared to play itself out. Although the national civil rights groups hardly communicated with each other, they experienced similar traumas in the immediate aftermath of King's death. SCLC suffered the national backlash against Resurrection City and the loss of its ally Robert Kennedy. SNCC's staff dwindled, and it lost its ally, the BPP. Both organizations also dramatically lost money and support during this period. As July ended and August began, the groups remained in a period of introspection, retreating within themselves to adjust to King's absence. Before the end of August, however, the organizations found themselves emerging from their seclusion to address a new threat—the rise of Spiro Agnew to national political prominence.

CHAPTER 5

A Hanging Judge

In July 1968, 12 months had passed since Spiro Agnew's response to Rap Brown's speech in Maryland. The governor, however, considered the SNCC speaker's year-old remarks relevant. Whenever an urban disturbance took place, Agnew received praise from his supporters for identifying Brown's July 1967 address as the foundation for the uprising. Even if Brown had nothing to do with the riots that the governor addressed, Agnew grew in national prominence by treating the Cambridge disturbance as a "one size fits all" reference for riots. Brown was Agnew's rhetorical one-trick pony, and the governor was playing it for all it was worth.

Agnew inflated the danger Brown's words posed by associating militant speech with major events concerning national security. On July 23, the day before the one-year anniversary of Brown's speech in Cambridge, the governor spoke at the National Governors' Conference in Cincinnati about his opposition to the findings of the Kerner Commission. "The Kerner Report neglected to credit the multiplicity of inflammatory statements such as Rap Brown's 'Violence is as American as cherry pie,'" he complained. He blamed Brown's statement for fostering "an aura of belief that rioting is the inalienable right of the ghetto resident." Agnew thought the commission was cherry-picking by only noting "the precedent in violence as 'created by white terrorism directed against non-violent protest.'" To be fair the commission should have also discussed "the pronouncements of the self-appointed black racist," according to the governor. After all, if only white terrorism created today's violence, why hadn't riots occurred in "communities renowned for white terrorism rather than the most liberal, progressive communities of North and South?"[1]

The governor's critique of the Kerner report was a departure from his anti-Brown stumping. To be sure, he repeated his theme from his April meeting that both European American and African American militants needed to be held accountable for their actions. On the other hand, he was now implying that the terrorism of both ethnic groups was interchangeable. Here, he was distorting history. Brown, Carmichael, and other militant speakers were only speaking; they did not actually kill people with their words or otherwise. European American terrorism, in contrast, had an extensive history of lynching and cross burnings dating back to the previous century. Moreover, Agnew was wrong; riots *had* occurred in enclaves of "white terrorism," but at the hands of European Americans. In Illinois, residents of the European American section of Chicago known as Cicero had terrorized an African American family out of their new house in 1951, and they threw rocks and bricks at open-housing marchers 15 years later.

Agnew's remarks during his brief tenure as governor received negative feedback from an increasing number of African Americans as he rose in national prominence. A SNCC branch in Maryland was one of the first respondents to Agnew's ascendancy. In a speech to the Greek Orthodox Youth of America on July 30 in New York, the governor stated, "One of the prime contributors to our age of anxiety is the insidious relativism that has crept into our thinking. Relativism is epitomized by the agonizing of a police officer who couldn't bring himself to kill a looter over a pair of shoes, or the youngster contemplating whether he will serve as a soldier in what he considers an unjust war." SNCC harped on part of that statement shortly afterward by producing a flyer that trumpeted, "Agnew says, 'Kill a looter over a pair of shoes.'" It echoed local activist Walter Lively's assertion that the governor "has brutally exploited the civil rights struggle to further his own ambitions." However, the document also deviated from SNCC's recent public apolitical remarks by suggesting, "We had better wake up and stop marching to the polls and voting for 'the lesser evil.'" It called on the community to elect its own political leaders instead.[2]

SCLC felt the same way as SNCC but decided to directly confront the Republican and Democratic conventions to voice their political opinions to the politicians themselves. "This is really one of the last chances for the Republican Party to win back the black vote," Ralph Abernathy warned. Reusing the PPC imagery of the mule train, SCLC trekked to Miami for the Republican National Convention. Upon arrival, Abernathy was saddened to see African Americans comprise only 2 percent of the party's delegates, and he called the convention "lily-white." He revealed his desire for a moderate—Governor Nelson Rockefeller of New York—to win the Republican Party's nomination for president. "Only the nomination of someone like Mr. Rockefeller can bring the black vote back to the

Republican Party," Abernathy advised. Richard Nixon won the nomination anyway.[3]

Soon afterward, the governor received a telephone call from the new presidential nominee, spoke briefly with him, hung up, and announced to his wife Judy that he was Nixon's choice for vice president. On August 8, Nixon told the Republican National Convention of his decision, and the convention endorsed a Nixon-Agnew ticket. Agnew's tough stance against Rap Brown and other demonstrators allowed Nixon to play to the South without resorting to race-baiting. During his first run for the presidency in 1960, the South had seen him largely as disinterested in the region, its handling of segregation, and its residents. While in Florida that year, a White House staffer claimed that Nixon did not visit with the locals. But now that his running mate for 1968 was publicly against civil disobedience, Southerners were heartened that Nixon was paying attention to their concerns. In Agnew's first press conference as the running mate, he reiterated both his support for civil rights and his opposition to civil disobedience. That combination allowed him to appeal to foes of the movement without the stigma that Southern anti-movement governors like George Wallace and Lester Maddox had faced from the nation for their deliberate discrimination against African Americans. After all, if Agnew wanted equality, how could he be called a racist?

Agnew was exercising Nixon's "Southern strategy" for votes. As Nixon observed his running mate's press conference, he was jubilant. "I think we've got ourselves a hanging judge," he beamed to Pat Buchanan, whose notification to Nixon of the "judge's" haranguing of civil rights workers helped make that moment of jubilee possible.[4]

Many African American Republicans, however, were disheartened. On the day after the nomination, Agnew's remarks during his previous 18 months as governor of Maryland received increasing scrutiny from African Americans nationwide. Several of them responded negatively to his nomination, and he was costing the Republican Party the support of nationally prominent African Americans who had previously shown support for the party.

By virtue of Agnew's placement on the ticket, he drove away one of the biggest African American GOP supporters. Former professional baseball player Jackie Robinson, who had desegregated major league baseball over 20 years earlier, was one of many African American public figures who supported the movement. He also periodically assisted with the political campaigns of Republican Party candidates, and he had endorsed Nixon for president in 1960. On the other hand, the 1968 Nixon candidacy repulsed Robinson. Agnew had been denigrating the very movement in which Robinson had given years of service. The civil rights icon called the Nixon-Agnew ticket "racist in nature." He said that by selecting Agnew, Nixon "has prostituted himself and sold himself out to the bigots in the South." He pledged instead to support whoever would become the Democratic nominee. Attempting to rally African Americans nationwide against Agnew, he also vowed to "pray to God that every black man and every minority in this country does the same thing."[5]

Robinson's rejection of Agnew set off a chain reaction. The national negative feedback from African Americans then affected the running mate's local African American support. On August 15, Gilbert Ware, the governor's only African American staffer, resigned out of frustration with Agnew's position on ethnic issues. Ware claimed to have felt discomfort with Agnew's ascendancy to a national ticket after the governor's scolding of Baltimore's civil rights activists back in April. The staffer had been willing to work for Agnew as long as the governor's influence had not extended beyond Maryland's borders.

Undaunted, Agnew continued to define African American activism for African Americans. On *Meet the Press* on September 8, he nurtured his reputation as a man unwavering in his convictions, no matter what detractors said. Concerning his remarks before civil rights activists, he admitted to having considered speaking to them in private. He had worried, however, about how the attendees would have relayed his remarks without the presence of the media recording the proceedings. A reporter then asked if Agnew was sorry for his remarks to the activists. He replied that he was not and that, if put in another similar situation, he would use the same words again.

The governor then widened his crusade against dissent, targeting other people besides Brown. He called Yippies and hippies "anarchists." He reasoned, "I haven't seen many people who align themselves with these undertakings who don't burn the American Flag, who don't fly the flag of the Viet Cong, who don't swear allegiance to Ho Chi Minh and Mao Tse Tung and do things that are calculated to disrupt the dignity and stature of the United States." Journalist Robert Novak then asked if the governor believed that student leaders of demonstrations were under the control of either Moscow or the domestic Communist Party. Agnew replied, "I think they are under the influence of them without any question," citing a news story about members of the SDS who called themselves Communists. His proof, however, did not show that non-SDS students who led uprisings did so in the name of communism. On the other hand, Agnew spoke in broad sweeps. During the campaign year, he refused to visit a poverty-stricken city because "if you've seen one slum, you've seen them all."[6]

The *Meet the Press* appearance continued with the panelists neglecting to follow up on Agnew's stereotyping, and newspaper reporters did not consider his remarks newsworthy enough to print the next day. On the other hand, his broad sweeps did not always serve him well. Days later he jeopardized his reputation for ethnic tolerance by publicly using ethnic slurs in the presence of the media. When telling reporters the ethnic makeup of his followers did not concern him, he said, "Very frankly, when I am moving in a crowd, I don't look and say, 'Well, there's a Negro, there's an Italian, and there's a Greek and there's a Polack.'" The following week he referred to Japanese American reporter Gene Oishi as a "fat Jap" twice.[7] Even worse, he was in Hawaii—a state significantly comprising people of Japanese heritage—while making the remarks. News commentators, Asian Americans, and prominent public figures immediately took him to task for his remarks and questioned his fitness for the vice presidency.

The governor addressed the controversy with remorse, defensiveness, and patriotism. He expressed disbelief that he, as a son of a Greek immigrant and as someone people had teased for being Greek, could possibly receive criticism for ethnic in-sensitivity. He offered his apologies to people he may have offended with his remarks. He was not sorry, however, for the spirit of play with which he made them. He warned that the United States was losing its sense of humor. "This is America," he proclaimed, "This is the melting pot of America! And if we are so ashamed of our background that a single word sets us in orbit, then the purpose of America, my friends, is beginning to fail."[8]

His response was a continuation of how he dealt with civil rights. He wanted to change how some people acted to solve the nation's problems. He tried to change what people said and thought about those problems. He wished ethnic minorities would lighten up about slurs. After all, *he* had done so. He attempted empathy by comparing his trials as a Greek American with the troubles of other ethnic groups. But by portraying the suffering of ethnic groups as equitable and interchangeable, he won over few minorities.[9]

SNCC was on the minds of several politicians in the fall of 1968. Congressmen followed Agnew's example of evoking the names of SNCC members in order to maintain political relevance and ensure reelection that year. The Republican Party leader of the House, Gerald Ford of Michigan, stated it was time to slam the door on H. Rap Brown and other Black Power advocates. Ford cited Republican backing of the House-passed antiriot bill, saying that the legislation could be used against Brown. His colleague, Everett Dirksen of Illinois, similarly professed that the nation's courts could prosecute the former SNCC chairman with other existing laws.[10]

The second-top Democrat joined them in damning SNCC. On September 16, Vice President Hubert Humphrey spoke out against Carmichael and Brown as extremists. As a result, SNCC activity became a campaign issue for the third presidential election in a row. In 1960, King had been arrested at a SNCC sit-in, which prompted a response from the Kennedy campaign. Four years later, SNCC's "Freedom Democrats" threatened to disrupt the proceedings of the Democratic National Convention (DNC) by challenging Mississippi's delegation. Humphrey helped broker the compromise that kept the challengers out of the DNC that year—an agreement that led President Johnson to make him the running mate. Now in 1968, Humphrey exploited SNCC to ascend to Johnson's position and demonstrate a tough "law and order" stance.

The following month on *Face the Nation*, Agnew further differentiated responsible militancy from irresponsible militancy. He noted the existence of both a civil rights movement and a civil rights revolution, and he professed a preference for the former. To him, draft-card burning constituted part of the latter. When an incredulous panelist asked him to elaborate, he said that the burning, like the civil rights revolution, resulted from the nation's current "total permissive atmosphere" that permitted "irresponsible protest."[11] The irony of his response was that, despite his favoring of the civil rights movement over the revolution, the former consisted of several activists disobeying laws. In contrast, the speakers of militant rhetoric comprising the latter were actually not breaking any laws while speaking, but rather exercising their right to freedom of speech.

However, for Agnew, the movement was simply the lesser of two evils, and he considered a civil rights protest an illegal act. When asked whether the Montgomery bus boycott of 1956 fell within the boundaries of responsible protest, he responded that it did not. He explained that "you cannot even allow that kind of thing to take place because it still leaves the determination of what is right and what is wrong, and which laws are just and can be broken for moral reasons, and which are unjust to the evaluation of an individual." The panel did not recognize Agnew's conflation of boycotts with civil disobedience. Instead the panelists pressed him on his claim that people should not have opinions about laws. A reporter asked, "Governor, you contend that the individual has no right to make up his own mind whether or not he thinks a law should be opposed or not?"

Agnew tersely replied, "Exactly."[12]

In October, SNCC's "irresponsible militants" inspired Pan-African protest at the Olympics. Two African American draftees with the National Football League—Tommie Smith and John Carlos—arrived in Mexico City to compete in track, and Carlos promised a "demonstration" at the games. Days later, Smith won the 200-meter dash, and Carlos placed third. The "demonstration" came at the medal ceremony for the event. Smith and Carlos approached the award stand, wearing black gloves, black socks, and no shoes. The winners received their medals. As the American flags rose on nearby flagpoles and "The Star-Spangled Banner" played, Smith and Carlos lowered their heads. Each of them raised a fist, giving the Black Power salute. At a press conference following the ceremony, Smith called the gesture his way of showing that "blacks are united." Smith said, "We're glad we did it."[13] Stokely Carmichael and Rap Brown joined Smith at another press conference later that month to support him, thus connecting the gesture to the group that had popularized "Black Power."

Detractors condemned Smith and Carlos in much the same manner as Governor Agnew lambasted Brown and for the same reasons. As with the former SNCC chairman, the athletes received accusations of treason simply for expressing their points of view. Fellow Olympian and pole-vaulter Bob Seagren told reporters that the gesture was "cheap" and improper of Smith and Carlos. "If it were not for the United States, they would not be there," Seagren opined curiously. "If they don't like the United States, they can always leave." With Seagren's echoing of Agnew's stance against any and all forms of dissent, the 200-meter race became a microcosm of the divide between the powers that be and the movement.[14]

The race also became a symbol of the split within the movement itself. Jesse Owens had been an African American track star at the Olympics in Germany 32 years earlier. His winning of the gold medal there became an ethnically political event on its own terms, because the country's Nazi leader Adolf Hitler refused to congratulate Owens for disproving ideas of Aryan superiority. Like others of his generation, Owens let his work speak for itself about equality. As a result, he did not approve of the gesture by Carlos and Smith in Mexico City. The veteran Olympian lectured, "These kids are imbued with the idea that there's a great deal of injustice in our nation." He called the 200-meter dash "the wrong battlefield" to fight against inequality.[15]

Despite the press's brief renewed attention to SNCC, the controversy over the Black Power gesture did little to attract new members or donors to the organization. The *New York Times* reported on SNCC's near demise ever since Carmichael's dismissal. The BPP received more media attention, and Carmichael was now generating publicity as a member of that group instead of SNCC. The article numbered SNCC's current membership at only 50 and consisting largely of veterans of the group's previous Southern projects. The periodical also referred to the organization's internal division. "We had so many factions," John Wilson sighed, "the Carmichael faction, the Forman faction, and so on." Still, he remained hopeful: "Now maybe we'll have just a SNCC faction, and we can get on with the program."[16]

The FBI did not think that SNCC had much of a "program" to resume. In a sense, SNCC's disorganization worked to its advantage, but the disorder made the group tougher for the FBI to monitor and disrupt. SAC–Atlanta told Hoover that SNCC was so without structure that COINTELPRO operations would be unsuccessful unless SNCC had more focus. On the other hand, the agent also reported that SNCC's Atlanta office merely facilitated the group's offshoot programs. The agent further claimed that National Black Antiwar Antidraft Union (NBAWADU) had folded, SNCC–Chicago had closed, and SNCC–Washington, D.C., was now dormant.[17]

Of all the SNCC branches, the one that attracted most of the federal government's attention was in Brooklyn. The branch's director, William "Muhammad" Hunt, issued leaflets that called the nation racist and declared that African Americans were shifting from resistance to revolution. He wrote, "Brooklyn SNCC has a four point program designed to open the eyes of the 'WALKING DEAD' i.e., the so-called negro. It is encumbant [*sic*] upon you as an African in America to seek liberation by any means necessary." Hunt's notoriety came despite his newness to SNCC. At least one associate remembered him as having come from Queens, New York, where he may have been a Black Panther. In addition, his presence was not too imposing. Although tall, he was reserved and quiet. Also, he was not too effective with his programming. He facilitated SNCC–Brooklyn's merger with the Student Organization for Black Unity (SOBU) and announced a forthcoming SNCC-SOBU Liberation School. His plans for the institution never quite extended beyond mere talk. Nevertheless, his talk was important enough to have the federal government concerned about him.[18]

Hunt's pamphlet revealed that the NOI had made a significant impact on SNCC. After the assassination of former NOI speaker Malcolm X in February 1965, a growing number of young African Americans, especially from the North, co-opted his rhetoric of self-reliance and self-defense and his catchphrases like "by any means necessary." SNCC's promoting of Black Power in 1966 had been merely the beginning of that transition. By using the phrase "the so-called negro," Hunt appropriated the language of NOI leader Elijah Muhammad, who often used the phrase in speeches and documents. As a result, Hunt linked SNCC rhetorically to the religious sect. Still, even by 1968, Fred Meely of SNCC–Philadelphia stuck out in the organization, because the way he carried himself reminded at least one associate of an NOI member. In terms of demeanor, he was polite, professional, never without a jacket, handsome, reserved, extremely smart, and very rigid. His inflexibility won him some supporters but also repelled some associates. Meanwhile,

COINTELPRO now had even more reason to neutralize SNCC, because it sounded like another organization that Hoover wanted to neutralize.[19]

Although COINTELPRO was convinced of SNCC's downslide, Hoover still felt the need to occasionally brief President Johnson on the organization's activities. On January 3, 1969, the FBI director told the president that SNCC's staff meeting of the previous week had 30 people in attendance and that infighting and monetary problems plagued the group. Many members were criticized for trying to start a BPP chapter in Atlanta. People also had intense feelings against James Forman. Irving Davis of SNCC–New York suggested that the national headquarters request financial assistance from foreign countries supporting American black nationalism because of SNCC's own low funds. The timing of the FBI's memo was awkward. President Johnson had very little time to deal with Hoover's bulletin because his presidency was going to end in 17 days. Any potential revitalizing of SNCC would have to be Richard Nixon's problem.[20]

On January 13, as Johnson started his last full week in office, President-elect Nixon met with six African American leaders he had invited to his headquarters in New York. When he had spoken on election night, he recalled a teenage girl's sign in Deshler, Ohio. It read "Bring Us Together," and Nixon promised to unite the country. His meeting with the leaders gave him an opportunity to make good on that promise. SCLC scored a major victory by receiving invitations for two of the slots. Jesse Jackson sent a non-SCLC representative, but Abernathy accepted his invitation. In addition, the SCLC leader was the only movement leader present because Roy Wilkins of the NAACP had to decline his invitation due to a prior commitment. The remaining guests were ministers and prominent journalists. Nixon announced the gathering as the first of many that he intended to hold throughout his tenure as president in order to establish communications between his White House and African Americans. He welcomed their "direction, advice, and criticism." They responded accordingly.

All of the attendees sensed Nixon's eagerness to end racial discrimination and assist the poor, but they criticized the absence of African Americans from his cabinet. Abernathy noted that President Johnson had appointed one for his. "Now we do not have a black man to represent the interest of black people in the cabinet of the United States of America. For me this is a backward step."[21] An African American member of Nixon's staff attended the meeting, but this official was not part of the president-elect's inner circle. Moreover, Nixon's naming of Pat Moynihan as chief adviser on urban problems irked the guests, one of whom coined a new word by calling the appointment "plantationist." In his 1965 study *The Negro Family*, Moynihan had written about poor African Americans as self-destructive and had criticized African American women for limiting the success of African American men. His critics considered his appointment by Nixon a sign that the Nixon White House would be unsupportive of the concerns of African Americans.

Abernathy's major contribution to the discussion, ironically, had little to do with poverty, hunger, or labor. Instead, he focused on political symbolism as a means of making amends for injustice against African Americans. He asked the president-elect to make King's birthday a national holiday. "I feel this is the first act of redemption that Mr. Nixon can make," he said. "Martin Luther King's contribution to America is just as significant as that of Abraham Lincoln, George Washington, Andrew Jackson, Benjamin Franklin, Thomas Jefferson or any other American," he continued. "Had he not armed black people with the weapon of nonviolence, blood would have flowed in the streets." He was under the impression that Nixon was 100 percent supportive of the holiday idea and eager to "narrow the gulf and even eliminate it as soon as possible between the haves and have nots."[22]

On the other hand, only the discontent of the leaders had made an impression on Nixon. He listened to them because they were successful communicators with African Americans. He knew that the "black extremists," as he called them, were at their peak of influence. He grew frustrated that after the federal government had passed laws and spent money on African American concerns and had yielded some improvements for them, African Americans seemed to him to be more dissatisfied with their lot as the decade ended than when it had begun. Upon his inauguration, he decided against addressing the concerns of African Americans through meetings, especially with "extremists" like the NAACP and white segregationists. He told his staff that his actions would speak for themselves. By lumping the NAACP—the most conservative of the civil rights groups—with "extremists," Nixon was now following Vice President Agnew's lead. The president's equating of the NAACP's supposed extremism with the violent system of Jim Crow came right out of Agnew's civil rights playbook.[23]

The judicial branch of the federal government interpreted the law through that playbook as well. Nearly a year after Congress had passed a law based on Agnew's pursuit of Brown, a federal court made indictments against people for having allegedly violated the federal antiriot law. On March 20, the court charged a group of people eventually nicknamed the Chicago Eight. The prosecution claimed that the defendants had crossed state lines, written articles, and spoken and otherwise encouraged others to come and disrupt Chicago during the DNC of the previous summer. The demonstrators responded to the defendants' rhetoric with "weapons to be used against the police" and had "directed loud profanity, projectile objects, threats and physical assaults upon policemen and National Guard troops." U.S. Attorney Thomas Foran also said that the Chicago Eight gave the activists lessons in karate, Japanese snake dancing, and defense against police aggression. The defendants were indeed dangerous. "Some of these men are highly intelligent, highly sophisticated agitators," noted Foran.[24]

The Nixon administration in particular had worked very hard to bring the Chicago Eight to trial. Foran had developed the eight indictments as Nixon's predecessor had prepared to leave office. He had also pursued cases against eight Chicago police officers for their conduct during the convention. Johnson's attorney general, Ramsey Clark, had refused to press the indictments against the activists, however. To him, the demonstrators had not violated the law but instead had exercised their constitutional right of free speech. In addition, attacking a police officer had not constituted a federal offense.

On the other hand, Nixon's attorney general, John Mitchell, chose to press the case. He used the antiriot law to ensnare the small contingent of hard-core agitators—a different breed from "conventional" activists. The administration wanted the "hard core" detained and punished. If they were to be freed, the government would look as if it had approved of the protests, Mitchell warned. Then, more and more demonstrations would take place. President Nixon just could not let that happen on his watch. The nation had to have law and order.[25]

SNCC did not publicly criticize the Nixon administration until nearly two months after the inauguration. Despite all the factions that had developed within the organization, the group managed to unite long enough to draft a response to the president's treatment of the impoverished. On March 6, SNCC released a statement from the Diplomat Hotel in New York condemning preventive detention as a way to scare the poor, African Americans, and activists. "We must understand that American fascism will be unique to this country. There will be no storm troopers, swastikas or brown shirts. The slogan for fascism in the United States will be 'law and order,' and that is what preventive detention laws are all about." Phil Hutchings and NBAWADU head James Johnson openly supported the statement. Brown did as well, which was only fitting because the declaration featured his tendency to draw a parallel between African Americans' conditions and the Holocaust. For all their effort, however, the statement did not generate much press interest.

In contrast, Wilkins attracted attention for meeting the president. The NAACP leader had decided not to attend the inauguration, but shortly afterward he and his wife accepted Nixon's invitation to dinner. After engaging in some conversation, the president turned to Wilkins to change the subject. "If I do anything wrong, I want you to tell me." His guest promised to do so, and throughout Nixon's first term, Wilkins kept his word.[26]

President Nixon scheduled a meeting with Abernathy for 10:15 a.m on May 13 at the White House. Unlike the January meeting Abernathy had shared with five other prominent African Americans, he was to have the president all to himself. The two had met privately in Washington, D.C., 13 years earlier, when Nixon was vice president. Back then, Abernathy and King had talked with him about civil rights, and the two activists had privately expressed their support for the Republican Party. SCLC had a policy of not endorsing presidential candidates, but the organization always tried to maintain communication with the White House—no matter who occupied it.

The scheduling of this new White House meeting was a major breakthrough for SCLC because of changes between the group and the executive branch since 1956. Now, in 1969, Abernathy was to arrive without his more influential best friend and to discuss poverty instead of segregation. He frequently and publicly expressed his skepticism of Nixon as president. In addition, the organization had not been welcomed to the White House since King had publicly broken with Nixon's predecessor on the issue of the Vietnam War in April 1967.

Nevertheless, Abernathy not only achieved a resumption of dialogue with the commander in chief, but accomplished this feat on his own. It was an unexpected additional opportunity for SCLC to bring the issue of poverty to the nation's capital for the first time since the end of Resurrection City the previous June, and SCLC was determined to make the most of it. He and some of his staff had to temporarily leave a monthlong strike it was helping hospital workers to conduct in Charleston, South Carolina, but the meeting would give SCLC an opportunity to directly ask the White House for help in resolving the strike. Also, Abernathy had a chance to show strong leadership in the movement by holding a private meeting with the Nixon administration.[27] Like the Charleston strike, the White House meeting had nothing to do with any planning by King before his assassination.

Nixon stood to benefit from the meeting, too. He needed to gain trust among African Americans after having lost ground by making Agnew his running mate, and Abernathy's name ran high in polls about civil rights leaders most accepted by Americans. The president was hesitant about inviting Abernathy, but his inner circle of advisers talked him into it. Sociologist Daniel "Pat" Moynihan strongly supported the idea. Chief of Staff H. R. Haldeman and White House counsel John Ehrlichman also encouraged the president to have the meeting despite their misgivings about reaching out to the movement.

Nixon assigned Moynihan to write to Abernathy. "On behalf of the President," Moynihan began, "I am writing to ask if it would be possible for you to join him at the next meeting of the Urban Affairs Council, on May 13 at 10:15 a.m., to discuss the Poor People's Campaign." He promised the attendance of the secretaries of seven cabinet departments, the vice president, and the president. "We very much look forward to this meeting with you," Moynihan gushed. Abernathy accepted and made arrangements to take himself, some staff, and a poor people's delegation to the White House.[28]

President Nixon put his best foot forward to receive Abernathy. The press was on hand to cover the White House's first meeting with SCLC since King's death, and Nixon never wanted to give reporters a reason to say negative things about him. Thus, when the clock struck 10:15 on the morning of May 13, the president, members of his cabinet, and the Urban Affairs Council were ready to welcome him. Even Defense Secretary Melvin Laird took time away from dealing with the Vietnam War to attend the proceedings. By reporting the administration's willingness to listen to the concerns of poor people, the press had the potential to make Nixon look good to African Americans.

The SCLC leader, however, had not yet arrived at the White House. He and his delegation of poor people kept Nixon, the administration, and the press waiting for several minutes. When SCLC arrived, the vice president and cabinet officials graciously greeted their guests. The visitors sat down, and the president extended his greetings to them. Then again, he had reason to be congenial toward them. Having patiently endured their lateness, the Nixon team was already in a more favorable light than SCLC.[29]

Abernathy started his remarks by slowly reciting a list of social grievances. It seemed to some in the room like a significant waste of time. The list was nine pages long, and he had already distributed the document to the council. Moreover, attendees thought he was trying to frame his concerns like King's "I Have a Dream" speech. He began each paragraph of complaints with the phrase "I am concerned." He was concerned about the war. He was concerned about the antiballistic missile. He was concerned about military spending. He was concerned about jobs. He was concerned about hunger. He was concerned about school desegregation. He was concerned about Title I school funds. He was concerned about equal employment opportunities. On and on he went, at times blaming the administration for the problems. He accused Nixon of neglecting ethnic minority groups and called the administration's hunger program proposal and its response to the Charleston strike "inadequate." Still, his hosts patiently listened to him.[30]

After the complaints, the civil rights leader recited a new list—a series of demands. Abernathy requested a "modest" $2.5 billion per year food program to be obtained by nixing ABM and SAGE or by deleting the farm subsidy. He wanted a new job program and better enforcing of Executive Order 11246. He asked Nixon to help Charleston strikers, to implement "immediate action on welfare reform," and to guarantee all U.S. citizens an "income above the poverty line." He concluded with a backhanded statement of optimism to the attendees: "Let history show that this Administration, of which little was expected, was the one which made America truly keep its long-deferred promise to all of its citizens."[31]

Nixon avoided addressing Abernathy's specific grievances and proposals. Instead, he thanked Abernathy for his "objective" criticism. He then offered his thoughts on the issue of poverty. "I don't go to bed each night feeling good about hunger, or poverty, or Vietnam," he began. "But we are developing policies to deal with these." He realized that for many African Americans, rising above poverty was only a recent phenomenon. He noted that although PPC men "now wore fine suits, drew good salaries, and had attained a comfortable station in life, they also had known poverty and want in their earlier years." He empathized, "Most of us haven't known the kind of poverty you have seen. We don't want other Americans to know it. We haven't known the prejudice you have seen. We don't want others to know it."[32] Instead of caving in to Abernathy's demands or agreeing with the activist's critique, the president chose to establish as much common ground with Abernathy as possible without losing face; they could at least agree that neither of them liked poverty.

Finished with his response, President Nixon rose to leave. Abernathy, however, immediately requested a rebuttal, and the commander in chief and the other attendees respectfully sat back down. The press was still in the White House, after all. The SCLC leader lamented how the administration's ineffectiveness made his organization's work difficult. He claimed that "such little progress" made people question nonviolence and refer to its devotees— like SCLC members—as "Uncle Toms." He tried to appease the president at the end of his remarks, vowing that despite the majority of African Americans and the poor not voting for Nixon, "you are our President, and you will have our support. We want to help you lead."[33] He then asked to meet cabinet secretaries individually and for the president to take time to greet another group of poor people who were waiting in the Indian Treaty Room.

The president then excused himself to let his visitors talk to his cabinet, saying in parting to the PPC members, "You have an hour, so have at 'em."[34] Agnew then presided, face-to-face with the same people he had publicly criticized 12 months earlier. This time he did not sling any accusations toward them of faking their poverty. He did not resurrect his claim of the PPC members having parked their Cadillac cars at Resurrection City the previous year. This time Agnew sat and listened.

Abernathy yielded the floor to his delegation of poor people. The delegates followed Abernathy's lead in reciting multiple grievances to the government officials. A woman from Birmingham, Alabama, named Mrs. Evans mixed gripes about her poverty—"I'm tired of living in three rooms with ten children"—with attacks on the president: "Mr. Nixon leave to avoid hearing our statements"—and bravado—"America black and white will come to Washington and wait till Mr. Nixon give us food and clothing"—and platitudes—"President Kennedy died for the Poor People's Campaign." She then declared a violent religious prophecy against the Apollo space program. "God ain't never told nobody to come and live on the moon," she proclaimed, "If you come up there God gonna destroy you. If God don't destroy you, we gonna destroy you."

Perhaps catching herself in the intensity of her speech, she suddenly concluded, "I better stop now before I say too much."[35]

The meeting continued as other guests spoke. An overweight European American woman presented her problems. A hefty European American man followed her, also listing demands. Then, with the witnesses having finished taking their turns to address Agnew and the cabinet, James Lowery of the SCLC board briefly spoke, as if summarizing the testimonies for a closing argument of a court case, asking for the Nixon administration's sensitivity and responsiveness "to the cries of misery that come out of the poor." It was an amiable conclusion to the White House proceedings.

However, Lowery did not get the last word. Immediately after he finished talking, Abernathy took the floor again and returned to his listing of his points of contention with the administration. This time he offered a new repetitive phrase for each individual offense against the poor. This time he replaced "I am concerned . . ." with "I don't see how . . ." He then demanded that the administration give him cabinet meetings and help with the Charleston strike. By this time some of his hosts had come to consider the dialogue worthless and "tiresome" and Abernathy as "pompous" and full of "invective."

Still, the hosts listened patiently a short while longer until Vice President Agnew brought the proceedings to an end. Offering an objective assessment of the meeting, he remarked on both Abernathy's and Nixon's eloquence. He then asked each cabinet official to speak to Abernathy's issues. A few officials spoke and answered questions from the PPC delegates. Then, Moynihan disturbed the meeting at 1:00 p.m. He announced that the poor people in the Treaty Room had been waiting for Abernathy since 11:00 a.m. and were restless, threatening a protest. The meeting immediately adjourned, SCLC and the PPC delegates left, and the Nixon administration turned to other matters.

As far as the Nixon administration was concerned, Abernathy's departure was good riddance. Haldeman thought the meeting was "[p]retty ridiculous." To him, Abernathy had attempted to trap Nixon into meeting with the rest of his delegation, or ordering cabinet members to do the same. He was glad that Abernathy did not succeed on either count and was impressed that Nixon had "handled [Abernathy] beautifully."[36]

Nixon speechwriter R. K. Price Jr, agreed. "From the whole tone and content of the session, it was clear that Dr. Abernathy's purposes were primarily political (in the sense of the internal politics of black militancy)," he argued in a briefing of the meeting to the president. Price believed that Abernathy was merely trying to show the nation that he had the clout to "deliver a President on demand to his assemblage in the Indian Treaty Room" or to successfully demand appointments with the cabinet. He had the cabinet's attention, and the council placed itself at his disposal, ready to discuss specifics. Instead, "he wasted its time with posturing, attitudinizing, sermonizing, and with pleading and wheedling directed not at the problems of poverty, but at the requirements of his own brand of confrontation politics." Abernathy revealed himself to be a mere "charlatan" who had the chance to present a strong case to the White House but "blew it." Price damningly concluded, "The poor deserve better."[37]

Abernathy, on the other hand, thought the poor deserved better treatment from the administration. He was furious that the president had made no commitments toward addressing poverty or helping the Charleston strikers. In addition, the activist bristled at the arrogance he had seen from the attendees, who had tried to convince him that they knew how to handle the problem and that it would soon end. After the meeting concluded, Abernathy talked to reporters. He called the proceedings "disappointing and fruitless." Because Nixon did not meet with the poor people in the Treaty Room after leaving the discussion, Abernathy claimed that the administration "did not have time for the poor."[38]

The White House was privately angry and incredulous about Abernathy's press conference. "Why, the son of a bitch!" exclaimed one staffer. "Went out and stabbed us on TV," Haldeman complained. The chief of staff felt validated about his reservations against meeting with the movement. "There's no use dealing honestly with these people," he concluded. "They obviously want confrontation, no [*sic*] solutions."[39]

Moynihan came to similar conclusions. His response carried significant weight because he was one of the few people in the administration who had conducted research on African Americans years earlier. Critics had lambasted his *Negro Family* study as too harsh toward African Americans and excessively focused on children born out of wedlock. However, he had agreed with Nixon on economic issues and was rewarded by him after the election with the Urban Affairs appointment. Incensed at Abernathy, Moynihan fumed to the president, "After the way you and the rest of us listened and indicated our sincere desire to find solutions to the problems, he goes into the press room and pisses on the President of the United States of America." He had attended the conference and believed that Abernathy had behaved rudely to the administration. Moynihan felt especially badly about the failed proceedings because of his support of the idea of the meeting. Abernathy's actions were "unconscionable" to Moynihan. "I promise you," he apologized to Nixon, "it will never happen again."[40]

The president refused to publicly engage with Abernathy. As was his way, he disliked addressing uncomfortable situations with people directly. Then again, he had nothing personal to say against Abernathy. He merely considered the SCLC leader in over his head and either unprepared or unwilling to have a serious discussion at the White House. To him, Abernathy merely postured and restated his demands in different ways. The meeting convinced Nixon not to entertain SCLC anymore. He wrote to Ehrlichman and Haldeman, "E-H, This shows that my judgment about *not* seeing such people is right." Consequently, SCLC was shut off from the executive branch. For the rest of his tenure as president, Nixon did not invite Abernathy or any SCLC member to the White House. His memo on the meeting dictated, "*No More of This!*"[41]

The remainder of the month of May did not go well for Abernathy. SCLC lost momentum after the disastrous White House meeting. The next day Abernathy conducted an individual version of the previous year's PPC by going to the Agriculture Department building. To symbolize the department's refusal to see him, he held a conversation with an empty chair representing Agriculture Secretary Clifford Hardin. The Nixon administration and the Republican Party, however, shrugged Abernathy off. They told the press that they considered him irrelevant and outside of the major African American leadership.

The SCLC leader spent the next few days running damage control. He offered a weak response to the Nixon administration's dismissive stance, saying that Nixon had treated him rudely. He also tried to divert attention from the abortive meeting by presenting a bold new national campaign—a PPC caravan from Alabama to the White House. "Governor Brewer and President Nixon can get ready for the poor people," he bantered. "We are now planning to raise the issue of hunger in a more dramatic way."[42] He was in no position, however, to plan such a demonstration. SCLC had already begun a series of marches in support of striking hospital workers in Charleston, South Carolina, and those demonstrations and an ongoing drop in donations to the group drastically thinned SCLC's resources for additional ambitious projects.

At least he had one friend in Washington. On the evening of May 14, he accepted an invitation to attend a senator's housewarming party there. The legislator was a longtime civil rights supporter and had voted for the Civil Rights Act of 1964. He also invited Abernathy to testify before his committee. The party and the congressional appearances allowed the SCLC leader to leave the nation's capital on a somewhat high note. The senator who extended hospitality to him was George McGovern.[43]

As politicians exploited the civil rights organizations to win the White House in 1968, the civil rights groups tried not to become distracted. By virtue of King's death during an election year, the organizations struggled to regroup as the candidates publicly criticized them. The civil rights groups remained committed to keeping their differences out of the spotlight as much as possible. Thus, they tried to privately solve problems concerning personnel, slogans, and programs as individual groups and then reconfigure as a movement.

CHAPTER 6

Manifesto

King's death coincided with the struggle of the civil rights organizations to adapt to social and political changes in the national landscape. For most of the groups, the problem predated the assassination. The press and militants had constantly attacked NAACP and the NUL as "out of touch" since the Black Power controversy, and SNCC still had trouble capitalizing on Rap Brown's celebrity over a year after his Cambridge speech. Only SCLC's problem of redefining itself resulted directly from King's passing. Nevertheless, the civil rights groups struggled to come to a consensus on issues, and some of them also suffered internal turmoil. In addition, new leaders took over three of the groups during 1968, and the changes they implemented made the movement's cohesion more difficult to accomplish.

CORE underwent a major transformation in 1968, when Floyd McKissick stepped down from the position of director due to illness. Roy Innis replaced him and took the organization in a new, separatist direction. In July, some members abortively tried to pass a new constitution that kept Black Power advocates from dominating the group, and two months later the organization adopted a constitution that banned European American membership. The once integrated pacifist group was now, like SNCC, open only to African Americans. Its members referred to the new policy as "black determinism" and rejected integration as a goal. "The melting pot theory for black people is a flop," declared member Wilfred Ussery.

Although the NAACP and NUL remained integrated, their leaders did not completely abandon CORE as it gravitated toward separatism. When Innis invited Wilkins and Young to the group's conference in July, they accepted. Wilkins boldly told his audience that he still rejected separatism, but both he and Young decided to finally publicly embrace Black Power—at least, on their terms. Wilkins defined the phrase according to African American "pride, . . . economic power and . . . political strength," and Young similarly applied the slogan to "self-determination—pride—self-respect—participation and control of one's destiny and community affairs." Now only SCLC remained uncommitted to the phrase, still holding on to "Soul Power."[1]

Meanwhile, SCLC had a much larger problem. In August, four months had passed since King's assassination, but Ralph Abernathy had yet to find his niche as the organization's president. For now he could still silence his doubters by reminding them that King had chosen him to succeed to the presidency. But now that his predecessor's last program—Resurrection City—had folded, Abernathy could no longer rely solely on King's memory for public validation. He would eventually have to deliver his own civil rights victories.

As the summer of 1968 concluded, SCLC prepared for its first annual convention without King. Despite the chaos of Resurrection City, the public overwhelmingly favored Abernathy as a movement leader. In a CBS News poll taken during Resurrection City, half of the African Americans surveyed supported Abernathy's views. Only 6 percent agreed with Stokely Carmichael, and 5 percent were for Rap Brown. Big-name celebrities like Bill Cosby, Robert Culp, Nancy Wilson, and Dick Gregory still promoted SCLC activities like the antihunger program Operation Breadbasket.[2]

Abernathy, however, was not president of the same SCLC that he had first led the previous April. When the annual convention met on August 14, the organization modeled itself after SNCC as a matter of policy. SCLC voted to approve both nonviolence and Black Power—the latter a marked departure from King's disapproval of the phrase. SCLC continued to shout "Soul Power" at its more public functions—the events most likely to receive mainstream media attention. However, despite whatever various interpretations the civil rights leaders made of Black Power, at least the movement was finally united around the phrase after a bitter two-year fight. The movement's important task now was to prevent Black Power and other slogans from replacing the development of programs—a fate that had befallen SNCC.[3]

SCLC also announced that it would not be responsible for the violence of nonmembers in its demonstrations. By doing so the organization avoided the risk of losing face if marchers turned to vandalism and looting, as in Memphis five months earlier. On the other hand, the decision was also an outgrowth of how King aligned himself with the frustration of the African American urban rioters of the past three years. From the uprising in Watts in 1965 up to his death three years later, King had never claimed that rioters were sinful or sick people. Rather, he had increasingly related to how militants and nationalists felt, using the pronouns "we" and "us" when talking about them.[4]

Abernathy's confidence in his leadership abilities did not rub off on everyone in SCLC. That night the group held a board meeting to discuss who would serve as its president. Reports about rumors of dissension within the group abounded. Was Abernathy "big enough and smart enough to fill Dr. King's shoes?," as NBC News put it.[5] Also, was Abernathy equipped to lead such a fundamentally different group from the one his predecessor had helmed? His colleagues concluded that he was, and they elected Abernathy to the presidency.

The next day the new president devoted part of his convention speech to addressing his detractors from outside the organization. While restricted from violence because of the organization's philosophy, he peppered his remarks with plenty of bantering and threats of destruction at the hands of the masses—not SCLC—if poverty and hunger continued. He reminded the audience, "We know that violence is not the way, and we will not turn to violence." But in confirmation of the new stance against ensuring nonviolence from African Americans overall, he warned the nation, "Do not expect us to be your babysitters, America!" He suggested that violence would end when the nation gave "jobs to the jobless" and fed the hungry. He also told the presidential candidates that they had to work to earn the votes of African Americans. Identifying himself as a gatekeeper of sorts, he declared, "You will have to come by Ralph Abernathy and others if you want that vote." His fiery rhetoric was effective; NBC News, after playing the speech, reminded viewers that despite Abernathy's "hard line," SCLC remained committed to nonviolence.[6]

In contrast to Abernathy's bombastic threats and demands, Coretta Scott King generated press for SCLC as a reserved and thoughtful speaker. She appeared on the cover of *Ebony* for the September 1968 issue. She was the subject of a biographical article that detailed her activism with her husband and some of the work she had done within and beyond SCLC since her husband's death. It was a sympathetic piece, making no mention of any problems taking their toll on the organization.[7]

Mrs. King's activism displeased some people in SCLC. When her husband was alive, he had been the undisputed leader of the organization. His inner circle in SCLC helped him run it. Mrs. King attended marches and ceremonies with him but had little voice in the group's affairs, and the men of SCLC were content with her role in the organization as the leader's helpmate. However, after King's death his widow's role in SCLC became much more important than anyone could have imagined, and at times it overwhelmed the organization. As different staff members competed to speak to the media on SCLC's behalf, they resented the high level of publicity that Mrs. King inherited from Abernathy's slain predecessor by virtue of her widowhood.

In addition, SCLC men bristled at having to allow time for her to discuss issues that meant more to her than to them. At an Operation Breadbasket event, Jesse Jackson called her "the first lady of the civil-rights movement." As she spoke she graciously admitted, "After my last visit to Breadbasket, I told my husband that Jesse Jackson will make a tremendous contribution to our society. I hoped then, and I still hope now, that he will remain with SCLC." But *Harper's* magazine reported that earlier that week, he had shown contempt for her by telling his staff, "We'll take care of our business and then Mrs. King can do her women-power thing."[8]

The men's conflict with Mrs. King was just a symptom of a larger problem. In late 1968, all was not well within the leadership of SCLC. Despite the show of solidarity toward Abernathy's presidency at the convention, the top officials in the organization were fighting among each other. Without King to moderate staff meetings, the volatile mix of personalities clashed multiple times—sometimes violently. In one meeting, Hosea Williams teased Young offensively for being middle class, at which point Young leaped over the table and grabbed Williams, and they rumbled while tumbling to the floor. Other times the abuse was verbal, as when Williams called SCLC education director Dorothy Cotton a "bitch" during a staff meeting.

Abernathy was of little help as president because he was among the principals who aired the grievances. He reprimanded his supporters for not according him the same respect as his predecessor, and he alienated them as a result. He accused Young of having written better speeches for King than for him. In his usual diplomatic fashion, Young claimed to only give talking points and that King's speeches resulted from his own work and creativity. Moreover, Young went out of his way to decline speaking invitations in order for Abernathy to have more opportunities to speak. On the other hand, when Abernathy repeatedly accused Harry Belafonte of having treated King differently, the entertainer and longtime movement supporter bluntly told Abernathy that King had earned the reverence. Belafonte challenged Abernathy to prove himself, but the minister did not offer ideas and a leadership style that appealed to him. Shortly afterward, Belafonte decided to sever his ties with SCLC.

SCLC recognized its splintering and made a drastic move to repair its internal relationships before the end of the year. The organization invited Dr. Price Cobb and his assistant Betty Browndon to facilitate a therapy session. For two days at Paschal's Motel, the therapists bluntly assessed each member. Abernathy admitted to having been jealous of King's international celebrity, but he insisted he did not want to be like King. By the end of the session, the organization had regrouped. Abernathy had entered the therapy principally aware of himself as SCLC's president but, as one witness put it, "came out a man."

The officials then went back to work. They needed each other, after all. Young was the one SCLC sent to meet with the business community. The organization sent Cotton to African American communities to teach the residents their citizenship rights. Williams's strength lay in organizing poor urban people for the group, and Jackson provided charismatic sermons to church audiences and organized people in the urban Midwest.[9]

SNCC also tried to settle its internal divisions once and for all. The organization suffered a terrible fall season. In September, the program secretary, Phil Hutchings, was arrested after a protest rally, found guilty, and fined $5,000. Meanwhile, factionalizing ran rampantly and now extended beyond the United States. Although several participants had complained in 1967 about Stokely Carmichael conducting too much overseas traveling, others continued to venture out of the country after Carmichael's firing. Julia Herve, daughter of the late novelist Richard Wright, facilitated a SNCC branch in Paris, and she and New York–based associate Irving Davis visited Cuba together during the fall season.

SNCC's Central Committee came to Agnew's state to meet in Baltimore between October 28 and 30. It decided that the organization needed another overhaul—the second one in four months. The committee elected to retain the multiple-chairman policy that SNCC had adopted in June, but it also structured the group into a near replica of the BPP by approving a proposed set of rules. The organization had prided itself for the past eight years on being without structure; one faction of the group was the disciplined "hard-liners," but the other was the "floaters," who did what they felt God telling them to do when God told them to do it. To Phil Hutchings, the organization's disorganization now hindered the group. He complained in the meeting that SNCC had been too "loose." Its members had committed themselves to struggle for liberation, but he characterized them as "misfits . . . who have given up on attaining any 'American Dream.'"[10]

Hutchings saw SNCC's bottom line in terms of programs and finances, and in both areas the organization was in deep trouble. He blamed John Wilson of SNCC's NBAWADU project for its "general fucked up state," as Hutchings put it. "NBAWADU has no money, no program and no real working staff," he lamented. An ambitious SNCC branch in New York, meanwhile, had acquired a significant amount of debt. Concerning the branch's headquarters, its members had not paid rent in two months, and they had decided to keep their cut-off telephone line permanently disconnected. The Central Committee agreed that SNCC–New York's office was not worth saving. "The lease runs out in March of 1969," Hutchings announced, "and we will leave then."[11]

The Central Committee also reorganized SNCC by distancing it from its rural, informal roots. After years of mostly Southern branches, the committee chose six major cities for SNCC to reestablish itself as a formidable national presence. The members determined that Atlanta, Brooklyn, Washington, D.C., Dallas, Los Angeles, and an undetermined midwestern city should be the new bases. In addition, the new hierarchy stressed different kinds of membership, thus overhauling SNCC's composition of "associates" who each had an equal vote in the group. Now SNCC was to have the levels of "staff" (full-time worker), "member" (honorary title), and "associate member" (via annual payment) for individuals, and "chapter" and "affiliate" for local branches. The Central Committee also approved a new code of conduct.

Hutchings especially was pleased with the resolutions that the Central Committee had passed. To him, they collectively formed "the new SNCC." In a direct attack on SNCC's previous overreliance on Brown's popularity, Hutchings declared, "Collective leadership over charismatic leaders. It is the basis of self-reliance." Announcing that the organization was "at a new stage," he more pointedly critiqued the former chairman, "Blacks don't need more leaders or 'rappers.'" Instead, African Americans wanted to know how to lead themselves, and it was SNCC's role to train them to do just that. Hutchings saw the organization's responsibility in terms of both ethnic self-pride and anti-authoritarianism. He asked the committee, "Do we want to be black, or do we want to be correct?"[12]

SNCC then attempted to revitalize itself through another partnership with a militant African American group, despite its recent failure to work with the BPP. Hutchings announced on November 27 that SNCC had formed an alliance with National Black Liberators (NBL), based in St. Louis. SNCC saw itself as based in the South, West, and East but not the Midwest. In turn, the Liberators were a relatively new entity, having just formed in 1967. Thus, they mutually benefited each other. NBL member Charles Koen became a Midwest deputy chairman for SNCC. And as with the BPP alliance, SNCC officers remained in the organization while joining the Liberators in high positions. Hutchings took on the role of NBL general field marshal, H. Rap Brown became the general of human justice, and James Forman served as the general of foreign affairs. Hutchings called the alliance the first of a potential series of alliances with militant African American community groups.[13]

As new members joined, older ones left, and not all of them departed voluntarily. In SNCC's national meeting between December 27 and 29, the group fired longtime participants Willie Ricks and Cleveland Sellers. They had helped develop and promote the organization's Black Power concept only two years earlier, but the group's membership significantly changed since then and did not want Ricks and Sellers as colleagues. On the other hand, for the first time, the meeting did not yield a major reorganization of SNCC. The organization remained intact but developed more factions that further disunited it.[14]

Fran Beal was one of the few attendees at the December meeting and one of even fewer women in attendance. Some of the organization's male associates there decided to support BPP member Eldridge Cleaver's recently published book *Soul on Ice*. Although he largely wrote about his life in prison, he also graphically illustrated violence against women and made disparaging comments about African American women in particular. Beal and her female associates in SNCC abhorred the group's endorsement of the book. The women had come to the conclusion that Cleaver's remarks would be detrimental to the implementation of Black Power.

For Beal, the embrace of Cleaver's book by her male comrades marked the peak of a series of slights against African American women within SNCC and without. She had disliked Daniel "Pat" Moynihan's claim in his report *The Negro Family* that African American women held back African American men's progress. SNCC's proposal in favor of *Soul on Ice* meant that the organization was internalizing Moynihan's ideas, and she saw the dignity of black women being impugned as a result. That was the proverbial "straw that broke the camel's back."[15]

SNCC's endorsement of Cleaver's misogynist fantasies in *Soul on Ice* resulted from the group's new composition. The organization consisted of more newcomers (post 1966) than longtime members, and many of the new male participants behaved like chauvinist cosmopolitans. Only 19 months earlier, the group's associates had seriously considered having the stalwart but terminally ill Ruby Doris Robinson succeed Stokely Carmichael as chair, and throughout 1968, Angela Davis in Los Angeles and Julia Herve in Paris created inroads for female colleagues in SNCC. By supporting *Soul on Ice*, however, SNCC clearly showed that it was more male oriented, anti European American, and oppressive to women. The group had come a long way from its embrace of the philosophies of Albert Camus and Karl Marx in the early 1960s.[16]

The controversy over *Soul on Ice* convinced SNCC's female members to caucus. At the meeting, Beal, Gwen Patton-Woods, and Mae Jackson formed the Black Women's Liberation Committee (BWLC) to confront the growing sexism they experienced in the movement. Shortly thereafter, Patton-Woods incorporated the organization. Beal took on an unofficial leadership role in the BWLC because of the deference and respect her female colleagues gave to her. She was a few years older than most SNCC participants and had been a single mother for years, and the years she had spent in Paris impressed her female colleagues.[17]

The SNCC women's response to *Soul on Ice* revealed that the group was still divided on the influence of the BPP. On the one hand, the national group increasingly supported self-defense, and the San Antonio group made itself a hybrid of both national organizations. However, the New York women saw Cleaver's book as problematic. Jackson saw her male colleagues projecting the author's attitudes about African American women to their female coworkers, especially in the case of one particular female associate from Queens, New York. Like some of the other SNCC women, the Queens attendee was young, attractive, light-skinned, and middle class. In addition, she expressed interest in SNCC's male colleagues. Men principally saw superficial value in her presence in the group and ogled her legs. She went to rallies but performed very little organizational work, and her associates questioned her commitment to the freedom struggle.[18]

Older male members gave their female colleagues more respect than the newcomers did. Rap Brown supported the women's side project. More importantly, Beal considered one of SNCC's elder statesmen, James Forman, to have a more progressive attitude among women than many of his male associates did. He and Beal served together on SNCC's International Affairs Commission and were constantly in dialogue with each other as a result. She asked for his approval of the BWLC, but a reluctant Forman initially hemmed and hawed. After she pleaded that SNCC would reject the committee proposal without his endorsement, he relented.

Forman soon found SNCC women a valuable resource for work beyond the BWLC, and he made their work crucial to his domestic and international projects for SNCC. He developed a major statement of protest that he intended to deliver to churches. He organized African American laborers at plants in Detroit and New Jersey. The workers collectively obtained "nongovernmental organization" status at the United Nations, which allowed them to meet with the president of Guyana and other international dignitaries. Patton-Woods and Jackson were responsible for putting the UN press kits together. The BWLC and Forman also went around the world together to promote his programs.[19]

Patton-Woods eventually followed Forman's lead by developing her own individual projects. She began to work closely with African American students, forming the National Association of Black Students (NABS) in 1969. The new organization worked closely with the BWLC to develop the treatise

"From Student to Student-Worker to Worker Consciousness." She and the students read a significant amount of literature on the political economy of capitalism. Through her efforts, NABS grew beyond Detroit and Washington, D.C., to affiliates nationwide, especially on European American college and university campuses. She marveled at the group's sophisticated regional and democratic structure, which was how SNCC had been in the years before the chairman position became nationally prominent under Carmichael and Brown. In addition, NABS owned two large houses, which were collectives. Those houses served as the embassies of the African American separatist group Republic of New Africa (RNA), and NABS allowed the RNA to hold its annual meeting in the houses.[20]

BWLC cofounder Mae Jackson also found an outlet for non-SNCC activism through the arts, writing poetry and reading it at colleges, community centers, and African American events. Her artistic gifts benefited SNCC by virtue of her membership in the group. The national African American magazine *Negro Digest* profiled her because of her literary talent. Aside from the BWLC and assorted speeches from Rap Brown, SNCC rarely received press coverage by early 1970, even from African American periodicals. The periodical announced that Jackson had recently won a $500 prize in writing—the Conrad Kent Rivers Memorial Award. *Negro Digest* reported that she had received the honor because she was "striving to achieve the highest literary goals despite economic disadvantages or against unusual odds." Most of the article was biographical and described the roots of her activism during her childhood, but the article only mentioned her current affiliation with SNCC in passing.[21]

Meanwhile, SNCC itself was losing steam. The New York City branch lost its office, and Mae Jackson and Carolyn Carter were among those who were present when SNCC was evicted. They were allowed to only pack a few papers in two shopping bags before leaving the premises. Jackson took everything that she could and caught a yellow cab to Brooklyn with tears in her eyes, devastated that the office had closed. The search for a new facility to rent distracted the branch from developing new programs.[22]

After a lull in publicity, SNCC members made major national news in April. The headlines they generated, however, were for individual projects instead of organizational programs. H. Rap Brown's autobiography *Die Nigger Die!* was published that month. It featured not only Brown's political views but also assorted photographs interspersed throughout the text. He wrote about his early years and about his time in SNCC before becoming the chairman. Much of the second half of the book concerned his speeches and his run-ins with the law. He provided full texts of all the letters he wrote to the public from jail. They were laced with profanity but also contained the humorous rhetoric that had earned Brown the nickname "Rap."

Brown's book offered a critique of how the press and politicians treated the movement. He made a point of saying that the media had portrayed SNCC's sit-in participants as wanting to eat where European Americans ate. He countered that he and his colleagues protested in order to show their unwillingness to have their choices and freedoms restricted. Brown's harshest words were for government officials, especially Vice President Agnew, whom he described as a cross between an elephant and a baboon.[23]

The book marked one of the few times Brown had communicated to the public since stepping down from the SNCC chairman position the previous year. Offering very few press conferences and interviews, he was yielding the organizational spotlight to program secretary Phil Hutchings. Moreover, Brown's book did not address events beyond his incarceration in early 1968. Therefore, readers still had no idea what he thought of President Nixon, SNCC's changes after he left the chairmanship, or how SNCC should move forward.

Only his criticism of the movement reflected his views of civil rights in 1969, and he was pessimistic toward it. With no one rising to take his place as *the* militant spokesman in his absence, he lamented that the current leaders of civil rights groups "diluted and prostituted" Black Power. In response, he dismissed NUL's leader as "'Whitey' Young, dictator of the urban league" and claimed that by associating Black Power with "black capitalism," Young was "still following his master." At least *Die Nigger Die!* allowed Brown to fill the void he himself had created with his hiatus. The positive reviews he received for his book suggested that many people had missed hearing from him.[24]

In Detroit, SNCC colleague James Forman caused a stir by taking over the National Black Economic Development Conference there. He had been working with the city's League of Revolutionary Black Workers on a document they called the "Black Manifesto." Their statement called for European American churches and synagogues to give African Americans reparations in ten specific ways. The manifesto claimed that the religious institutions helped contribute to the centuries of abuse that African Americans had experienced since the beginning of slavery. When he interrupted the conference to read the demands on April 26, the conference voted to support them. That victory led Forman to directly confront organized religion.

Forman had been in SNCC for eight years by the time he entered Riverside Church in New York City on May 4. He had started in the organization with faith in politicians and religious leaders to support the group's stand against segregation's immorality. Over the years he and others in SNCC grew increasingly angry and disappointed at the reticence or opposition from both groups of people. When he disrupted Riverside's worship service, the pastor announced that the service was cancelled and then left the building. The church's combative organist played loudly to drown out Forman as he spoke, but the activist simply waited out the musician and then proceeded to speak. As he delivered the manifesto, he became more and more enraged at his thoughts of Christian enslavers, the killings at the hands of Lyndon Johnson, Richard Nixon's trickiness, and even Spiro Agnew. In a sense the disruption was typical of Forman, for he had made news four years earlier in Selma, Alabama, for using profanity at a church during planning for the Selma-to-Montgomery march. He had proclaimed, "If we can't sit at the table, we'll knock the fucking legs off!" Back then, he had asked for forgiveness immediately after cursing, but now in New York he made no apologies for offending anyone.[25]

The manifesto was not an official SNCC document, and it reflected very little of SNCC in its current form. Some of the language had roots in earlier speeches from ex-SNCC associate Stokely Carmichael. Just as Carmichael had talked about African Americans being ready to die after King's killing, the manifesto similarly says, "[T]here is only one thing left that you can do to further degrade black people and that is to kill us. But we have been dying too long for this country." He ended the statement with the same closing that Brown often wrote in his letters: "We shall win without a doubt."[26] Other parts of the manifesto suggested that Forman was influenced by the current campaigns of SCLC. The organization had been tackling the issues of poverty and labor since the previous year. Likewise, Forman claimed solidarity with the National Welfare Rights Organization, which had participated in Resurrection City. He also called for $20 million for the establishment of a National Black Labor Strike and Defense Fund to protect African American strikers.

Despite the tension he had experienced in the BPP, he drew mostly from that group when constructing the manifesto. The statement contained a list of 10 demands, not unlike the 10-point platform of the BPP. The manifesto itself was merely an extension of the BPP's third demand in its platform, which stated, "[W]e are demanding the overdue debt of forty acres and two mules." Whereas the BPP vaguely described how the "racist government" would disburse restitution to all African Americans, Forman offered a specific sum—$500 million—and apportioned it to "$15 per nigger." He also provided detailed uses of the funds such as four African American television networks, a "Black University," and printing presses. Moreover, the rhetoric of the BPP appeared in the manifesto. Just as the BPP platform called U.S. society "decadent," so did Forman's statement.[27]

The popularity of the manifesto lay not in its content but with Forman's dramatic delivery of it. Over the next few months, the press identified him more often as the promoter of the manifesto than as a member of SNCC. News of the Riverside disruption led to discussions in churches about the demands of the statement. Meanwhile, Forman continued to interrupt other churches' services. In addition, the reparations movement went overseas, as Julia Herve of SNCC–Paris interrupted services at American Church in Paris to read the "Black Manifesto," demand $500, and call for the use of church facilities. These later disruptions received less press attention than Forman's actions at Riverside. Still, Forman had enough confidence in the momentum of the reparations campaign to take his idea to the next SNCC meeting, scheduled for June.

Among the ministers who opposed the manifesto, some of the sharpest criticism came from African American circles. Stephen Spottswood, the NAACP board chairman and a bishop of the African Methodist Episcopal Zion church denomination, dismissed Forman's idea as "emotionally appealing" but unfair. His remarks constituted the latest battle of the ongoing NAACP-SNCC feud. "The Association has never subscribed to the reparations concept," he noted in a speech to his fellow NAACP members. He reprimanded European American devotees of the manifesto for overlooking its revolutionary content. Moreover, Spottswood found Forman's work too unstable. If European Americans wanted to donate money anywhere, they should give it to established civil rights groups instead of a "paper organization," as he put it.[28]

SCLC's two most prominent women developed different approaches to activism. Mrs. King remained constantly busy by virtue of the public's demand for her as an eloquent speaker, a devotee to several causes, and King's widow. She was no longer the "First Lady" of SCLC, but the public treated her as an unofficial First Lady of the movement. On February 5, 1969, she led an antiwar march sponsored by the Clergy and Laity Concerned about Vietnam and also spoke at the march's destination—the Justice Department building. She was named an honorary chairman of the New Mobilization Committee to End the War in Vietnam. She also divided her time between fundraisers for the King memorial and events facilitated by SCLC.

In contrast, Juanita Abernathy, the wife of the current SCLC president, kept a low profile. Her relative invisibility removed the threat of competition with her husband and the other SCLC men for media attention. She only occasionally appeared with her spouse at various organizational events and attended those functions solely in the role of the president's wife. In stark contrast to Mrs. King, she conducted few activities without him and rarely participated in programs outside of his organization. She explained to *Ebony*, "I'm not active in the SCLC administration at all, and I don't plan to be. I like a housewife's role."[29]

Mrs. Abernathy was one of very few people who publicly celebrated her husband's leadership qualities. As SCLC internally fought over his presidency and the public waxed nostalgic for King, her compliments marked a rare moment of positive publicity for her husband in the media. "He never really relaxes," she said of his work ethic. About his job as a pastor, she revealed that ministers comprised the center of African American church activities. As a result, ministers had to play leadership roles. Her husband's work as SCLC's leader kept him from interacting with church members as often as before, but the members knew that he had another responsibility and believed that he was with them in spirit. "They're proud of him," Mrs. Abernathy noted. As for her thoughts on the movement, she deferred such talk to her husband and was content to be "just a helper."[30]

Her concept of the woman's role in the movement borrowed significantly from Daniel "Pat" Moynihan's recommendation in *The Negro Family* that African American women let their men strut like bantams. She claimed that women helped African Americans achieve their goals, but she also noted that African American women were "more free" than African American men. "It has been said that the only free people in the South are the black women and the white men," she observed. "In a sense, that may be true. The white man has always dominated his woman. The black man could not; he didn't have any authority to—he came from slavery. The black woman could be impudent and not be lashed, but the black man would be strung up for just looking resentful." She also recognized that European American men dominated both European American women and African American women and allowed African American women to say things that they prohibited African American men from saying. "This is part of what the black man faces today," she explained. "He has never been permitted to be a man." Then in an almost subconscious answer to the criticism of Abernathy as egotistical, she declared of African American men in general, "He has to have his ego. If you take that away from him, he can't function as a man." Thus, her stroking of her husband's ego reflected her responses to the discrimination he faced as an African American man and to the public's frequent, unfavorable comparisons of him to his predecessor.[31]

SCLC's inability to redefine itself without King softened the impact of its activism. His identity remained central to the organization, and on April

4, 1969, the group launched a long-term campaign toward preserving the fallen leader's memory. Until then, the organization's marches and sit-ins had addressed specific social issues and had stirred the nation's conscience. Now, SCLC led nationwide demonstrations to mark the one-year anniversary of King's death, and the events were in cities of major significance to the fallen leader's work for SCLC. However, they did not rouse masses of people to sympathy with the organization's work against poverty and violence. Abernathy and Senator Ted Kennedy of Massachusetts led a march in Memphis to remember the last campaign King had lived to see. Similarly, in Alabama, demonstrators recreated the Selma-to-Montgomery march of 1965, in which television cameras had captured the graphic violence of policemen on horseback gassing and charging at activists. The policemen did not re-create their roles four years later. Meanwhile, in Washington, D.C., where King had given his famous "I Have a Dream" address almost six years earlier, motorists turned on their headlights while driving during the day.

In the meantime SCLC found an opportunity to conduct a protracted nonviolent campaign of civil disobedience to highlight the issue of labor. In late March hospital workers in Charleston, South Carolina, started a strike. Employees of Medical College Hospital had tried to create a union there—Local 1199B of the Retail, Wholesale and Department Union at Charleston. The hospital fired them for their efforts. Esau Jenkins, a longtime local movement activist, contacted Abernathy. "Ralph, come to Charleston," he implored.[32]

The situation was similar to the previous year's strike in Memphis, in which a movement veteran had asked King to lead marches with the striking sanitation workers. Despite the setbacks SCLC had experienced with that strike, Abernathy agreed to go to Charleston. After all, Jenkins was on the SCLC's board of directors. "I have sense enough to please my boss," Abernathy later quipped in an address to the Charleston strikers.[33] It was an odd remark, because the workers he supported were definitely not pleasing their boss by striking.

SCLC's involvement in the strike made sense for several reasons. The strikers were conducting themselves in ways that mirrored how the organization protested. The workers marched nonviolently, and their protest concerned the issue of economic justice. In addition, if SCLC were to have a successful campaign there, it would be the first victory to have occurred without any input from King whatsoever. Resurrection City had tested how well Abernathy could implement what King had planned. Charleston was a test of how well Abernathy could create and run his own demonstrations.[34]

On April 25, Abernathy demonstrated there despite an injunction. He told the police chief that he had a duty to disobey unjust laws. As a result, he was arrested and sent to jail there. The strike continued without him, but his arrest had consequences beyond the city limits of Charleston. An SCLC branch in Mississippi had attempted to conduct a "poor march," but it was a disaster. The local activists had borrowed some of the tactics of the previous year's PPC. Abernathy failed to attend because of his incarceration in Charleston, leaving the Mississippi march restricted to only local coverage. The participants failed to generate much newsworthy drama, especially because the local government refused to engage with them.[35]

While incarcerated Abernathy decided to borrow a tactic from his predecessor and compose a public letter to the Charleston community. It appeared on May 2 in the *Charleston News and Courier* newspaper. He called for a nonviolent end to the labor dispute. He also asked local citizens to support the strikers. He demanded that the United States end hunger, poverty, and slums. He suggested that the nation create a fair welfare system. "There is still much work to be done on the 2nd chapter of the Poor People's Campaign," he wrote.[36]

The letter was a rebuttal of a statement by the Clergy Concerned Committee. Abernathy addressed allegations the group had made about SCLC. He said that his group did not create violence. Moreover, because of SCLC's presence in Charleston, domestic unrest had been curbed. Still, there was only so much that the organization could do. "We cannot control everybody any more than you can," he noted, "but I will say that unless this strike is settled, you will have much more violence." He also responded to the ministers' accusation of communism among the activists. He stated that SCLC wanted neither "a godless, atheist, totalitarian form of Communism" nor "a dictatorial repressive so-called Democracy." He vowed that the strike would continue until the workers could unionize.[37]

Upon the letter's publication, Abernathy received criticism for it. People accused him of trying to be like King. The comparisons were more numerous than what Brown had received for writing letters in prison. On the other hand, Brown was SNCC's leader—a group King had never led. Abernathy was the president of the group King had fronted. In addition, Abernathy's letter did not cover new ground. He was making the same demands that he had made in Resurrection City the previous year. Then again, in Abernathy's eyes, the Charleston strike was a continuation of the PPC from the previous year. But if a mule train, an encampment, and a strike did not get Abernathy's antipoverty message across to people, perhaps a letter would.

That night Abernathy posted $500 bond, and the police released him from jail the next day. He emerged from incarceration to give his followers a pep talk that doubled as a lecture. He promised victory for the strikers but only "with a great deal of suffering and sacrifice." It was a message King had preached many times before with other protestors. And just as King had done in his campaigns, Abernathy placed the onus of the strike's success on the demonstrators. If they remained nonviolent, they would win.[38]

In the aftermath of King's death and the prominence of militant rhetoric and unrest, SCLC struggled to keep the strikers faithful to nonviolence in Charleston. Workers at the County Hospital struck with the Medical College strikers as a gesture of solidarity, but they lost their jobs, too. More importantly, the longer the strike lasted, the more trouble SCLC experienced. Younger marchers joining the campaign that month were throwing stones and bottles. Their actions validated Abernathy's prediction in his letter a prolonged strike would lead to more violence. On the other hand, his campaign was coming unglued. He wanted publicity for the strike, but not in this way.

Making matters worse, many of the locals vehemently resisted SCLC's efforts. Abernathy received harassment that focused as much on the residents' distaste of the marches as their dislike of the SCLC leader as King's successor. As a result, some proponents of segregation mocked his leadership as badly as civil rights colleagues had done. Charleston's branches of the Citizens' Council, John Birch Society, and Royal Knights of the Ku Klux Klan addressed their collective death threat to "False Prophet Ralph," attacking his personality. "Mr. King was a gentleman, just the opposite of what you turned out to be," they sneered. "You are losing your *grip*, Old Boy, so you better quit while you are even," they warned. "It would be a sad tragedy if Charleston was further *polluted* with the rotting flesh of David Ralph Abernathy [*sic*]." The city's Republican chairman, Ray Harris, made some of the same complaints that Dixiecrats had raised years earlier. "They claim to be nonviolent," he observed, "but where ever they carry their nonviolence, there is violence and discord." He also felt sorry for SCLC: "All it has is Ralph David Abernathy, who twists and misquotes the scriptures, the Constitution, and history for whatever cause he happens to be champion of for the moment."[39]

Fortunately, major entertainers and politicians lent their presence and support to SCLC at the strike, just as they had done at Resurrection City 12 months earlier. Walter Reuther of the United Auto Workers, Michigan congressmen John Conyers and Charles Diggs, and activist Allard Lowenstein were among the luminaries who joined 12,000 people at a rally in Charleston on May 11. Their participation showed that they supported not just King but SCLC overall, and by marching in Charleston they suggested their approval of Abernathy's first original protest and, by extension, his leadership of the group. His supporters remained in the city when he went to visit the White House on May 13, and they were there when he returned.

As the strike dragged on, SCLC won support from a fellow civil rights leader. Whitney Young of the NUL assessed the state of the movement in his new book *Beyond Racism*, and he predicted that SCLC would "continue to challenge the conscience of the country and particularly its religious institutions." He saw potential in the group's organizing of local boycotts because the churches comprising its membership knew how to do the work involved in running an effective boycott—focusing on one business, recording its discriminatory incidents, calculating its African American capital, and informing the African American community. He also declared, "SCLC's many young activist ministers can also play a major role in organizing the black community and in articulating its needs and desires."[40]

Although Young boasted that all of the civil rights groups were "uniquely equipped to deal with certain problems facing black citizens," some were better equipped than others. He found Black Power a useful slogan but felt that CORE made better use of it than SNCC did. The former group worked toward creating "expanded ghetto entrepreneurship, consumer co-operatives, and economic development," all of which the NUL leader considered "real black power." Of the latter group, the author lamented its "transitional period," saying, "SNCC lost much of its following because it was unable to find a role for itself that would make its Black Power sloganeering relevant to today's realities." Instead of offering hope for SNCC's future, Young identified the group's best attribute of its past—its ability to "involve young people in programs of social change."[41] Thus, he saw little promise for the group's survival, except through a takeover by young adults.

Unsurprisingly, Young saw the most promise in the NUL and in the NAACP. He led the former group, and his close friend headed the latter. Young discussed those organizations in the context of having successfully met earlier goals, unlike the other groups. Wilkins had helped African Americans win "the legal battle for civil rights" and should try instead "to get out the vote, register people, and to apply political pressure." Similarly, the NUL had constructed the movement's "strongest contacts with the Establishment" and could best "challenge white leadership when challenge is needed" but needed to "develop an organizational base in the black community."[42]

Aside from his assessment of the movement, Young offered few new ideas in *Beyond Racism*. As in previous years, he only saw potential for African American uplift in 1969 through an integrated effort. He acknowledged that time had changed. African Americans held positions in the Senate and the Supreme Court and had just begun to expand the middle class. In addition, civil rights laws had "neutralized" blatant repression, launching the beginning of a "post-civil-rights period." Also new was Young's willingness to discuss power, writing that "America must share with black people the power and the privileges now held only by white Americans." Still, he claimed that African Americans' work with "concerned white people" would yield "an open Society, free of racism, free of poverty."[43]

Young's integrationism, however, also extended to assigning blame for the slow progress of African Americans. European Americans unwilling to share power with African Americans perpetuated repression against them. African American students crying for separatism played "right into the hands of bigots." And at the risk of offending the previous year's presidential candidates, Young referred to their use of "law and order" as "a thinly veiled code phrase for 'keep the niggers in their place.'"[44]

Young did not waver much from the arguments of King's final book, *Where Do We Go from Here*. Young echoed King's two-year-old warning of America headed toward either "nonviolent coexistence or violent co-annihilation," stating instead, "We can work together to create an Open Society which brings dignity to all men, or we can die together in an agony of hate and violence." Young differed from King, however, in focusing solely on domestic turmoil. King fretted over domestic ethnic relations; war in Vietnam; and poverty in Asia, Africa, and South America. Young, on the other hand, described America as on "the brink of disaster," heading toward "police-state repression." Moreover, by barely mentioning Vietnam, Young portrayed domestic unrest as the more urgent crisis and avoided upsetting the White House about the war as King had done.[45]

By the middle of 1969, the civil rights organizations had effectively redefined themselves and charted their courses after King's assassination. They now shared a sense that violence in the United States was a foregone conclusion, but disagreed as to what it meant. Wilkins, Young, and Abernathy wanted to prevent it, while Brown considered it "necessary." The groups found several opportunities to test their approaches to violence when state-sponsored shootings of young people plagued the country over the next 12 months.

CHAPTER 7

No Peace in This Land

On the same day as Ralph Abernathy's abortive White House meeting, a small-town Southern election produced a major civil rights advancement. In Mississippi, the state NAACP leader Charles Evers won the mayoral election in the town of Fayette. The town itself was unremarkable, barren of industry and full of African Americans. And before May 13, 1969, it was ruled exclusively by European Americans, just like all the other communities in the South. However, by winning the election that day, Evers became the first African American mayor in the state since the end of Reconstruction. The Voting Rights Act of 1965 helped African Americans begin the process of wresting complete governmental control of the South from European Americans. The legislation provided opportunities for African Americans to vote for candidates and run for offices without fear of legal disenfranchisement, and Fayette's new mayor-elect was one of the first African American electoral beneficiaries of that act.

Evers's campaign was not without struggle. He had received death threats from the Ku Klux Klan. In addition, the Mississippi Sovereignty Commission, a state government agency that had conducted COINTELPRO-style activities against civil rights activists since its formation in 1956, ran an investigation of him in May 1969. The agency contacted Jefferson County's sheriff and tax assessor and Fayette's city clerk, police chief, and mayor to collect as much data as they could about the candidate. The commission combed through his tax records and his paid bills, and the investigators asked the county officials about his "personal habits." The agents published their findings in a memorandum to the commission's director and concluded that the candidate was self-interested and "bad for the community," but the agency did not prevent Evers from winning the election.[1]

Ironically, although civil rights activists had helped persuade Congress to pass federal legislation that protected African American political participation, a growing number of people now considered electoral politics a preferable alternative to struggling for change from outside the system. The press noted how different Evers was from contemporary movement leaders. He spoke against violence and talked about working with people of all colors. His victory-night address resurrected much of the spirit of the civil rights struggle of years gone by. Evoking King's dream of multiethnic community fellowship, the mayor-elect stood at the podium and told his audience, "We are going to show the nation that even in rural southwest Mississippi, black and white can work together." The crowd then began singing "We Shall Overcome" as he left the podium.[2]

On the other hand, Evers had much in common with Abernathy, too. After all, the current president of the SCLC had spent that day trying to accomplish what had eluded his predecessor. He wanted to bring SCLC back into a working relationship with the White House. It was part of his greater hope to someday lead people into the "Promised Land" that King did not live to see. Meanwhile, Charles Evers tried to bring about the political progress that his late brother Medgar had worked to facilitate before his assassination in 1963. Medgar's avenue for change had been the NAACP, and Charles became the organization's state leader upon his brother's death. Charles then used the stature from his position to launch a political career. But as Evers succeeded within the system, Abernathy failed to find his niche in battling outside of it.

Evers also connected with the current movement by publicly expressing disagreement with President Nixon's policies. The mayor-elect suggested that the president renew the Voting Rights Act without altering it as it approached expiration in the following year. Also, when Nixon announced his intent to delay the desegregation of some schools, Evers assailed him for showing Mississippi's African Americans "unjust disrespect." He bantered, "We've been knocked down before, Nixon, but we're coming back at you."[3]

Still, Evers was the kind of African American leader that Nixon preferred African Americans to have—the low-key, noninflammatory integrationist. The NAACP leader's victory showed that some African Americans still approved that style of leadership, too. Meanwhile, the growing militancy of the movement and the intense rhetoric of emerging speakers from the SNCC and the BPP also brought the issue of post-King African American leadership to the cultural forefront. Two new television situation comedies for the 1969–1970 season did not say which person should lead African Americans, but rather how African Americans should lead. Reflecting the more conservative side of the movement, both shows were set in integrated public schools. Lloyd Haynes played a highly respected high school teacher who taught a diverse group of students and worked well with European American colleagues in *Room 222*, and Bill Cosby played a high school coach in *The Bill Cosby Show*. Both actors offered low-key performances and dry humor for their roles. They sported small "naturals" and wore suits and ties. As educators instead of militant separatists, their characters represented Black Power for Nixon-era television.

The promotion of mild-mannered, integrationist African American male figures came at a time when the federal government worried about the rise of outspoken nationalists. On June 13, Attorney General John Mitchell ordered the creation of a task force to gather information for prosecuting the primary people responsible for campus unrest. He claimed that the H. Rap Brown Act gave him the authority to do so. When discussing how to finance the new task force, the Appropriations Committee stated that the Brown Act "will be utilized to the fullest extent" against campus demonstrations. Meanwhile, the Senate Permanent Investigations Subcommittee, headed by segregationist John McClellan of Arkansas, launched a study on campus disorders, naming SNCC and the BPP among the likely causes of the unrest.[4]

One month later the FBI raised the stakes. On July 15, J. Edgar Hoover publicly announced that the BPP was the number-one threat to the internal security of the United States of America. The group conducted programs that attracted Hoover's attention and aroused his ire. The organization and police officers engaged in shootouts against each other across the country, and the Panthers allegedly served children breakfast in order to brainwash them. Meanwhile, over the past few months, the organization had surpassed both SNCC and SCLC in media attention. The BPP also dominated attention from COINTELPRO agents. Nearly every COINTELPRO memorandum related to the Panthers, and reports about SNCC and SCLC were few and far between.

Not to be outdone by the BPP, exactly one week after Hoover's declaration, SNCC members Rap Brown and Muhammad Hunt, now head of the Revolutionary Political Council (RPC), held a press conference at Holy Apostles Church in New York at 11:00 a.m. Brown announced the demise of SNCC's organizational name. The word "nonviolent" had become a hindrance to SNCC, and Hunt said that SNCC would not yield to "the concept of nonviolence as a solution to the problems of oppressed people." Brown then unequivocally repudiated nonviolence on behalf of the group while launching into his standard theme of violence as cultural. "We do not accept unconditional nonviolence as a tactic," he declared. "All tactics must be considered and all violent tactics must be considered, because we're living in a world of violence."[5]

The members had actually discarded the old name at a national meeting of the organization one month earlier. At the meeting they had considered renaming themselves the Revolutionary Action Party, whose initials spelled out Brown's nickname. But at the July 22 press conference, Brown stated that the group was now to be called the Student National Coordinating Committee. That way, the members could keep the famous acronym while simultaneously disposing of one of the group's fundamental principles. To Brown, conscious struggle among people of African descent against oppressors of European descent was constant, but changes in the struggle allowed various phases of struggle to come and go. Like these phases, SNCC also was subject to the rules of life and death. Replacing the "N" in SNCC was simply a part of the movement's process of existence.[6]

Brown claimed at the press conference that he had once again been elected chairman of SNCC. Concerning other personnel, Phil Hutchings was now assigned to start a new "propaganda network" for making an all-black political party, Irving Davis headed International Affairs, and Jimmy Johnson led the group's NBAWADU project. Brown also mentioned new long-term organizational projects such as a campaign to free the Cleveland-based imprisoned militant Ahmed Evans, a People's Medical Center, the monitoring of violations of the United Nations Charter on Human Rights, and the empowering of welfare mothers. Hunt announced that SNCC had secured doctors to offer free medical care in Bedford-Stuyvesant and Brownsville, Brooklyn.

The returning SNCC leader was as fiery as ever. Brown's time away from the media spotlight had not taken away the intensity of his rhetoric. Going beyond his usual theme of color-based warfare, he called for African Americans to channel their energies against the White House. "Tell Nixon we are going to put violence in his home, not only in the streets," he vowed. "He should be concerned about violence in his home." Brown admitted that African Americans were already violent, but that their energy was misdirected toward themselves. "We are talking about re-directing our violence," he noted.[7]

SNCC's name change gave the organization the most widespread the media coverage it had experienced in two years. Brown's celebrity and the group's official turn from nonviolence guaranteed attention from the press. However, the reports on television and in newspapers did not mention anything beyond Brown's return to the helm and the group's reorganization. Despite the SNCC chairman's apparent threat to attack the president, reporters neglected to mention it; apparently, violent rhetoric from Brown had itself become routine. The new name merely confirmed what people had already long suspected about the organization.[8]

SNCC's transition was also somewhat standard. The group was only a part of a wave of activist organizations that dramatically shifted tactics during the summer. The establishment of Nixon's "law and order" rule inspired new ideas from dissenters. The group SDS split into two factions. Its members who organized the working class became the SDS–Progressive Labor Party branch, but other members plotted to conduct bombings to overthrow the federal government. The latter faction eventually became its own organization—the Weathermen.

Meanwhile, Stokely Carmichael gave up the struggle in the United States. He relocated permanently to Africa in the summer of 1969. On June 25, he wrote from Conakry, Guinea, to announce his resignation from the Black Panthers. His wife, Miriam Makeba, read the letter to the press in New York on July 3. Carmichael could no longer reconcile himself to the organization's willingness to welcome European Americans into the African American struggle for liberation. In addition, he disliked how the group characterized people who disagreed with the idea of an integrated activist organization. "All those who disagreed with the party line are lumped into the same category and labeled 'cultural nationalists,' 'pork chop nationalists,' and 'reactionary pigs,'" he revealed. "This may be a very convenient tactic," he reasoned. "However, it is dangerous and vicious."[9]

As Carmichael departed, Roy Wilkins continued to rail against the ex-SNCC chairman's generation of Black Power activists. Almost a decade after praising the sit-in students of 1960 and feeling their pain of segregation, Wilkins washed his hands of the young separatists. "These black youngsters who today are seeking absolute blackness in all things don't know, of their own experience, what racial segregation can do to a people," he wrote. "They think they know." Admitting that America was far from perfect, he did acknowledge "many flaws in the system" and, hinting at revolutionary rhetoric, suggested, "They cry for overturning." Ironically, to warn people against Carmichael's kind of separatism, Wilkins relied upon Pan-Africanism. The NAACP leader told the "youngsters" to consider Britain's African colony of Rhodesia as an example of the dangers of separatism by skin color. Rhodesia proved to him that "racial separation is the basic requirement for control."[10]

Instead of discussing Rhodesia, Rap Brown concerned himself with running the organization he had just taken over. He consolidated control of many of the programs that the factions of "Nonviolent" SNCC had run. The new name mattered little to the members themselves, who referred to the group by its acronym anyway. In addition, Brown altered the name in order to attract young students to the organization but did not make the new name the focus of his chairmanship.

James Forman was gone from the revamped group. His colleagues chose not to endorse the manifesto at the June meeting, and his diminished power in the new SNCC convinced him to leave. On the other hand, his contributions influenced the remaining associates for a long time. Irving Davis, a protégé of Forman's, shared leadership duties of the new SNCC with Muhammad Hunt.

In addition, churches continued to extend support to the group long after the release of the manifesto. Rector Weeks did not receive the grant he had requested from Bishop Donegan back in June 1969. However, when SNCC was soon evicted from its office on Fifth Avenue, St. Peter's Episcopal Church in New York welcomed the organization. The group had significantly dwindled in size since its renaming. Nine members from across the country attended a national meeting in November. At the time, the group had six members in the New York branch alone. During the first year of the new SNCC, the organization was too financially strapped to pay its telephone bill and the rent. St. Peter's placed SNCC offices in the church's parish house, which was on the opposite side of the church from the rectory. Church staff did not cross paths with SNCC on a regular basis as a result, and St. Peter's did not often discuss the organization's affairs. Church personnel mentioned Brown's name at times and even made occasional references to the departed Carmichael.[11]

Some people took SNCC's name change as a signal that it was time for them to move on to other projects and away from SNCC forever. Unlike the contentious firings of associates in the 1968 organizational meetings, these departures were voluntary and—for the most part—without hard feelings. Maria Varela moved to New Mexico to work full-time with Reies Tijerina in the Southwest Hispanic Land Grant. When Forman left, so did his close colleague and BWLC cofounder Gwen Patton. Longtime supporter Harry Belafonte, who had given SNCC a $40,000 check in 1961 to help the group launch its organizing programs, was disheartened by the organization's new disavowal of nonviolence and ended his relationship with the group.[12]

The programs that survived the name change focused on domestic and foreign political issues. The organization retained an international presence through a Scandinavian branch run by Sven Hedman and Sara Markstrom. From New York, Fran Beal and Judy Sullivan facilitated an H. Rap Brown Defense Fund—a revival of SNCC–Los Angeles' "Let Rap Rap" campaign. Most importantly, the BWLC remained a part of SNCC. It was the one program from the organization that attracted stalwart female veteran activists. Longtime SNCC member Eleanor Holmes Norton served as the BWLC's legal adviser. Another important link the BWLC had to its parent group was through Ella Baker, who had been present at the "Nonviolent" SNCC's first meeting in April 1960.[13]

The most ambitious new project from the new SNCC was the Agrarian Reform Program. The organization wanted to create a cooperative farm system throughout the South and Southwest. The group wanted tenant farmers to be able to provide for themselves through their work. SNCC considered implementing artificial insemination on the farm in order for cattle to give birth faster and for the farms to be hygienic and have sufficient milk, leather, and meat. The group also proposed to raise funds for the construction of housing for the tenant farmers. SNCC envisioned day care and health facilities on the farms. It also intended to "raise the political consciousness of this segment of the Black Population and turn them on to the road of constructive radical change." As of November 1969, the organization was looking for two hundred acres of land to buy, but it had already started facilitating donations of cattle and chickens.[14]

The new SNCC also distinguished itself from the old by eliminating its restriction of membership to African Americans. The organization became open to all people of color. SNCC–New York had already become allied with Arab Americans, Asian Americans, and—through the socialist protest group Young Lords Party—Puerto Ricans. The diversity of the New York branch reflected Brown's control of that faction of the old SNCC. Now that Brown controlled all of the organization, all of SNCC could be multicultural. The change marked a significant shift from the one-color focus SNCC had first adopted in 1966. Years after Stokely Carmichael and others had started speaking in support of "Third World" people, SNCC now included people of various "Third World" ethnic groups. In a way, therefore, SNCC became more like SCLC, which had already actively recruited support from various ethnic groups. European Americans were still prohibited from SNCC, however.[15]

In contrast to the upheaval in SNCC and the BPP, SCLC experienced a period of stability and momentum. Ralph Abernathy was leading the group on his terms, and he still enjoyed the same inner circle of staff that had made the transition from King's leadership to his. In addition, he earned his first campaign success that had not originated with his predecessor. On June 27, the Medical College workers in Charleston won their demands and finally stopped striking. Andrew Young of SCLC was jubilant. "We won this strike because of a wonderful marriage—the marriage of the SCLC and Local

1199," he beamed. "The first of many beautiful children of this marriage is Local 1199B here in Charleston, and there are going to be as many more children like 1199B as there are letters in the alphabet."[16]

Abernathy could only enjoy the news from jail. One week before the agreement, he and Hosea Williams were arrested at another demonstration in Charleston. On July 2, still incarcerated, Abernathy wrote a letter to his staff, encouraging them to stay at work in South Carolina. He acknowledged that SCLC won "an historic accomplishment on behalf of the nation's poor" but reminded his colleagues that the County Hospital strikers remained unemployed. In addition, concerning himself and Williams, "We are completing our twelfth day here in the jail under the ridiculous charges of 'inciting to riot.'"[17]

He received letters of encouragement in the immediate aftermath of the strikers' settlement from a diverse and powerful array of people. Hawaii congresswoman Patsy Mink and Missouri congressman William Clay wrote to support him. One person informed the SCLC leader that he had appeared in the June 10 issue of *Look* magazine. Columbia Pictures invited him to a screening of the movie *Castle Keep*. He was further encouraged when the County Hospital workers were rehired later, by the end of July.

Even the Nixon administration extended olive branches of sorts to SCLC. Labor Secretary George Shultz wrote a response about Abernathy's written complaints to him in an affirming manner. "I welcome the opportunity to comment on the issues you raise," he said, "and I look forward to a continuing dialogue with you and your immediate staff." Meanwhile, the Civil Rights Division of the Department of Health, Education, and Welfare went even further. Division Director Leon Panetta, in office for less than three months, named his staffer Waite Madison as the "special liaison" with civil rights groups. Concerning Madison's qualifications, Panetta explained in his letter to Abernathy, "Before assuming duties as Northern Compliance Coordinator, he worked for many months in the southern states." After he acknowledged "the need for better liaison and improved exchange of ideas with organizations involved in civil rights activity," he invited the SCLC leader to "call on Mr. Madison and myself and know that we will be asking for your views on the administration of Title VI [of the Civil Rights Act]."[18] Letters to Shultz and calls to Madison and Panetta were now as close as Abernathy would ever get to Nixon's White House.

SCLC also had some unexpected luck with the media, winning prime-time television exposure for the first time since the news bulletins about King's assassination. On July 7, the ABC network presented a documentary about Operation Breadbasket, which featured some footage from Resurrection City and some scenes of SCLC in Chicago. In a sense, the movie was an in-house effort. SCLC supporter and *I Spy* star Robert Culp wrote, produced, and directed the film. Although NBC had cancelled *I Spy* in early 1968, Culp still wielded enough clout for his movie to air on network television. Also, SCLC's recent success in Charleston certainly did not hurt the film's chances for respectable ratings.[19]

The organization also capitalized on its positive press from the Charleston victories by launching yet another march against economic inequity. This time the group chose to target Florida. The reason did not have to do with the discrimination, labor, or poverty in that state. Rather, the United States prepared to launch the Apollo 11 rocket to the moon, and the organization tried to benefit from the worldwide attention the launch would receive. Abernathy, newly released from the Charleston jail, led a mule train of 150 poor people to Cape Kennedy to protest what he called "a distorted sense of national priorities."[20] In dramatizing the need for the nation to pay more attention to the problems of hunger and poverty, however, he did not want SCLC to disrupt the launching of the rocket.

Thomas O. Paine, a NASA administrator, softened the impact of SCLC's demonstration with warm Southern hospitality toward the PPC. He met with Abernathy in a field close to the main entrance of the John F. Kennedy Space Center and asked the minister to pray for the astronauts. Paine acknowledged the existence of rampant hunger and poverty, but he took issue with Abernathy's claim about distorted priorities and said that lunar exploration was not hindering the nation's progress in ending social ills. "If it were possible for us not to push that button and solve the problems you are talking about," Paine reasoned, "we would not push that button." As a further gesture of goodwill, he offered 40 "VIP" seats to the marchers, allowing for Abernathy and 10 of the poor families to watch the launch. SCLC accepted the offer, and NASA was saved from a depiction as an enemy of civil rights. Abernathy himself conceded that he was glad that the nation was going to the moon.[21]

On the other hand, Abernathy tried to save face by trumpeting SCLC's accomplishments at the launch. "SCLC formed the conscience of the nation and the hearts of the world upon the forgotten poor of our country whose anguish deepens daily because of this nation's tragically misplaced priorities," he loquaciously bragged. "The Poor People's Campaign won a moral victory at Cape Kennedy," he declared. Abernathy himself won a victory by showing that even after his abortive discussion with President Nixon, he still had enough clout to successfully get a meeting on demand with a federal government official. His glee, however, was dissonant with the anguish that his impoverished demonstrators illustrated on their signs. One sign displayed a countdown to "genocide" instead of a launch. Another rhetorically asked, "What do I care for space when my insides are empty?"[22]

After the launch, SCLC bore more substantial fruit from its political organizing. On July 29, the group's voter registration efforts in Greene County, Alabama, enabled people to elect African Americans to county political control. African Americans won control of the city commission and the county board of education. The election results were a major milestone in the South overall because Greene was the first county in the Deep South since Reconstruction to elect both a school board and a county commission run by African Americans. In addition, 15 SCLC members had helped voter registration efforts there, and the election signaled that perhaps the organization could carry on well without King.

SCLC had predicted those election results. The organization figured that with African Americans registered to vote there, the residents would elect African Americans. As early as July 3, while still in jail in Charleston, Abernathy and Hosea Williams had sent telegrams to invite people to Greene County for an inaugural celebration later that summer. They curiously sent invitations to militant and nationalist African Americans—even some who had rejected nonviolence. Ron Karenga and SNCC's James Forman and Rap Brown were among those on SCLC's list.

Abernathy was understandably giddy in the speech he gave on election night. Some of his remarks were quite serious. Despite Williams's concern for the small (200-vote) margin of victory, Abernathy candidly countered, "I'm just thankful to God that we beat these white folk once in our lives, here in Greene County." But most of the address was celebratory. He proclaimed that "poor people everywhere, black and white, can look to Greene County as an inspiration to gain political control and representative government so that governments will save them, not exploit them." Using hyperbole, he said that "the step that Armstrong made on the moon was not as great as the step these six black men have made in Greene County." He boasted that he was "a prophet sent by God," and he predicted more African American elected officials for the county in the future.[23]

However, Abernathy's strangest behavior in Eutaw was yet to come. On August 11, Greene County's African American officials were sworn in, and Abernathy led between 700 and 800 African Americans on a "freedom march" outside in celebration of the event. Suddenly the milestone was marred by civil disobedience. A crowd of about 100 African Americans broke off from the march and went to Greene's county seat of Eutaw to break into the segregated swimming pool facility there. Some climbed over the fence that had kept people of their skin color from entering. Others busted open the door to the bathhouse and concession stand with an iron bar. They grabbed whatever food and soda they could take from the concession stand.

Abernathy claimed to not have been with the vandals and looters when they wrecked the facility, but he took advantage of their mayhem. He soon caught up with them on the pool grounds. "This pool is now *yours*," Abernathy beamed as he addressed the crowd from inside the fence.[24] Then he commandeered a swimsuit, changed out of his clothes, and joined the others in the county pool. It was a small-scale rural uprising. It lacked the arson and killings of the urban disturbances of recent years, but had in common the vandalism and looting of the city "riots." As a result, by participating in an uprising, Abernathy had just done in Eutaw what Rap Brown was merely accused of doing in Cambridge only with words.

The Eutaw pool incident was as close as Abernathy had come to violating the H. Rap Brown Act. Abernathy was a Georgia resident who had crossed into Alabama, and he not only encouraged those committing destructive civil disobedience at the pool but also was physically with them while they did it. His involvement was a significant break from Martin Luther King's stance on uprisings. Abernathy's predecessor had spent the last year of his life repeatedly speaking out against urban disturbances. When his marchers in Memphis had turned to vandalism and looting in March 1968, King immediately left the demonstration. In contrast, Abernathy reveled in the disorder at Eutaw and verbally justified it with the faulty logic that African American control of county government allowed African Americans to break in and steal from the county's pool.

He also offered a pithy explanation for joining the swimmers: "It was hot."

The day's events were also SCLC's latest example of conducting its own activity during a community's high-profile incident. But in a reflection of the nation's familiarity with movement tactics, the county government and the media refused to take Abernathy's bait and make a big story out of the break-in. NBC News only devoted 90 seconds to coverage of the event, and did not include Abernathy in its footage of the disturbance. Local law enforcement made no arrests, claiming that no good would have come from making any.

With Abernathy's conduct at the pool, SCLC had overstayed its welcome in Greene County. The incident displeased local citizens, including the African Americans who had just won their electoral offices. One of the new officials called the incident "very upsetting." Abernathy had his electoral activism victory, giving him another accomplishment that had nothing to do with his predecessor. After scoring impromptu media coverage with the disturbance, he had nothing else to gain in Greene. Now that people were turning on him, it was time to go.[25]

SCLC had national business to address, anyway. That same month the organization held its annual convention and decided to play upon its strengths in the immediate future. Andrew Young advised his fellow members to scale down marches and demonstrations and focus on voting, politics, and labor. On the strength of the Charleston victory, Abernathy vowed to lead workshops for African American hospital workers in Petersburg, Virginia, and Tallahassee, Florida, and other cities.

Abernathy offered a contradictory performance at the convention. Some parts of his speech appropriated his predecessor's rhetoric. Borrowing directly from King's Memphis speech of April 3, 1968, Abernathy announced, "I'm going through to the Promised Land." He then talked about joining King in heaven. He declared, "I have a rendezvous with destiny and a date with eternity."[26] On the other hand, he tried to differentiate himself from King. He called himself the "Joshua" to King's "Moses." The speech reflected Abernathy's internal struggle as the leader of SCLC. He tried to establish his own successes in the organization, but the group promoted itself as carrying on King's work. Its official button displayed images of King and Abernathy side by side.

The new SCLC president was best able to distinguish himself from his predecessor by criticizing the federal government more forcefully than his old friend had. Abernathy especially took a harder line against President Nixon than King had with President Johnson—a reflection of his bitterness concerning the administration's treatment of him and his poor delegation at the White House back in May. He associated Nixon with segregationist politicians through the phrase "the Nixon-Agnew-Thurmond Administration." In addition, he referred to the president as "Tricky Dick"—an unflattering nickname that Helen Gahagan Douglas had first coined in 1950, when she ran against Nixon in California for a seat in the Senate. Abernathy's personal attack was unprecedented, but the White House had never been so publicly dismissive of the movement or hostile toward it before Nixon's inauguration.[27]

After the convention, SCLC immediately went to work on a long-range campaign. In October 1969, the group started organizational efforts in Sandersville, Georgia—a town with a significant African American population. Four years after the Voting Rights Act's passage, no African Americans held elected positions in the city government. SCLC's campaign there not only emphasized the deeply entrenched disenfranchisement that still plagued the South but also demonstrated why the act's federal supervision of local polling places needed to be renewed when the supervision was scheduled to expire the following year.[28]

Meanwhile, Coretta Scott King remained the most visible face of SCLC, although her publicity did not usually result from her work on the organization's current projects. As King's widow, all of her activities generated significant press coverage, but the press gave her even more attention whenever she either memorialized her husband or discussed her life as his wife. In September, *Life* magazine devoted two issues to publishing some of Mrs. King's memoirs. Her appearances there were a significant achievement for someone still involved in the movement. *Life* was a major weekly pictorial news magazine that had a large readership and mainstream appeal. Through the periodical's printing of her memoirs, Mrs. King gave the movement substantial national exposure on her own terms.

Later that month, it was television's turn. Mrs. King appeared on *Face the Nation* on September 28. While presenting her views with her usual eloquence and clarity, she sounded less hopeful about the country than anyone in SCLC had publicly been. She claimed that the United States was turning back the clock on African American progress. She promoted her late husband's organization as a crucial resource in stopping the reversal. "The programs of SCLC are extremely important to keep pressures, you know, on the administration and to keep the problems before the Nation," she noted. "I think we must continue our marches, we must continue our picketing, we must continue our sit-ins, we must continue all forms of pressure, nonviolent pressure." She promised to continue supporting working women and participating in peace demonstrations. Still, echoing SNCC's sense of futility toward President Nixon, Mrs. King declared, "I think that his administration is really asking for trouble unless it changes its policy, and I can't predict what kind of trouble this is going to be."[29]

Not all of her questions focused on social causes. The press also broached the subject of internal disagreement within SCLC. She was asked about Abernathy's appeal for people to donate to the organization. He had been publicly complaining that donors were mistakenly thinking that contributions to Mrs. King's memorial project for her late husband went to SCLC, too. The widow saw no conflict of interest, however. "I am for contributing to both, because I think they are both very important," she announced. "I think there is enough money for both."[30]

Whereas reporters wanted Mrs. King to talk about herself or her husband, the press gravitated to Andrew Young for interviews specifically about the current state of SCLC. NBC's *Today* show invited him by letter to appear in a year-end episode to be taped on December 29 and to air on New Year's

Eve. The network planned for him to take part in a panel discussion with Archbishop Fulton Sheen, Margaret Mead, and Secretary Robert Finch of Health, Education, and Welfare. The panelists were to answer questions from a diverse collection of high school seniors on how to address issues of skin color, peace, population, and environment in the 1970s. Hugh Downs, as program host, was to moderate.[31]

SCLC members spent part of the fall speaking out against the Vietnam War. In mid-November, Mrs. King made good on her promise to become involved in peace protests. That month the New Mobilization Committee to End the War in Vietnam demonstrated against the conflict in Washington, D.C., and she spoke at the demonstration. Abernathy, meanwhile, spoke at that group's antiwar rally in San Francisco. He gave his remarks while surrounded by the cast of the antiwar, countercultural Broadway musical *Hair*.

His speech was one of his most creative addresses of his presidency. Still sore at the White House, he claimed that "Richard Nixon has failed to move this country forward and to move this country out of Vietnam," before adding the punchline, "so we must move him!"[32] Then, borrowing Rap Brown's signifying tactic, Abernathy played upon the president's campaign slogan from the previous year:

Who is trying to keep black men and white men together in Vietnam and trying to keep black children and white children apart in Mississippi?

Nixon's the One!

Who continues the killing in Vietnam instead of healing in America?

Nixon's the One!

After another joke—calling Nixon's Vietnamization policy "Nixonization"— Abernathy then concluded on a more serious note. He urged his audience to remain vigilant in demonstrating for the end of the war. He said that they could not rest until "no citizen is deprived of freedom because of the color of his skin, or his sex," and then added as a nod to modern times, "or the length of his hair." Only at the end did he mimic King's "I Have a Dream" speech. In place of King's concluding call for diverse people to sing "Free at Last," Abernathy implored, "GIs, workers, businessmen, black people, brown people, white people, old people, young people—raise with me a mighty chorus and sing it out: 'Let There Be Peace'—*now!*"[33]

Meanwhile, the NAACP and the NUL finally joined the rest of the civil rights organizations in calling for an end to the Vietnam War, thus thoroughly linking civil rights work to antiwar activism. The NAACP issued its antiwar statement before the NUL did. At its annual convention, the NAACP passed a resolution that qualified its antiwar statement by reminding the public that the group was still primarily a civil rights organization. The resolution called the war "cruel, inhuman, and unjust" and demanded the "speediest measures" for removing U.S. troops from the conflict. Like King and SCLC two years earlier, the NAACP reasoned that war funding needed to go to the "domestic war on poverty." For the national antiwar moratorium in October, Whitney Young issued a statement in support, similarly advocating for the war's end to invest "into our own land, our own cities, our own people."[34]

The civil rights and antiwar movements also converged in court. On September 24, the Chicago Eight trial began. The prosecution placed civil disobedience of the 1960s on trial. The defendants were known demonstrators against the Vietnam War. They were part of what The *New York Times* had recently identified as the nation's prominent collective of agitators: "antiwar protesters, Black Panthers, Students for a Democratic Society, the Student National Coordinating Committee, antidraft groups, and radicals in general."[35] The jury, however, consisted of people known then as the Silent Majority. They did not protest in order for their needs to be met. None of them were ethnic minorities. The men did not have long hair. President Nixon was actively seeking the support of the Silent Majority for his handling of the Vietnam War and referred to them by that collective name in a televised speech about the war later that fall. The trial seemed to try to resolve the generation gap as well as determine the guilt of the Chicago Eight.[36]

Julius Hoffman, the presiding judge, was charting new territory. No court had ever tried anyone for violating the H. Rap Brown Act. The movement, especially SNCC, shaped the proceedings. Some of the defendants had been involved in the student-run organization years earlier. As a result, when lawyers examined the background of each defendant, they determined whether his participation in SNCC had in part contributed to his alleged crimes at the DNC. In addition, the defendants occasionally sounded like SNCC leaders. Yippie leader Abbie Hoffman, borrowing from Brown's likening of African American social conditions to the Holocaust, referred to the courtroom as a "neon oven."[37]

The trial provided an opportunity for movement activists to unite against excessive force in the trial itself. Judge Hoffman ordered defendant and BPP member Bobby Seale bound and gagged during the proceedings. Seale had been speaking too much for Hoffman's comfort, and the judge implemented the gag as a means to silence him. The courtroom sketch of Seale's physical silencing appeared in newspapers the next day and outraged African Americans nationwide. SCLC official C. T. Vivian immediately and publicly condemned the judge's action, calling it representative of the treatment of African American men caught in the judicial system. "Black men in our courts *are* gagged," he lamented. "Black men in our courts do not feel as though there is any justice."[38]

One specific judicial decision that had offended African Americans in recent years was from the Supreme Court. One year after the court had unanimously decided in *Brown v. Board of Education* that segregated schools were unconstitutional, the court ruled in 1955 that states could take "all deliberate speed" necessary to desegregate. Many of the segregated areas interpreted that phrase to mean "never," and several of them either closed their schools to avoid forced integration or simply defied the original *Brown* decision. However, on October 28, 1969, the court decided in *Alexander v. Holmes County Board of Education* that "all deliberate speed" had run its course and was no longer constitutional. Segregated areas now had to produce solutions to integrate their schools "at once," as the Court put it. As with *Brown v. Board of Education*, the NAACP's legal defense team had been involved in the *Alexander* proceedings. The verdict was, therefore, a major judicial victory for African American civil rights.

On the other hand, the *Alexander* decision made the Nixon administration look good, too. *Alexander* was one of the first civil rights cases of the Supreme Court under a chief justice appointed by President Nixon. Warren Burger followed the example his predecessor Earl Warren had set in the *Brown* case. The new chief justice waited until securing the same decision from the other justices. The verdict, therefore, was unanimous—a clear declaration of where the federal judiciary stood on the matter of school desegregation. In addition, *Alexander*'s outcome validated Nixon's claim that the federal government did not need civil disobedience from demonstrators in order to advance the cause of equality. To any naysayers with complaints about the president's handling of African American concerns, he could now point to *Alexander* as something progressive that had happened on his watch.

The naysayers still had traction against Nixon on the issue of hunger, however. Three thousand people heard him speak at the opening of the three-day Conference on Food, Health, and Nutrition in Washington, D.C., on December 2. The president asked the delegates to support his three anti-hunger ideas: a commission on population growth and the nation's future, expansion of the Food Stamp program, and a family assistance plan with a $1,600 ceiling. He predicted that passage of these bills "should virtually eliminate the problem of poverty as a cause of malnutrition." As he spoke, no one applauded.[39] Only after he concluded his remarks and left the stage did the clapping begin. The attendees were disappointed that he did not call for immediate emergency distribution of food to the impoverished or a $5,500 guaranteed annual income for them.

Ralph Abernathy was one of the delegates who witnessed Nixon's speech. As Nixon departed, the SCLC leader shouted, "For God's sake, feed the hungry!" The audience exploded in applause. This time Abernathy was surrounded by supporters, and the president was out of his element. The Nixon administration was frustrated by the outcome, and the president vowed never to participate in such gatherings again. Daniel "Pat" Moynihan sniffed that the delegates were ungrateful.[40]

Abernathy, however, was not as big a problem for the federal government as the BPP. BPP–Chicago's leader Fred Hampton, a former NAACP youth organizer, was developing a large following at 21 years old. As a very popular leader of a part of the top threat to the nation's internal security, Hampton threatened to become the African American savior that Hoover feared would rise. As a result, COINTELPRO used data from an African American informant to tell the police how to maneuver through Hampton's apartment to shoot him. On December 4, the police did just that, killing both Hampton and fellow BPP member Mark Clark. Hoover then paid the informant for helping COINTELPRO eliminate Hampton.

His killing provided a dissonant context for a major civil rights collaboration three days later. Over 100 activists and allies gathered at a studio in New York at the behest of an advertising agency to participate in the filming of commercials that promoted interethnic harmony. For one commercial, musician Mitch Miller led all of the participants in the singing of "Let the Sunshine In" from the musical *Hair*. The show's entire cast participated, and among the movement's singers were Ossie Davis, Ruby Dee, Dick Gregory, Roy Wilkins from the NAACP, Whitney Young from the NUL, SCLC's C. T. Vivian, ex-CORE member James Farmer, and ex-SNCC associates Julian Bond and Fannie Lou Hamer. Perhaps only a few years earlier, Miller would have led his makeshift chorus in "We Shall Overcome," but the civil rights leaders were now in the "Age of Aquarius." After having introduced sit-ins and freedom songs into American culture, the movement followed trends instead of starting them.

The utopian optimism of *Hair*'s music did not transfer to Chicago, where civil rights figures joined the Panthers for Hampton's funeral on December 9. Both Panthers and civil rights leaders gave fatalistic predictions of genocide when addressing the audience of 5,000 people. "We will be wiped out," a BPP member prophesied. "We won't have anything left." Likewise,

Ralph Abernathy called Hampton's killing part of a "calculated design of genocide in this country," claiming that "America is doing everything within its power to destroy us and to kill us." He then tried to rally the congregation to keep marching for liberation. While not disclaiming nonviolence, he vaguely threatened that "there will be no peace in this land until freedom comes to all."[41]

The media noted how similarly the BPP and SCLC sounded that day. The funeral, however, was just the beginning of an attempt by SCLC to present itself as an ally of the Panthers. The BPP, however, did not need SCLC's approval. The Panthers had plenty of influential, wealthy supporters, especially from Hollywood, and its membership was growing. SCLC had none of those things but positioned itself to acquire them by establishing similarities with a well-known and hip organization. Consequently, shortly after Hampton's funeral, at a memorial event for King in Washington, D.C., local SCLC member Walter Fauntroy proclaimed that although the organization did not share the BPP's rejection of nonviolent civil disobedience, "The goals of the SCLC are the same as those of the Black Panther Party."[42]

The movement further associated with the BPP on December 15, when Roy Wilkins decided to look into complaints of police harassment of the group. At a press conference with former Supreme Court Justice Arthur Goldberg, he announced a commission of private citizens "to direct a searching inquiry into the incidents in Chicago, Los Angeles, Detroit, New York, and elsewhere in which Black Panthers have become the object of attention by law enforcement agencies." He portrayed the commission as business as usual, promising objectivity and clarifying that his project did not represent an alliance between the two organizations. Remaining consistent with the organization's stand against lawless killing, he stated that "the process of justice cannot proceed on the basis of predawn raids and killings." He reminded the press that the NAACP had always served as "a consistent champion of the disadvantaged." He had a point, because nearly a decade had passed since he had expressed solidarity with another group of "youngsters"—the sit-in students of 1960. In addition, he established philosophical differences with the BPP, declaring that the Panthers "will continue to fight in their own way."[43] Nevertheless, he was starting to bridge the generation gap that Black Power had widened.

Wilkins won the commitments of several civil rights leaders to serve on the commission. Although they represented various interests, all of them were integrationists. Whitney Young and A. Philip Randolph most closely reflected Wilkins in political viewpoint, and Jack Greenberg of the NAACP's Legal Defense Fund signed onto the project. George Wiley of the National Welfare

Rights Organization and former SNCC member Julian Bond were politically to Wilkins's left. No current members of CORE, SCLC, or SNCC were on the commission. CORE and SNCC were separatist groups, and both SCLC and SNCC had aligned with the BPP. Their absence underscored the movement's increasing internal polarization.

The federal government offered a mixed reaction to the shooting. Four days after Wilkins's conference, Attorney General John Mitchell formed his own commission specifically on Chicago to "end rumors and speculation" about the Hampton case. Hoover, however, treated the incident as a launching pad for intensified monitoring of the movement, alerting the president to the activities of African American organizations it considered threatening. The FBI director had not sent the executive branch any correspondence on SNCC since the previous year, and even the organization's name change had not motivated him to contact President Nixon. But five days after Hampton's death, Hoover informed Nixon that SNCC leaders had held meetings in New York City "with a number of the organization's representatives from throughout the Nation" discussing "reorganization, directives, and acquisitions of weapons."[44] He made a point of observing SNCC's presence in three major cities from three different regions: New York, Cincinnati, and New Orleans.

Hoover also noted the organization's new focus of discipline. In a sense, SNCC was becoming more like the BPP. "SNCC chapters will henceforth operate with at least fifteen dedicated members conforming to strict standards of conduct and under rigid control of national SNCC headquarters in NYC," reported Hoover. The group had a new program of "weekly work and study classes on tactics and strategy" and new requirements for associates to "enroll in a karate class and achieve a 'black belt' degree of proficiency." Another requirement to have participants "obtain weapons" further solidified SNCC's transformation into a BPP-like paramilitary group. Hoover warned that in addition to "training sessions" for the weapons, SNCC wanted in the future to establish a "first aid and/or medical center," a "black library," and "the buying of farmland for black tenant farmers for agrarian reform in Morristown, Tennessee.[45]

Nixon did not immediately act upon Hoover's warnings. He had personally made few gestures to African Americans, militant or otherwise, because he believed that he did not have to do so. As a "moderate conservative" Republican, he could accommodate both European Americans and African Americans. To him, liberals and Democrats were too loyal to a particular side. He could not please either side of the civil rights struggle, dissatisfying "the people on both extremes," as he put it. "I could deliver the Sermon on the Mount and the NAACP would criticize the rhetoric," he complained. "And the diehard segregationists would criticize it on the grounds that I was being motivated solely by public pressure rather than by conscience." Now that he was catering to the Silent Majority, any African Americans who wanted to benefit from his policies would have to belong to *that* group—not to the civil rights groups.[46]

In contrast, SCLC operated outside of the Silent Majority, making itself visible and heard in local campaigns. In early 1970, the group's major project in the South was its long-term campaign in Sandersville, Georgia. By January, the organization had been helping the locals protest discriminatory hiring and discrimination in public works projects for six weeks. In that time, two African Americans had been shot, including a woman driving away from a church meeting in a nearby town. Sandersville imposed an 11:00 p.m. curfew to thwart any late-night violence. The residents came out in large numbers to demonstrate, and during one protest local police officers arrested 300 marchers. Meanwhile, in one month the organization helped register 1,200 African Americans to vote.[47]

On the other hand, federal officials still branded Abernathy as unpatriotic because of his civil disobedience. When he traveled to Sweden at the invitation of the country's Martin Luther King Fund and the Swedish-American Foundation, he received a public reprimand from the floor of the House of Representatives. John Resnick, a congressman from Louisiana, mused that the day of the SCLC leader's visit coincided with the day that North Vietnam had asked Sweden for $1 million in aid. The legislator considered the coincidence "appropriate" and called Abernathy a "perverted, rabble-rousing jailbird."[48]

Shortly after New Year's Day 1970, Abernathy further agitated the White House. He demanded that the president propose legislation for a national holiday in memory of King. Unsurprisingly, Nixon was resistant to any idea from Abernathy and sharply responded in writing on a memo, "No! Never!" Undeterred, the SCLC leader simply bypassed Nixon's blessing and publicly declared January 18, 1970, a "national people's holiday . . . by the power vested in me."[49] His proclamation had little merit, because he had no authority to speak a national holiday into existence. It did not even have the approval of the King family.

The president's rejection of Abernathy's demand reflected more than hard feelings. Nixon could not appear too supportive of civil rights leaders if he wanted to secure the support of Southern European American voters. In February, he removed Leon Panetta from the directorship of the Division of Civil Rights in the Department of Health, Education, and Welfare, and Panetta's replacement did not extend any invitation for communication with Abernathy. Some longtime supporters of segregation had groused that Panetta had been too committed to his job. When the president announced Panetta's departure, Senator Strom Thurmond of South Carolina could hardly contain his glee, and he hurried to share the news with his fellow Dixiecrat in the Senate—Richard Russell of Georgia.[50]

SCLC's excommunication from the White House was just as well, because the group had started unraveling. Andrew Young thought that the civil rights struggle needed new approaches, and he felt that his experiences in the movement and the skills he had learned in it still had social relevance. He wanted to exercise those skills as a politician, but that activity clashed with King's philosophy about politics compromising activism. In addition, he did not consider Abernathy a leader or an inspiring figure commanding nearly the same amount of authority that King had.

Thus, in March 1970, almost two years since Mrs. Jay Davis had encouraged Andrew Young to enter politics, he finally took her advice to heart. He announced his candidacy for Congress at the Paschal Motor Hotel in Atlanta to an audience of 200 people. NAACP–Atlanta's Lonnie King had also announced his run, making the contest a symbolic battle between the two premier civil rights groups. However, Young resigned from SCLC in order to focus on his campaign.

To him, SCLC was like family, and he found it difficult to explain his decision to Abernathy and the senior staff. His colleagues were not surprised, because they had known of his investigating of a congressional run. Still, they reacted coolly to his decision. Young had the impression that they felt that he was deserting them. He explained to them that he was not leaving the movement but merely taking it to a new arena.[51]

Civil rights organizations entered the new decade by trying new approaches to activism. The movement showed solidarity with the counterculture in both substantial and superficial ways. It had grown increasingly confrontational against federal and local authorities, whether by shouting down the president, upstaging a rocket launch, or simply challenging the police's report of a killing. Nixon, Agnew, and Hoover, however, did not let the challenges go unanswered, and their responses sometimes produced fatal consequences for the challengers.

CHAPTER 8

Heads-Up Murder

Near the end of a February 1970 episode of *Rowan & Martin's Laugh-In*, African American comedienne Teresa Graves opened a pair of psychedelically painted shutters to tell the audience a quick joke. "What Vice President Agnew *really* means is, 'Do your own thing,'" she began before singing à la Frank Sinatra, "'but do it *my way!*'" In addition to cleverly referring to the vice president's real-life friendship with the crooner, the one-liner accurately captured Agnew's place in American life at the time. Graves did not have to mention the vice president's previous statements that needed clarifying because his views on issues and his bluntness in delivering them were familiar to the public. The episode was taped weeks in advance, but the joke proved prophetic in relation to how both Agnew and the federal government at large handled civil rights activism in early 1970.

On February 18, the nation's attention was focused on 12 jurors from the Silent Majority and seven male activists on trial. A federal court found five of the Chicago Eight—Rennie Davis, David Dellinger, Tom Hayden, Abbie Hoffman, and Jerry Rubin—guilty of violating the H. Rap Brown Act and sentenced them to five years in prison. A gloating Agnew called the court's decision "an American verdict." He had good reason to gloat, because with this conviction, the Rap Brown Act on the books, and Agnew as second in command, the speaker-as-violent concept won support from all three branches of the federal government.[1]

Civil rights organizations frequently tackled issues of justice over the next few months. Their discontent with the Nixon administration's implementation of "law and order" after Fred Hampton's killing significantly intensified when more young adults died at the hands of the police throughout the spring season. On the other hand, in their frustration they were divided as to whether to completely stay the course on nonviolence, align themselves with militant figures, or abandon the justice system altogether. Still, their wide range of responses showed their worry that no one from any political persuasion was immune to the state-sponsored violence of that period.

As spring 1970 began, SNCC's chairman prepared to go to court. On March 8, Rap Brown left New York for Bel Air, Maryland, in order to stand trial on the incitement charge after nearly three years of the denial of a speedy trial. However, the "American verdict" of the Chicago Five case did not bode well for Brown. After all, people who had never met together were just found guilty of collectively violating the law unofficially named after him.

People in the movement closely followed the case. Brown's close longtime associates in SNCC—Ralph Featherstone and Che Payne—arrived from out of town to offer support to him during the trial. Featherstone had been in SNCC since 1964 and was one of the oldest members to stay there after the group's name change. As late as 1969, he was in Mississippi, organizing people and conducting fundraising work. Payne's involvement in SNCC dated back to as early as 1965, when he had participated in its political organizing of local African Americans in Lowndes County, Alabama.[2]

Brown's attorney William Kunstler spent March 9 at a preliminary hearing, trying to convince circuit court judge Harry Dyer to relocate the trial from Bel Air. Cambridge, after all, was where Brown's infamous speech took place. That city also had a substantial African American population, which would allow the SNCC chairman to be tried by a jury of his peers. Bel Air, Kunstler contrasted, had much smaller African American numbers, and the locals showed what he called "paranoiac fear" that uprisings would take place there during the trial.[3] The town was staunchly conservative; the local movie theater did not even admit young people with long hair.

Most importantly, the residents were largely ignorant of African American concerns. As a result, he devised a questionnaire for prospective jurors. He wanted to know if they knew what he thought they should know about African Americans in order for them to judge his client fairly. Questions like, "Would you object if your son or daughter dated a black person of the opposite sex?" and "Has a black person ever eaten at your dining room table?" would allow him to know how closely a European American could associate with an African American before becoming uncomfortable. Political questions that let Kunstler know how similar the people's views were to Brown's included, "What is your opinion about American involvement in Vietnam?" and "Did you ever vote for Spiro Agnew when he was candidate (A) for Governor of Maryland (B) for Vice President of the United States?" The Agnew question was especially important because the vice president had been the one to publicly call for Brown's incarceration even before he had been charged with a crime.

Some of Kunstler's questions were superficial. He offered them in order to find out which prospective jurors could understand the defendant on his own terms. By determining which of the interviewees were familiar with the African American culture that had produced Brown and his followers, Kunstler could more aptly form a jury of the SNCC leader's peers. The lawyer asked, "Do you know what a dashiki is?" and "Can you define the following terms (a) cool it; (b) right on; (c) playing the dozens; (d) up tight; (e) pigs; (f) he dig no black folks; (g) stop jivin' around; (h) honky and/or peckerwood; (i) the man; (j) handkerchief-headed nigger." After mentioning this set of questions to the mostly European American reporters surrounding him, he told them the answers because of the high likelihood that they had no idea what he was saying.[4]

As Kunstler labored in court that day, Featherstone and Payne spent time with each other instead of Brown. The two visited at Featherstone's Drum and Spear bookstore. After 2.00 p.m., Featherstone borrowed his neighbor Jean Wiley's car—a white 1964 Dodge Dart. Wiley was his neighbor and an old SNCC colleague, and he often borrowed her car. About six hours later, he closed his bookstore for the day while visiting with Payne and then went to visit his father. Afterward, he left alone in Wiley's car. Shortly before midnight he and Payne started driving from Bel Air to Washington.

Then the car exploded.

When dawn broke early the next morning, what remained of the car was still burning. The blast tore all four limbs from Payne's body, and his face was so badly disfigured that he was not immediately identifiable. Featherstone's corpse was missing an arm.

In New York at 2:00 that same morning, Lynne Doswell received a telephone call from her husband's lawyer. Kunstler was asking about Rap Brown's whereabouts. He then announced, "There's been a car explosion. I'll call you right back."[5] Minutes later, he called her again but to bear the bad news that her husband may have been in the car. Doswell immediately made preparations to attend the funerals of her fallen comrades.

Meanwhile, police officers and others were quick to lay the blame for the explosion upon the activists themselves. When authorities later reconstructed the blast, they stated that the Dart's speedometer indicated it had been traveling about 55 miles an hour when the explosion took place. Both police officers on the scene and the FBI stated that Payne had been carrying a dynamite bomb on the floor between his legs and that it accidentally exploded. Officers said that Featherstone and Payne had driven undetected into Washington, toured Bel Air briefly, and started back to the nation's capital. As a result, due to their short time in Bel Air and their constant driving, no one would have been able to plot successfully to kill them. The police offered evidence to reporters in the form of a note they claimed to have found attached to Featherstone's body:

To Amerika,

I'm playing heads-up murder. And I'm playing for keeps cause when the deal goes down I'm gon be standing in your chest screaming like Tarzan, and the looser [*sic*] pays the cut. Dynamite is my response to your justice. Guns and bullets are my answers to your killers and oppressors and victory is my sermon in your death. For my people I'll chase you into pit of hell with both barrels smoking and may the best man win and God bless the loser.

Power than peace.[6]

Those who knew the pair, especially their present and former movement colleagues, begged to differ with the official accounts. They argued that European American extremists had either ambushed the two or booby-trapped their car in an attempt to assassinate Brown. Former SNCC chairman John Lewis did not believe the FBI. He thought Featherstone would have been the least likely person to do what the bureau said he had done. Also, prominent African American politicians and movement figures displayed a rare show of solidarity by publicly calling for an investigation into the bombing. They included Representative John Conyers of Michigan, ex-SNCC associates Fannie Lou Hamer and Julian Bond, Dr. Kenneth Clark, Maryland state senator Clarence Mitchell III, and Mayor Richard Hatcher (Gary, Indiana) and Mayor Charles Evers (Fayette, Mississippi).[7]

The night after the Bel Air bombing, it was time for Cambridge, Maryland, to explode again. Shortly after midnight, an explosion in the women's restroom of the Dorchester County courthouse tore a 20-foot hole in the building where Brown's trial was originally scheduled. No one was injured in the blast, which happened 100 miles from Bel Air. Police began seeking a young European American woman seen at the courthouse before the incident.

For the first time since July 1967, Cambridge was back in national news because of violence associated with civil rights workers. The bombing was the lead story of *the Huntley-Brinkley Report* that day. The following week's issue of *Time* eulogized the SNCC bombing fatalities as part of a "frightening trend." The periodical assured readers that bombing was not taking place throughout the nation, but it did warn that the incidents had happened in "widely separated parts of the country." The politics of the locations had been diverse as well. "New York and San Francisco, both areas of left-wing extremist activity, have been particularly hard hit," noted *Time*, "but so have less electric cities, including Seattle, Denver and Madison, Wis."[8]

Several people responded to Brown's trial and the deaths of Featherstone and Payne with demonstrations. One of the most peaceful of them took place in Featherstone's community in Washington, D.C. On March 11, 200 students at Federal City College walked out of their classes and marched. Some of them put a sign on the main classroom building and unofficially renamed it in Featherstone's memory. Then, they all walked to nearby Howard University and D.C. Teachers College and gathered a few more marchers. The calmness of the event was a testament to the cool, relaxed demeanor of the man they honored.[9]

In contrast, students and police clashed in the Midwest and the South. Fifteen students picketed in front of Samuel Ach Junior High School—a mostly African American facility in Cincinnati—to protest Brown's trial. As a crowd of 100 people gathered outside the school, two police officers in the crowd fell and were kicked. More officers arrived to disperse the crowd, and they arrested two adults and three children as the protest dissipated. In Jacksonville, Florida, European American and African American students clashed at Highlands Junior High School on Friday, March 13. When classes resumed the following Monday, less than half of the student body was in attendance.[10]

On March 14, the movement reunited to bury its own. The funeral for Ralph Featherstone took place in Washington, D.C., at the Stewart Funeral Home. About 800 people attended the 90-minute service, including Walter Lively, SCLC's Walter Fauntroy and James Bevel, ex-SNCC's Julian Bond, John Lewis, Cleveland Sellers, Courtland Cox, Charles McDew, Ivanhoe Donaldson, James Forman, and H. Rap Brown's wife. Charlotte Featherstone—Ralph's widow—had only been his wife for three weeks. Outside Stewart Funeral Home were still 300 others. Despite the damage of the blast to Featherstone's body, mourners at the funeral saw his remains in an open mahogany casket. Ever since the funeral for the teenage lynching victim Emmett Till in 1955, many activists and their relatives had chosen open-casket funerals for movement martyrs in order for the public to see racism's physical toll. After Featherstone's funeral ended, his remains were cremated.[11]

Around the same time, the body of Che Payne, who had most recently taken up permanent residence in Atlanta before his death, returned to his hometown of Covington, Kentucky. His funeral was at the Ninth Street Baptist Church, where he had taught Sunday school many years earlier. Although his service did not receive as much media attention as Featherstone's had, figures from or related to the movement still attended. Ralph Featherstone's older brother, Lynne Doswell, and James Forman went to the funeral. The mourners then went to Mary E. Smith Memorial Cemetery and laid Payne to rest.[12]

Brown was out of public view after the bombing, choosing not to attend the funerals for Featherstone and Payne. In addition, he did not personally announce SNCC's response to the Bel Air bombing. Instead, that task fell to Fran Beal. With no visible chairman in SNCC, Beal was now the group's only national officer as secretariat. She had moved beyond her unofficial role as the BWLC leader by taking on unofficial leadership in SNCC itself. For one of the meetings of the organization's Secretariat Conference, Beal had hosted the proceedings at her home, and people came from as far away as Cincinnati to attend it. She, however, displayed no pretensions about leadership and did not inject her personal views when representing the group on March 15. Sporting an Afro and identifying herself as the chair of SNCC's National Women's Committee, she merely read from the text of the group's "Statement to the Black Communities in the United States" and did nothing more.

Through the statement, SNCC sought to build a strong argument for the significant influence of Brown's leadership of African Americans. The statement began with a quote from Brown's February 1968 letter from prison in Louisiana, as if suggesting that he was prophesying when he wrote, "America, if it takes my death to organize my people . . . then here is my life." Brown's letter had already been a tactic borrowed from King. Now SNCC framed Brown's words as his foreshadowing of his death, just as many people thought that King had foreseen his death with his "Promised Land" speech on the night before his assassination. After calling for "massive retribution and revenge" because SNCC believed someone had killed Featherstone and Payne, the organization introduced the theory that Brown had also died in the bombing. The group did not rule out "the very real possibility that the body of H. Rap Brown was removed from the scene of the murder by the racist white power structure in order to avoid massive reprisals in the United States."[13]

SNCC then blamed the Nixon administration for the explosion. Once again resorting to coded rhetoric about genocide that suggested an African American holocaust, the organization asserted that the deaths of the activists were "a small part of the systematic extermination of Black people that is the basis of the call for law and order." Perhaps because of Brown's longstanding quarrel with the vice president, the group made a point to emphasize what it saw as the latter's responsibility for the bombing when referring to "the dirty bloody hands of Richard M. Nixon and especially Spiro Agnew."[14] As far as the organization was concerned, the Nixon administration had just conducted an act of aggression against it, and the group somehow had to respond.

The organization was not sure of how precisely to fight back. Its statement could only provide familiar militant platitudes, neither of which seemed poised to draw masses of people to SNCC's struggle. The group's address quoted Brown's warning of a "major confrontation" to come sometime in the future—a confrontation that even Martin Luther King Jr. had predicted when he had worried about the ability of Stokely Carmichael and Rap Brown to reach out to people. SNCC saw the role of African Americans in this confrontation as "trying to destroy the racist, capitalist and imperialist government of the United States." The organization, however, did not offer any specific tactics as to how to bring the country to revolution. SNCC squandered an important opportunity to promote itself coherently and attractively to the public at a time when the bombing had increased the media's interest in the group.

Another statement from SNCC's RPC the next day did not differ much from the previous day's address. The RPC repeated the hypotheses of Brown's death in the explosion and the hiding of his body. The document claimed that the bomb was meant for him. Whereas SNCC had accused and threatened the government in its earlier statement, the RPC's address primarily called for accurate reporting about the incident. It specifically demanded that the media stop saying that Brown was alive and well at home. "These totally unfounded stories are dangerous to the morale of Brother Rap's family and friends," it noted. It then borrowed from the BPP when requesting that Brown not be tried at all for his July 1967 remarks in Maryland. Like the Panthers, the RPC believed that "no Black man can get a fair trial under this judicial system."[15]

SCLC, in turn, acted as if it agreed with SNCC and the Black Panthers about American justice, especially concerning the SNCC chairman. SCLC joined SNCC for the first time in publicly advocating the defense of Brown. He had been in legal trouble for almost three years, but now that he was on the run, he was less of a competition for movement leadership. Also, whereas King had disassociated himself from Brown because of the rhetoric, the surviving SCLC officials now saw how militant speech had reached young people. As a result, in March 1970, SCLC tried to sound just as militant without endorsing violence. Jesse Jackson supported Brown's right to say what he had said in Cambridge in July 1967. The SCLC official announced a 30-city drive to gain amnesty for him. "I salute you for hurling yourself as a flaming force for freedom against such engrained racism," Jackson said to Brown in a public statement. Making light of Agnew's nearly three-year-old charges against the SNCC fugitive, Jackson affirmed Brown's rhetoric of July 1967. "Of those whom you allegedly 'incited,'" he began, "let me say, it is better to burn for justice than to be afraid or coolly complacent or guiltily involved—as is the white power structure—in perpetuating the freezing, exploitative, inhumane state of injustice in Cambridge and throughout Maryland and racist America."[16]

Meanwhile, part of the "white power structure" saw a different conspiracy at work. When the Senate met on March 16, Senator Gordon Allott of Colorado spoke from the floor about Brown's trial. The senator claimed that recent events in Maryland demonstrated a "new way of avoiding trial and punishment." He noted that the car bombing had precipitated the recent Cambridge bombing and that a rash of bombing threats throughout Maryland followed the Cambridge incident. Now people were complaining that the local unrest would prohibit Brown from having a fair trial. Allott argued that if the missing SNCC chairman had not caused any delay in the trial, none of the events leading to complaints of a biased public would have happened. He demanded an immediate trial for Brown. "The tactic is simple," he observed when describing the current legal strategy of radicals. "They refuse to come to trial or, failing that, they behave like the defendants in the Chicago conspiracy trial and refuse to allow the trial to proceed."[17]

The Bel Air explosion and the public's response to Brown's trial led Judge Harry Dyer to reexamine William Kunstler's request for the relocation of the trial. Two years earlier, the previous judge had worried that Brown could not have an orderly and impartial trial in Cambridge. Now disorder had come to Bel Air, too. Consequently, Dyer decided to postpone the trial until March 24. Shortly thereafter he moved Brown's case again—this time to Ellicott City, Maryland. He believed the defendant would receive as fair a trial as possible there.[18]

During the spring of 1970, President Nixon sought to stay above the fray, not offering any leadership in relation to any of the movement fatalities since the administration had begun. On March 22, the president announced to the public his intent to stay uninvolved. He released a statement on civil rights, in which he said he was against segregation but also against busing. Further, he repeated his oft-stated preference for resolutions to civil rights matters on the local government level instead of federal involvement. Except for the reference to busing, he said very little that he had not previously said during the 1968 campaign.

The media wanted to know how civil rights activists felt about Nixon's speech, but that night Coretta Scott King wanted to talk about something else. Amid the reports about SCLC's defections and SNCC's fatalities, *The Ed Sullivan Show* provided a rare opportunity for the movement to appear on prime-time television. Long before 1970, the program had functioned as a cultural surrogate of the movement by frequently providing a television venue for African American entertainers when other series rarely did. Participants in civil rights demonstrations did not appear on television outside of news telecasts, and movement leaders were not often invited to shows besides Sunday morning news series. However, on March 22, 1970, Sullivan allowed Mrs. King to preview the new documentary film *King* for a television audience two days before its premiere in 1,000 theaters in 300 cities.

The Ed Sullivan Show couched the documentary's preview in nostalgia for the definitively nonviolent movement of King's lifetime. After a brief introduction by Sullivan with his usual awkward swaying and his hands clasped behind his back, Mrs. King walked out on stage. The host shook her hand, patted her back, and yielded the stage to her for the next five minutes. Looking straight ahead to the camera, standing erect and poised as usual, she addressed the audience. "My husband had a dream," she said to the hushed crowd, "but he was no dreamer. He moved, and he did." She then noted the inner strength necessary for pacifist activism: "He preached nonviolence, but he lived day by day with the real courage that violent men really do not have." Next, she said that in his 1963 speech at the Washington Monument, he expressed "the true American dream"—not just for "the black people of America" but "all free men." A clip of that address aired before the show returned to Mrs. King. She then jumped five years ahead to his "Mountaintop" speech. "The last night my husband spoke in Memphis, Tennessee, even in his last public words, weary and troubled as he was," she confided, "the dream, the confidence, the hope for America was still alive." She ended her remarks, and footage of his final speech played.[19]

The audience applauded the preview and Mrs. King's presentation of it. A genuinely moved Sullivan walked back on stage to her right side, patted her back again, and held her right hand in his left. He then addressed her, "All of us in the country and Canada, all of us sympathize with your terrible grief, and everyone in America envies your courage. Thank you."[20] He concluded by leaning over and kissing her right cheek. It was a bold gesture that capped a bold segment.

Still, the focus on the King years allowed *The Ed Sullivan Show* to ignore the movement in its present form. Mrs. King's segment provided escapism from the reports about Rap Brown as a fugitive or the deaths of Featherstone and Payne without completely escaping from the movement itself. As the press and politicians still used the word "Negro," Mrs. King uttered the then provocative phrase "black people" only once. Sullivan only mentioned the social problems of poverty and injustice to say that the proceeds from the movie were to go to the Martin Luther King Special Fund to address those concerns. Neither the host nor Mrs. King disclosed her current and frequent antiwar activism, nor did they discuss her membership on the board of SCLC. Moreover, no one spoke of SCLC at all.

SCLC, however, did not have to wait too long to have its own televised forum. On March 29, Abernathy appeared on *Face the Nation* to talk about civil rights progress in light of Nixon's March 22 statement and the upcoming second anniversary of King's death. Throughout the interview Abernathy was verbose but rarely made points clearly, directly, and concisely on the program. When the first question was about the pace of African American progress, he answered, "Well, I would think that the pace is following in the very same direction that it has been moving during the administration of President Nixon, and that is in a backward direction." In response to whether schools are desegregating quickly enough, he rambled, "It is my position that we are not making enough progress, and that you just do not say to an individual who is choking you to death, 'Gradually release your hands from around my neck.' You want him to get his hands from around your neck entirely, so that you will be free, and you can exercise your neck as you choose to exercise your neck."[21] Also, Abernathy did not go into particulars when asked about the president's message on desegregation. Instead, he talked about how tired African Americans were, how Nixon needed to do less talk and more action, and 244 years of slavery. He offered generalities and platitudes but little of substance.

Abernathy's clearest and most concise statements concerned his own role in the movement. During the interview he implied that he possessed a significant amount of political power as a civil rights leader. He considered himself capable of thwarting the Nixon administration's suppression of African Americans. "President Nixon has tried to turn back the clock of history. And that is not going to happen," he boasted. The SCLC leader still saw himself as the federal government's liaison to the African American community, bragging that "Mr. Nixon will have to come forth with some program to really win my confidence, before I can say to my people that we have to do any more bearing and waiting hopefully for something to happen."[22]

On the other hand, the SCLC leader was evasive and noncommittal on questions about his organization. It spoke to his inexperience concerning the planning of the group's programs. When pressed on what exactly were SCLC's current activities, Abernathy noted vaguely that the group was organizing the poor. When asked how, he responded, "To organize them into unions, labor unions . . . the laborers who are not covered by the National Labor Relations Act. The Southern Christian Leadership Conference is working daily to organize these people so that they can have collective bargaining rights and they can have a union to speak for them." On politics, he announced, "[W]e have gone into marginal districts and we are organizing now for the '72 elections."[23]

Questions arose about SCLC's problematic relationship with Coretta Scott King, but Abernathy glossed over the issue. "No, there is no friction between the foundation or the Martin Luther King Center and the Southern Christian Leadership Conference," he declared. "I think there is not clarity." He differentiated both activities, saying that SCLC worked on "the action phase of the movement" while the memorial strictly concerned itself with "the life and works of Doctor King."[24] He agreed with Mrs. King on the importance of both programs to continue. Then again, being agreeable with SCLC's most visible and most popular member was in the organization's best interest.

Abernathy's toughest questions came from CBS reporter Mike Wallace, who quoted the SCLC leader's reference to the group as an exhausted organization. "Where was I quoted in saying that?" Abernathy asked, caught off guard. After Wallace cited the quote, he asked if time had passed the minister by and if civil rights leadership was more militant now. Abernathy defensively replied that a poll had predicted either he or Julian Bond would be the first African American president. When Wallace asked about the BPP's importance, Abernathy called it a "very fine group of dedicated individuals" who ran a "very fine program." He called Stokely Carmichael a "very fine young man."[25]

During the interview, Abernathy revealed that he was not completely reactionary against the Nixon administration. Despite his disagreements with the White House, he at least tried to establish some common ground with it—something the president and vice president had not tried to do with the movement since May 1969. When explaining SCLC's recent absence from news coverage, Abernathy said that he agreed with Agnew that the media sensationalized specific issues. However, the SCLC president provided a humorous caveat to his comment, demonstrating the movement's continued frostiness with the Nixon administration. "Far be it from me to have to agree with Mr. Agnew on anything," he quipped. He had never before publicly tried to see matters from the administration's point of view. And he never would again.[26]

Three weeks after his television appearance, Abernathy became more combative against the president. In an address at Yale University, the SCLC leader went beyond criticizing Nixon's policies by calling for his ouster. He predicted that the demonstration would signal "the beginning of the end of the Mitchell-Nixon-Agnew-Thurmond era."[27] It was a further rhetorical shift away from King. Abernathy's predecessor had pushed for more laws from Congress or specific policy changes from presidents. But just as SCLC had never endorsed a presidential candidate, King had never called for a president not to be reelected. Abernathy was personalizing the civil rights struggle by stressing personalities over laws and policies, giving the organization a political slant in the process. More importantly, he allowed his grudge against the White House to fester in ways that diminished himself and SCLC.

Almost as if to flaunt his distaste for Nixon, Abernathy publicly celebrated people whom the federal government had dubbed "enemies." Just as Walter Fauntroy had done back in January, Abernathy embraced the FBI's top target—the BPP—as part of the movement. He called for liberal and progressive support for a pro-BPP rally in New Haven, Connecticut, scheduled for May 1. He labored to establish a connection between the "racist justice" that had led to the Montgomery bus boycott in 1955 and the proposed rally. However, both events were starkly different. The boycott was a yearlong protest of Jim Crow, but the rally was a one-day gesture of support for a militant African American group.[28]

Meanwhile, Rap Brown's trial was scheduled to begin in Ellicott City on April 19, and on that day the judge and lawyers waited for the defendant's arrival. He never appeared.

Senator Allott was apoplectic. Once again taking to the Senate floor to condemn the SNCC fugitive, the senator observed that April 19 was also the one-thousandth day since Brown had spoken his controversial words in Cambridge. Allott noted the anniversary by renewing his call for Brown's trial to start as soon as possible. The senator argued that the trial's delay adversely affected law enforcement, claiming that police officers became bitter when people like Brown escaped punishment for making police work difficult. "When this happens, the police feel a strong temptation to take on the punishing function of the law," he observed. This development was "understandable" but not "pardonable." To Allott, the preservation of "law and order" rested on when Brown could face a judge in court.[29]

On the other hand, the vice president had a different idea on how to keep "law and order" intact. As the federal government either arrested or killed several major activists during Nixon's first year in office, the number of demonstrations and the size of each protest dramatically fell. But the absence of dissent left Agnew unable to talk as often about the issue that had allowed him to rise from Maryland governor to vice president. Now that violence was escalating to the point of activists bombing buildings, dissent was once again a relevant topic. In order to stop the violence, Agnew had to do more than speak out against protest. Thus, he chose to put dissenters on notice that the Silent Majority was going to dissent against them. It was time for what he called "positive polarization."

He spoke at a Republican fundraising dinner on April 28. When he offered advice for his "friends in the academic community," he made a reference to the waning campus disorders. "Next time a mob of students waving their nonnegotiable demands starts pitching bricks and rocks at the student union," he stated, "just imagine they're wearing brown shirts or white sheets and act accordingly." To him, student activists who vandalized were more than mere criminals; they were now the enemy. He ironically sounded just like his nemesis Rap Brown by showing that he also knew who his enemies were and what to do with them.[30]

Two days later, President Nixon appeared on television to announce that the nation had another new enemy. He announced his decision to send ground troops into South Vietnam's neighboring country Cambodia. Illustrating the incursion as a show of national strength, he said that doing nothing would have turned the United States into a "helpless, pitiful giant." Cambodia, however, played against Nixon's recent handling of the war. Since the previous summer, he had been lowering the number of U.S. troops in South Vietnam and, by extension, lowering the number of U.S. casualties. As a result, fewer antiwar demonstrations had taken place nationwide and in smaller numbers.

Agnew's rhetoric and the Cambodian incursion immediately reignited the antiwar movement. Protests erupted on campuses nationwide in the first week following the president's announcement. However, counter demonstrators were also on hand at some of the protests, and construction workers enforced the vice president's values with their fists against the antiwar marchers. It was not unlike the urban disturbances of 1968 in Chicago, except that the vigilante "hardhats" had replaced the overzealous policemen, and they were on orders from Agnew instead of Mayor Daley. "Act accordingly" was less direct than "Shoot to kill" but not without similarly grave consequences.

That week of demonstrations following Nixon's address reached a deadly conclusion on May 4. In Ohio, Kent State University's antiwar demonstration lasted two days. It ended when the Ohio National Guard killed four students. The public reaction showed how well Agnew's goal of polarization had reached fruition. On the other hand, it was not positive. While some people mourned the losses of the students, others considered their deaths the price paid for violently confronting authority figures.

Much of the African American response, especially among students, consisted of numbed sorrow. They mourned the loss of lives, but they did not participate in reactionary demonstrations dominated by European Americans. The Kent State shootings had happened to African Americans several times before and had just taken place in Orangeburg two years earlier. As a result, the killing of students at the hands of the police was not a novel concept to young African Americans. As one of them put it, "I kind of feel like if you're black, no matter where you go, no matter what you do, you're going to run into problems that are common to Blacks everywhere."[31]

That statement rang true exactly one week after Kent State, when an uprising in Augusta, Georgia, brought more fatalities. Following a now familiar pattern, a crowd's outrage over one person's killing led to the deaths of several others. A 16-year-old African American convict named Charles Oatman lost his life after a beating in prison. Although news reports blamed two of his African American cellmates for the killing, some African Americans heard that prison officers were responsible. Upon hearing the latter claim, a group of African Americans protested by setting 50 fires downtown and engaging in sniper fire. Governor Lester Maddox called in National Guardsmen to restore order. Six African American men were shot dead before order was restored.[32]

The anger expressed by some African Americans that day at Augusta was no isolated incident. Another disturbance involving African Americans erupted in Mississippi later that week, showing that some African Americans were trying to apply the advice of Northern insurrection by Rap Brown and Stokely Carmichael to Southern communities. On the night of May 13 at Jackson State College, a crowd of African Americans gathered on the street in front of the dormitory Alexander Hall, throwing rocks at passing European American motorists. The police arrived to form a barricade, and the campus president imposed a 10:30 p.m. curfew. Some people in the crowd left, but a small remnant remained and tossed rocks at the police vehicles. Over the next few hours, people hurled bottles, and one person fired a few shots at a traffic light elsewhere on campus. Still, the police were able to calm the crowd without violence.

The campus president took measures to keep the students pacified. Shortly after midnight, he hosted a gathering of about 25 students at his house. Like the Kent State students, this group expressed frustration over the Indochina War and with the continuation of the military draft, but they did not have any problems with the college itself. A couple of hours later, the state's adjutant general warned the campus president of the possibility of the use of tear gas if a disturbance were to happen the next day. He promised to provide gas masks for the president and his family in case of such an occasion. Still, as a precaution, on the afternoon of May 14, the president asked the police chief to barricade the street in front of Alexander Hall upon nightfall.

The police opened the street to city traffic anyway. By 9:30 p.m., rocks hurled from demonstrators once again streamed across the campus sky, and 90 minutes later someone set a dump truck on school grounds afire. Bricks, rocks, and bottles now sailed through the air outside of the dormitory Stewart Hall. Firefighters moved from the extinguished dump truck to battle a bonfire elsewhere on campus. After the firefighters put it out, the policemen went on to Alexander Hall, where disorder had begun barely 24 hours earlier. Chaos returned—this time with the crowd in the street taunting the police with the insult made famous by the top threat to America's internal security.

"Pigs!" they shouted. "Pigs!"

The sounds of unrest then escalated in a matter of seconds. A bottle dropped by a television cameraman before a rock nearly missed him. A police officer then heard a shot fly by him, and another policeman advised a nearby African American, "You niggers better get from up here. We're getting ready to kill up a bunch of you."[33]

Then, over the next 28 seconds, 150 rounds of double-0 buckshot—the heaviest buckshot for shotguns—launched from police firearms and lit Jackson State's sky. Four hundred of the bullets directly hit Alexander Hall, but one officer lost count of how many times he had reloaded his shotgun. Near Alexander's doorway, college student Philip Gibbs suffered wounds to the armpit and brain, and he died. High school student James Earl Green was shot in front of another dormitory across from Alexander and succumbed from the buckshot's damage to his internal organs. Green was 17 years old—4 years younger than Fred Hampton's age when the Chicago Police had assassinated him. The Nixon administration's hard line on protest suggested that no dissenter was too young to die at the hands of a police officer.

"Cease fire! Cease fire!" a lieutenant finally yelled to the officers after the 28 seconds. The firing ceased. In addition to the two fatalities, the police wounded 12 other people at Jackson State that night.

As an on-campus shooting, the Jackson State killings had many elements similar to the Kent State killings. As in Ohio, the events in Mississippi had started with students demonstrating against the Vietnam War. Students at both campuses had grown angry about the presence of the police at demonstrations. At both schools, students hurled objects at the officers. And at both institutions, armed officers fired upon unarmed students.

On the other hand, what happened in Mississippi also contained elements of the violent repression based on skin color—repression that African Americans knew all too well by 1970. In addition to protesting the war, the Jackson State students had also been demonstrating against the killings in Augusta, Georgia. Immediately after the shooting ended in Mississippi, the

African American victims were denied dignity because of their brown skin. Police radio recorded an officer's crude description of the aftermath. "I think there are about three more nigger males over there," he noted. "Them gals, it was two nigger gals, two more nigger gals from over there shot in the arm I believe."[34] Also, just as the Cambridge uprising of July 1967 had begun on Race Street, the Jackson State incident featured its own grim geographic irony. The street in front of Alexander Hall—the scene of the massacre—was Lynch Street.

Local politicians offered different responses. Jackson mayor Russell Davis sat at his desk and gave a television address. He reminded his constituents that the facts of the event had not yet been determined but that the incident constituted "a dark day in the history of this city." In contrast, Mayor Charles Evers of Fayette went to see the damage at Jackson State on May 15. He had two daughters who were students there at the time, and he traveled there to make sure they were unharmed. Indeed, they were safe, but Evers was still unnerved by the bullet holes that pocked Alexander Hall. "We're gonna let 'em know we're not gonna take this," he vaguely but angrily threatened. "You just don't shoot a dormitory—period."[35]

Meanwhile, civil rights activists watched helplessly as events unfolded. Lacking influence in the Nixon administration and coming apart internally, the civil rights organizations had no means to directly pressure the White House to stop the domestic killings. The shootings of unarmed students threatened to destroy whatever limited appeal nonviolence still had to activists after King's death. Thus, the civil rights coalition spent the rest of the year searching for a way to unite to save nonviolence.

CHAPTER 9

Times Have Changed

The killings of students in May 1970 inspired a collective outcry from civil rights groups and their allies in a manner unseen since King's assassination. They sensed an immediacy to address the violence and made bold, dramatic statements when responding to it. To them the country was out of control, and no one—from the local authorities to the White House—seemed to offer leadership to stop the shootings. The organizations presented a uniform message to the world if not a uniform presence at demonstrations.

Of all the civil rights groups, the SCLC crafted the first response. SCLC decided to lead a demonstration in mid May in its home state of Georgia—an unusual choice in that the organization tended to travel out-of-state to confront government officials about inequality and violence, just as it had done in Birmingham and Selma. By operating so quickly after the Jackson State incident, SCLC was not giving itself time to send some of its members out in advance to its marching destinations to teach people about nonviolent protest. Then again, time was of the essence, and the group did not have time to wait for another series of killings. Thus, on May 19 the group began its March against Repression in the small town of Perry. Its destination was 110 miles away in Atlanta.

The demonstration was not unlike another protest that had served as the Movement's answer to a shooting. For the March against Fear in June 1966, SCLC had marched with other civil rights groups from Memphis, Tennessee, to Jackson, Mississippi. The Movement conducted the March against Fear in response to the assassination attempt of activist James Meredith, who had tried to encourage African Americans in Mississippi to exercise their voting rights. Back then, King was still alive, students had not yet introduced Black Power, and the country had experienced only one summer of nationwide urban rebellions. Four years later SCLC was gambling on marching to remain relevant in a new, more militant and less nonviolent climate of African American activism. Moreover, many of the demonstrators carried on as if little had changed since 1966. Most of the elements of the marches of the past decade appeared in this new march. People carried banners, sang or chanted while they walked, and—most importantly—refrained from violence.

Nevertheless, something was different in the March against Repression. The violence of May 1970 triggered a sense of futility among the participants. SCLC had been able to recover from its utter emotional devastation during King's funeral two years earlier, but the recent killings started a relapse into hopelessness. The demonstrators in Georgia were more weary and sad than usual. The power in the singing and chanting voices came more from desperation than from self-confidence. The mule train from the PPC was back, but this time the mules were draped in black. A banner over one of them read "Six Murdered in Augusta." Over another was the message "Two Murdered in Jackson."

SCLC leaders were just as dour as the mules. Only one year earlier in Charleston, the organization had told strikers that success depended on their ability to remain nonviolent. Now in Georgia, SCLC spent more time warning America to stop its violence than advising activists not to start theirs. The demonstrators promoted their march as the nation's best hope for salvation from self-destruction. Several activists expressed fear that the United States had passed a violent point of no return. "I don't know how much longer we can keep raising our nonviolent voices against this repression," Abernathy sighed. Hosea Williams felt similarly and came very close to legitimizing the SNCC's militant rhetoric. He was so pessimistic about nonviolence that he quoted the very man whose provocative words Martin Luther King had abhorred. "Our actions will determine whether America lives as a democracy," Williams cautioned, "or whether H. Rap Brown is right—that you must burn it down and hope to build a new nation."[1]

Meanwhile, Georgia's head of state shut his ears to the nonviolent raised voices. Governor Lester Maddox called a news conference on May 19 to discuss his opposition to the march. He stated that he was not taking any measures to prevent SCLC from marching, but he vowed that the demonstrators would be prohibited from protesting on the grounds of the capitol in Atlanta. He also rejected SCLC's request for a state police escort for the marchers. Connecting the march to the Cold War, he called the protesters "Communist enemies of freedom." His rhetoric was on par with what other governors facing civil rights activism had said throughout the movement's lifetime. Then again, Maddox had always been a staunch segregationist, and Jim Crow defined his political career. In 1964, he had chased African Americans out of his restaurant with a pistol after they had tried to integrate the eatery. Two years later he parlayed his fame from that incident into an electoral victory for the position of governor of Georgia.

While speaking to reporters about the March against Repression, Maddox revealed that he had sent SCLC a telegram, requesting the cancellation of the protest. In the telegram Maddox borrowed Vice President Agnew's tactic of blaming nonviolent African Americans for not keeping violent ones under control. In addition, he went even further than Agnew in blaming nonviolent demonstrations for causing their participants to become violent. Without mentioning specific examples, Maddox claimed, "Previous nonviolent demonstrations by your group and similar groups . . . have spurred the hate and prejudice among some of your followers which later led to the violent death of six people in Augusta."[2] He neglected to mention that when he was governor during SCLC's funeral procession for King in Georgia two years earlier, no violence from those marchers had taken place.

Nevertheless, Maddox was dealing with an "enemy." If he had admitted that SCLC did not always foster violence, he would have portrayed the "enemy" in a favorable light. Perhaps the governor honestly thought that his holding SCLC responsible for the Augusta deaths would shame the group to stop the march. More likely, he lambasted public dissent in the fashion of the vice president in order to score political points. Although the state forbade any governor from serving two consecutive terms, he was running that year for lieutenant governor. Agnew's popularity as vice president that spring taught Maddox and other politicians that anti-Movement speech was still the key to electoral victory.[3]

On the next day, Abernathy added to Williams's SNCC reference with some of his own. The SCLC president drew from ex-SNCC chairman Carmichael's remarks from the day after Martin Luther King's death, calling the repression of the past month "part of a calculated program of genocide against black people and poor people in this country." He also resorted to Brown's tendency toward ad hominem attacks on the president and vice president. Unlike Brown in the Johnson administration, Abernathy did not refer to the president as a "honky" or "cracker," nor did he threaten to shoot the First Lady. Instead, Abernathy called Nixon and Agnew "wrinkled old souls." As with his reference to the president as "Tricky Dick" in August 1968, this new name-calling attack signaled a clear, final shift in rhetoric that moved away from King's philosophical and intellectual meditations on justice and toward politically partisan, emotional insults.[4]

Williams was more subdued than Abernathy in his invective toward the Nixon administration. However, his speaking style reflected his confidence in his position of leadership in SCLC. For the first time ever, he compared himself to the biblical figure Moses—a connection previously made only between Moses and King. At best, Abernathy's supporters had regarded him as Moses's successor Joshua. In addition, Williams tried to establish a similarity between the Israelites' trek out of slavery in Egypt and the March on Repression. While trying to paint the governor and the president as the antagonists fostering the repression, the SCLC organizer gravitated toward hyperbole by suggesting that he had larger obstacles to overcome than Moses had. "I can tell Moses one thing," Williams remarked. "He may have had a Red Sea to contend with, but he didn't have a Lester Maddox and a Richard Nixon."[5]

The next day it was Governor Maddox's turn to intensify the rhetoric, telling reporters that people associated with the march had threatened his life. His claim of a death threat dovetailed well with his assertion days earlier that the nonviolent demonstration would cause the participants to become violent. As proof of the threat, he held up a letter with a signature from the Deacons—most likely, a reference to the armed African American self-defense group Deacons for Defense. The letter's author said, "[I]f another black is shot in Georgia, you better be careful about where you show that bald head. It will come up with a bullet in it."[6] Maddox expressed worry that someone among the marchers was plotting to kill one of their own and then to place blame on the governor. As a result, he decided to give the marchers police protection.

Williams did not consider the protection necessary, and he said so. He suggested that the police just go home, because there was no disorder. Reinforcing the group's nonviolent reputation, he promised that "we didn't come here to break windows, loot, and burn." He also made a reference to the violent means by which segregationist officeholders often intimidated movement activists and other dissenters into silence. He claimed that the power to keep violence from erupting rested solely with Maddox. "If Governor Maddox doesn't send someone down here to kill us, no one will die," Williams predicted.[7]

The marchers were indeed exercising restraint, but observers in the media were unimpressed. On May 22, NBC reported on the four-day-old march in a pessimistic and nostalgic manner. "Martin Luther King is dead, and times have changed," the narrator solemnly began. The news report noted the absence in the demonstration of "the spirit of the mid-'60s" and the rare presence of a European American marcher. As bystanders watched the march go by, they were indifferent—that is, if they noticed the marchers at all. Calling the protest a "straggling little march," the network complained, "The Southern Christian Leadership Conference put it together hastily . . . and it shows." Many of SCLC's veterans were gone. The march lacked organization, with the demonstrators starting several hours late and ending early each day. As footage aired of the Georgia marchers climbing aboard a bus at the end of a marching day, the network wistfully observed, "In the old days, they walked all the way."[8]

The marchers finally reached their destination of Atlanta the next day. There, all 10,000 of them stopped, and a mixture of old and new luminaries of the movement gave speeches. As usual, Mrs. King and the SCLC leaders were on hand, but so were Gary, Indiana, mayor Richard Hatcher, Atlanta mayor Sam Massell, antiwar activist David Dellinger, Pan-Africanist Imamu Amiri Baraka, and David Hilliard of the BPP. SCLC's invitations to Dellinger and Hilliard showed how much contempt the organization had for the Nixon administration—because Dellinger was one of the Chicago Eight who had received Agnew's "American verdict" of "guilty," and Hilliard was a member of what Hoover had called the top threat to national internal security. Hilliard's presence was especially ironic and uncharacteristic for the nonviolent SCLC, because he had just threatened to kill President Nixon when he had spoken the previous November at an antiwar rally in San Francisco.[9]

Abernathy used the occasion to promise a nonviolent electoral revolution. "Today we are marching against repression, and tomorrow we are going to be registering people to vote against repression. The day after, we will be casting our votes to sweep out of office the racist politicians and political hustlers who have created the present situation," he told Atlanta attendees. Abernathy worried that the White House had not only taken the segregation-era repression tactics of Southern officials but had also applied them on a national scale. "The South has traditionally been a center of militarism and the police-state mentality, which is now increasingly becoming the life style of the government in the country as a whole."[10]

The SCLC leader was a less violent version of H. Rap Brown that day. Abernathy only wanted the removal of the presidency from Nixon—not removal of Nixon's life, as Brown had intimated in July 1969. Still, both agreed in wanting someone else besides Nixon in office. Abernathy called for the "ten most unwanted politicians in America" to be replaced by people who would "tear this country upside down and right side up." Predictably, the president and vice president were among the "most unwanted." Governor Maddox, four Dixiecrats in Congress, and three conservative officeholders rounded out the list. However, Abernathy did not specify who exactly should replace the undesirables. As a general rule, SCLC never endorsed presidential candidates.[11]

Some of the other speakers at the March against Repression sounded like former SNCC leaders. Hosea Williams announced there that SCLC would start a summer community organizing and political education program, "recruiting students who want to work against repression and against the war in Vietnam."[12] The project was reminiscent of SNCC's Freedom Summer from six years earlier, in which the organization had recruited students nationwide to converge in Mississippi to attack segregation's oppression of the state's poorest and most isolated residents. Meanwhile, Baraka called on the demonstrators to communicate with their fellow Africans and support their struggles for political independence. His Pan-Africanist rhetoric recalled Stokely Carmichael's speeches for SNCC.

Between the SNCC-like addresses of the March against Repression and Fauntroy's likening of SCLC to the BPP the previous January, SCLC was evolving in the absence of King by imitating other organizations instead of developing its own identity. It set itself apart from the others by remaining committed to nonviolent civil disobedience and carrying out King's "dream." But as people soured on how the group carried out the "dream" without the dreamer, the organization tried to show how much it had in common with more popular groups that had their own identities. Abernathy was content to say that he shared the frustration of the militants in watching defenseless African Americans die, but he always stopped short of saying that he would give up nonviolence. Still, he spent less time specifically reminding audiences that he was still committed to it.

Many people noticed the change in Abernathy's rhetorical style. Of all the people who sent letters to him about his remarks at the march, very few people expressed support for what he said. A branch of the Women's International League for Peace and Freedom sent him a letter in which the organization declared its solidarity with him. Meanwhile, Diahann Carroll— star of the television sitcom *Julia*—wrote to him both to apologize for her absence from the march and to say that she supported him. At the time, she was breaking new ground as the first African American woman in a leading television role in over a decade and the first to have a regular role that was not a "mammy," and her series had just won a third season of episodes for the upcoming 1970–1971 season. Viewer discomfort with her marching alongside antiwar radicals and militant African Americans was the last thing her career needed.

Most of the letters Abernathy received came from people taking exception to his harsh critique of Nixon. "For God's sake, what is he supposed to do for you people?" asked one exasperated person. Another writer noted his sympathy for the killed students but opined that "when these spoiled brats go out on a rampage to riot and destroy, then the guilty ones ought to be shot." After his backhanded eulogy, he blamed Abernathy for the current domestic unrest and rebuked the insults toward the White House. "I'm glad that we have a president like Richard Nixon and a vice-president like Spiro Agnew who will stand up to these folk," he wrote—simultaneously comforting himself and threatening Abernathy in the process.[13]

For all SCLC's problems, the organization still had enough clout to attract a U.S. senator. Democrat George McGovern of South Dakota accepted the organization's speaking invitation to the March against Repression. He was one of Abernathy's very few allies in the Senate, having opened his home 12 months earlier to the SCLC leader during the organization's disastrous Washington, D.C., visit. In addition, the senator had just coauthored a bill in Congress to cut off funding for the Vietnam War, making him an ideal speaker for a nonviolent organization's event. "The kind of Southern Strategy that makes sense is the kind that we have here today," he beamed to the crowd. Addressing the recent violence, he implored, "We cannot afford to expend our energies hating each other." Attempting to counter Agnew's "positive polarization," McGovern sought unity: "We cannot afford to set worker against student, youth against age, white against black."[14]

Roy Wilkins did not attend the march, but the killings of May 1970, especially at Jackson State, had profoundly affected him. His response to the deaths marked a turning point in how he illustrated the "youngsters" he so often treated condescendingly. For the first time since the Black Power controversy of 1966, he acknowledged the legitimacy of the anger of young African Americans. He said that African Americans over 30 years of age understood "the anger and frustration of Negro youth." Concerning Jackson State, the young people had a right to be angry. "The building was literally sprayed with bullets," he lamented. Then, after observing that "no one has claimed that the girl students were firing on the state highway patrolmen" from the dormitory windows high above Lynch Street, Wilkins harshly concluded that "the Mississippi highway patrol came to the Jackson State campus determined to kill black students. They were out for blood, not for keeping the peace."[15]

The NAACP president went a step further by recognizing the constructive legacy of the African American militants, especially the cultural militants. He credited the "youngsters" for stimulating "racial pride." He noted that his group had tried for years to help instill self-pride and ethnic pride in African Americans but admitted that "in four short years, the black militants have made race pride a household word." Moreover, he saw lasting positive potential in their work. "If pride can be kept from becoming arrogance, we will leap forward as never before," he glowingly predicted.[16]

On the other hand, Wilkins did not want the killings to prove to young people that the separatists were right. He mildly echoed the sentiments of "youngsters" like Rap Brown when hinting that the country was in a season of genocide against African Americans. In addition, he claimed that the officers who had killed the students had committed a crime. Still, the NAACP leader gave an unusually qualified recommendation for African Americans and European Americans to work together. He announced that "in this day of death and obscurantism in a highly-charged emotional atmosphere generated by viciously executed murders of Negro young people, such as those at Jackson State, we make it clear that our stand is for integration and against black separatism."[17]

Whitney Young provided the most incendiary reaction among the civil rights leaders. He claimed that the president and vice president had created a political climate that led the officers to shoot the Jackson State students. To the NUL leader, speeches by Nixon and Agnew gave the lawmen license to kill the young African Americans. Young's remarks made the news on all three television networks, and reporters generally interpreted the comments as Young changing his mind about the Nixon administration and now opposing it. With the president's most supportive civil rights contact turning against him, the movement had become uniformly anti-Nixon at the start of the summer of 1970.[18]

That summer was poised to be the vice president's time to shine. He had Rap Brown on the run and an army of "hardhats" on his side. Agnew, however, struggled with the harsh comments that Abernathy had made during the march in Georgia and now considered the SCLC leader even more of an "irresponsible militant" than before. The vice president phoned Hoover and directed him to find information to discredit Abernathy, and Hoover complied. Civil disobedience was bad enough, but disregard for the law *and* disrespectful statements about the White House were too much.[19]

For all of Agnew's antagonism against dissenters, the violence against them unnerved Nixon. The president had always seen himself as a man of peace. He had referred to a teenage girl's "Bring Us Together" sign in 1968 in order to say that he would indeed unite the country. Now, just as he had a lock on the Silent Majority, the children of that majority put his plans for domestic peace in jeopardy. He looked for answers to the uprisings on colleges and universities, and he formed the Commission on Campus Unrest on June 13 to find them.

The commission's junior member had his own ideas as to possible responsible parties. Joseph Rhodes Jr., a 22-year-old African American student at Harvard, was an acquaintance of Nixon's assistant for domestic affairs, John Ehrlichman. Since the start of the administration, Rhodes had been giving Ehrlichman updates on the student mood and the attitudes of young Americans. He did not mince words in the updates, and in an interview one day after his naming to the commission, he spoke bluntly to Robert Reinhold of The *New York Times*. Concerning his role in the commission, he was single-mindedly focused on stopping killings of college and university students—no matter what it took. "When parents send their kids on campus they wonder whether they will get killed," he observed. "What do you do so those parents can sleep at night?"[20]

It was a question that public servants across party affiliations had a responsibility to answer, according to Rhodes. "If somebody gets killed next year I'll feel responsible," he admitted. In his opinion, Republicans and Democrats had done very little toward stopping the campus violence. After having relayed the thoughts of students in California to the Nixon administration the previous year, Rhodes was convinced that Governor Ronald Reagan was "bent on killing people for his own political gain." The commission member did not even spare the Administration's highest officers from criticism, and they received the strongest rebuke. Referring to Nixon's slur against students from the previous month, Rhodes announced, "One of the things I want to try to figure out is who gave what orders to send police on campus and were they thinking about campus 'bums' when they pulled the trigger." He then noted the possibility of the administration's rhetoric being violent. "If the President's and Vice President's statements are killing people, I want to know that."[21]

Agnew's line against civil disobedience had come full circle. It had been almost three years since he had linked Brown's words to violence in Cambridge. In the interim, the federal government and several governors started using force to discourage activists from verbalizing their dissent. The officials ostensibly wanted to prevent violence from erupting from the dissenters. Meanwhile, Agnew encouraged "positive polarization" and denigrated demonstrators with various slurs; and governors and mayors who supported him allowed the armed forces at their disposal to crush street protests. Now, an African American with considerable influence like Brown, although not a leader or a member of any movement group, associated the vice president's words with the previous month's killings. Moreover, as a quiet and reserved Harvard-based Nixon official and not a confrontational "outside agitator" of the streets, Rhodes—unlike Brown—could not be dismissed as a radical militant.

Agnew was livid, but Rhodes had not broken any laws. The student had spoken to a reporter and not an excitable crowd. Also, no one rioted after having read his words. Nevertheless, Rhodes was as critical of the United States as Brown had been. If Agnew could not lock up the commission member and throw away the key, he could at least use the power of his office as a bully pulpit to punish Rhodes somehow. Thus, the vice president spoke to reporters to address Rhodes's remarks.

Agnew followed his usual formula for attacking verbal dissent: quoting the offensive remarks, reprimanding the offender, and calling for some kind of consequence to the speaker. The vice president restated Rhodes's comments. Agnew then said that anyone who would make those comments "does not possess the maturity, the objectivity, and the judgment to serve on a fact-finding body of national importance." Therefore, Rhodes did not deserve to wear "the cloak of dignity that a presidential appointment would throw around him."[22] For punishment, the vice president demanded the student's immediate resignation.

Shortly thereafter, Rhodes addressed reporters about the vice president's speech. On a national scale, few people had seen African Americans speak against Agnew unless the critics were militants of nationally known movement groups. On television, however, viewers saw the image of Rhodes— bespectacled, wearing a short and parted "natural," and smoking a pipe while typing in a Harvard office. It contrasted sharply with the images of shouting, denim-clad advocates of revolution. In addition, unlike Brown's tendency to threaten and insult the vice president, Rhodes responded to the criticism with nonchalance. He portrayed his adversary's remarks as less of a personal affront than the result of an annoying personality flaw on Agnew's part. Standing outside with journalists on the Harvard campus, he calmly told them, "The Vice President's given to making such comments about a variety of people." After the nonplussed reporters asked him to elaborate, he added, "We have to tolerate it." He said with a mixture of bemusement and futility, "It's unfortunate, but it happens."[23]

Vice President Agnew placed President Nixon in the uncomfortable position of choosing between him and Rhodes. The president, however, chose Rhodes. He claimed to have named Rhodes and other students with an awareness of their views. He fully expected them to play to whatever constituents they needed to appease. He did not think that Rhodes's remarks warranted concern. He sent his press secretary, Ron Ziegler, to the press corps to deliver the final verdict: "Mr. Agnew was only speaking for himself."[24]

Agnew lost heavily by challenging Rhodes. The vice president failed for the first time to convince his colleagues in the federal government to denigrate someone he had identified as troublesome. He annoyed Nixon by criticizing a presidential appointment. Also, as a result of Agnew's public confrontation with Rhodes, the president ordered his inner circle of advisers such as Ehrlichman and Chief of Staff H. R. Haldeman to put the vice president on a short leash and keep him from giving speeches. His style, which had lifted him from governor to the second-in-command, now made him a liability, and he lost the respect of the inner circle. Ehrlichman later concluded of Agnew, "Maybe he was just a dedicated public servant who wasn't too bright."[25]

The vice president was reluctant to admit defeat against Rhodes, however. On the Fourth of July, he spent part of the national celebration rehashing an old point of contention. The president of the American Bar Association had recently rebuked Agnew for confronting Rhodes, saying, "[W]e've got to show the youth of this country that we welcome their involvement." Ironically agreeing with Agnew about the power of rhetoric, he told reporters that the vice president and other high officials should "exercise restraint and realize that more weight is given to what they say." Agnew did not revisit the entirety of Rhodes's remarks but cherry-picked the statement about Reagan to lambaste the comment as a "sour-stomached statement" and a "hairy-brained, unprovable bluster." He then proceeded to once again criticize the president's appointment of Rhodes to the commission, calling the student's remarks "disqualifying" and a sign of "a transparent bias and a closed mind on the subject matter under examination."[26]

The next day Rhodes talked to reporters a second time about Agnew. This time he seemed genuinely perturbed at having to do so. He expressed having been let down by the Nixon administration. He mentioned having promised the administration he would refrain from mentioning the disagreement because an administration official had agreed to keep Agnew from talking about it, too. "It bothers me the President hasn't been able to quiet the Vice President down," he lamented. Then, he noted the seriousness of his appointment and the frivolity of Agnew's persistence: "I'm working very hard on this commission, and I just don't have time to get into this kind of an exchange with the Vice President."[27]

President Nixon wasted little time on the disagreement, too. As Agnew sparred with an individual African American, Nixon made an overture to African Americans en masse. On June 22, he extended the Voting Rights Act to 1975. It represented his commitment to carrying forward the political progress that the movement had helped to facilitate under Nixon's predecessor. After all, he had admired the work of Dr. King. On the other hand, his extending of the act also showed that he did not need the Movement's help in leading African Americans to progress. Upon signing the extension, he gave statistics on how many African Americans had voted and won elections since the act's implementation in 1965. The numbers were "dramatic evidence that the American system works," said Nixon. "They stand as an answer to those who claim that there is no recourse except to the streets."[28]

For the Nixon administration, support for voting rights did not extend to the movement itself, however. On his watch, the FBI continued to keep close tabs on activists. Even some of the more conservative, nonviolent speakers in the movement were targets. On the day the president extended the Voting Rights Act, the FBI reported that SCLC's Coretta Scott King was a cochair of the antiwar group Clergy and Laity Concerned about Vietnam and was a sponsor of the National Council to Repeal the Draft.[29]

The White House remained concerned about its image concerning civil rights, however, and reached out to Whitney Young. The administration revealed to the press in July that it wanted the NUL leader to serve in a position. Nixon did not officially immediately extend an invitation to him, and Young made no public comments about whether he wanted the job. He believed, however, that the estrangement between the African American community and the White House produced "nothing constructive." Remaining open-minded about the rumored offer, he vaguely announced to columnist Nick Thimmesch, "I would be happy to participate with the black community in an effort to open up the lines of communication with the administration."[30]

Civil rights officials were skeptical. Stephen Spottswood of the NAACP board aligned the organization with the anti-Nixon SCLC and SNCC in his keynote address at the group's annual convention. He lamented, "For the first time since Woodrow Wilson, we have an administration that can be rightly characterized as anti-Negro." He also accused the Nixon administration of "calculated policy to work against the needs and aspirations of the largest minority of its citizens." He cited the president's "benign neglect," attempts to weaken voting rights and support of exempting private all-white schools for taxes as examples of "anti-Negro" activity.[31] A White House official called the remarks unfair, and several editorials in newspapers nationwide complained, but the organization stuck by Spottswood.

In response, Young once again changed his position on the administration. At a press conference on July 19, he disagreed with Spottswood's opinion. He diplomatically called Nixon's conduct toward African Americans "pro-majority vote-pro-political," designed to win the most votes for the president. He admitted that the White House was fostering an "anti-Negro" reputation but that it did not consciously maintain a "deliberate policy of hating black people." Young did not say that the president supported African Americans, but the comments marked a definite improvement from his opinion that rhetoric from Nixon and Agnew killed African American students.[32]

Some of the feelings the movement had expressed about the government were reaching a wide audience, even within the government itself. Very few people would have confused Joseph Rhodes Jr. for Malcolm X. The Harvard student did not repeat the late NOI speaker's public calls for African American self-defense "by any means necessary," nor did Rhodes refer to "the white man" as an evil monolith. However, he expressed opinions that echoed passages from *The Autobiography of Malcolm X* when he and two of his commission colleagues appeared on *Meet the Press* on September 27 to talk about their findings. The commission had concluded days earlier that rhetoric from the Nixon administration had contributed to the violent climate between students and the police. Rhodes, like Malcolm X before him, was blunt and matter-of-fact when condemning state violence against African Americans and against students overall. As a result, he offered some of the most poignant comments of the televised panel discussion. On the Jackson State killings of last May, he said that the commission had ruled that the law enforcement officials in Jackson had "demonstrated a remarkable lack of concern for the human life of black people." The officials had treated Mississippi's African Americans as "fair game for their missiles, for their weapons." Local law enforcement had behaved completely unprofessionally, because their lives were not threatened. They were "taunted more than anything else by the students, and shot over 300 times into a girls dormitory at unarmed people, killing two, wounding nine, for no obvious reason." On Kent State, the young commission member said the students had felt invaded by an extension of the military. He concluded that in both incidents, "the use of deadly force that was used was completely unjustified."[33]

Rhodes also borrowed Malcolm X's linking of violence against European Americans with a similar African American precedent. Back in November 1963, Malcolm had claimed that the federal government's inattention to African American deaths at state "hands" over the years led to President John F. Kennedy's recent assassination. Seven years later, Rhodes saw a familiar connection. When addressing how African Americans felt about media attention to Kent State in contrast to the inattention to the Orangeburg killings of 1968, he replied,

> Black people perceive that the reality of America is that it is racist and that it oppresses black people and represses their leadership and kills its young men whenever it can—at Jackson State, in South Carolina. I don't think many black students were surprised that repression had spread now to those white students who had attempted to affect an equal change in our national policy toward Vietnam.

He may as well have said that "the chickens were coming home to roost."[34]

Unsurprisingly, the "law and order" Nixon administration was incensed about the commission's brutal critique of "law and order" as it was implemented against student dissenters. Even less surprising, Vice President Agnew immediately spoke out against the commission's findings. He called the report "imprecise, contradictory, and equivocal." Blaming the president for the climate was "unfair, outrageous, and unacceptable." He disapproved of the commission's implication that racism and poverty justified the campus protests. He called the commission members "self-appointed interpreters and translators," again failing to acknowledge that Nixon had appointed them. It was part of his standard procedure of portraying people who disagreed with the White House as outsiders.[35]

Moreover, the vice president relayed that message constantly that year. During the midterm elections of 1970, he gave speeches in support of Republican candidates all over the country. He had Nixon's permission to do so because the president had appointed Bryce Harlow—with Harlow's reluctant willingness—to oversee Agnew's addresses. The vice president continued to use alliteration, and he invented the word "radic-libs" to denigrate Democratic opponents. Also, in Agnew's opinion, the sympathy of the Commission on Campus Unrest toward the students marked the latest manifestation of society's excessive permissiveness.[36]

The vice president believed that the exploitation of his handling of Rap Brown still made effective politicking in the fall of 1970. Now he used the FBI fugitive to try to help other Republicans win electoral contests. The governors who had first won their elections in 1966—the year that the movement backlash began—were now running their first reelection campaigns. Claude Kirk and Ronald Reagan had built their constituencies over their terms by denigrating dissenters, especially African American ones. As a result, their electoral contests in 1970 served as referendums on demagoguery against Brown and the movement in general. Although Agnew was part of the class of 1966, his election to vice president in 1968 excused him from having to run in 1970. However, his continued stoking of anti-Brown fires showed his willingness to see if the issue that fueled his rise to the second-highest national office would also enable his contemporaries to keep their jobs.

On October 15, the vice president went to Florida to campaign for the reelection of Claude Kirk. Although Kirk had publicly dismissed Agnew's notion that Brown was a threat and had said that the militant could not incite anybody, the vice president still offered his support to the governor. After all, now Kirk had faded from national consciousness, and Agnew was the more famous of the two. The vice president called Kirk a "born leader" who "took the wind out of Rap Brown's sails" by confronting him face-to-face in August 1967. Agnew spoke for the Nixon administration by calling upon the crowd to reelect Kirk.[37]

One of Agnew's foes tried to speak against those efforts. Now out of the service of the Nixon administration, Rhodes became more blunt and direct in his criticism of Nixon and Agnew. Also, as a former member of the commission, he could speak to audiences with authority on protest. Addressing the NAACP–Cincinnati on November 1, he said that they had "sought to play on our fears and hatred for his own political gains." Calling this trend "tragic and monstrous," he continued, "Mr. Nixon has the incredible ability to speak of violent protestors as the major threat to justice in America when daily black Americans experience injustice and exploitation on a massive scale." He was one of the few public speakers to relate the Nixon-Agnew strategy with African Americans without resorting to name-calling bluster or threats of violence. He was pessimistic in his assessment of Nixon. "This president," he lamented, "has clearly written off the black community."[38]

Agnew's efforts yielded mixed results on election night. His attempts to bring about the defeats of Joseph Duffy, Charles Goodell, Albert Gore, and Joseph Tydings—people he had labeled "radic-libs"—were successful. He helped facilitate the victory of James Buckley, whose brother William F. Buckley was a staunch conservative and the founder of the magazine *National Review*. However, several Republican gubernatorial candidates lost. One of them was Claude Kirk, and his defeat suggested that Agnew's strategy of exploiting Brown to garner votes would not work anymore.[39]

President Nixon had already learned that lesson by then. He implemented "benign neglect" by avoiding public discussions of civil rights leaders while privately monitoring them. As Moynihan had predicted, the White House's silence toward them led reporters toward the causes the administration promoted. Meanwhile, the White House wrote a classified memo each time a civil rights leader criticized the federal government. In August, Nixon received a news summary in which Abernathy had announced a march by SCLC to Washington, D.C., within the year "to liberate and occupy the Justice Department and Congress." Nixon underlined Abernathy's quote, "This fascist domination has got to go."[40]

Abernathy's criticism of the president revealed weakness in spite of its sharpness. No matter how militant SCLC sounded or behaved, the group could not escape from the precedents of more militant groups and offer original ideas or positions. Especially concerning the Vietnam War, the organization continued to play the role of "follower" instead of "leader." On August 15, for example, SCLC called for African Americans to be exempt from the draft. The BPP had taken that same position four years earlier, and SNCC had started the NBAWADU at the same time.

In addition, the departures of key people were weakening SCLC's creativity. By 1970, longtime member James Bevel had become estranged from the group. He was conducting programs independently of SCLC. He wanted Abernathy to quit so that Jesse Jackson could replace him as president. Bevel lacked tact when expressing his preference for Jackson, and his colleagues quickly dismissed the idea. At that moment he became a liability in the organization. SCLC resolved this latest internal conflict in August by voting Bevel out on a separate issue. He had written on the wall of a hotel room, and the organization was displeased at having to pay the expensive bill.[41]

SCLC's continued associations with the BPP kept the FBI interested in the civil rights group. On August 21, Hoover told Chicago's special agent to be alert for any need of COINTELPRO activity concerning Jesse Jackson, who had recently expressed support for Huey Newton and Bobby Seale. Hoover said Jackson "appears to have taken a more extreme position with regard to racial matters and appears to be attempting to form some type of relationship with the Black Panther Party." Jackson had sent a telegram to BPP–Illinois upon Newton's release, saying, "We now join hands and lock arms to make his cause known throughout the nation. Let us know if there is anything we can do to assist you." Hoover was especially leery of Jackson because the minister had given the eulogy at Fred Hampton's funeral eight months earlier.[42]

SCLC squandered whatever goodwill it may have gained after the March against Repression from the previous May. Trouble began in October, when the organization protested the absence of African American promoters of a series of Jackson Five concerts in Texas. Rather than hire African American promoters, Berry Gordy of Motown simply canceled the concert dates. He preferred to shy away from militant groups or causes. He refused to allow his performers to engage in political activism, and he bristled when reporters asked his artists questions specifically about African American issues or African American identity. He was not about to let SCLC use the Jackson Five for radical purposes.

Gordy's cancellation of the concerts did not endear young African Americans to SCLC. The musical group was at its peak of popularity at the time. Its first three songs had topped *Billboard*'s pop charts. When Gordy called off the Texas engagements, the fourth song had just topped the charts. Ironically, it was called "I'll Be There."[43]

That same month, the November 1970 issue of *Ebony* was published, revealing internal conflicts that plagued SCLC. The issue featured another interview with Coretta Scott King, and she appeared on the cover just as in her previous interview for the September 1968 issue. The article about her said that the SCLC snubbed her when she attended board meetings and that the organization treated her as a "stepchild." Some in SCLC "vacillate between respect for her and loyalty to the people who actually are in charge now," said a King assistant. She chose not to be the 1969 SCLC convention keynote speaker because she did not discuss policy. She spoke at Cultural Night instead. For the 1970 convention, she was asked not to be involved but to chair the annual banquet instead. "They finally got around to asking her to work in the kitchen and dining room," said a King assistant.[44]

On November 3, former SCLC member Andrew Young lost the election to Congress. His ties to civil rights had damaged his ability to relate to the electorate at large. He had condemned the Chicago police's killing of Fred Hampton, and his support for the end of Western civilization in order for the Third World to emerge had also hurt his campaign. Also, he had lost by 20,000 votes, and only about 40,000 of his district's 70,000 African American voters went to the polls that day. It was a cruel irony for a man who had helped organize voter registration drives in the movement to lose because of low African American voter turnout. Perhaps Martin Luther King had been right all along. Maybe a civil rights activist could not effect change politically after all.[45]

Young's defeat was a tacit validation of Abernathy's continued involvement in civil rights activism. The SCLC leader did not gloat about his former colleague's failed campaign but rather extended grace to him and even made an offer for the politician to come back to the fold. "Andy, you never know what God might want us to do," he said, "but if it be His will that you return to hazardous duty in SCLC, we welcome you."[46] Young, however, declined Abernathy's offer and looked ahead to the 1972 election.

Whitney Young indirectly strengthened the notion that civil rights progress lay outside politics. He met with Nixon and the cabinet on December 22, and he emerged from the proceedings with renewed confidence that the administration was not anti-Negro. The NUL leader looked forward to working with the White House to improve African Americans' conditions. His optimism drew skepticism from prominent African Americans. On the other hand, the violence of the spring having tapered off by the end of the year, and people believed that the upcoming new year of 1971 could prove Young correct. "Even allowing for the possibility that Young was suffering from intoxication brought on by the high altitude of the White House," columnist Carl Rowan snickered, "let us hope he is right." Still, Nixon and Hoover had exhibited anti-Negro behavior throughout 1970 by attacking civil rights groups, and the factionalism that plagued the Movement from within made the organizations more vulnerable to sabotage from without.[47]

CHAPTER 10

The Revolutionary Army

As Rap Brown remained absent from the public eye throughout 1970, new militants emerged with the potential to become the "messiah" figure that Hoover tried to prevent through COINTELPRO. In May, the Court of Appeals of the State of California reversed charges against BPP leader Huey P. Newton. In early August, the court released him from the Alameda County Prison as he awaited a new trial, but the celebrity status that Newton had attained during his incarceration did not follow him upon his release. Speakers like Bobby Seale and writers like Eldridge Cleaver had helped popularize the BPP during Newton's incarceration, but the newly freed chairman considered the hype a false image. He decided not to live up to it but to promote his own vision of the BPP, but he had problems in verbally expressing himself. He lacked the conviction of Seale's voice and the clarity of Cleaver's arguments. In addition, Newton spoke in a high-pitched voice and often gave philosophical ramblings. Even Panthers themselves were disappointed by how he talked.[1]

Another African American convict, on the other hand, was able to raise eyebrows while incarcerated. George Jackson was not the leader of a self-defense group or a paramilitary organization. His book *Soledad Brother* was published. The release of a nationalist, militant tract was now at least an annual event. *Soul on Ice* had entered bookstores in 1968, and *Die Nigger Die!* appeared the following year. Now in 1970, it was Jackson's turn, but his writing was different than the others. The book consisted entirely of letters he had written during his incarceration over a six-year period. That period coincided with the increasing militarization and Pan Africanism of the movement's rhetoric. Consequently, between 1964 and 1970, Jackson's correspondence grew more radical in tone.

One example of the evolution of his politics was in how he regarded the movement. On April 11, 1968, Jackson had told his father in a letter a week after King's assassination, "The concept of nonviolence is a false ideal." Jackson wrote that King, Roy Wilkins, and Whitney Young had promoted turning the other cheek. "Well, that is good for them perhaps," the inmate surmised, "but I most certainly need both sides of my head."[2] At the time he did not see the movement as relevant to his personal struggle.

However, by 1970 he had had a change of heart. On June 4 of that year, he wrote to former SNCC member Angela Davis about his feelings on Malcolm X and King. He argued that the two speakers had died for specific political reasons, based on the timing of their deaths. Jackson noted that when "Muslim nationalism" gained momentum among African Americans, Malcolm was killed. "The professional killers could have murdered him long before they did," he reasoned. Jackson said that King similarly was reaching audiences with radical rhetoric just before his killing. "You remember what was on his lips when he died," he recalled, "Vietnam and economics, political economy." Jackson then admitted that King "was really on our side (the billions of righteous)" and immediately began imagining the possibilities of exploiting the SCLC founder for revolutionary purposes. "I mean we can just claim him, and use his last statements and his image to strengthen ours," he planned. "I'll be easy with it, slip it in, like it was just common knowledge that King was a Maoist."[3]

Soledad Brother became a best seller and, according to former SNCC member Julius Lester, would make people almost nostalgic for the days when Stokely Carmichael and Rap Brown had been the country's biggest worries. Carmichael and Brown had held that distinction only because federal officials had singled them out as "militants," but their alienation from the government and from other civil rights leaders further radicalized that. On the other hand, now that President Nixon had distanced himself from all of the leaders, the groups had to figure out how to produce progress from completely outside the administration. However, they shared only animosity toward both the president and the war, and they could get rid of neither despite their best organizing efforts. As the exhausted peace activists branched out to new causes such as the ecology and amnesty for draft dodgers, the burned-out civil rights workers looked more intensely inward toward such identity issues as feminism and African alliances. Their introspection led to further dissension within the organizations and in the movement at large, and the coalition grew more vulnerable to COINTELPRO's neutralizing activities.[4]

SNCC entered a slump during the first summer of Rap Brown's absence. The group's antiwar National Referendum had not aroused much public interest. The press covered SNCC in May only because Hoover added the missing chairman to the FBI's list of the "Ten Most Wanted." De facto cochairman Irving Davis took on SNCC's position of director of international affairs, and he had been planning to start a liberation school in Atlanta. However, he had a falling-out with Muhammad Hunt and suddenly resigned. His departure delayed the planning for the school, and no one immediately replaced him in the positions he had held.[5]

With two leaders gone, the group met in Croton, New York, on June 19 to plan its future. With Hunt leading the proceedings, SNCC underwent a reorganization of hierarchy. Hunt remained the head of the RPC, but Fran Beal and Bruce Allison joined him there. Jimmy Lytle of Ohio served as the organization's photographer. Terry Ardrey, formerly of the NAACP, became SNCC's new secretariat. He was tall, dark, and thin, and suffered from a heart condition. He was a poet who wanted to venture out and give spoken-word performances. Fellow SNCC poet Mae Jackson secured his speaking engagements, but she sent him to perform in cold New Paltz once because he tended to annoy her.[6]

Beal wanted SNCC to reconsider the role of women in the group and in the country. After giving her colleagues the latest news on the BWLC, she read aloud from her article "Double Jeopardy." She began by noting the problem of African American male unemployment and its effect on the African American family. She squarely blamed capitalism for "destroying the black race's will to resist its subjugation" and developing "a situation where the black man found it impossible to find meaningful or productive employment. More often than not, he couldn't find work of any kind." She considered African American women to be victims of governmental manipulation, "economically exploited and physically assaulted." To her, the widespread African American female domestic labor "in the white man's kitchen" and the African American woman's position as "the sole breadwinner of the family" proved her point. "This predicament has led to many psychological problems on the part of both man and woman and has contributed to the turmoil that we find in the black family structure," she argued. Many African American women internalized capitalist interpretations of gender and subsequently thought of African American men as "shiftless and lazy" and unwilling to "get a job and support their families as they ought to." The domestic discord from these interpretations then led to "the separation of man from wife, mother from child, etc."[7]

Beal then refuted the recent militant posturing of male spokesmen for the African American struggle, noting that it did little to liberate women. "Unfortunately, there seems to be some confusion in the Movement today as to who has been oppressing whom," she charged. The African American man had been accurate in rejecting many mainstream ideas about struggling for equality ever since SNCC's initial popularizing of Black Power in 1966. "He sees the system for what it really is for the most part," she admitted. "But where he rejects its values and mores on many issues, when it comes to women, he seems to take his guidelines from the pages of the *Ladies Home Journal*."[8] What SNCC—and the movement as a whole—had failed to do was include women prominently in that struggle after 1966.

She made the argument that the political rise of African American men did not have to come at the expense of African American women. Moreover, the women did not begrudge any gains made by the men. Repudiating Moynihan's claims that the women were too domineering and needed to let the men "strut" like peacocks, she declared that "it is a gross distortion of fact to state that black women have oppressed black men." Rather, the African American woman was "a slave of a slave." In addition, Beal believed that the movement was incomplete without full participation of women. The African American men who told African American women to abandon activism in favor of submissive domesticity were working against the revolution. "If we are talking about building a strong nation, capable of throwing off the yoke of capitalist oppression, then we are talking about the total involvement of every man, woman, and child, each with a highly developed political con-sciousness," she argued. "We need our whole army out there dealing with the enemy and not half an army."[9]

Beal then directed her remarks to specific women's issues. She provided detailed information about discrimination concerning birth control, and she noted problems in the relationship between African American women and European American feminists. By mentioning these concerns, she informed her male colleagues of how they could show solidarity with SNCC's women. She wanted the men to fight alongside the women to end the sexism they faced. After all, the women had been supporting the men's calls for power and revolution over the years.

Beal's reading of "Double Jeopardy" in its entirety at the meeting marked a major turning point in the movement. Although African American women had publicly addressed similar concerns over the years, no one had made the argument to have civil rights organizations support their female members' positions on them. Moreover, Beal was not asking for permission to tackle the issues; she merely let SNCC's men know that SNCC's women would not stop the African American women's struggle anytime soon. Her recitation of her article at Croton reflected the power and respect that she had attained in the group over the years. Also, the fact that Beal's paper reflected the views of the BWLC as a whole showed that African American feminism had won the support of a significant part of SNCC membership. The ideas in "Double Jeopardy" won over few male SNCC comrades, but Beal and the BWLC agreed to move forward with or without them.[10]

Also at Croton, SNCC decided to actively recruit younger and more diverse new members from across the country. They approved plans for a research department and the organizing of high school students. In addition, after three years of largely urban, Northern programming, SNCC chose to reestablish itself in the South through agrarian reform, student organizing, and industrial worker organizing. Ardrey was to start work on a liberation school in Atlanta. Attendees wanted to organize GIs in Georgia by establishing a coffeehouse there—the Third Eye Lounge. SNCC–Atlanta stalwart William Coleman was assigned to that project, and on Independence Day the facility opened. Members also proposed organizing up north in Newark, because they had heard of "revolutionary" organization of "Third World workers" there. Hunt tried to establish a political party, and his wife Barbara became SNCC's liaison to the Latino group Venceremos Brigade—a resumption of the interethnic alliances that SNCC had undertaken under Brown's leadership.

After having learned of the Croton meeting, Hoover sought to crush as much of the organization's ambitious agenda as he could. He started with the Agrarian Reform Program. SNCC had made some headway in the project, making plans to solicit funding from the Interreligious Foundation for Community Organizing (IFCO). Thus, on July 26 he approved a COINTELPRO proposal from New York's special agent to send two letters from phony people to the IFCO. The FBI aimed to "cast doubt in the minds of those IFCO personnel who deal with SNCC as to the sincerity of SNCC members in actually working their proposed 'Farm Project.'" The agency drafted one letter to address SNCC's plan to buy land in Knoxville and another letter to discuss the group's intent to buy farm equipment in Atlanta. Agents in those cities were directed to write their letters within eight days of each other "in order to provide additional security and realism for the counterintelligence technique."[11]

Both of the fictional writers described themselves as having upstanding reputations and refused to involve themselves with SNCC, but they felt that they needed to inform the IFCO about the organization. From Atlanta, COINTELPRO wrote a letter pretending to be a man in the used farm equipment business. The fictional man warned the IFCO that "a Negro who calls himself Muhammad" asked him to sell the phony salesman used equipment at a new price. The imposter then claimed that Muhammad intended to get reimbursed by the IFCO and split the money with him. From Knoxville, a phony real estate agent wrote to IFCO that "Muhammad" asked him to sell 200 acres of land to him for $5,000. "Muhammad" would then report the price to the IFCO as $50,000 and split the reimbursement with the fake land agent. To cause further discord, the Knoxville letter accused "Muhammad" of calling the IFCO "a bunch of Honkie and Uncle Tom Churchmen who were real liberal with money and never asked questions."[12]

SNCC's travels throughout and beyond the country reflected the group's lack of focus without Brown. Barbara Hunt traveled to Cuba in August, but Lynne Doswell's summer in Tanzania suggested a return to Pan-Africanism for the group. The organization attracted new members to Northern branches such as Charles Brodnax in New York and Dan Brown in Milwaukee. Meanwhile, the group bolstered its faltering Southern presence via SNCC–Atlanta's new members Cecil Carter and Jimmy Lytle and SNCC–Houston's "Brother Scrooge." That summer was also a time of loss, because Dan Aldridge and Judy Sullivan left the group.

Women continued to play crucial roles in the new SNCC. Mae Jackson became finance officer of New York's branch, which meant that she was the bookkeeper. Although Hoover and COINTELPRO mostly discussed the activities of men, they monitored what the women were doing just as closely. When Jackson opened the SNCC office door every day at 9:00 a.m., two FBI agents watched her from a nearby car parked outside the office building. Sometimes the African American agent would leave the car and stand by the office entrance.[13]

Moreover, if Hoover considered a woman dangerous to internal security, he would make an example of her, as he did with men. Former SNCC–Los Angeles associate Angela Davis kept the organization in the limelight that summer in the same way that Brown had during the spring—by becoming a fugitive. Authorities sought her arrest after discovering an African American teenager named Jonathan Jackson had used her firearms in a deadly courtroom shootout. On August 18, the FBI placed her with Rap Brown on the 10 Most Wanted List merely because of her ownership of the firearms. She became the third woman—and the first African American woman—ever placed on the list.

Her sisters in SNCC rallied to support her, exacerbating an ethnic rift in American feminism in the process. The BWLC joined women across the country that month in marching to observe the fiftieth anniversary of the ratification of the Nineteenth Amendment. At the march in New York, the organization carried signs that said "Hands off Angela Davis," but some of the European American feminists objected to the gestures of support for the fugitive.

A member of the National Organization for Women claimed that Davis's struggle was irrelevant to women's liberation. Fran Beal tartly replied, "It has nothing to do with the liberation *you're* talking about, but it has everything to do with the kind of liberation *we're* talking about."[14]

The BWLC fundamentally differed from European American feminism concerning relationships with men. The latter found problematic the acquisition by men of rights and power, and they expressed specific concerns about African American men rising socially and politically before all women were able to do so. Beal did not see the rise of African American men as a point of resentment. Instead, she approved it, for without their ascension, the lifting of African American women would not happen either. She saw potential for both genders of African Americans to help each other overcome.[15]

The BWLC's successful programming was the bright spot of an otherwise disappointing summer for SNCC. The organization's New York branch failed to secure funding from the IFCO for the proposed cooperative farm. Meanwhile, SNCC–Atlanta faltered, too. On September 3, COINTELPRO reported that its efforts kept the executive council of the Episcopal Church in New York from funding SNCC's H. Rap Brown Liberation School in Atlanta. SNCC had asked the council for $67,000 early in 1970. When Hoover found out, he put his agents to work. On June 8, COINTELPRO drafted letters from two phony people writing to the church to say that the school was just a scam and that SNCC wasn't going to use the money to buy anything for the school. SNCC was informed on August 27 that funds from the church weren't likely in the immediate future.[16]

That fall SNCC's future further dimmed. Between September 8 and October 9, the Third Eye Lounge temporarily closed. The business had amassed thousands of dollars in debt, and the organization was unable to settle its accounts. Then again, SNCC's national headquarters in New York was a few rooms in a church at a reduced rate. With the group financially unable to gain a strong footing in the South, its outreach remained confined to cities in the North.

Meanwhile, the organization made more news through the activities of its fugitives than with current members and programs. Reporters asked constantly about the whereabouts of Rap Brown and Angela Davis. Then, after authorities captured Davis on October 13, her trial generated further headlines. Meanwhile, SNCC tried to address the problem of publicity by generating its own media outlet. The group's new newsletter *National SNCC* launched, and the members published it bimonthly. It was a largely editorial newsletter, because the activists contributed to the periodical by espousing their political views.

SNCC's leadership vacuum also proved problematic for the group. No one had groomed Muhammad Hunt of the New York office for succession in case anything happened to Brown. As a result, even people within SNCC did not see him as the legitimate successor. He was never even close to gaining acceptance as the de facto national chair of SNCC, as far as they were concerned. He served as the spokesman of the New York branch but certainly not on the national level. In addition, members were aware of FBI infiltration of militant groups, and some of them thought Hunt was an informant. By this time, Lynne Doswell in particular had no idea who in SNCC was "genuine" and who worked for Hoover.

Hunt tried to compensate for what he lacked in Brown's charisma and leadership skills. The de facto chairman demonstrated extreme loyalty to the organization. He relished having any kind of authority in SNCC at all. He went to excessive measures to ensure that the members adhered to his policies and politics. In addition, he was a careful and methodical organizer. But with SNCC membership reduced to a single-digit number in the main branch at New York, no one could figure out why exactly he wanted to be chairman of the organization. At the time, Muhammad Hunt and two or three other people were essentially SNCC in New York.[17]

Mae Jackson considered SNCC on its last legs and left the organization after Hunt assumed command. However, she did not completely cut her ties to her former comrades, for she was friends with the mother of Hunt's child. Both women remained members of the BWLC, and Jackson's friend supported her during her pregnancy. Still, her continued presence in the BWLC pointed to a glaring problem for SNCC. Brown's takeover of the group did not prevent it from factionalizing, and the side project of the BWLC took people away from the main organization.[18]

Another recruitment issue involved SNCC's conflicting actions regarding protest. For the past 10 years, the organization had prided itself on confronting authority. Its participants had dared to go to jail instead of accepting bail, and they had knowingly risked their lives by traveling into remote areas to challenge segregation and its repressive enforcement. Now, high-profile members like Brown and Davis were doing neither of those things by becoming fugitives. Then again, the earliest members of SNCC had believed in the overall morality of the laws of the United States. They had defied local segregation laws, considering them denials of constitutional guarantees. But now that the SNCC associates of 1970 were against the federal government, they desperately tried to avoid getting into federal custody.

SNCC's women embraced Brown's support of multiethnic protest for their independent group. The BWLC became the Third World Women's

Alliance (TWWA) that fall when Puerto Rican socialist women joined it. Before the end of the fall, the New York branch of the TWWA had grown to 200 members. The organization began publishing its newsletter, *Triple Jeopardy*. The rapid growth of the alliance attracted attention from reporters, especially those in New York. Fran Beal now spent more time speaking to the media there on behalf of the offshoot group than on behalf of SNCC.[19]

The TWWA filled a void for feminists who were not European American. "There really is nothing out there for women of color," Beal complained. In addition, to her and other TWWA members, the "Black Power" mindset remained chauvinistic against women. Many of them argued, "Women should step back and have babies for the revolution." The TWWA challenged the "Black Power" advocates about the hypocrisy of restricting part of an ethnic group in order for the entirety of the group to progress. "You can't be revolutionary and talk about setting women back," Beal noted.[20]

Beal not only saw the chauvinism as hypocritical but also impractical. "The idea that women's only role is breeder in the revolutionary army is nonsense," she said. To her, the very act of reproduction had no politically redeeming value on its own merit. "Lots of women have been breeding children, and it hasn't liberated us yet," she quipped.[21]

The TWWA criticized European American feminists for only seeking European American female empowerment. Their avoidance of color-based discrimination meant the continued oppression of minority women. Beal claimed that European Americans who struggled for gender-based equality merely sought the equality to murder and exploit Third World inhabitants. She did not believe that European American feminists would sacrifice their privileged class status to get rid of a narrow kind of discrimination. Therefore, she called for the organizing of feminist African Americans, Chicanas, Puerto Ricans, and Native Americans.

Several African Americans met in Georgia over Labor Day weekend to attend a meeting—the Congress of African Peoples (CAP). CAP organizer Haywood Henry claimed that people of African descent could start to cure the evils they faced by meeting as a people. It was not a new argument, for several African Americans had called for unity and separatism among African Americans for many generations. When all of the civil rights groups were integrated and fought to desegregate public facilities and enfranchise African Americans before the late 1960s, they rejected the concept of organizing solely among African Americans. By the fall of 1970, however, the organizations had already united behind Black Power. CAP facilitators wanted to build upon that unity and reintroduce the idea of black nationhood.

Civil rights figures Ralph Abernathy, Julian Bond, Jesse Jackson, and Whitney Young went to the CAP meeting, and their attendance signaled the movement's readiness to at least entertain the idea of black nationhood. For Abernathy and Jackson, CAP marked the latest opportunity for SCLC to express solidarity with separatist African Americans, and Bond was a former member of SNCC—the group that had popularized Black Power. However, Young's presence, despite his longtime opposition to separatism, extended from his patronage of CAP cofounder Imamu Amiri Baraka's recent efforts to organize African Americans. The NUL leader was impressed by Baraka's willingness to produce programs instead of relying on inflammatory rhetoric, and Baraka sought Young's support because of his ability to generate large funds from his network of European American contacts.[22]

Baraka's speech at CAP called for a new direction for African American activists in a manner that repudiated the evolution of the freedom struggle after the mid-1960s. He first lambasted militant speech for its own sake. "Many people think that once they get a .22 rifle and go and shoot once a month that they are skillful enough to overtake and overthrow the United States Government which is the most powerful force on this planet," he observed. "But that is not the case. Just being angry at white people will not overthrow them." He admitted that the struggle needed to involve all African Americans, but he acknowledged that some were more revolutionary than others. To him, strength lay in numbers. "There are more Black people involved with Roy Wilkins than are involved with the Congress of African Peoples," he noted. "There are more niggers who think like Whitney Young than think like we do." He wanted them in the Pan-African struggle. "You cannot merely say, 'You're corny, nigger.' You got to get him and embrace him and make him be with you."[23] With Young remaining in the room while Baraka uttered those remarks, the speaker appeared to accomplish just that.

Baraka then closed with his poem "It's Nation Time"—an artistic call for ethnic solidarity. He repeatedly cried, "Come out, niggers" to reinforce his idea of strength in numbers. He wanted them out "when the brothers take over the school," to "help us stop the devil," and to "help us build a new world." The poem also referred to division among African Americans. The people he called "us" and "brothers" already supported skin-color solidarity, but the "niggers" still needed convincing. Moreover, Baraka called out specific "niggers" like Roy Wilkins and Diana Ross to "come out," which hardly had potential to attract them to future CAP meetings. Still, the civil rights leaders had not unified to create their own new program for struggle, leaving CAP as the best option for the Movement to follow instead of to lead.[24]

As 1970 became 1971, Brown received potentially good news out of Maryland. Richard Kinlein—the state attorney for Howard County—accused Brown's prosecuting lawyer of fabricating charges against the fugitive. Kinlein claimed that William Yates II, the lawyer prosecuting the case against Brown, had admitted to making up the charges back in April. The report was an indication that a growing number of influential people were having second thoughts about the significance of militant African American rhetoric. Perhaps the words a person spoke were indeed not powerful enough to make a crowd riot hours later.[25]

At the end of 1970, President Nixon slightly hinted as much at a press conference. Earlier in October, he had publicly congratulated the FBI for its "remarkable" capture of Angela Davis. He marked the occasion to warn her and other radicals that "we shall see to it that those who engage in such terroristic acts are brought to justice." But in December a reporter called the president's remarks part of Davis's "pretrial publicity." He pointedly asked Nixon, "How do you reconcile your comments with your status as a lawyer?" A humbled Nixon acknowledged the reporter's "legitimate criticism" and admitted that lawyers make mistakes. Then he admitted of his own remarks about Davis, "I think that kind of comment probably is unjustified." His disclosure signaled that the time for inflammatory rhetoric from government officials against the movement had passed.[26]

By January 1971, many people considered various elements of the movement interchangeable, but the activists themselves were partly responsible. Militants in SNCC and the BPP toned down their references to violence, while conservatives in SCLC spoke more militantly. Also, the groups self-consciously drew from each other's strategies and slogans. George Jackson's goal of using King's memory for militant purposes became a reality in South Vietnam. On the occasion of the late SCLC leader's birthday, African American troops wanting to celebrate the occasion there demanded passes in order to do so. Then 20 African American soldiers at the Newport dock in South Vietnam began marching. They carried a wooden cross, a Black Power flag, and a banner that said "Honor Dr. Martin Luther King." They met 20 other African American servicemen at Long Binh, and together they marched to the U.S. Army headquarters in town. They stayed in front of the building for half an hour, raising their fists and chanting, "Stop discrimination in the Army," and "Free Angela Davis."

The U.S. media reported the event as the first Black Power incident of the Vietnam War. However, despite the African American demographic of the demonstrators, the concept of Black Power had little to do with the event. The march combined honor for the movement of the distant past through the tribute to King, the superficial elements of the recent past such as the raised fist, and the issues of the present like the Angela Davis case. In a sense, the media had bought into Vice President Agnew's contention that any African American political expression fell within the confines of Black Power. As prominent speakers about injustice, King and Davis were both "irresponsible militants"—two sides of the same coin.[27]

Nevertheless, the demonstration was significant in that it demonstrated the long-range impact of the movement. Although King had disliked both the Black Power slogan and the Vietnam War, soldiers of that war made him relevant to their causes. Moreover, despite the war setting and the participation of combat-ready troops, the protest was nonviolent—a validation that SCLC's devotion to nonviolence was not in vain. If armed troops could set aside their weapons and remember a pacifist for half an hour in South Vietnam, perhaps there was hope that the "law and order" White House could also set an example for peacemaking.

SCLC certainly had hope that the Nixon administration would eventually set aside its enmity toward the group and honor King with a national holiday. SCLC returned to Washington, D.C., on King's birthday and led 1,500 people in a 12-block march from a church to the Capitol steps. As usual, Abernathy drove a mule train to lead the way. He carried petitions of 3 million signatures in support for a King holiday. No honor from the federal government was forthcoming, however.[28]

Undaunted, SCLC returned to the theme of economic inequality for yet another march series two weeks later. On January 30, the group led African American hotel maids on a march from Daytona Beach to Cape Kennedy before the Apollo 14 liftoff. The organization was once again highlighting the problem of labor exploitation; having advocated for sanitation workers in 1968 and hospital workers in 1969, SCLC chose hotel maids as their example of the working poor. The group was also attempting to share the spotlight with a major national event, although television viewership of moon landings had steadily declined since the first one in 1969. In using humor to call attention to SCLC's repeated claim that the Apollo space program hardly addressed poverty, one sign read, "You can't eat rocks."

The next day, SCLC continued its protest with 200 demonstrators in number. They walked from Titusville to the Kennedy Space Center. The march itself was the only part of the event that the group did of one accord. When SCLC members began talking about the demonstration, they disagreed with how to explain its significance. "We are not protesting America's achievements in outer space," Hosea Williams said. "We are protesting our country's inability to choose humane priorities. He echoed previous complaints from SCLC about the country spending billions of dollars on Apollo "to get some moon rocks for Vice President Spiro Agnew to hand out to heads of states." However, Williams became distracted by the Apollo liftoff, showing that SCLC itself could not keep its own members focused on poverty when a NASA rocket launched nearby. Although the marchers did not get to see the launch from inside the Kennedy Center, as promised, Williams allowed, "I thought the launch was beautiful. The most magnificent sight I've seen in my whole life."[29]

SCLC member Joseph Hammonds was less charitable than Williams and made a comparison that yet again SNCC had made first. "America is sending lazy white boys to the moon because all they're doing is looking for moon rocks," he claimed. "If there was work to be done, they'd send a nigger." It was another incoherent message from the organization. On the one hand, Hammonds disapproved of the Apollo program. On the other, he decried the segregation within the program that he found useless. Moreover, four years earlier, Rap Brown had made a similar point when he had spoken in Detroit. "They gave Negroes an astronaut, but I bet they lose that nigger in space," he predicted. In actuality, the astronaut died in a jet crash landing without having gone to the moon, and NASA did not appoint an African American for any of the Apollo missions.[30]

SCLC appeared to not take this Apollo march as seriously as previous marches. The titles of earlier protests corresponded to specific social conditions. The March against Fear in 1966 was to inspire Mississippi's African Americans to stop being afraid of reprisals from registering to vote. The March against Repression from last May addressed the killings at Kent State and Jackson State and in Indochina. In contrast, SCLC called its demonstration at the Apollo 14 launch a "March against Moon Rocks"—a title for the sake of giving a march a title. The name did not call attention to a social ill, for moon rocks were not a problem in and of themselves. The "March against Moon Rocks" name suggested that SCLC was slipping into self-parody.

The descent continued two days later, when Abernathy announced SCLC's support for Angela Davis at a rally sponsored by the Angela Davis Defense Committee. The announcement was significant, because the organization had not publicly endorsed the release of an individual African American woman since the arrest of Rosa Parks on a Montgomery bus in 1955. But there the similarities ended. SCLC had used Parks's arrest to launch a fight against segregation, but it mobilized people around the cause instead of the victim. In contrast, Davis already had a broad, massive network of support by the time SCLC advocated for her four months after her arrest. Abernathy was one of several prominent speakers at the rally that day. The venerable civil rights activist Ella Baker served both as a cochair of the Defense Committee and as a speaker at the demonstration, and longtime movement ally Anne Braden introduced Abernathy. This event allowed SCLC to retain national media coverage immediately after the March against Moon Rocks.

Abernathy's participation in the rally reflected the high regard he maintained in activist circles, but his speech was an end in and of itself. SCLC did not start any new projects when it announced its support for Davis. Moreover, he did not deeply delve into why he took up her cause. Instead he offered routine condemnations of the country and pleas for mass activism. "A racist, oppressive, criminal society is attempting to kill a militant, black, woman activist because of her political beliefs and her commitment to those beliefs," he complained. "Ladies and gentlemen there are *thousands* of political prisoners in America," he observed, "and the only way to free them is to get out and *struggle* in a mass movement of people. We need fund-raising for Angela Davis, but we also need hell-raising for millions of people."[31]

Only the first one-third of Abernathy's address focused on Davis. The remainder of his remarks contained little more than boilerplate about the usual topics with his standard phrases. It was essentially a typical Abernathy stump speech with an added slight nod to political imprisonment. He demanded that the people "free the nation" of poverty, war, and a "Nixon-Agnew-Reagan Administration." As usual, he decried the "law and order" culture and the fighting in Indochina, too. He challenged his listeners, "Let us speak until we can roam the streets of America and there will be no policemen to beat our heads and we will not have to raise our sons to go off and be slaughtered somewhere in war." His only additional reference to Davis was near the end: "Let us speak until Angela Davis is as free as a bird in these United States of America."[32]

His platitudes in his address were also derivative from other speakers. He borrowed the BPP's "Power to the People" slogan. Referring to the television program *Laugh-In*, he told his listeners to "sock it to America." He also used language reminiscent of a play from the NOI. "The Trial" had been part of the 1959 CBS News broadcast on the NOI—*The Hate That Hate Produced*. The report showed Louis Farrakhan intoning, "I charge the White Man with being the greatest liar on Earth," among other crimes. Abernathy instead stated, "I charge America," and listed hypocrisy, murder, conspiracy, "being a liar," and "robbery of the Puerto Ricans, the Mexican-Americans" as the charges.[33]

Overall, his announcement of support mattered little to the Davis case. SCLC was just one more organization supporting her, although it was the first mainstream civil rights group to do so. Abernathy's statement did not move the federal government toward freeing Davis, especially because the SCLC leader had aroused the anger of the Nixon administration. More importantly, his call for people to have power whether their skin was white, black, yellow, or "polka-dot" diminished the gravity of his statement. The "polka-dot" reference was one further example of SCLC's self-parodying.[34]

In the meantime, both SNCC and the BPP continued to spiral downward, plagued by disappearances and defections. Eldridge Cleaver left the Black Panthers to start the Black Liberation Army. Huey Newton had begun steering the BPP from its popular image of urban militarism, but Cleaver disagreed with the organization's new direction. He had been one of the people primarily responsible for promoting the Panthers' militaristic image during Newton's imprisonment.

Hoover pounced on the vulnerability of both groups. On December 10, 1970, New York's special agent sent to COINTELPRO affiliates in other cities a draft of a letter made to be from Muhammad Hunt criticizing the BPP and Eldridge Cleaver. The letter is "aimed at disrupting any relationship which might exist between SNCC and the BPP." The agent recommended sending the letter from Atlanta because of Hunt's current residence there, and suggested the letter be mimeographed because SNCC's "poor financial condition" would have kept it from affording to duplicate the documents any other way. The bogus letter perfectly captured Hunt's language, down to his standard signature line "Love and Revolution." In the document the FBI portrayed Hunt as upset with Cleaver's comments about SNCC member Phil Hutchings. In addition to calling the BPP "Panther pussys" [sic], the phony Hunt referred to Cleaver as an "intellectual pimp" and a "coward" for not engaging in revolution but living in "safe and ineffective" exile. Although the letter was addressed to SNCC personnel, New York's special agent suggested sending it only to BPP chapters nationwide and to Huey Newton's home.[35]

The federal government continued its surveillance of SNCC in Atlanta, as well. The Senate Appropriations Committee reported, "The Student National Coordinating Committee has embarked on a program to increase its local membership cadres and to promote guerilla warfare training and the development of political awareness among its members." The FBI revealed that the Third Eye Lounge had permanently closed and that the Southern Workers Coalition had become SNCC–Atlanta's new project. On February 10, the city's special agent informed Hoover in COINTELPRO that the Black Panthers were using a local organization to attempt to acquire SNCC's former national office in Atlanta. The agent then suggested drafting a letter to SNCC in New York, informing the national office there of the BPP's plans. In so doing, "this would cause considerable conflict between SNCC functionaries and the BPP."[36]

The FBI's monitoring of a barely operational SNCC branch in Atlanta proved how serious Hoover was about keeping militants neutralized. None of SNCC–Atlanta's three members—William Coleman, William La Trane, and Ricky Reed—generated local or national headlines for statements or events in early 1971. The branch had been out of the limelight ever since Brown had relocated the national headquarters to New York in June 1969. In addition, three active members marked a significant decline from the years when Atlanta had been the group's national base. Still, three members were not zero. As long as SNCC had a presence in Atlanta, COINTELPRO treated it as a threat.[37]

The FBI was succeeding in keeping civil rights groups from uniting among themselves and forming new alliances, but the bureau could not crush the organizations themselves. Their shutout from the White House emboldened them to try new ideas for organizing African Americans. However, the old conflict of integrationism versus separatism limited the potential for Pan-Africanism in the movement, and male chauvinism in the groups led activist women to depend on their own power and talents. The coalition struggled harder to stay together as the disputes grew more pronounced.

CHAPTER 11

Same Old Thing

For all of the efforts by the Nixon administration and J. Edgar Hoover to discredit "irresponsible" civil rights activists, the movement's "responsible militants" still had some political clout in early 1971. On January 28, Roy Wilkins met with Housing Secretary George Romney. The following month, both the NAACP leader and the Urban League's Whitney Young attended the president's two-hour briefing on revenue sharing. Romney headed the proceedings, and John Ehrlichman and the president addressed the audience. While there, Wilkins said that African American voters should carefully study Nixon's proposal but that safeguards should prevent states from distributing federal money on a discriminatory basis. Other civil rights groups represented at the briefing were the National Council of Negro Women (NCNW) and the National Business League, and African American mayors Richard Hatcher and Robert Blackwell also participated. The gathering was the largest movement presence in the White House during Nixon's presidency.

Ralph Abernathy did not attend the briefing because Nixon's banning of him from the White House was still in effect. However, that same month the SCLC leader spoke before the Senate Armed Services Committee and left a good impression upon at least one congressman. Abernathy relayed his organization's demand that the federal government end the draft and establish an all-volunteer army. Taking a patriotic tack, he claimed that the draft was "totally antithetical to the concepts of freedom and democracy upon which this country was founded." He then paraphrased from the BPP's slogan by saying that a force of volunteers was about "returning the war power to the people." Representative Spark Matsumaga of Hawaii was so impressed by the testimony that he included it in the *Congressional Record* on February 26.[1]

Matsumaga's support hardly dissuaded Hoover from trying to "neutralize" the movement, and the FBI continued its surveillance of the activists. Suddenly, on March 8, a subversive political group having nothing to do with the movement caught Hoover and his agents off guard. An organization calling itself the Citizens' Commission to Investigate the FBI invaded a small FBI office in Media, Pennsylvania, removed documents from the office, and distributed them to news periodicals. The documents taken by the vigilante group exposed the bureau's secret COINTELPRO operation to the public for the first time. Most of the public, however, did not immediately see the paperwork. The press did not publish any of the content from the documents.

Still, the covert operations were now compromised. Now people knew that COINTELPRO existed, even if they did not know exactly what the program did or who the targets were. The FBI's immediate response was to distance itself from its disclosed secret. On April 28, 1971, Hoover ordered the discontinuation of all of the COINTELPRO projects, including the "Black Extremist" one that had targeted SCLC and the SNCC for nearly four years. The FBI still kept active files on movement organizations and individual activists, but the director no longer dictated any activity against them in the name of COINTELPRO. Any further counterintelligence by Hoover against the movement would have to take place through a new secret program.[2]

Whitney Young tested Nixon's commitment to civil rights on February 8, 1971, by calling him to advise him on judicial appointments. He informed the president that no one had ever appointed an African American federal judge from the South. The NUL leader suggested one to fill a vacancy in the Eastern District of Louisiana. He also asked Nixon to consider Clyde Ferguson, former dean of Howard University Law School, as William H. Hastie's replacement on the U.S. Court of Appeals for the Third Circuit. In a letter to John Ehrlichman, Nixon revealed that he saw an opportunity to show support for African Americans by following Young's advice. "[Deputy Attorney General Richard] Kleindienst, of course, will understand that we do need some appointments of this type," the president wrote, "and if we could make one that happened to be suggested by Young and who also was qualified, this would kill two birds with one stone."[3]

Four weeks later Young joined other African American activists in Lagos, Nigeria, to engage in dialogue with African leaders. After CAP's success last fall, civil rights workers were content to relinquish the movement's vanguard position of the African American struggle and to see where Pan-Africanism would lead them. Having failed to domestically mobilize many people through Black Power and opposition to the Vietnam War, civil rights leaders now looked outside of the United States for assistance. Bayard Rustin, SCLC's Jesse Jackson, and ex-SNCC member John Lewis were among the movement's representatives there with Young. The African-American Institute sponsored the gathering.

The meeting was low-key, escaping the media radar. None of the network television news programs covered the proceedings, because the meeting only offered content that various civil rights leaders had already mentioned over the past few years. Stokely Carmichael had cried for Pan-Africanism since 1966, and movement officials had already gathered for the Pan-Africanist cause in September 1970. In addition, the Lagos gathering did not feature the intense rhetoric and confrontational attitude that had previously characterized separatism, and the participants expressed more concern for themselves than for their relationships with others. Instead of making violent calls against "whiteys" and "honkies," they promoted self-uplift.[4]

The press eventually covered the meeting, but under tragic circumstances. On the conference's fourth day, Young joined Ramsey Clark and his wife for a swim out in the ocean. The NUL leader was overcome by a wave, his lungs filled with water, and he stopped swimming. Clark pulled him to shore and tried to resuscitate him, but Young was dead at the age of 49. Conference proceedings ground to a halt, and the civil rights activists prepared to bury another fallen comrade.

The public outpouring of grief was immediate and powerful. *Jet* magazine identified him as the fourth civil rights leader to die since John F. Kennedy's assassination in 1963, counting only King and Senator Robert Kennedy as the other losses. Wilkins remembered Young's energy and mourned him as "one of the most dynamic and effective leaders in this struggle for human dignity" who gave the Urban League "a new sense of urgency" and "a new image of vigor." Meanwhile, former SNCC member Julian Bond felt that he and his colleagues had lost a valuable ally, someone who could move easily in the passages of power as few in the movement could or would. Despite all of Young's work toward civil rights, his remains were laid to rest in a segregated cemetery.[5]

President Nixon's reaction to Young's death was unprecedented in the movement. When previous leaders died, presidents had issued statements of condolence and either attended funerals or sent representatives to them, but did little else. Nixon, however, made a public statement, sent a plane to Lagos to retrieve Young's body, sent seven cabinet members to the March 16 funeral, and gave the eulogy at Young's grave during the next day's burial service. The president stood in silence before the grave for two minutes before eulogizing the activist. "Thousands of men and women in his own race will have a chance, an equal chance, who otherwise might never have had a chance except for what he did," Nixon noted. "And thousands of others, not of his own race who have an understanding in their hearts which they would not have had except for what he taught."[6] The president was especially moved by Young's willingness to help everyone in America achieve liberty and justice.

Nixon's elaborate sendoff of Young reflected a continuation of his recent attempts to increase support among African Americans for the administration. He positioned himself next to the widow at the burial and did not correct press accounts that she had embraced him during the service; she had merely spoken to him about honoring his promises to Young. On the other hand, below the surface of the president's showiness lay little of substance. Lyndon Johnson may not have done as much to bury King three years earlier, but he had effectively used the nation's grief to yield the Civil Rights Act of 1968 from Congress. In contrast, no new landmark civil rights legislation emerged immediately after Young's death, nor did President Nixon appoint any of Young's recommendations to federal benches.

With Young dead and Jackie Robinson and Roy Wilkins becoming elderly and less active, the proponents of civil disobedience were the only national civil rights leaders left to converse with the White House. Nixon, however, did not want to converse with them and shut the administration off from them. In doing so, he made civil rights workers more vocal against him, and thus less attractive to him, but their vicious circle meant the perpetuation of poverty and violence for African Americans throughout 1971.

SCLC pursued political influence despite its shutoff from the White House by running for public offices. In February, Jesse Jackson's run for mayor of Chicago as an independent candidate allowed him to break from Abernathy's shadow. The press remained relentless in their coverage of tension between him and Abernathy. Jackson was able to secure interviews without Abernathy, and many reporters considered him an authority figure not only on SCLC but also on the movement itself. Still, he needed the publicity that SCLC's "Operation Breadbasket" gave him. As a result, unlike Andrew Young, Jackson did not quit the organization to run his campaign. Instead, he referred to himself as on temporary leave.

Jackson's campaign was an uphill battle, considering the popularity of incumbent mayor Richard Daley. The current mayor also wielded tremendous power over the city, although his political "machine" had started to decline in recent years. In addition, Jackson had to go to the Supreme Court to challenge a state law requiring him to acquire 58,000 signatures for his nominating petition. In Illinois, any independent candidate for mayor had to gain a number of signatures equal to 5 percent of the total plurality vote in the previous mayoral election. When the court upheld that law, Jackson lost his opportunity to challenge Daley.[7]

Walter Fauntroy had better luck in Washington, D.C. The district was deciding on its first congressional delegate in decades. Fauntroy entered the race as a Democrat. Although both he and Jackson were in the movement, the former had political experience that the latter lacked. While in SCLC, Fauntroy also served as the vice chairman of the district's city council. Also, unlike Jackson's relatively small African American constituency in Chicago, Fauntroy had cultivated a following among the sizable African American population in Washington, D.C., over the years. In January he won the district's Democratic primary election, and he handily defeated his Republican opponent in March.[8]

That same month SCLC underwent an overhaul. As people started leaving the organization, Abernathy started to form a new "inner circle" of people. Bernard Lee became the executive special assistant to Abernathy. Stoney Cooks entered a program relations position in the group, and Tom Offenburger became Abernathy's research assistant. Also, the group had to fill the vacancies from the recent political defections. David Clark started serving as head of the Washington, D.C., branch while Fauntroy ran for Congress. Calvin S. Morris similarly began his role as the acting director of Operation Breadbasket while Jackson campaigned for mayor of Chicago. With Jackson and Fauntroy joining Andrew Young in political activity, SCLC moved further away from King's mindset of discouraging political involvement as a vehicle for social change. In addition, the continued involvement of Jackson and Fauntroy in the organization during their campaigns meant that the activists did not see politics and protest as separate entities. After Jackson dropped out of Chicago's mayoral race, he endorsed Mayor Daley's Republican opponent—a significant break from SCLC's policy of avoiding political endorsements.[9]

Meanwhile, as civil rights activists gained political legitimacy, established politicians sought support from the movement. Senator George McGovern announced his decision to run for the presidency in January, and Hosea Williams of SCLC soon received a copy of the candidate's campaign statement and a request for feedback. McGovern considered Williams one of his "friends and potential supporters," as he put it. In turn, activists wooed by politicians cultivated relationships with them, thus nurturing the movement's new access to powerful government officials. On March 1, Williams replied to the senator, saying that he approved McGovern's determination to stop both poverty and the Vietnam War. "For as long as you continue to work aggressively to end war, discrimination, and poverty in this country, your goals and those of the movement I represent will be the same," he told McGovern. "Having such common goals, you may be assured of my personal support and my voice and efforts in your behalf," Williams promised. As a matter of policy, the organization did not endorse presidential candidates, but Williams was now the first individual in the group to independently do so.[10]

Some people in SCLC still deliberately tried to adhere to King's ideas. His widow continued to associate the civil rights struggle with the anti-war struggle. On March 26, Coretta Scott King accepted an invitation to speak at a peace demonstration. "I think this is the single most important thing that I could do at this time toward fulfilling my husband's dream," she wrote to Ruth Gage-Colby, national coordinator of the National Peace Action Coalition. Paraphrasing the Black Panther slogan, she concluded her letter, "I still believe that the power to bring about positive, lasting change rests with the people."[11] The Spring Demonstration against Poverty, War, and Repression was scheduled for April 1971—four years to the month that King had first publicly opposed the country's role in the Vietnam War. By 1971, however, more people had begun agreeing with King's point of view. In fact, most people wanted the United States out of Indochina. The question now rested on when—immediately or after the release of the American prisoners of war in North Vietnam. Nevertheless, now that members of the Silent Majority wanted the war to end, their backlash against antiwar activists was abating.

However, on April 19, five days before the scheduled Spring Demonstration, one particular antiwar group tested that majority's tolerance for antiwar dissent. Fifteen hundred veterans of the Vietnam War assembled in Washington, D.C., to air their grievances to the federal government in person. They marched up Pennsylvania Avenue. Some walked. Some hobbled. Some wheeled themselves. They carried banners that decried the conflict and called for peace. Bystanders lined the streets to see the veterans pass by. The demonstrators stopped at the Washington Mall and set up camp there. Nearly three years after SCLC had launched its Resurrection City, the Vietnam Veterans against the War (VVAW) now had its own occupation. They called it Dewey Canyon III, derived from the name of America's secret invasion of Laos.

Borrowing from the movement, the VVAW conducted dramatic but non-violent protests throughout the week. Moreover, the group decided not to conduct civil disobedience but instead to exercise their right to dissent to the fullest extent they could. The members had felt unheard throughout the existence of the war. People did not want to listen to the concerns of the veterans, and the press struggled to grasp the concept of former soldiers publicly objecting to the war in which they had fought. The veterans considered a mass march in Washington, D.C., the only way to express their views in a manner that guaranteed the attention of government officials.

In addition to marching and camping, the veterans legitimized their grievances by participating in government activities. They lobbied to Congress. They sat in a Supreme Court session. When President Nixon tried to discredit the activists as hippies, they presented their combat cards to reporters and discredited Nixon instead. When the Justice Department threatened to arrest the campers for sleeping in the park, they promised not to sleep. One of them proposed taking "speed" to stay awake that week. Some legislators joined the president in condemning them, but a few others, like Ron Dellums and Ted Kennedy, expressed solidarity with them. The VVAW now had allies within the federal government.

On April 23, Dewey Canyon III climaxed with 700 veterans marching to the steps of the Capitol. They lined up to the fence at the building. They gathered to tell "a story of Vietnamese people whose nation was torn by an army not concerned with human lives," as a VVAW leader put it, "but with body counts."[12] The first veteran introduced himself by name and rank. He recalled how the government had medaled him for his service in Vietnam. Then, he tossed his reward over the fence.

Then another identified himself and pitched his medals over. "Right on!" yelled his brothers in arms.

Then another: "Here's my merit badge for murder!" he roared.

Onlookers were stunned. Some of them berated the veterans for exercising their right to protest. "I wish you'd go out and get a job and *work*!" an exasperated elderly woman shouted at the demonstrators. "I'm *tired* of you!" Her complaint reflected fatigue from the domestic unrest of the past few years more than it concerned the specific actions of the veterans. After all, this demonstration was only the first time that the VVAW had marched in Washington, D.C. Nevertheless, it was yet another new group of activists conducting the same kinds of activities that the African Americans and the students had previously done. Like many in the Silent Majority, the disgruntled woman had seen enough marches over the years and just wanted them to stop.[13]

The next day the Spring Demonstration against Poverty, War, and Repression took place in Washington, D.C. About 200,000 demonstrators from several different organizations marched through the streets that day. However, they did not offer new rhetoric or new solutions to the same old problems. In many ways it was a typical march. SCLC, as usual, represented the movement and concentrated on the issue of poverty, and Abernathy and the mule train were back. The SCLC leader called for the government to guarantee a $6,500 income for a family of four. The folk music trio Peter, Paul, and Mary sang "Blowin' in the Wind," just as they had done at the March on Washington in 1963. Elements of the 1969 moratorium also returned—the photos of Chairman Mao, the flying of Viet Cong flags, the wearing of American flags.

SCLC also treaded familiar ground by painting the White House as villains. Mrs. King blamed both Nixon and Agnew for keeping people impoverished in order to control them. Abernathy resurrected the movement's likening of oppressed people with the Israelites. In the previous decade, activist speakers had referred to segregated African Americans as the biblical group of escapees. Now Abernathy broadened the interpretation to mean each U.S. citizen under Nixon's rule, implying that everyone in the country was a slave under the president's policies. "We've come here today to the court of Pharaoh, Richard M. Nixon," Abernathy declared, "saying to him, 'Let my people go.'"[14]

One new aspect of this march was the political diversity of the participants. The Spring Demonstration revealed that support for SCLC's causes had expanded beyond the usual suspects. Now showing public solidarity with the movement were elected officials who had supported civil rights before becoming politicians. A new representative—Bella Abzug—spoke at the rally, telling the attendees that they possessed the power to "undeclare" the Vietnam War. Vance Hartke, the lone U.S. senator in attendance at the demonstration, made an impassioned plea for immediate withdrawal from the war. "We have bled too much, committed too many horrors, and the time to get out is now," he declared. "The only way to bring our prisoners of war home is to get out now; the only way we can renew our commitment to mankind is to get out now."[15] The newest allies were, of course, the veterans themselves. The VVAW members wore their olive drab military uniforms and held toy weapons. Showing solidarity with SCLC, they also wore blue denim.

Before King's assassination, the SCLC founder had provided the most eloquent, impassioned addresses at the antiwar demonstrations the organization attended. Now, with King dead, no one in SCLC had been able to lead antiwar coalitions with oratory for the past three years. This particular day was no exception. Instead, VVAW member John Kerry stole the show with his graphic yet hopeful speech—an excerpt from remarks he had given earlier in the week to Congress. "Thirty years from now, when our brothers go down the street without an arm or a leg or a face and the children ask 'Why,' we will be able to say, 'Vietnam,'" he predicted. "And we'll mean a place where America finally turned and where soldiers like us helped in the turning."[16]

The VVAW instantly became the new stars of the antiwar set, outshining SCLC and its contemporaries. Whereas SCLC had suffered a plunge in donations after King's April 1967 antiwar speech, the VVAW experienced an influx of money and recruits. While encamped in Washington, D.C., the locals donated food to the veterans. Taxi drivers picked up hitchhiking veterans needing a ride to a nearby destination. SCLC, who witnessed the VVAW co-opting the nonviolence and marching that day with great success, was reduced to watching another organization enjoying the fruits of the movement's labor.[17]

Still, the Spring Demonstration provided a triumph of sorts for the movement. The event's success validated the nonviolence of the civil rights activists, and the VVAW contributed significantly to that validation. People who had been trained for combat demonstrated peaceably. They had the skill and the means to conduct violence but did not practice it. Although a former part of the military, they were not militant. With SNCC's Rap Brown still missing and the BPP's Huey Newton steering his followers away from the group's gun-toting imagery, the VVAW's military pacifism was replacing militant rhetoric as the newest activist fad.

The movement immediately seized upon this successful comeback of ethnically integrated nonviolent protest. The following month SCLC participated in May Day demonstrations—the largest antiwar protests since the moratorium of late 1969. Abernathy worked with longtime ally George Wiley of the National Welfare Rights Organization and with new partner Cesar Chavez of the National Farmworkers Organizing Committee to organize massive protests for the first week of May. They wanted to use nonviolent civil disobedience to mark the one-year anniversary of the killings at Kent State and Jackson State. The groups were part of a new coalition that formed for the occasion—the May Day Tribe. By organizing a follow-up protest so quickly, the Tribe stood to preserve as much momentum as possible from the Spring Demonstration. By the end of April, SCLC's mule train had returned to Washington, D.C., for a new round of activism.

The usual pattern of civil disobedience and police violence transpired over the next three days. May Day action began on May 3, with demonstrators filling the streets to pass out antiwar literature and to keep government officials from arriving at work to conduct their business. Over the next two days, the police arrested 9,000 demonstrators—2,000 on May 4 alone. On that day, activists stopped traffic between the Justice Department and Internal Revenue Service buildings. SCLC members tried to disperse the crowd and redirect people to West Potomac Park, but the activists who remained were bludgeoned by police officers' clubs. The demonstrations continued until

SCLC member William Dothard announced on May 6 that they had ended, but by then fatigue had already set in among the dissenters. "A lot of people want to go home," sighed one of them.[18]

Ironically, one of the more impactful civil rights events of the spring of 1971 was not in the streets of Washington, D.C., but rather in one of its hallowed government facilities. On April 20, in *Swann v. Charlotte-Mecklenburg*, the Supreme Court unanimously voted that busing was a legal option in facilitating the integration of schools. For schools that practiced de facto segregation, districts could legally transport children from a European American neighborhood to a school in an African American neighborhood, and vice versa. Schools would then have more diverse demographics. Busing was not a new practice, but African American children who lived close to European American schools had been driven to African American schools during the days of de jure segregation. Now, the *Swann* decision involved both groups for the purpose of stopping Jim Crow.

The *Swann* decision showed that the Supreme Court's verdict on Mississippi in 1969 was no fluke. The court was committed to desegregation, and "all deliberate speed" was not fast enough. On the other hand, the South responded to the *Swann* case the same way that it had responded to the Mississippi case—replacing cries of "Never" with compliance. The region was changing, after all. The media had extensively covered the electoral victories of "racially moderate" politicians to Southern offices in late 1970. These candidates differed from previous winners due to the absence of promises to preserve segregation. So many of these candidates won their elections that some reporters called the region below the Mason-Dixon line the "New South."

Although they did not generate much publicity during the years of the civil rights movement, sparsely populated rural towns frequently served as the birthplaces of major advancements in African American empowerment. In Fayette, Mississippi, Mayor Charles Evers symbolized the promise of the "New South" in the spring of 1971, when he won the Loyalist Party's nomination for governor of the state. He was not only the first African American to run for the office but the first candidate who was a former activist in the movement. As the first African American mayor of a Southern city since Reconstruction, he certainly knew how to win difficult elections. As with the mayoral contest, he ran for governor just to show that it could be done.

The Mississippi Sovereignty Commission kept surveillance on Mayor Evers during his gubernatorial candidacy. On April 23, Commission director Webb Burke published a report about the mayor's campaign staff, travel plans, and security concerns. Burke noted that Evers's office had received bomb threats since the gubernatorial campaign had begun earlier in the year. Three months later, Burke reported on the low turnout of people at Evers's celebration of the second anniversary of his mayoral inauguration. The mayor spent the evening recalling his administration's accomplishments and criticizing his supervisors.

The *Memphis Commercial Appeal* newspaper revealed that the commission was investigating him, but Burke immediately issued a public, untrue denial on behalf of the agency. The state was trying to save face in a "New South" climate. "This state agency does not operate along racial lines," the director lectured, "but has from time to time checked into the activities of black and white persons when their conduct appeared to be detrimental to the peace and domestic tranquility of any Mississippi community." Burke falsely claimed that the commission had not investigated any of the candidates seeking public office. He then offered another lie: "As concerns Mr. Evers, no agent of the Sovereignty Commission has ever had his activities under surveillance."[19]

Meanwhile, in Mississippi's much larger city of Jackson, William Waller also represented civil rights progress in the state. He had not been a member of the movement, but he had associated himself with it. After the shooting of NAACP–Mississippi field secretary Medgar Evers in 1963, Waller was the prosecuting attorney who tried to have Byron de la Beckwith convicted for the killing. As the Democratic Party candidate for governor, he was a far cry from the party's segregationists who had ruled the state for generations.

Mississippi's current governor John Bell Williams was part of the "Old South," serving a term that he had won in 1967. He had been a segregationist state legislator years before becoming the governor, and he never publicly repudiated the old politics. However, even he had started to display some of the attributes of the "New South" politicians as the 1970s dawned. After attending the first few Sovereignty Commission meetings of his administration, he stopped going and sent a representative instead. When the Supreme Court ordered school desegregation in Mississippi in October 1969, he chose not to continue the state's defiance of the Court's 15-year-old *Brown v. Board of Education* decision. Sounding like a minister presiding over a funeral, he counseled segregation's mourners: "Make the best of a bad situation with God's help."[20]

Jo Etha Collier was one of the first beneficiaries of the Court's 1969 decision and Mississippi's reluctant compliance. She integrated the high school in the small Delta town of Drew in the 1970–1971 academic year. She liked to smile a lot, and that year she had plenty of opportunities to smile in her new school. She was an award-winning student, the girls' track team's Most Valuable Player, and the winner of a basketball letter jacket. She capped off the year by graduating from the high school on May 25, 1971, breaking the longstanding color barrier of Drew High School's diploma-awardees. After the hour-long graduation ceremony ended that night at 8:30 p.m., Collier went downtown with her friends to go celebrate.

Also in town that night were three inebriated European American men. They were riding in a green Ford car—a vehicle whose driver the locals knew all too well. One of the occupants of the Ford was a field laborer in Drew. Inside the car with the trio were loaded weapons. As they parked outside the Billups Service Station at 9:00 p.m., an African American approached the car and asked for a cigarette light. An occupant refused by pointing a shotgun and threatening, "I'll put all your God-damned lights out."[21] The African American wisely retreated, and the green Ford left the station.

Collier was still out around town, chatting with other African American locals in front of a grocery store. At 9:45, the green Ford approached her. Then one of the occupants fired a .22 caliber pistol from the automobile. The bullet struck the high school graduate in the neck. She bled profusely at the scene and died later that night.[22]

Collier was the third African American killed by a European American in Mississippi that week. The other two fatalities were men—one at the hands of a grocer in Ecru and the other by a night watchman in Sumner. Even the Sovereignty Commission had been preparing itself for unrest that month, as people observed the one-year anniversary of the Jackson State killings. The past 12 months had not eased the suspicions of some people that those deaths and the fatalities from Kent State shared a connection of some sort. In fact, two speakers from Kent State came to Jackson State's one-year commemoration of the deaths of Phillip Gibbs and James Green. The commission was relieved to report to the state attorney general that the event had led to "no problems . . . no signs of emotionalism or unrest."[23]

Emotionalism and unrest swept through the town of Drew when Collier died, however. The acts of urban insurrection that had plagued major Northern cities in the late 1960s had now reached a small town in the Deep South. For the next two days, some local African Americans vented their frustration and grief through vandalism. They threw bricks and rocks into store windows in Drew, causing some damage. Just as some African Americans had produced unrest out of a sense of futility concerning police discrimination or brutality in the urban rebellions, now Drew's African Americans rioted after having realized that once again peaceful means for social change led to death. In addition, local authorities imposed a curfew on the town, not unlike the curfews placed on Detroit and other enflamed cities of the 1960s.

Local activists offered few solutions for the town except more of what the movement had previously done. On May 27, Cleve McDowell, a local attorney and the second African American to enroll in Ole Miss just eight years earlier, sounded like a Delta version of Ralph Abernathy. In the tradition of the SCLC, he spoke to 200 African Americans in a church, calling for a march in Drew. On the other hand, he wanted this demonstration to convey a new attitude. "We want to make it perfectly clear that in 1971 you can't shoot a black person in the street and get away with it," he warned. Not only were the politicians new in the "New South," but the confrontational response of African Americans to violence was new, too—at least, in Drew, Mississippi. McDowell then appeared to endorse nonviolent protest but with caution, just as SCLC had done after King's assassination. He explained, "We are not suggesting or endorsing violence, but we won't always be on the receiving end of it."[24]

The mayhem that had engulfed Drew subsided that day, giving way to a combination of sadness, poise, and self-determination. Three hundred African Americans marched through the downtown area for 45 minutes. Strictly in terms of size and duration, it was not a notable march. However, the mere existence of the protest in one of the state's most oppressive areas—Sunflower County—made it a triumph. It was the county of segregationist senators James Eastland and John Stennis. It was the home of former SNCC ally Fannie Lou Hamer, who had been beaten at the county courthouse nine years earlier for the offense of attempting to register to vote. Still, no violence from the European Americans or the African Americans of Drew marred the downtown march. Even the local law enforcement was impressed. Police Chief J. D. Fleming complimented McDowell, "It was mighty good. You did a nice job. . . . It was a quiet and dignified march."[25]

By the end of the month, the townspeople of Drew no longer worried as much about potential violence as negative publicity. One resident was exasperated not so much by the shooting but by its location in his town. "Hell, why did it have to happen in Drew?" he complained. "We were all getting along so well. Now everybody thinks we are at each other's throats." He had a point, because despite the town's location in violent Sunflower County, Drew had not experienced a violent death since World War II. Moreover, the incident had attracted the attention of President Nixon, who called the incident an "unnecessary tragedy."[26]

In addition, the local citizen's remarks partly reflected the "New South." In earlier times, segregationists had defended segregation by saying that they got along with "their Negroes." They had only expressed concern about outside agitators or the media coming in to stir up trouble. But by worrying that Drew would project an indigenous image of interethnic discord, the resident tacitly admitted that Collier's death and African Americans' angry responses had nothing to do with outside agitators. This time, the anger was homegrown.

Still, town officials did not take any chances about outside agitation from the movement. To try to fend off accusations of racism, Chief Fleming told reporters that Collier's killing had nothing to do with her skin color. As far as he was concerned, three men had simply driven into her neighborhood and decided to shoot someone. He concluded that if anyone else had just happened along where Collier had stood, that person would be dead instead of her. As the town braced itself for the girl's funeral, African Americans requested that it take place at the high school instead of a church. The all–European American school board of Drew reluctantly capitulated—a victory for local African Americans. Reporters were banned, however, from filming the funeral inside the church. Town officials did not want major civil rights leaders to gain political mileage from having their remarks aired on national television. As a result, no one outside of Drew High School would be able to watch SCLC president Ralph Abernathy speak—a victory for local European Americans. "In a sense, the score is even," noted the NBC news reporter Steve Delaney. Nevertheless, European Americans' control of Drew was no longer "quite so comfortable or quite so complete."[27]

Around 1,300 people—four times the number of the Drew march—made their way to Collier's funeral on May 30. For many of the attendees, the service was an occasion of déjà vu. Just as *Jet* magazine had photographed the corpse of 14-year-old lynching victim Emmett Till in his open casket in 1955, the magazine now did the same for Collier's open-casketed remains 16 years later. In the article in which the photograph eventually appeared, the magazine offered the mournful, bitter headline: "Same Old Thing, Same Old Place." Movement veterans were once again on hand to bury yet another martyr for the struggle. Charles Evers, former SNCC ally Fannie Lou Hamer, and Ralph Abernathy were among those on hand to say goodbye to Collier.[28]

"The Delta has made its way onto the map again," Abernathy preached. He asked the same questions that movement leaders had inquired at funerals for fallen comrades. "How long will black people be mistreated in Mississippi? How long will black people be shot down in the Delta?" This time, however, the hope that had fueled activists was gone. In the early 1960s, if a movement minister asked, "How long?" the congregation would reply, "Not long," because of their certainty of Jim Crow's imminent demise. Now in 1971, Abernathy's question was rhetorical. Nobody answered. They apparently did not think that "not long" was accurate anymore. Or perhaps they were silently seething, because in 1971 the question still had to be asked.[29]

Time magazine still projected hope. It portrayed the South from the viewpoint of a glass half full instead of half empty, even when considering the Collier shooting. The periodical still supported the idea that the "Old South" was gone. The high school graduate's assassination was an aberration in the otherwise progressive new direction the region was taking in terms of civil rights. At the time it was a novel way to look at the area. But as the last of the "white only" and "colored only" signs disappeared and African Americans won more elections to offices in rural counties and small towns, the viewpoint gained traction. *Time* summed up the South's transition period: "Amid the bright promise of the new South, the murder was a tragic reminder of the old."[30]

On the other hand, the killing confirmed for Hamer that the South had not changed from its "old" violent ways. She made a reference to recent shootings to prove her point. "It's a damned shame that kids were killed at Jackson State and nothing ever done, and now this," she sighed. Then echoing Abernathy, she also rhetorically asked how much longer such incidents would happen. She also took a fatalistic tone, not unlike her former SNCC colleague Stokely Carmichael after King's death. "It was Jo Etha Tuesday," she noted, "but it might be me tomorrow."[31]

Perhaps to find relief from the lingering oppression that African Americans faced in the South, SCLC conducted campaigns outside of the region. On June 19, the organization held a Solidarity Day rally in Cairo, Illinois, where a two-year-old boycott of downtown businesses was still in effect. Considering that Northern states had traditionally expressed hesitancy about SCLC's faith in nonviolence, the event was a modest success. About 1,200 people marched—an impressive number for a movement activity in 1971. Longtime ally Nina Simone sang there later that evening. The group called for the "overthrow [of] this capitalistic, racist society," which would then lead to "a just society."[32]

Despite Collier's death, some young people in the South still saw value in nonviolent civil disobedience. On September 11, a small group conducted a sit-in on a street in the rural town of Butler, Alabama. They were protesting that a school had fired four African American teachers, although the school had received orders to integrate. A European American man named Gladden Smith deliberately drove his car over one of the demonstrators—an Afro'ed 19-year-old woman named Margaret Ann Knott. She died within hours. Her last words were, "I know that I am dying, but I am dying for my freedom."[33]

Abernathy and SCLC immediately went to Butler to organize demonstrations there. One of the group's first activities in town was its participation in Knott's funeral. Once again drawing from the PPC imagery, the SCLC leader drove a mule-drawn cart that carried the body of Knott to her gravesite. On the other hand, this time the organization carried itself differently than before. Abernathy himself was increasingly pessimistic about redeeming America's soul. He was almost as fatalistic as SNCC had become after Martin Luther King's assassination in 1968. Abernathy considered Knott "one more black martyr [in] the struggle for what is right." He blamed "white racist America that preaches one thing and does another" for Knott's killing. He complained that African Americans were tired of "mean vicious white men who decide they are going to kill a nigger." To be sure, it was one of the most ethnically charged speeches he had given, but it also showed that he echoed the sentiments of *Jet* and Fannie Lou Hamer that this kind of killing meant that there was no "New South." Knott's death was still the "same old thing."[34]

On September 15, 160 marchers in Butler defied an anti-march injunction. SCLC offered support to them with its resources. The organization distracted from the issue, however, by verbally taunting the town's powers that be. Joseph Lowery, drawing from the group's history, threatened that without justice for Knott, the Alabama town of Butler will be "the Selma of the '70s."[35] He was suggesting that SCLC's marches would goad Butler's police into clubbing and trampling over demonstrators, as Selma's officers had done. However, Lowery assumed that Southern officials had not learned how to handle demonstrators without violence in the six years since Selma. He also implied that he would be able to organize masses as sizable as the crowd in Selma to submit to nonviolence and absorb that physical brutality. With the movement having become more militant by 1971, Lowery's promise would be difficult to keep. After all, only three years earlier, SCLC had announced that it would not guarantee nonviolence from every demonstrator in its marches.

Abernathy offered a similar problematic historical analogy—one that implied killing people. He warned that if the community did not follow through with the desegregation agreement that local officials had made, he would "march through Choctaw like Sherman through Georgia."[36] Considering the death and destruction that Sherman had inflicted during the Civil War, Abernathy's analogy was among the most violent statements that he had spoken in public. However, because he was still committed to SCLC's nonviolence, the threat amounted to little more than bluster.

In victory, SCLC was especially susceptible to exaggeration. By the end of the month, the organization and the local officials had brokered a resolution. The town's agreement included the rehiring of the teachers, the hiring of an African American officer to the segregated police force, the hiring of an African American deputy sheriff, the appointing of African Americans to school administration positions, and the creation of a human relations committee of diverse membership. Abernathy called the subsequent settlement between African Americans and European Americans the "greatest victory ever for SCLC."[37] The protest, which James Orange, Ben Owens, Lester Hankerson, and Willie Tabb had helped start, lasted for 15 weeks. At one point, when the jails were filled, a Jim Crow public swimming pool became a makeshift desegregated jail for the demonstrators. Still, Butler never became the movement flashpoint that Abernathy's rhetoric seemed to suggest, in contrast to such previous "victories" in Alabama as Montgomery in 1956, Birmingham in 1963, and Selma in 1965.

SCLC's involvement in Butler guaranteed that the town would be under the glare of the media spotlight but less intensely than the group's campaigns of the 1960s. As with Jo Etha Collier's killing, *Jet* magazine provided the most extensive reporting on the events in Butler. The periodical covered Knott's funeral, publishing a photograph of her remains in her casket as her parents looked on in grief. CBS News reported about the Butler demonstrations on September 13 and 15. Still, most of the media coverage concerning Knott's death resulted from SCLC having joined the protest after her killing. Even then, Abernathy's presence in Butler did not attract much of the press. Most journalists were not as interested in this story as in the previous events of the movement—including the killing of Collier four months earlier. The victim had not participated in a major newsworthy protest before her demise. She was not a symbol of "race relations," unlike Collier's distinction as having broken Drew High School's color barrier of graduates.[38]

More importantly, Knott's death was in the middle of a hostage crisis at Attica in New York, and the events there dominated the news of that week. About 1,000 inmates there held 33 prison staff hostage for four days. Their actions were in response to the death of George Jackson, the author of *Soledad Brother*, who had been shot and killed by prison officials in California the previous month. Governor Nelson Rockefeller brought in the state police to bring the standoff to an end, but 9 hostages and 29 inmates died before the police restored order to Attica. Thanks to Angela Davis's public statements while incarcerated and the popularity of *Soledad Brother*, prison reform was a major issue covered by the media in 1971. That development and the intensity of the Attica uprising naturally pushed SCLC's Butler campaign to the back pages of newspapers.

Civil rights organizations hardened against President Nixon as African American fatalities mounted and problems remained unaddressed by the administration throughout 1971. The dissolution of COINTELPRO and additional civil rights marches failed to alleviate African Americans' dire conditions. The killings at Attica showed that Southern locations such as

Drew, Mississippi, and Butler, Alabama, hardly monopolized violence against African Americans. Thus, despite the "New South" governors like Waller in Mississippi, Northern governors like Rockefeller in New York also called for brute force upon African Americans. Civil rights activists could only hope that the "law and order" White House and its supporters would soon overreach their enforcement of the law to the point of a strong national outcry.

CHAPTER 12

Run by Dictators

Despite Vice President Agnew's enduring popularity with the "Silent Majority," by mid-1971 he had also become a much-lampooned figure in national popular culture. On television, the jibes at his expense were mostly tongue in cheek. During the 1970–1971 season, *Laugh-In* often featured Barbara Sharma as a patriotically dressed tap dancer delivering backhanded odes to the vice president. She performed her routine in front of an enormous American flag and an equally large photograph of Agnew. Meanwhile, some music of the period was much less subtle. African American spoken-word artist Gil Scott-Heron made unflattering references to him in his songs "The Revolution Will Not Be Televised" and "Comment #1." Tom Lehrer's "The Ballad of Spiro Agnew" proposed to name the vice president's accomplishments but then abruptly ended without having listed any.

Like Agnew, President Nixon only spoke with movement leaders he considered responsible, but he welcomed a new figure into that exclusive group in the middle of 1971. He met with Vernon Jordan—the new leader of the NUL. The NUL was one of the few civil rights groups that Nixon still publicly respected, especially while Whitney Young had been alive. Young's successor got off to a good start with the Nixon administration, having a cordial conversation with the president. The NUL leader thanked him for speaking at Young's funeral. Jordan said that he would mention any disagreements he had with any of the president's policies, but he hoped that they could maintain communication with each other when differences arose. Nixon, in turn, promised him accessibility to the administration through domestic adviser John Ehrlichman. Shortly thereafter, Ehrlichman and Jordan began meeting periodically to play tennis and discuss policy. After only a few weeks on the job, Jordan already had the White House access that still eluded CORE, SCLC, and SNCC.[1]

Civil rights groups found their organizing work supplanted by others throughout 1971. Legislators publicly denounced Agnew's civil rights harangues, and their criticisms on the floor of the House drove Nixon to rein in the vice president. Entertainers addressed problems that only the activists had discussed, and the mainstream approval of their songs and movies brought civil rights further into the mainstream. Just as SNCC had tried to catch up with Brown's celebrity, the civil rights organizations struggled to take full advantage of the new audiences for their issues.

Throughout the year Nixon did not use Agnew as the administration's megaphone nearly as often as before. The vice president, as a result, became a victim of his success in putting down the movement. The absence of high-profile civil rights demonstrations left him without a target to attack. Even the antiwar demonstrations did not happen as often, nor were they as populated. In addition, the president did not trust the vice president as much as before. Agnew's efforts at helping Republican candidates in the 1970 elections had fallen far short of expectations, and he was on a tight leash anyway after his disastrous campaign to have Joseph Rhodes Jr. removed from the Commission on Campus Unrest.

Nixon loosened the leash enough to permit Agnew to travel to Asia, Africa, and Europe on official business in July. Once again, the president appointed Bryce Harlow to monitor the vice president. After having visited Ethiopia, Kenya, and the Congo, Agnew talked to reporters on July 17 as his plane headed to Spain. He used the words "dedicated," "enlightened," and "dynamic" to gush about the African leaders he had met.[2] He liked how they related to the rest of the world, and he considered them capable of solving their problems. The vice president's remarks about the continent were some of the most complimentary to have come from any presidential administration in years.

Agnew, however, then curiously diverted to Pan-Africanism. While praising African heads of state, he took an opportunity to juxtapose them positively against the African American movement leaders he had long abhorred. He noted that the quality of African leadership contrasted sharply with "many of those in the United States who have arrogated unto themselves the position of black leaders." Unlike the Africans who could solve their own problems, African American leaders merely "spend their time in querulous complaint and consistent recriminations against the state of society." Reverting to his 1968 role of counseling the movement on how to behave, the vice president suggested, "The black leadership in the United States, not all but most of it, could learn much by observing the work that has been done in these countries by people like Haile Selassie, his Prime Minister, President Jomo Kenyatta, and his distinguished ministers, and of course President Mobutu and President of the National Assembly Bo-Boliko." At the time he made his remarks, public officials rarely took public swipes at the movement anymore. Consequently, he went against Nixon's policy of "benign neglect."[3]

On July 21, Representative Charles Diggs, an African American representing Michigan, brought Agnew's remarks to the attention of his colleagues in the House of Representatives. He considered the vice president's statement a direct contrast to the president's recent words of encouragement to Diggs and his African American colleagues. The Congressional Black Caucus (CBC) had formed earlier in the year to focus on issues concerning African Americans, and Nixon said that he understood why the caucus existed. "Black people in America have not received a fair shake in America," the president had told the CBC in his first meeting with the group. "If I were you, I would be on the other side of the table pleading this case."[4] Diggs called on Nixon to clarify as to whether Agnew spoke for the White House.

The representatives who responded to Diggs's remarks in session agreed with him. Each of them repeated his request to the president. Some of them tried to make sense out of Agnew's harangue. Charles Rangel of New York thought that the vice president had spoken spontaneously and had been "thinking out loud." John Conyers of Michigan declared, "Mr. Agnew is to be pitied." They accused the vice president of fostering divisiveness among Americans, especially on the basis of skin color. Both European American and African American representatives criticized him. They expressed emotions ranging from frustration to embarrassment, as when Ed Koch of New York complained, "Mr. Speaker, the Vice President makes me feel so ashamed at times."[5]

In the process of rebuking Agnew, the House validated the work of the movement. Rangel echoed Rap Brown's associating of the government with Nazis when saying, "It seems inappropriate that the President's alter ego should incite domestic discord by stomping and storm-trooping over our black leaders at home." Ogden Reid of New York mentioned specific current leaders with pride. He noted, "I have had the privilege of working closely with Rev. Abernathy, Roy Wilkins, George Wiley, Whitney Young, and the late Martin Luther King as well as Jesse Jackson and others to secure economic, social and political rights for all Americans." He also acknowledged the difficulty and continued necessity of the movement's work, saying that "the fight has not been an easy one and is not yet won."[6]

James Abourezk of South Dakota employed a current movement tactic in his criticism of the vice president. He illustrated Agnew as a villain of the activists, just as SCLC and SNCC were doing. Moreover, Abourezk specifically compared the vice president with the segregationist Southern officials that the freedom fighters had formerly portrayed as their antagonists. "If he were not in the high office of the Vice President of the United States, his remarks about everybody, including the black leaders of this country, would be taken as nothing more than the bad-mouthing of a redneck," he surmised before politely adding, "if I may be permitted to compare him to a redneck."[7] The ad hominem attacks from the likes of Brown and Abernathy had risen to the highest levels in the federal government.

Of all the comments from the representatives, only those from William Clay of Missouri immediately made national news. He thought it was crazy of the vice president to make the Pan-African comparison, and he said as much to his colleagues. He had started in a low-key but pointed manner, cautioning Agnew against celebrating authoritarian regimes of the worst order. "Does the Vice President want us to emulate nations such as Russia, Yugoslavia, or Spain—run by dictators—where a No. 2 man is expendable?" he rhetorically asked. But then Clay intensified his rhetoric with barbs about Agnew's mental state on the House floor, "In my opinion, Mr. Speaker, our Vice President is seriously ill. He has all the symptoms of an intellectual misfit." He also referred to the vice president as "this buffoon." Then turning to crude sexual metaphor, Clay broke new ground in anti-Agnew rhetoric by lamenting, "His recent tirade against black leadership is just part of a game played by him—called mental masturbation. Apparently Mr. Agnew is an intellectual sadist who experiences intellectual orgasms by attacking, humiliating, and kicking the oppressed."

After Clay finished, Diggs gave a pithy yet supportive reply: "I thank the gentleman from Missouri for his constructive criticism."[8]

This exchange was too much for House minority leader Gerald Ford. The next day he complained to the House about Clay's complaint of Agnew. "I have never before heard such language in the House," Ford fumed. He claimed that Clay had violated House rules with the words he had chosen to personally attack Agnew. "It seems to me," Ford concluded, "that the gentleman from Missouri, for having used that language, owes an apology to the House and an apology to the Vice President."[9]

Ford's tactic did not work, however, and Clay instead stood by his statement. He was prepared to go the distance. He had once spent 116 days in jail because he had disobeyed a court order and refused to apologize to a St. Louis judge he had considered racist. "I have no intention of apologizing to Vice President Agnew," the congressman announced. After three years of the vice president's remarks against African Americans, Clay had had enough. "Agnew owes an apology to every Black leader in the country," he declared. He then applied his controversial comments to the minority leader, claiming that "Gerald Ford suffers from the same illness Agnew suffers from." He then repeated a joke that he had heard from former president Lyndon Johnson. "Part of his problem," Clay diagnosed of Ford, "is that he played football in college without a helmet."[10]

Ironically, the movement offered the most muted criticism. Taking a cue from Joseph Rhodes, Abernathy avoided attacking the vice president in a defensive manner. In fact, when responding to Agnew's remarks, the SCLC president did not even mention his feelings about the vice president's opinion of the movement. Rather, Abernathy said that in addition to African American leaders being more like African ones, Agnew himself could learn from the examples from the continent's dark-skinned leaders. As usual, Abernathy saw his public condemnation of the vice president as another opportunity to highlight the problems of poverty and income inequality. "It is my hope," he stated, "that as the number-two chief executive, he will have learned human decency, the right of all citizens to participate in a democratic society and the right of all citizens to be fed, properly housed, adequately educated and employed, from the leaders of the nations with whom he has visited."[11]

In a complete reversal of 1968, Nixon himself was impressed by the restraint of the movement's spokesmen while frustrated by his vice president's explosive rhetoric. He told John Ehrlichman how glad he was that Roy Wilkins had just begun to publicly to favor cooperation with the administration. As the vice president's comments made the rounds of the delegates of the NAACP convention, they responded with remorse for Nixon. They felt sorry for him having an "albatross" like Agnew around his neck, bringing his stature down. Nixon considered the NAACP's stance "more effective than if they had been strident about it."[12]

In contrast, he did not understand why Agnew felt the need to criticize African American leaders. The vice president should have stopped at his praise of African leaders. If he had to make any comparisons, he should have merely suggested that African Americans had a right to be proud of their African heritage. Moreover, whom exactly was Agnew trying to impress? He was not going to add to the administration's small percentage of African American support, and no other constituency genuinely cared about how much better Agnew thought African leaders were than African American ones.

Months later, Vice President Agnew found ways to tie the Attica uprising in with the movement. Instead of an anti-dissent stump speech or press conference, he took to the pen. Writing a special column for The *New York Times* on September 17, he offered the argument that perhaps the Silent Majority had grown too silent. Three years earlier he had made the same point while lashing out at civil rights activists in Baltimore, and his tirade there had helped him become Nixon's running mate. Now he was working hard to secure his second GOP nomination to the vice presidency in 1972. "What happened in Attica proves once again that when the responsible voices of society remain mute, the forces of violence and crime grow arrogant," he preached. The fact that a BPP member served as a negotiator and intended to call for uncompromised demands on behalf of the convicts provided the grounds for Agnew to resurrect his grievances against the movement, specifically SCLC. He recited one-year-old quotes from the organization's leaders, in which they had announced their support of the BPP. He called one of them a "heretofore responsible Negro leader."[13]

After associating the Attica riot with SCLC's support of the BPP, Agnew concluded his column by borrowing a tactic from his nemesis H. Rap Brown. In a variation of the SNCC leader's equating of African American repression with the Holocaust, the vice president claimed instead that the Attica disturbance exemplified Nazism. "One need only recall the era of Hitler's Storm Troopers to realize what can happen to the most civilized of societies when such a cloak of respectability is provided thugs and criminals," he warned. Flipping one of Brown's catchphrases on its head, Agnew was apparently threatening that if mostly African American radicals were going to play Nazis, the vice president was not going to play Jews.[14]

The column provided Agnew with a much-needed opportunity to prove his relevance to the Nixon administration. At the time the president was still seriously considering replacing him with John Connally as a running mate. Nixon, in fact, privately told the Texas Democrat that he was his choice to succeed him. In addition, Nixon continued to limit his vice president's speaking engagements. On the other hand, as much as Nixon and his inner circle shut out Agnew, he was still the vice president. He was still a popular public, political figure. In addition, although he was the most powerful critic of The New York Times, he was also very newsworthy. With the press at his disposal and the public ready to read his views, Agnew made the most of his opportunity by resorting to what had lifted him to the vice presidency in the first place—publicly criticizing the movement.[15]

Agnew's comments stirred the anger of one of his most prominent critics— Joseph Rhodes. In his own special column five days later, he sharply criticized the vice president's column. Now that Rhodes no longer worked for the Nixon administration, he did not need to mince his words about the second in command. Using Agnew's tactic of quoting from speeches to make a point, Rhodes argued that the Attica remarks provided the rationale behind Agnew's speech about African leaders from last May. To Rhodes, both addresses exemplified the vice president's "detachment from the reality that is the common experience of millions of impoverished and helpless Americans." On Agnew's specific complaints about Attica, Rhodes facetiously observed, "Nothing infuriates our Vice President more than all the fuss over the deaths of the black prisoners." He could not believe that "Mr. Agnew holds the black leadership of America responsible for the violence at Attica." He reminded the vice president that convicts were people, too. He wrote that police officers and guardsmen could be prone to violence. He ended his column with a corrective on Agnew's depiction of Nazism that simultaneously damned the vice president's intolerance for dissent. Rhodes observed, "The 'storm troopers' were not criminals in prisons; they were officers of the law and carried out their horror under the 'civilized rationale' of upholding law and order."[16]

The first and second in command in the White House were now humiliating each other in their dealings with the movement. Agnew's statements about civil rights leaders became a liability for the Nixon administration, whereas only three years ago they had helped him earn enough favor from Nixon to become his running mate. The media picked up on Nixon's dissatisfaction and reported on it, causing embarrassment to the vice president. Agnew had taken the slack Nixon had given him on the leash and had hung himself with it.

The lack of response among civil rights groups to Agnew's antics was part of a larger problem of the movement's invisibility throughout much of 1971. The activists offered little for the public aside from local-level protests, an antiwar march, and sporadic television appearances. Some people in the media cared about the fate of the movement but wanted to move beyond the usual faces of Wilkins and Abernathy and find a fresh face for civil rights. Reporter Ralph Novak tried to generate excitement about SCLC by focusing on one of its national officers. "At 29 Jesse Jackson is heir apparent to Dr. Martin Luther King Jr. as the leader of America's blacks," he proclaimed. It was true, Novak acknowledged, that Abernathy was higher than Jackson in SCLC's hierarchy, but that fact did not take away from the reporter's point. Jackson, after all, had the clout to call a meeting of African American elected officials, which resulted in serious discussions among them about the formation of an independent political party. "There is only one man who could have gathered all of these leaders here," said Mayor Carl Stokes of Cleveland. "That man is Jesse Jackson."[17]

The drive to bring new faces into the movement limelight reflected that many public figures, especially African American musicians, were incorporating civil rights themes into their art. The year 1971 was a watershed time in rhythm and blues, when the movement's influence upon commercial recording artists peaked. Several songs in recent years had either reported generic instances of poverty and violence or had issued calls for peace, love, and brotherhood. In 1971, however, the lyrics became more detailed. Instead of lamenting war, the title of Freda Payne's song pleaded, "Bring the Boys Home." Promoting the idea of a New South, the Staple Singers' song "Respect Yourself" contained a call for a Klansman to remove the sheet from his face because a new era had dawned. Also, some songs quoted directly, if superficially, from the movement. From the Chi-Lites, the hit "For God's Sake" had a subtitle straight from the BPP: "Give More Power to the People." James Brown offered the song "Soul Power"—SCLC's three-year-old catchphrase—but his song used the slogan more as a euphemism for sex than for political organizing. The songs crossed over to become pop hits that year, showing that the movement's issues had become more palatable for commercial consumption, even as lyrics had grown more militant.

Popular music had never been this vocal about the issues of the movement. The acceptance of musical criticism by African American voices meant that the public could tolerate dissent if it entertained people, too. Perhaps the downslide of the movement had made the music safe; after all, BPP chapters were closing, and SCLC and SNCC had long lost media attention. Then again, more people were against the Vietnam War, wanting the removal of U.S. troops instead of a prolonged campaign to victory. The publication of the Pentagon Papers added to the public's frustration by the war.

Even H. Rap Brown's popularizing of the image of the African American fugitive from justice received a glossy treatment from Hollywood. In Melvin Van Peebles's film *Sweet Sweetback's Baadasssss Song*, an African American man named Sweetback ran away after having killed several European American police officers. Along his sojourn he engaged in sexual intercourse with multiple women of different skin colors. He wore a bushy Afro and a droopy mustache, just like the former SNCC chairman. The movie was a hit, but not everyone approved of its stylized, sexualized militancy. Lerone Bennett of *Ebony* magazine reminded his readers that "nobody ever f***ed his way to freedom."[18]

Sweet Sweetback's Baadasssss Song was a product of the movement aside from the fictionalizing of the militant fugitive. SCLC supporter Bill Cosby loaned Van Peebles $50,000 to make the picture. Fictional Black Panthers appeared in the movie, and BPP leader Huey Newton heavily promoted the feature upon its release. Also, in a celebratory twist to the BPP's catchphrase "Off the pig," the movie allowed its protagonist to kill policemen without suffering any legal consequences. In addition, Brown's rhetoric shaped the film's ending. Upon Sweetback's successful escape from the United States, the closing title read, "A Baadasssss Nigger Is Coming to Collect Some Dues." The former SNCC chairman had called for collecting "dues" through violence back in July 1967 in Cambridge, Maryland.[19]

By the summer of 1971, militant posturing had become an integral part of the movement. At the NAACP's annual convention, the organization repeated its opposition to the Vietnam War. The group boldly expressed dismay at the federal government's "duplicity and misinformation" on the war, "as exposed in recent newspaper articles" such as the revelation of the Pentagon Papers.[20] In addition, this time the organization did not qualify its antiwar stance by claiming to be a civil rights organization first. The omission suggested that the NAACP had finally embraced King's uniting of civil rights with the antiwar cause.

That same summer the First Lady of the movement declared her individual support of an imprisoned African American female Communist. On June 4, Coretta Scott King observed, "Increasingly in recent years the basic American legal tradition that a person charged with a crime is presumed innocent has come under diverse forms of attack, especially for black people." She hinted that such a fate may have befallen Angela Davis. Unlike Abernathy, Mrs. King did not make a judgment on the case itself. In addition, she acknowledged, "I have clear differences politically with Miss Davis." However, she believed that Davis deserved "bail and a fair defense" for her case. "If her Blackness, her womanhood and her politics are being judged," Mrs. King warned, "then all Americans will lose some of their liberties along with her."[21]

Mrs. King's statement on Davis was especially significant. Abernathy had spoken in favor of Davis first, but he was constantly aligning himself and SCLC with radicals who were media magnets. In contrast, Mrs. King was already a beloved popular figure and had nothing to gain from advocating for the prisoner. The widow's extension of goodwill meant that members of the movement's old guard were more willing to associate themselves with the new guard.

Nevertheless, some of the defiant posturing by middle-aged African American civil rights leaders was superficial. Whether they were trying to be fashionable or had truly embraced new ways of discussing struggle, the impact of SNCC and other younger activists on them was clear. The self-pride that Wilkins credited the "youngsters" for giving to the elders was now in full bloom. An increasing number of longtime civil rights veterans, like Mrs. King, started identifying themselves as either "black" or "Afro-American" instead of "Negro." Ralph Abernathy, at age 45, was beginning to grow out his "natural." In August, at SCLC's annual convention, 58-year-old Rosa Parks—the woman who had refused to give up her bus seat in Montgomery in 1955—gave the Black Power salute while on stage.[22]

SNCC, meanwhile, was keeping a relatively low profile, largely by relocating to the South. Despite its shrinking numbers, the organization's associates felt that expansion beyond New York, Atlanta, and Cincinnati would revitalize the group. SNCC–New York's Muhammad Hunt and the Atlanta cadre's William La Trane initially went to Chicago to start a new chapter there in the spring of 1971. As the month of May came to a close, Hunt tried starting more chapters in Tulsa, Trenton, and Gainesville while revitalizing the group's presence in San Antonio, Baltimore, and Washington, D.C. Only those in Tulsa and San Antonio yielded positive results.[23]

The San Antonio cadre did not need much encouragement from Hunt to stay active. Although the branch had maintained very little contact with the national office, it remained a vibrant part of the national organization. Even throughout the disarray caused first by Brown's takeover and then by his disappearance, Mario Salas and Carlos Richardson—SNCC–San Antonio's cofounders in 1968—remained involved in coordinating demonstrations there. Their stability ultimately paid off. By 1971, SNCC–San Antonio was as active as its major counterparts in New York and Atlanta. In fact, it recruited participation from college students, a demographic that the national organization sorely lacked at the time.

Ironically, the New York branch inadvertently demonstrated most dramatically how far SNCC had strayed from its former self. George "Fidel" Love started the Revolutionary Youth Organization—SNCC's youth program. His task was to organize high school dropouts and any students up to age 22. These young adults would then become SNCC's youth faction—a division the group had not previously needed. When SNCC had begun in 1960, young adults up to age 22 had comprised the organization's participants. Eleven years later, the group now consisted of people in their late twenties or their thirties, and most of the members were not students. Indeed, the missing H. Rap Brown turned 28 in 1971 and had not been enrolled at a school at the time of his disappearance. Moreover, by trying to draw in young people and factionalize them, the older people in SNCC were doing what Ella Baker had accused the NAACP and SCLC of trying to do with the original SNCC students.[24]

However, current SNCC members in New York continued to make major headlines only when working on outside campaigns. The organization's female participants busied themselves with projects concerning African American feminism and criminal justice. For a project in the fall of 1971, they capitalized on the notoriety of one of their alumni. Through the TWWA, they sponsored and organized Angela Davis Day—an afternoon rally scheduled for September 25 in Central Park. Calling themselves the United Coalition for Angela Davis Day, they advertised the event in the *Village Voice* as a call to "demand bail for Angela" and "indict Rockefeller for the Attica Massacre." They attracted major civil rights activists to their program, showing that they were on a par with the strongest movement groups. Ossie Davis and Dick Gregory, both of whom had demonstrated with King, spoke at the event, as did Representative Ron Dellums. "Fight racism and oppression," the advertisement demanded. "Get it together at Central Park Mall."[25]

Three days after the rally, SNCC–New York associate Fran Beal kept up the momentum from the event. She was part of a group of people giving a press conference to announce a national collective demonstration against U.S. prison conditions on October 2. New York's Harrisburg Defense Committee coordinated the protests, and the TWWA was a cosponsor. As with Angela Davis Day, the SNCC women once again had the clout to provide nationally known activists like the Chicago Eight's Tom Hayden and David Dellinger to serve as speakers. When the scheduled day arrived, the protests took place all across the country as planned. Demonstrations were in the West (California's San Quentin Prison), the Midwest (Chicago's Cook County Jail; Kansas City, Missouri; Sandstone, Minnesota); the South (Texas's Bexar Travis and Dallas County Jails), and the East (Vermont's Windsor State Prison and Danbury, Connecticut's Federal Correctional Institute). Over 1,000 people participated in Danbury alone.[26]

As much as SNCC tried to do to highlight present concerns, the group's past continued to haunt it. In the early morning hours of October 16, New York City police officers responded to a tip about a robbery at the Red Carpet—a bar of mostly African American customers. Twenty-five of the customers had reportedly just been forced at gunpoint to lie on the floor and remove their valuables. After the patrolmen arrived at the bar, four African American men left the building. Three of them were former SNCC associates: Sam Petty, Arthur Lee Young, and Levi Valentine; Petty had come into SNCC through the organization's alliance in late 1968 with the NBLs. As the men fled the scene, bullets flew toward the officers. The policemen fired back and chased the fugitives into a nearby apartment building. The officers arrested three of the runaways there.

Patrolman Ralph Mannetta ran after the fourth person still at large, considering him an armed threat. The policeman went to the roof of the building and found the runaway. The officer then immediately shot the culprit twice in the stomach, and the wounded man fell to the floor of the roof. According to Mannetta, a .357 Magnum, a fully loaded carbine clip, a bandoleer with 24 bullets inside, and a loaded banana clip were near the fallen casualty. The police then took the runaway to Roosevelt Hospital to allow him to recover from his wounds.

By dawn, Mannetta was back at the police station. A detective asked him in a whisper, "Do you know whom you shot?"

"No," the officer replied.

The detective revealed that the Red Carpet patrons had identified the man. "They say it's H. Rap Brown," he disclosed.[27]

Mannetta spent the rest of the dawn trying to remember who Brown was. Only later that morning at a press conference did he learn that he had just caught one of the FBI's Most Wanted. By that morning Brown had been in hiding for 19 months. Authorities identified Brown by his fingerprints. His wife was contacted, and she went immediately to visit him at the hospital.

The shooting was only the latest of a yearlong chain of tragedies for Lynne Doswell. In the previous October, she had returned from Tanzania, and the FBI temporarily detained her at the airport. COINTELPRO had not targeted her as much as it had monitored her husband and other SNCC members. On the other hand, Angela Davis had just been arrested that month, and Doswell not only had worked in SNCC during Davis's tenure in the group but also was married to one of the bureau's most wanted. For months afterward, Hoover's men maintained relentless contact with her parents— hounding them at their respective jobs. She thought that the bureau had flattened the tires of her father's car the following February and that he died within days of some kind of poisoning by the agency.

Over the next several months, Doswell's suffering came full circle. In March 1971, Brown's mother died, and her condolence letter to Doswell's mother arrived posthumously. Later that spring, Mrs. Doswell's own health deteriorated, and she succumbed to an aneurysm in June. Now, in October, an orphaned Lynne Doswell stood at the bedside of her wounded husband on the same floor of the same hospital where her mother had spent the last three months of her life. Moreover, the former SNCC chairman was now a prisoner of the same agency that had detained his wife at the airport 12 months earlier.[28]

Within days of Brown's shooting, The *New York Times* published a sketch that was eerily reminiscent of the courtroom drawing of the bound and gagged BPP member Bobby Seale. This time, the picture was of a sickly, vulnerable Brown. The drawing depicted him lying in his hospital bed. His head was shaven, he was emaciated, and he breathed through a plastic tube inserted in his nose. The image was a far cry from the typical photograph of him as Afro'ed, denim clad, and standing erect with a finger of indictment extended against "white America" while speaking to a crowd.

Also unusual was the company at Brown's bedside that day. A criminal court judge arraigned him on his sickbed. Lynne and her brother-in-law Sam were in the room watching the arraignment. The judge did not allow the *Times* to photograph Brown, but he did permit a sketch of the fugitive's arraignment at the hospital.[29]

Twelve months after the arrest of Angela Davis, Brown's capture ended the "fugitive era" of the movement. Although his physical appearance had started to change during his hospitalization, he continued to transform himself behind bars as if marking the end of that era. Shortly after his incarceration began, he started to shed some of the persona that had contributed to his popularity. He converted to Islam, and he changed his name to Jamil Abdullah Al-Amin. He became more reclusive as well. Unlike the letters he had written during his incarcerations in 1967 and 1968, he wrote nothing for his followers now.

Journalists, however, did not seem to miss him. Brown had only aroused media interest as long as he was a hunted man. Once captured, reporters only paid attention to him when he appeared in court. Now that he was less of a firebrand and did not give explosive statements from prison, the press had less incentive to report about him. Concerning his personal transformation, the news outlets hardly mentioned the conversion and continued to identify him as H. Rap Brown. Exhibiting some lack of fight after becoming detained, he did not bother to correct anyone who called him by his old name.

His arrest left people, especially his supporters, completely disillusioned. To some people, the firebrand who talked about revolution and burning America down did not seem like the kind of person to rob a bar. Holdups of taverns were not part of "the revolution." It was such an ordinary, common fate, and it seemed beneath Brown to have to experience it. To others, he was yet another militant who had tried to outwit governmental oppressors and had even seemed successful in doing so. For still others, the robbery simply represented Brown's criminality, as did his "violent" speeches. Vice President Agnew's dream had finally at least partly come true; his adversary was locked up. The subsequent trials for the multiple charges he had accumulated since July 1967 would determine whether the judicial system would throw away the key.

Authorities transferred Brown to Bellevue Hospital Prison Ward later that fall. As his robbery trial began, the activist only saw his hospital room and a courtroom. On the day he entered his plea of "not guilty," he left the hospital to limp into the Manhattan Supreme Court. He was still gaunt and sickly, but the dozens of supporters in the courtroom praised him with cheers, anyway. They had not seen him in 21 months, after all. After he finished, he returned to Bellevue and lay back on his sickbed, awaiting his legal and physical fates.[30]

Meanwhile, SNCC's legacy received a much-needed boost beyond the confines of Brown's prison walls. The organization was able to indirectly claim electoral victories that fall. On November 2, the state of Mississippi elected William Waller the new governor. Like his "New South" predecessors, he wanted to revise the region's image. He also wanted to change how the state operated by eliminating traditions that were holdovers of segregation. As a result, he championed within the system some revisions that civil rights activists had long sought from the outside. He prioritized the dismantling of the Sovereignty Commission, of which he saw no use. He sought to desegregate various state government entities. He even preferred replacing the adopted segregationist anthem of "Dixie" for another, more inclusive song during official functions like his inauguration. His victory, as well as Charles Evers's respectable showing, demonstrated that the African American vote had won more respect from state politicians. Organizations like SNCC had gone into Mississippi in 1964 for Freedom Summer to encourage African Americans to exercise political power, and the group's efforts planted the seeds for the electoral fortunes of Wallace and Evers in 1971.

SCLC spent the last months of 1971 engaged in outreach activities. Jesse Jackson facilitated the Black Expo—a major gathering of African American entrepreneurs and entertainers—in Chicago that October, and he invited a possible presidential candidate for the next year's election to speak. Congresswoman Shirley Chisholm, an African American representing New York since 1969, promoted ideas more similar to the TWWA than to SCLC in her Expo address. She made some frank remarks about her candidacy and her life as an African American female politician. She revealed that she suffered sexism from not only European American men but also African American men, and she chalked up the refusal of African American male politicians to endorse her as a matter of jealousy on their part. To her, their male egos were wounded because she had not consulted them before considering her campaign. She warned African American women interested in politics to prepare themselves to face sexism as well as racism. She had a point; in recent weeks, African American men were publicly saying that the first serious African American presidential bid should have come from a man and that she was a "little black matriarch . . . messing things up."[31]

Jackson also invited Wilkins to the expo in order to give him a prize for his work. In keeping with SCLC's incessant memorializing of its founder, the group named the tribute the "Martin Luther King, Jr. Award." Jackson cited the NAACP leader's compliment of King as one who "always kept his hands on the plow," and he respected Wilkins's willingness to praise a leader from another civil rights group. Wilkins graciously accepted the award, glossing over the group's well-known spats with SCLC over Black Power and Vietnam. "There has never been any conflict in our organization with SCLC," he stated. "We're both working for the cause of freedom." Wilkins's presence there not only connected the NAACP to SCLC once again but also brought two civil rights generations together. His attendance at Jackson's event, moreover, spoke highly of the SCLC official's ability to draw prominent leaders to him.[32]

Meanwhile, Abernathy returned from a two-week trip abroad that same month. Having just won a hard-earned victory in Butler, he attempted to enhance SCLC's global image by visiting several countries in Eastern Europe. Although they were Communist countries, the SCLC leader marveled at the religious freedom that the people there were able to experience. He announced that the Communists made him feel like a human being. Considering the demonstrations he had conducted to protest the brutal killings of unarmed teenaged African American girls earlier that year, it was natural for him to feel relief from that in places where he did not see people dying because of their skin color.

For many people, Abernathy's remarks sounded treasonous. By implying that Communists treated African Americans better than the United States did, he was aligning himself further with the most leftists of radicals. Even as King had grown despondent over the Vietnam War and urban disturbances in his last months, he had still held out hope that the United States would live up to its promises. "All we say to America is that you be true to what you said on paper," he had intoned in his final speech.[33] On the other hand, in that same speech King had compared Memphis's injunction against a second march to the actions a totalitarian regime would have undertaken. Still, he had not gone to Abernathy's extent to hint that totalitarianism would be better for African Americans.

Despite the backlash against Abernathy's remarks, the organization saw tremendous value in reaching out to Communist countries. Between July and November, Hosea Williams and his wife embarked on a global excursion to several African and Asian countries. Abernathy's duties as the SCLC leader kept him from extensively traveling, so he asked Williams to represent the organization for the Brotherhood Trip of SCLC. One of the places Williams visited was China, where Nixon was trying to strengthen commercial and diplomatic ties. In June, one month before the president announced an impending trip to the country, Abernathy wrote a letter for Williams to deliver to Chairman Mao. The SCLC leader said that he saw Williams's trip to China as part of the organization's efforts to establish global dialogue with people of African descent and poor people. In a sense he was making the PPC an international program. Just as SNCC had tried to cultivate a global political struggle in the late 1960s, SCLC was now launching a worldwide antipoverty campaign. "Third World Peoples must unite," he wrote to Mao.

Williams arrived in China on September 19, and he spent three weeks there. He promised to give the chairman a documentary film about King and talk to the nation's leaders about "the struggle to liberate black people in America." He believed that the Chinese had strengths and values that African Americans sorely lacked. "We wish to learn about the origin and environment of the Chinese cultural revolution. We are interested in how the Chinese developed leaders and followers," he announced to reporters. "We want to study how the Chinese develop individual self-pride, self-respect, and how they developed mass participation of the bureaucrats and laboring people." He expressed hope that when Nixon visited China, the president would talk to the country's leaders about similar issues.[34]

Williams's trek to China opened up new opportunities for SCLC to attract the American media. He invited newspaper editors to publish his weekly columns about his Brotherhood Trip, and they accepted. Moses J. Newson, the head of the organization Afro-American Newspapers, had been trying to secure a weekly column of any sort from SCLC for years without success. The leaders of the NAACP and the NUL already wrote weekly columns, and Newson hoped that Williams's foreign reports would lead to further weekly entries from SCLC after the activist returned stateside. For all of the group's complaints about news organizations neglecting to cover the movement, Newson's letter was a reminder that SCLC's lack of publicity was partially self-inflicted.

On October 5, Premier Chou En-lai hosted a party for more than 70 people. The Williamses attended, as did several other American visitors to the country. The politics of the minority invitees was wide in range. Representatives of militant groups and street gangs joined the nonviolent Williams at the gathering. Pablo Guzman of the Young Lords and the Black Panthers Huey Newton, Elaine Brown, and Robert Bay partied with the SCLC official. The event demonstrated that China was not as restrictive in its visitation ban against U.S. citizens as before. It also showed that SCLC was more willing than ever to openly socialize with militants, gang members, and Communists.[35]

Ironically, by considering China a model, SCLC indirectly followed Agnew's suggestion that civil rights leaders run their groups like Communist dictators. When Williams left China to tour other countries, he concluded that the movement stood to benefit greatly from the Chinese. He realized that civil rights activists had made "many mistakes" while struggling for freedom. He considered current activism too rigid to produce significant social change. "In the civil rights movement, we just did not shift to enough strategies," he admitted. "We found a good thing—marching in the street—and we continued to march." He marveled at how Chairman Mao was "fluid enough to shift to new strategies" to stay one step ahead of opposition. SCLC and the movement needed to be fluid now, too.[36]

The China trip also provided the organization with prime-time television exposure for the first time since Coretta Scott King had visited *The Ed Sullivan Show* over one year earlier. In late November 1971, CBS aired an episode of the news program *60 Minutes*, in which Hosea Williams talked about his visit to China. He stated that he was there to talk to the Chinese about nonviolence and Christianity. The broadcast raised little controversy, and no more opportunities for prime-time television exposure were immediately forthcoming after the episode. But many people had written congratulatory letters to Williams and described the trip as a major political development for African Americans.[37]

When Williams returned to the United States a few weeks later, he asked to meet with President Nixon to discuss the trip. The activist believed that he had information that Nixon should know when visiting China. "We feel certain that America, the world and the cause of peace would benefit if you would allow us to share our findings with you," he wrote. The president, however, disagreed with SCLC's sense of self-importance. Nixon did not seek the movement's advice on civil rights and certainly had little inclination to request its insight on foreign relations. Moreover, the president did not want to meet with SCLC. He had already tried that at the White House in May 1969, but had received insults from Abernathy at a press conference after their meeting. Nixon never met with Williams.[38]

On the other hand, SCLC did yield a significant accomplishment as Williams wrapped up his trip. Thanks in part to the organization's efforts, the people of Sandersville elected three African Americans to the city council on December 6. The win was a long time in coming. SCLC had conducted voter registration campaigning there for the past two years. Coming on the heels of Walter Fauntroy's entrance into Congress, SCLC's accomplishment in Sandersville illustrated that programs about voting could produce tangible results. On the other hand, calling attention to poverty only made the poor more visible but not less poor. Electoral power was giving the organization more success than PPC street demonstrations had yielded in recent years.

With victories in Butler and Sandersville, Abernathy was now able to claim two more fruitful SCLC campaigns that had started during his presidency. The projects received little publicity, and the organization was unable to take the limelight from Brown's capture or Davis's trial. On the other hand, SCLC was now able to use its small political victories to gradually restore its reputation as a significant force in the movement. The group certainly did not need to jeopardize its resurrection by trying a new national recruiting project. Its recent track record of disorganized encampments, toothless anti-moon marches, and controversial global missions was not encouraging toward such an event.[39]

The movement, as a whole, was not faring much better by the end of 1971. President Nixon vetoed a child development bill that civil rights leaders had supported. Wilkins, Jordan, Abernathy, and five other activists sent him a letter, urging him to sign it, but the president did not budge. As Nixon's reelection campaign lay ahead the next year, the civil rights groups struggled to balance their collective commitment to avoid political endorsements with their frustration with the incumbent's inaction on their issues. Some groups would succeed better than others.[40]

CHAPTER 13

Explode All over the Landscape

Shirley Chisholm, a former schoolteacher, had only served the Brooklyn district of New York as its congresswoman for four years before announcing her candidacy for president of the United States in 1972. Her ethnicity and gender made her an unlikely choice; no African American woman had previously run for the office. On the other hand, no African American woman had served in Congress before she ran for the office. She doomed her candidacy for the highest office, however, by primarily courting African American votes and by failing to generate support from the major civil rights organizations.

The NAACP refused to support her because the organization saw her candidacy as separatist. Bayard Rustin claimed that "black voters were asked to support Mrs. Chisholm precisely because she was black." He acknowledged that she did not preach separatism on the campaign trail, and he noted that the NAACP did not repudiate her as a person. Still, her "campaign predicated on consciousness-raising" did not sit well with the organization. Moreover, for all her work in attracting African American voters, they only significantly turned out for her in North Carolina.[1]

SCLC did not outright refuse to endorse her but did not immediately commit to a candidate early in 1972. Ralph Abernathy stated, "I cannot give my support to Shirley Chisholm until she is loud and clear on the issues."[2] Speaking at a luncheon, he gave higher praise for candidates George McGovern and Hubert Humphrey than for Chisholm. He claimed that minority voters were rejecting Nixon, but in the absence of a favorable candidate, the SCLC leader did not rule out rejecting the Democrats and voting for a third party. Considering that he saw himself as the nation's likely choice for its first African American president, his hesitancy to support Chisholm was unsurprising.

Despite the movement's reluctance, Chisholm embraced several of the causes of the civil rights groups. On the traditional end, she shared SCLC's concern for poor people, claiming that "the have nots need someone on the national scene who is responsive to them." Just as both nonviolent and violent African American activists supported Angela Davis, Chisholm also publicly called for the former SNCC associate to be freed while awaiting trial. On the more radical end, she echoed the sentiment of the African American feminists of the TWWA by gently chiding men for their misuse of power. "I love them," she said, "but they've messed up."[3]

Abernathy met Chisholm in Quincy, Florida, in early March for a campaign rally that 1,000 people attended. It was an advantageous photo opportunity for both. Chisholm stood to benefit from sharing the stage with a nationally known community organizer, and Abernathy received guaranteed national publicity by meeting a presidential candidate. In his remarks the SCLC president marveled at the impossibility of a rally for an African American presidential candidate in the recent past. Comparing Chisholm to other candidates, he gave George McGovern and John Lindsay grades of B but declared that Chisholm earned an A for "Able." The crowd roared in approval, and spectators of all ages gave the Black Power salute in agreement. SCLC and Abernathy remained noncommittal as to her candidacy, but he at least stood next to her and said nice words about her. No previous presidential candidate had received that much support from the organization.[4]

Meanwhile, the Nixon administration struggled to rally people on the basis of issues involving African Americans. Four years earlier, Nixon had been able to lure the Silent Majority by harping on "law and order" as an alternative to the urban disturbances of that period. During his presidency he allowed COINTELPRO to help him maintain order by neutralizing those he had considered responsible for the unrest, and he sent military-trained police officers all over the country to crush social agitators in African American areas of cities. As a result, he became a victim of his own success. Without militants and uprisings to exploit in order to scare people into voting for him, his old warnings about the spread of urban violence outside of ghettos would not resonate with his supporters.[5]

The White House lost one of its longtime boogey-women early in the campaign year. The trial of Angela Davis also put the Nixon administration's ideas about dissent on trial. On February 23, she was released from incarceration, thus ending her time as a political prisoner. The ex-SNCC associate was now able to await her trial in less than four months in the comfort of her own home. By freeing her, the judicial branch repudiated the White House's threat from October 1970 to put away people like her.

Nixon needed to rally people because he had decided to run for reelection. He was so focused on securing a second term that he was willing to lose one of his top soldiers in the administration's ongoing war against the movement. He asked Attorney General John Mitchell to run the campaign, and Mitchell accepted. He announced on February 15 that he would depart the Justice Department on March 1. Having brought the Chicago Eight to trial and arrested others for violating the H. Rap Brown Act, Mitchell would be a tough act for his successor to follow. Nixon chose Deputy Attorney General Richard Kleindienst to take over the reins. The deputy was extremely familiar with how Mitchell ran the department, and the Justice Department's campaign against dissent continued.

Meanwhile, Nixon found a new bugaboo for the voters. Instead of scaring people about riots spreading beyond ghettos, the president warned people that judges were about to try to bring children to the ghettos for educational purposes. Ever since the Supreme Court had declared in 1969 that the time for "all deliberate speed" in school desegregation had run out, various courts throughout the country had generated controversy by transporting children of one skin color to a school dominated by children of another color in order to accomplish desegregation. On January 28, 1972, Nixon predicted to John Ehrlichman that busing would become a big campaign issue. The president confided to Ehrlichman, "We cannot sweep this issue under the rug. It is going to explode all over the landscape during this next year."[6]

Actually, the issue was not so new to Nixon. The previous year, Roy Wilkins had called out the president for playing both sides of the busing controversy. The NAACP leader noted, "To please Northern whites who have many all-black neighborhoods and schools (the devil take the Negroes), he re-emphasizes his personal opposition to busing, even though the Supreme Court has ruled otherwise." Also, Nixon was a "law and order" president who refused to enforce the law and cut off funds to school districts that refused to integrate. The president had no authority over how the courts interpreted the law, but he did have the power to play into the deep reservations that people had about busing.[7]

However, the vice president beat the president to the punch, deciding unilaterally to announce the administration's position on busing. If he were to discuss busing in a way that rallied the Silent Majority, then he would become a valuable asset to the White House. Then, perhaps, the president would allow him to speak on behalf of the administration more often. Nixon might even stop teasing him about appointing John Connally instead of him as a running mate for the reelection campaign. Thus, on February 15, the vice president went on a Washington, D.C., television show to vocally oppose a constitutional amendment concerning forced busing to desegregate schools. "I think it fuzzes and obfuscates the entire issue," he reasoned. "I think these things are capable of being handled within the normal statutory framework and constitutional framework of our existing constitution."[8] He did not specify which laws addressed busing, but that was beside the point. As usual, he was embracing the status quo, saying that the Constitution was fine the way it was.

The vice president, however, spoke only for himself and embarrassed the Nixon administration once again. President Nixon had not dismissed the busing amendment idea at the time but had not yet announced his opinion of it. Agnew put Nixon in the awkward position of having to state where he stood on the amendment, because the press held the president accountable for the vice president's remarks. Agnew's comparison of African leaders to African American activists had not even happened an entire year ago, and only 20 months had passed since his diatribe against Nixon appointee Joseph Rhodes. Moreover, the vice president's busing statement did not make his position in the administration any less tenuous. Nixon was still considering Connally to replace Agnew.

Meanwhile, one of Nixon's opponents defined his presidential candidacy by his views on the matter. Alabama governor George Wallace ran on an anti-busing platform, which allowed him to play to his anti-integration base without alienating other people with pro-segregation rhetoric. He called busing "the most asinine, callous, atrocious thing I ever heard of in the United States." He then offered a bitter quip: "It's when 20 million school kids and 60 million taxpayers get taken for a ride."[9] He was doing what he did best— poking fun at the federal government's ineptitude and enlightening people about being cheated by the system. And he elicited very favorable responses.

To mainstream America, Wallace had completed his transformation from segregationist to populist. Newspaper columnist Nick Thimmesch called him "the champion ventor of . . . 'ordinary people.'" In addition, he saw African Americans as part of his Silent Majority now. He had made a point of asking for everyone's vote, "whether white or black," and he warned African Americans that liberals were not really interested in them.[10] In addition, by focusing on busing, Wallace addressed a topic that affected people all across the skin color spectrum. African Americans as well as European Americans opposed busing as a solution to school segregation. However, Wallace prioritized discussing how not to integrate schools instead of how to desegregate them.

Wallace's campaign quickly gained momentum. Some people saw the tactic as business as usual for someone with a pro-segregation career. Indeed, he still spoke at segregationist venues such as the private North Florida Christian School, and the adopted segregationist anthem "Dixie" still played at his rallies. Other people, however, considered his busing rhetoric a natural extension of his resentment of federal intrusion into state affairs. Regardless, his strategy played very well in the South. On March 14, he won Florida's Democratic Party primary in a clean sweep. All 67 of the state's counties voted for him.

The Nixon administration was publicly cordial to its adversary. Wallace was, after all, enjoying remarkable success with the "wedge issue" that the president intended to exploit that year. Nixon would have been hypocritical to paint Wallace as a segregationist bigot for his opposition to busing. Instead, the White House expressed empathy, if not support, for the governor. On March 15, the vice president affirmed Wallace's victory in Florida. Giving an address at Drake University in Iowa that day, Agnew resented criticism by Wallace's Democratic opponent Edmund Muskie about the Alabama governor's exploitation of busing. "When a man wins an election, he shouldn't be referred to as a demagogue," Agnew reprimanded. "It seems to be the general impression—and this is again characteristic of the political innuendo that streaks back and forth across the nation—that he is somewhat of a reactionary person who is trying to deprive the minority groups of their freedom and bring out the worst of their emotions, causing us to divide as a people." In Agnew's opinion, "I haven't heard him say anything that I would consider radical during that campaign." He had a point; if he and President Nixon felt the same way about busing as Wallace did, the Alabama governor's views would hardly be radical to Agnew.[11]

Still, Wallace was Nixon's adversary, and the president did not want him to have an advantage in the election in relation to the busing issue. Thus, on March 16, in response to Wallace's massive win in Florida, Nixon spoke against busing in a 10-minute speech on network television. He called for Congress to improve the education of inner-city minority children. That way, with education comparable across ethnic neighborhoods, no need for busing would exist. Nixon also advised federal courts against ordering the busing of students. Just as "law and order" had defined the previous presidential contest, the busing issue was this year's all-encompassing African American issue with politicians. The difference, however, was that four years earlier, Nixon had pledged to take an active role in implementing "law and order." But in 1972, he preferred to let Congress and the courts keep busing from becoming a federal law that he, as president, would be forced to enforce.[12]

Now that the president had taken over the public discourse about busing, he did not need the vice president to comment further on the matter. As a result, Agnew needed to latch onto another political issue in order to remain a viable choice for Nixon's running mate. He played it safe by going with what had worked for him before. "Law and order" still had a place in the campaign, as far as Agnew was concerned. He promoted the same themes in 1972 as in 1968, showing that he had not grown in his office over the previous four years. On March 20, he spoke at the police department's Holy Name Society in New York, once again espousing the virtues of law enforcement. He announced that "appreciation for law enforcement people" was "on the rise." Turning to attack critics of the police, he bemoaned, "I'm sick and tired of reading that when a policeman goes into the streets to fight crime and takes his life in his own hands, that he's overreacting." He then dismissively denounced the movement's recent attention to misconduct of law enforcement. "There's too much talk of police brutality and overreaction," he professed.[13]

Political developments in March were not encouraging for the movement. Just as the previous presidential contest had avoided civil rights issues through "law and order," the 1972 campaigns seemed destined to do the same through opposition to busing. School desegregation was the only civil rights issue that received considerable attention due to the candidates' public resistance to it. On the other hand, the movement itself was not united in support of it; both SNCC and CORE had long ago disavowed integration in general. In addition, a foe of the civil rights leaders stood to occupy the White House the following year, no matter who won in November. A long-time movement enemy from Alabama had just won Florida's Democratic primary, and more recent nemeses of the civil rights coalition—the Republican incumbents—were doing their best imitations of the Alabama adversary.

Still distrustful of the White House, SCLC members took matters into their own hands in ending the war in Indochina. That April, SCLC met with people who wanted to discuss possibilities for peace in the region. Stoney Cooks joined other U.S. citizens in Paris to hold discussions with Vietnamese peace negotiators "so that the Vietnamese people can maintain communications with Americans in the peace movement and so that the American public will not have to rely on the statements about the war by the Nixon Administration."[14] Cooks and the others, however, had little influence on the president's war policy. Nixon began intensifying the bombing and mining of North Vietnam shortly after the unofficial negotiations had taken place.

On the other hand, that same month Dave Clarke of SCLC brought promising news to the group. He had visited presidential candidates George

McGovern, Hubert Humphrey, and John Lindsay and presented his list of election-year concerns to each of them—but only McGovern wrote back to him. Clarke was encouraged by the senator's reply, especially because the legislator had already proven himself to be a strong ally for civil rights. For a campaign poster, McGovern used a photograph of himself and Abernathy marching together in the March against Repression during May 1970. "I think we have a particular interest in maintaining close communication with Senator McGovern," Clarke concluded.[15]

SCLC's political influence was on the rise. At the end of April 1972, politicians expressed interest in Abernathy. African American representative John Conyers asked him to meet with Bella Abzug, John K. Galbraith, and Gloria Steinem the following month. He considered Abernathy one of the nation's "progressive political leaders." With his input, the participants could successfully "explore political alternatives open to us in 1972."[16]

The group also found more success with labor issues. In April, the newly formed Atlanta/DeKalb branch of SCLC led a strike against local chain Church's Fried Chicken. Seventeen stores closed, costing Church's $150,000. The branch and the boycott provided an opportunity for Hosea Williams, the chapter's leader, to shine apart from Abernathy without leaving the organization. Having helped organize the PPC and conduct other anti-poverty marches over the last four years, Williams proved to be a formidable foe against Church's. He was one of the last remaining members of King's inner circle to stay in SCLC, and the group benefited from his experience and expertise.[17]

Ironically, some of the "Black Extremists" were exercising their influence by traditional political means instead of the terrorism the FBI feared. As May 1972 began, the presidential campaign of Democratic primary candidate Senator George McGovern of South Dakota won the support of civil rights veterans Julian Bond and Jesse Jackson. During the month, Mrs. King endorsed McGovern, too. She agreed with most of his ideas on domestic and foreign policy. She predicted that he would "bring an end to the era of division in our nation and . . . usher in a new era of reconciliation." Moreover, she illustrated him as on a par with the highest esteemed of movement royalty, claiming that "the McGovern campaign has, from the beginning, struck themes which have paralleled my own views and those causes to which my husband gave his life force."[18]

Mrs. King's endorsement of McGovern did not bode well for Shirley Chisholm's presidential aspirations. The congresswoman had expected African American men to support other candidates. She had heard their excuses—that she had not paid her dues as an African American leader or that she had to wait her turn and let an African American man run first. She had weathered the refusals of European American feminists to endorse her because of her skin color. But now a prominent African American woman had shunned Chisholm's campaign. As a civil rights activist who supported feminist causes, Mrs. King had the potential to give the candidate's campaign legitimacy with both the movement and the feminists. Her rejection ultimately doomed Chisholm's run, but she chose to defiantly stay in the race until the DNC began in a few weeks.

The month of May started badly for Governor Wallace, too. The vitriol that he had attracted from young detractors during his 1968 presidential run continued to follow him four years later. At one campaign stop in Maryland, he had to abbreviate his speech because hundreds of African Americans had shouted him down with profanity. At other stops in the state, people hurled rocks and popsicles at him. Undaunted, he kept traveling throughout Maryland, determined to win the state.

Overall, Governor Wallace looked at the spring of 1972 as "my time" and saw his campaign as unstoppable. He had good reason to believe so; he had made such a strong showing in Florida and had forced the opposing party to publicly address the momentum of his campaign. He and his wife Cornelia stopped in the town of Laurel, Maryland, on May 15. The location was unremarkable, but it provided yet another opportunity for Wallace to play to his strengths—greeting a European American crowd and harping on busing. He gave an address at the local shopping center in the late afternoon. When he finished, he and Cornelia walked through the crowd, shaking hands.

The madness that had plagued his campaign seemed absent in Maryland. The turnout in Laurel was respectable, and no hecklers had ruined his speech. As the Wallaces mingled with supporters, a clean-cut, smirking young European American nudged through the crowd to approach the candidate. Suddenly, five bullets from a .38-caliber gun entered the governor's body. He fell on his back, arms splayed to his sides. Cornelia rushed to his side and took off her suit jacket to sponge up her husband's blood. Arthur Bremer, the smirking young man, had just shot the candidate at close range.[19]

The assassination attempt inspired journalists to yet again revisit Rap Brown's assessment of violence as "American as cherry pie." One article used his quote as a context for studying how many public figures died by assassination or were wounded by assassination attempts. The article noted that since 1963, "the faith of many Americans in the reasonableness of their country's politics has been shattered by assassins' bullets six times." As in Ronald Cohen's piece of June 1968, this article quoted both Brown and historian Arthur Schlesinger Jr. The press no longer debated Brown's statement but rather accepted it as a given; Bremer's shooting of Wallace was merely the latest proof of the ex-SNCC leader's point.[20]

Such public validation of Brown mattered little to him in court. On June 2, he returned to New Orleans to face sentencing for his conviction on the four-year-old charge of having carried a gun on a flight from New York to Louisiana. Judge Lansing Mitchell still presided over the court, and he sentenced the defendant to five years in jail and a $2,000 fine. Brown's long-time lawyer, William Kunstler, decried the punishment as having come from a biased judge who was sentencing "not because of the crime involved, but because [Brown] was a black militant." He had a point, because Lansing had confidentially promised to "get that nigger" before the start of the 1968 trial.[21]

Brown was no longer gaunt, but he still looked different than usual. He appeared in court in denim jeans, part of the old SNCC dress code. On the other hand, he had started wearing wool hats, and in court his accessory was a purple cap. He also sported a beard to surround his droopy mustache. His new look was a far cry from the hip, stylized image he had fostered during his tenure as SNCC chairman. Then again, two years had passed since he had left that role, and he did not reclaim it in prison.

Some things about Brown, however, had not changed. The defendant still possessed an anti-authoritarian streak, and he exercised it in court. Even as Kunstler tried to explain Brown's behavior in recent years, his client undermined the efforts with his trademark plays on words. In reference to the delay in sentencing because of Brown's year in hiding, his lawyer explained that the defendant feared for his life. Judge Mitchell did not think the explanation was good enough. "I told you," he reminded Kunstler, "that if he would come above ground at that time, [the court] would have taken care of him—to protect him and see that no harm came to him."[22]

At this revelation of uncharacteristic goodwill from the government towards Brown, the defendant quietly laughed and mocked Mitchell's promise by telling him, "I'll take care of you, too."[23]

In response, Mitchell stared icily at Brown and smiled. Evidently pleased that the SNCC leader had just defiantly said what he had said in court, the judge ordered a court reporter to record Brown's announcement, word for word. Lansing had gotten "that nigger" again.

Brown then continued, as if not finished with his statement, "To see that no harm comes to you."[24]

Brown's remark sealed his fate. Having waited for four years to sentence the ex-SNCC chairman, Mitchell gave him a punishment for a longer time than the waiting period. Meanwhile, the press manipulated the defendant's statement to enhance his reputation for violence. On NBC, the news report of the trial only featured Brown's "I'll take care of you," and left out the other part of the quote.[25]

Even in New Orleans, Brown attracted a following. As a dozen federal marshals whisked him out of the courtroom, they encountered 200 demonstrators. Reusing the rhetoric of the BPP, of which Brown had briefly been a member in 1968, the protesters chanted, "Death to the fascist pigs!" They alternately shouted, "Free Rap Brown," which corresponded to Brown's position as the last of the major political prisoners of the late 1960s to remain incarcerated, now that Huey Newton and Angela Davis were out of prison.[26]

Although no longer incarcerated, Davis still wanted liberation from the criminal justice system. She returned to court on June 4. In contrast to the tension and sneering during Brown's sentencing, Davis's proceedings fostered hope among her supporters. For a brief moment, her trial had the air of a movement mass meeting from the early 1960s, when movement activists had been proudly nonviolent and devoutly Christian. From a corridor connected to the courtroom of Davis's trial, an anonymous voice started singing, "Woke up this morning with my mind / stayed on freedom."[27] Soon, others in the room joined in the impromptu performance. The singing of a spiritual during a trial for a radical activist of the Black Power years seemed to have brought the movement full circle.

The verdict on African American radicalism now rested with the jury. After they arrived at their decisions, they entered the courtroom stone-faced, which worried Davis. Their expressions led the defendant to prepare for her incarceration. However, the court clerk read "not guilty" for the murder charge, the kidnapping charge, and conspiracy charge. A jubilant Davis left the courtroom with her freedom intact.[28]

The jury's "not guilty" verdicts validated Davis's earlier activism in SNCC and other organizations. The jurors ruled radicalism as legal and not a criminal offense in and of itself. They also legitimized the movement itself. SCLC had publicly supported Davis, and now it was publicly proven right in its maintenance of her innocence. For some people, her acquittal was not good news. Representative Joe Waggonner of Louisiana called the outcome "a sad day for America and a banner day for international communism." He lamented that "those bent on the destruction of our form of government and our free society have been rewarded for a job well done."[29]

Elsewhere in the federal government, the outcome of the trial yielded mixed results. The jury's granting of legal legitimacy to Davis's views and activism was a heavy blow to the White House's three-year-old campaign against dissent. Someone who had been affiliated with two African American organizations that COINTELPRO had profiled—SNCC and the BPP—avoided the imprisonment that the FBI had long sought for people in those groups. On the other hand, Davis's victory came in a courtroom and not through a violent attempt at revolution. Contrary to Waggonner's conclusions, the defendant had won within the system. The government was not destroyed. In a sense, "law and order" had worked for Davis.

"Law and order" did not work for everyone, however. As high-profile SNCC veterans faced courtrooms, current SNCC associates in Texas attacked problems in the criminal justice system. On May 30, the Southwest Texas Methodist Conference approved a proposal to create a legal assistance fund that was designed to give San Antonio's poor people another option besides court-appointed attorneys. The local SNCC branch had pushed for it at that year's conference and the previous year, when the organization had accused the conference of not meeting the needs of the poor.[30]

By this time, SNCC's presence in Texas had diminished considerably from its peak in the late 1960s. As of 1969, the FBI had successfully neutralized nearly all of the branches that had started in the state. SNCC–San Antonio had escaped the FBI's attention and survived. But in the middle of 1972, it also was under the bureau's watch. The branch's members and the United Committee to Free All Political Prisoners in Texas announced their intention to cosponsor a "benefit soul concert" at Brackenridge Park's Sunken Gardens on June 15 in order to celebrate Angela Davis's acquittal and Texas convict Lee Otis Johnson's release. The cosponsors agreed to use the event's proceeds to fight sickle cell anemia, which local SNCC associate James Alexander had contracted. When a newspaper in the city reported the announcement, the periodical identified one of the sponsors as the state branch of SNCC—not the city branch. The article listed T. C. Calvert as "head of the state political affairs of SNCC" and Mario Salas as "state coordinator of SNCC." By inferring that SNCC–San Antonio was now SNCC–Texas, the newspaper unwittingly confirmed that branches that had emerged in Dallas and Houston only a few years earlier no longer existed.[31]

Amid all the excitement about Chisholm's candidacy, busing, and Angela Davis, SCLC's longtime concern for the poor became lost in the shuffle. Reporters barely paid attention to the group in terms of activism and programming. The organization tended to make news when it associated itself with people and groups attracting more attention. Only four years earlier, King had been able to attract people to his causes, but now Abernathy sought people with whom to make alliances.

SCLC was very busy that year with political organizing. Some of the organizing was traditional, especially in the form of campaigning, because several people with ties to SCLC switched from activism to politics. Andrew Young made another run for Congress, and Hosea Williams ran for the Senate while retaining his position in SCLC. Through the past and present electoral campaigns by Fauntroy, Jackson, Williams, and Young, the organization had effectively broken from King's view that activists should not become politicians. Of the present major leaders of the organization, only Abernathy had not yet run for office. If he indeed believed in people's predictions that he would be the first African American president, 1972 was not the year he would try to bring that prophecy to reality.

He laid out his plans for the immediate future in a speech to an audience of about 200 at Brown University on March 2. The three goals he announced were the ending of the Vietnam War, the freeing of all political prisoners, and the organizing of the poor to vote President Nixon out of office. Abernathy offered very few new comments in his address. Then again, many of the problems he discussed had existed for years. The United States entered its seventh year of the war. If the country was still dropping too many bombs over Vietnam, he had to keep addressing it. If Vice President Agnew continued to distribute moon rocks to foreign officials instead of feeding the poor, Abernathy had to say so.

Ironically, Abernathy sounded like the vice president when talking about prisoners. Four years after both people had instantly started new leadership positions under prolonged heavy public scrutiny, they unwittingly developed the same speaking style when addressing social issues. Neither person had developed a thick skin in the time since they first came under intense public criticism, and their rhetoric often reflected defensiveness. As a result, they tended to lament their depictions in news reports and blame only others for the nation's problems. The SCLC leader complained about the unfair treatment one of his strongest allies received from both the justice system and the media. He alleged that "Angela Davis is on trial simply because she is black." He blamed her imprisonment on her status as "a black individual who did not hide behind a desk somewhere and because of her political beliefs."[32] He claimed that reporters were also putting her on trial and that Nixon already found her guilty. Similarly, Agnew occasionally groused that the news media possessed a liberal slant that gave conservatives like him unfavorable coverage, and he said that his outspokenness attracted media criticism. He took dissenters like Davis to task for causing domestic unrest instead of addressing the issues they protested. As much as Abernathy and Agnew may have hated to admit it, by 1972 they were two sides of the same coin.

Abernathy made his clearest points in his speech when talking about his political plans for that year. He unequivocally called for the removal of Nixon from office. However, he believed that such an outcome could only result from SCLC's political organizing of the impoverished. He said that the group would try to build a coalition of poor people. That coalition would, in turn, become a political force strong enough to vote the president out of office. "We have the opportunity to seize nonviolently the government by marching on the ballot box," he claimed.[33]

Despite Abernathy's use of the march as a metaphor for voting, he had no intention of abandoning the marching tactic in 1972. Keeping in line with the organization's recent trend of diverting attention from major national events, SCLC intended to take the nation's poorest people to the national political conventions scheduled for that year. On March 8, Abernathy announced that SCLC would have its own "poor people's" convention in July at the DNC in Miami. As in 1968, he planned to lead the poor in marches. He intended to have the impoverished sojourners speak about their plights to people in powerful positions. Some of the people involved from four years earlier would join the Miami demonstration. Abernathy even considered dubbing his program "Resurrection City II." Ironically, with SCLC calling for an infiltration of poor people into DNC proceedings to offer testimonies, Resurrection City II was more similar to SNCC's "Freedom Summer" than to the first Resurrection City. SCLC, therefore, was now not only repeating its own previous program ideas but also recycling ideas it had already borrowed from SNCC.

On the other hand, Resurrection City II also promised to be starkly different from the first Resurrection City. In contrast to Abernathy's attempts to give the poor an audience of different federal officials, he now wanted to give poor people a political voice. He intended to march them into the DNC, just as he had marched the PPC into the nation's capital. "We'll have as many delegates as they do," he boasted. Still, his drive to have the poor speak to politicians carried greater risk than four years earlier. In 1968, the PPC activists aired their grievances to members of federal governmental agencies—people with the means to address the PPC's complaints of national structural inequality. In contrast, the candidates running for president did not run agencies, which meant that the PPC would complain to people who—if they were to lose the presidential election—would have no way to fix the structural problems that caused poverty. In addition, all of the Democratic Party's candidates struggled to effectively campaign against the Nixon administration that year, which left the chance for a Democrat to control the departments of the presidential cabinet a remote possibility.[34]

On June 7, the SCLC leader went to Chicago to promote the event and raise money. Speaking at a $25/plate Breadbasket dinner there, Abernathy offered his standard bombast and banter to his audience. He predicted that 3,000 people would encamp at the DNC "to highlight the need to quash poverty." He also claimed that the Democratic Party could not take the votes of poor people for granted. "Poor people must give the message to the Democratic Party that it cannot have our support in exchange for the same old crumbs they've handed out before," he declared.[35]

To Abernathy, the political involvement of the poor was part of the dream of his predecessor. Although his friend had been dead for nearly four years, the needs of the poor were as pressing as when SCLC had planned the first Resurrection City. "We don't want to give up because Martin Luther King is not with us," he said. "Let us transform our love for Dr. King into an effort to take action."[36] Still, the organization's dedication to King's dream retarded its development. Abernathy rhetorically and strategically was imprisoned by King's vision. By continuing to talk about the slain minister's ideas and create programs based on them, Abernathy was unable to fully address problems as they currently existed. SCLC treated the issues of 1972 as if nothing had changed about them since April 4, 1968.

The only original contribution Abernathy consistently made to the struggle was his public criticism of the Nixon administration. King did not live to see Nixon become president, but he had not personally attacked former President Johnson. Abernathy's insults of Nixon were no better or worse than those from other contemporary African American leaders. On the other hand, the barbs from SCLC were especially personal, because Abernathy in part was revisiting his old grievance against the president for their abortive May 1969 meeting in Washington, D.C. Casting the White House yet again as the enemy of the poor, Abernathy told his audience in Chicago to "retire Richard Milhous Nixon and send Spiro Agnew back to Maryland to draw his pension."[37] By offering no ideas as to who should replace the incumbents, he suggested that no one could do any worse than they had done.

Nevertheless, such a suggestion compromised SCLC's ability to raise money. The group had never alienated people on the basis of political affiliation. But by publicly damning Nixon and Agnew, the organization shut itself off from many potential supporters. Only four years earlier, an ally had taken an SCLC official to task for publicly questioning Nixon's honesty. Now Abernathy was making much worse comments about the president, and the rhetoric did little to alleviate the group's longstanding financial problems and stop the gradual dwindling of support.

But all was not lost for SCLC. In terms of programming, the organization was still on a roll. It had not suffered a major setback in its campaigns since the March against Moon Rocks in early 1971. Instead, the group was collecting victories in Butler, Alabama, and Sandersville, Georgia. The defection of Jackson caused some unwelcome publicity for Abernathy, but that split had nothing to do with programming. As long as Abernathy achieved success by trying to apply his predecessor's ideas to new problems, there was no need for him to try anything different. And now, no one remained in SCLC to challenge his leadership. Abernathy's interpretation of King's vision became the guiding force of the group for the duration.

The SCLC leader tried to reassure people who were skeptical of the chances for Resurrection City II to succeed. In a rare moment of acknowledging a personal imperfection, Abernathy revealed, "I will admit that the first Resurrection City four years ago in Washington, DC is remembered by many people in terms of one single word: mud." But then he blamed the media for talking more about the mud than the poverty of the occupants. He said he was constructing another encampment because poverty still existed. "Four years later in 1972, the agenda for ending poverty is far from completion," he noted. "And we know that there are too many politicians and too many men at the command posts of power who wish that the poor people would just go away—that the poor would vanish, and the country could go back to business as usual." He did not say how he would make the protest attractive to reporters. Indeed, in the four years since the first Resurrection City, takeovers of college buildings and other institutions by activists had become more frequent. Nevertheless, he was successful in arousing the media's curiosity as to how he would pull off an encampment at a political convention.[38]

As SCLC tried to effect political change from outside the system, some of COINTELPRO's former targets attempted to change the system by infiltrating it. Their efforts were not unlike SNCC's unsuccessful attempt in 1964 to have its multiethnic "Freedom Democrats" replace the all–European American delegation from Mississippi. Jesse Jackson participated in an effort to unseat delegates from Cook County, Illinois, to the DNC. The county's party boss, Mayor Richard Daley of Chicago, had chosen the delegates himself, but they did not reflect the party's new mandatory diversity standards. Each state's delegation was to have African Americans, women, and young people "in reasonable relationship to the group's presence in the state population."[39]

Nearly repeating history, Illinois's regular delegation and the reform delegation pleaded their cases of legitimacy before the Credentials Committee on June 30. Eight years earlier, the Freedom Democrats had tried to become DNC delegates despite not having been able to officially register as Democrats in Mississippi; they framed their quest for participation as a moral issue. Similarly, Jackson and six others claimed that their adherence to the diversity standards made their delegation the rightful one for Cook County, although only Daley's delegates had been elected by county residents. SNCC was not able to convince the Credentials Committee of 1964 to support their moral campaign, but Jackson did in 1972. SNCC could only enjoy Jackson's victory in reflected glory, because no current members of SNCC were part of Chicago's new delegation. The Windy City did not even have a SNCC branch. Still, SNCC's moral cause now had national political validation and the support of a candidate who could potentially win the November presidential election.[40]

In terms of both national political influence and mainstream acceptance, the movement peaked as the first half of 1972 came to an end. The justice system validated an ex-SNCC member's rights, and popular culture celebrated her. SNCC's concept of Black Power was now embraced by African American politicians of diverse stripes, and the press continued to affirm Rap Brown's statement on national violence. Meanwhile, SCLC was poised to enter the Democratic Party either by protest or by election.

Civil rights leaders had every right to be hopeful. Agnew appeared less frequently in public, Southerners voted for "New South" politicians instead of segregationists, and the number of U.S. troops in Vietnam was declining. African Americans suffered fewer violent reprisals for exercising their political rights, and some were winning elections. As a result, civil rights activists were not speaking as violently that year as they had during the previous four years. The 1968 campaign season had focused on who would more effectively crush Brown and other militants, but the 1972 elections were poised to become a collective referendum on the movement at large and its causes. In the meantime, the civil rights organizations developed new ways to work collectively in order to capitalize on their political gains.

CHAPTER 14

Nation Time

In January 1972, pollster Louis Harris revisited the age-old question, "Who speaks for the Negro?" He did not specifically use the word "Negro" because over the past two years, people had increasingly used the term "black" or "Afro-American." However, his method of polling African Americans about their tastes in leadership remained the same. Every year or so, he compiled a list of prominent African American organizations and individuals. He then approached African Americans and informed them of the poll. "I'd like to read you a list of some black leaders and organizations," he said to each person. "For each, tell me if you respect them a great deal, some but not a great deal, or hardly at all."[1] In recent years the names on his list included movement leaders, elected officials, entertainers, and athletes.

Only two movement groups—the NAACP and the SCLC—appeared in the 1972 survey, but they topped the list among all the groups and individuals. Although the NAACP ranked higher than SCLC, Ralph Abernathy's ranking of third bested fifth-place Roy Wilkins. The poll showed that not much had changed since the first year after Martin Luther King's assassination. Despite the rise of militant speakers and the successful elections of some African American politicians, people still considered the directors of civil rights organizations to be the nation's dominant African American leaders. Those findings were very good news for Wilkins and Abernathy.

However, the Harris Poll also revealed that the two group presidents did not have a monopoly on respectable leadership. Politicians Charles Evers and Carl Stokes scored nearly as highly as Wilkins and Abernathy had. Lowest on the list were Muslim converts like Muhammad Ali and Kareem Abdul-Jabbar—neither of whom were presidents or chairmen of any organizations—and such militants as Angela Davis, Eldridge Cleaver, and the BPP itself. Still, even the lowest-ranked had won at least "some—not a great deal" of respect of at least 40 percent of those surveyed. People did not have to lead groups and push for civil rights in order for African Americans to follow them.[2]

African American journalist Tony Brown illustrated that point for an episode of his weekly public television series *Black Journal*. In January 1972, he asked nationally prominent African Americans to appear on a live 90-minute special episode. The title "Is It Too Late?" symbolized the precarious state of affairs Brown sensed for African Americans during the Nixon administration. The following month the episode aired, and it featured a panel of 10 people: 2 congressmen (Charles Diggs and Ron Dellums), 1 Pan-Africanist activist (Imamu Amiri Baraka), 2 Muslims (Elijah Muhammad and Louis Farrakhan), and 5 civil rights activists. Among the activists, 1 was a comedian (Dick Gregory), 2 were women (Fannie Lou Hamer and Dorothy Height), and 2 were male leaders of groups (Ralph Abernathy and Vernon Jordan). The fact that half of the panel came from the movement demonstrated that the host considered civil rights work important to African American uplift, but the other half's composition of people outside of civil rights proved that the movement was not the only game in town.

Civil rights organizations still enjoyed some successful campaigns, but their individual effects on the movement were negligible. As a result, no one person had been able to cross organizational boundaries and mobilize diverse groups of African Americans. On the other hand, that development may not have been a problem in and of itself. "We have no superstars at the moment in terms of the civil rights and peace movements," ex-SNCC participant Ivanhoe Donaldson admitted before adding, "And maybe there's no need for one."[3]

The movement was at a crossroads. Despite its victories with civil rights legislation, ex-SNCC associate Vincent Harding complained that the civil rights coalition overall had not progressed with the times. It had become hampered by its overreliance on "strategies no longer adequate to the present and future of black America," as he put it. The challenge for civil rights activists was twofold: come to a consensus on which issues to tackle and develop new strategies to address them. In addition, with Rap Brown's arrest, no one in the movement remained who had nearly as much influence across all the organizations. A single and clear agenda for the movement proved extremely difficult for civil rights activists to accomplish. New groups were forming, and more African Americans were becoming leaders.[4]

Jesse Jackson of SCLC was emerging as a leader in his own right. He still had to answer questions about whether he wanted to be the organization's president and replace Abernathy. Jackson consistently maintained that he did not harbor such aspirations. After three years, his relationship with Abernathy remained a dark cloud that hovered over his activism. As other people had steadily left SCLC since 1968, the media covered the tension between Abernathy and Jackson more intensely, almost as if by default.

On December 10, 1971, Jackson sent Abernathy a telegram. SCLC had just suspended Jackson for two months with pay because he had incorporated the Black Expo without the organization's approval. Never before had SCLC so publicly reprimanded him or given him such a grave consequence. He considered the organization's punishment too severe. "I consider 60 days too long for this vital work to be endangered by my 'leave of absence,'" he complained, "and hereby submit my resignation for the good of the organization, effective Friday Dec. 17, 1971."[5]

Two days after the telegram, Jackson's entire Operation Breadbasket staff announced their intention to leave with him. Word of his defection soon leaked to newspapers in Chicago and elsewhere, and SCLC went into immediate damage control. On December 13, Abernathy released a press statement that confirmed Jackson's resignation. In his remarks he severed ties with the new upstart but acknowledged him as part of the movement, thus presenting the split as an amicable divorce. The SCLC president graciously complimented him: "Reverend Jackson has made a valuable contribution to the struggle for economic justice for black and poor people. We are confident that he will continue in this struggle."[6]

SCLC's supporters in Chicago were stunned. Daisy Marshall expressed hope that Abernathy and Jackson would "forget all diversities and unite again," but such requests were futile. A few of them wrote to Abernathy to support him. Ollie Smith even congratulated him for suspending Jackson, declaring, "I believe in my heart that God is pleased." Most of the letters Abernathy received about Jackson's resignation ordeal, however, were negative. Geraldine Riley of Operation Breadbasket reprimanded the SCLC president for going "to our enemy the white media" to publicize his issues concerning Jackson. She concluded, "[I]n this you are wrong."[7]

Jackson's solo civil rights activism immediately got off to an impressive start. On December 12, a group of people met at the Commodore Hotel in New York to show support for him. Among the attendees were politicians Richard Hatcher and Carl Stokes, entertainers Ossie Davis and Roberta Flack, Harvard professor Alvin Pouissant, and SCLC member W. A. Saunders. Jackson had not officially left SCLC yet, but he had already acquired the clout to attract influential supporters. Perhaps the guests saw a dynamic energy in Jackson that they had missed in the movement since King's death. On the other hand, they may have been primed for Jackson's leadership by all the press coverage that had preferred him over Abernathy for the past three years. Regardless, the attendees made a point of noting that their support of Jackson was not a rejection of Abernathy. There was room enough in the movement for lots of people.[8]

In the last week of December, Jackson started Operation People United to Save Humanity (PUSH). He modeled it after SCLC to an extent. PUSH was based on his vision of how to improve the lives of the oppressed, just as SCLC was based on King's vision. Jackson no longer had to suppress his vision in order to help carry out Abernathy's interpretation of King's dream. Instead, the PUSH leader could work to make his own dreams come true.

Now that Jackson had created a new force in the movement and had established independence from SCLC, newspaper journalists tried to introduce him to readers. Many articles described his early life in Chicago and his years in SCLC. They compared him favorably to King. They talked about how many people he had been able to lure away from Operation Breadbasket to PUSH. "Rising black leader" and "top-name" were among the phrases newspapers used when identifying him. Editor Gus Savage of Chicago's newspaper *Citizen* pledged support for him in an editorial titled, "Stay on the Case, Jesse." Several African American institutions sought Jackson's oratory services. As he launched his organization, he spoke at multiple functions. These appearances gave him experience as an independent movement leader, and they allowed him to promote his new group.

Meanwhile, Abernathy was now free to run SCLC without rumors of internal dissent and leadership power struggles. All of the people the media had blamed for dividing the organization—Bevel, Young, and Jackson—were gone. To Abernathy, the latter two had seemed especially annoyed by his succession to the organization's presidency, and he did not think that they considered him qualified for the position. He thought that both of them were natural leaders—Jackson for his oratory skills and Young because of his charm and light skin color. The SCLC leader felt that their ambition for leadership also caused their discontent within the group. But with their departures, Abernathy effectively became solely responsible for the development of the organization. He could take sole credit for successes but also was subject to sole blame for any failures.[9]

Reporters still talked about competition between Abernathy and Jackson. The cover of the January 13, 1972, issue of *Jet* magazine was a split photograph of the conservative, clerically robed Abernathy and the Afro'ed, medallion-wearing, fringe-vested Jackson. With 16 years of age separating the two figures, the cover illustrated the cultural generation gap that divided them. The rural Abernathy identified with the last generation of African Americans who had migrated from plantations of sharecropping to urban areas. In contrast, the Chicago-based Jackson, not yet 30 years old, represented the generation that had grown up in the cities. Spending their adolescence reading about sit-ins and boycotts and desegregated facilities, Jackson's generation took immediate civil rights progress for granted. Small wonder that Jackson had become impatient with the slow progress he had perceived from SCLC.

However, *Jet*'s cover was somewhat misleading, because the periodical had used an old photograph of Abernathy to accentuate the generation gap. Abernathy had actually become slightly more countercultural in appearance by the start of 1972. His sideburns were long, and his "natural" was large and bushy. His Afro was not as large as Jackson's. Nevertheless, Abernathy was not the close-cropped man that *Jet* had presented as Jackson's opposite that January. The African American press was starting to portray Abernathy—and SCLC, by extension—as passé.

One week later *Jet* further elevated Jackson over Abernathy by surveying the new leader's impression upon his colleagues in the other civil rights groups. He had called for coalitions between PUSH and any interested organizations in order to "influence national legislation like Dr. King, John Lewis, James Farmer [formerly of CORE], Whitney [Young], and James Forman did."[10] His belief in strength in numbers failed to take into account the power of the current civil rights leaders. In contrast to the figures of the early 1960s that he had cited, only Wilkins and Jordan enjoyed significant influence in Washington, D.C. Moreover, the president directed them to visits with White House advisers, and SNCC and CORE had no stature in the nation's capital except as targets of FBI surveillance.

Civil rights leaders' different opinions of Jackson highlighted how his defection from SCLC split the movement. Wilkins made no commitment on his group's behalf to associate with PUSH but affirmed the possibility "to get blacks from organizations as diverse as the Panthers and the Urban League to agree on certain aspects of black unity." Jordan said that the NUL would work with PUSH but also maintain its relationships with other groups, and Dorothy Height of the NCNW also expressed willingness to team with Jackson. SCLC was noncommittal, and *Jet* failed to reach Abernathy for comment. Roy Innis, however, coolly dismissed PUSH as superfluous. He noted that his group had called for "liberation" before Jackson had, and Innis saw "no difference in what CORE is doing and what he says PUSH will be doing." Innis announced that if Jackson also were to denounce integration, then "there is plenty of room for him in CORE."[11]

As the widow of an iconic movement figure, only Mrs. King equaled if not surpassed Jackson in terms of celebrity status among civil rights workers at the time. The First Lady of the movement brought major celebrities to her events that were independent of SCLC, such as the first annual Martin Luther King Jr. Birthday Commemoration Concert. Representative Ron Dellums spoke, and humorist Moms Mabley performed her stand-up routine. Mrs. King secured commitments from SCLC defectors like Andrew Young, and over a year after SCLC demonstrations had led Berry Gordy to cancel concerts by the Jackson Five, he allowed that group and Gladys Knight and the Pips to sing at the concert. That night, Mrs. King raised $47,600 in proceeds for her King Center project.

Angela Davis was one of the few high-profile activists to publicly prefer Abernathy to Jackson. She believed that the SCLC leader was closer than the PUSH leader to fulfilling the goals King had sought before his assassination. "Rev. Abernathy has taken, I think, the most consistent position on political prisoners of any group or organization of that character in this country," she declared in an interview. In contrast to Abernathy's constant addresses on the subject and his visits to her in jail, Jackson appeared too focused on African American capitalism to her. Ironically, although she was born two years after the PUSH leader, she said he—not Abernathy—represented "the old and traditional." Her views did not dissuade people from becoming excited about Jackson's emergence and giving his leadership a chance. Still, as a political prisoner, her opinion that Abernathy was more radically relevant than Jackson was a strong validation of the SCLC leader's activism.[12]

With Jackson gone, Hosea Williams was now SCLC's most vibrant speaker. Before 1972, he had not been a minister and was the only member of King's inner circle who was a layman. However, he accepted his call to the clergy when the year began, and soon thereafter Abernathy ordained him. To Williams, Christianity and activism were one and the same, and they had to be synonymous in order to attract young African Americans. He echoed the late Whitney Young's warning from nearly five years earlier that the adolescents and young adults had grown tired of hearing just talk. But instead of demanding action from the federal government, Williams stated, "The church must take on the drug addiction problem, police brutality, and prostitution." Still, even his willingness to use the church to address those issues brought to fruition the role that Young had wanted ministers in SCLC to play.[13]

Williams also made news for starting another new look of SCLC activism. He had always been savvy as to the physical attributes of activism, for in 1968 he had been the one to insist upon SCLC members wearing the denim of the PPC for King's funeral. But in 1972 he began wearing the kind of jacket that

Chairman Mao wore, showing that he remained excited about the trip he had taken to China the previous fall. He continued to praise the country for carrying on a more successful freedom struggle than civil rights activists in the United States were conducting. The *New York Times* observed that Williams "tells audiences that the Chinese have 'more freedom than a black living in the ghettos of New York City or Denver.'" His jealousy of China, however, did not alter SCLC's fundamental goal. It was the only civil rights group still committed to "Dr. King's central idea—nonviolent social change."[14]

SNCC had trouble courting a public following, especially because its chairman was now in police custody. Nevertheless, in early 1972 a loyal remnant remained. Several members of SNCC, the BPP, and the TWWA attended Rap Brown's trial in criminal court in New York for the holdup of the previous October. Some of Brown's supporters claimed that the robbery trial was the latest example of the federal government treating Brown like a political prisoner. They claimed that while Brown had been in hiding, he had tried to convince people not to sell drugs. They also said that at the bar he had allegedly held up, he was actually trying to persuade the heroin and cocaine dealers there to repent that October night. Julian Bond, a former SNCC colleague of Brown's, said that Brown was leading a movement against drugs, in which he not only told pushers to stop selling drugs but also called for the removal of drugs from African American neighborhoods.[15]

Some of Brown's supporters vowed to carry on his work against narcotics. His wife Lynne Doswell and brother Ed Brown teamed with ex-SNCC associate Mae Jackson and her brother to form the H. Rap Brown Anti-Dope Movement. The group worked to "eliminate people dealing in dope," as Bond put it during a press conference. The organization would start with "moral persuasion," and then resort to "more forceful deliberate means" if dealers refused to give up their trade. Bond announced that the group would conduct its own surveillance on the dealers, facilitate its own tribunals, and issue its own punishments to the offenders in order to prohibit outside interference. The organization attracted movement veterans like Imamu Amiri Baraka and former SNCC colleagues like Fred Meely. At 17 years old, the youngest member of the group was a minister who led another organization called the National Youth Movement. His name was the Reverend Alfred Sharpton.[16]

As for Doswell, she had become an anomaly in the civil rights movement, as far as the media were concerned. By this time newspapers, radio, and television had divided their coverage of African American women in the movement. Young militant feminist activists appeared in major headlines and on television news reports. On the other hand, entertainment outlets profiled stoic, reserved middle-aged women such as grieving widows. While Walter Cronkite talked about Angela Davis on the *CBS Evening News*, Coretta Scott King conversed with Johnny Carson on NBC's *Tonight Show*. Doswell, in contrast, bridged both groups. Despite her youth she was a stoic, grieving figure because her husband was incarcerated. Small wonder that the media largely ignored her; she did not fit the stereotypes.

One of the few people who publicized her was an African American television producer named Ellis Haizlip. Ever since 1968, his weekly hour-long public affairs program *Soul!* had provided viewers of public television with a diverse assortment of African American culture and politics. He booked gospel singers, rhythm-and-blues artists, poets, nationalists, and movement activists, among others. Previous guests included former SNCC members Julius Lester, Stokely Carmichael, and Mae Jackson. Haizlip also tackled contemporary news stories. He controlled the content of his program and was unafraid to provide a forum for people with countercultural ideas.

He asked Doswell to appear on his show shortly after her husband became incarcerated, and she accepted. In a way, she was carrying on her husband's tradition, for he only gave interviews with African American reporters. For Doswell and Brown, an African American journalistic perspective was important. She also took pains to protect him as he awaited his trials; his lawyer William Kunstler accompanied her to the taping of the interview.

On January 19, 1972, the national public television network NET aired her guest appearance. Haizlip and his guest sat in chairs facing each other on a sparse stage in front of a burnt orange background. He dressed casually in a button-down shirt and slacks, and she wore a bright orange head-wrap and a dark green robe. His interview with her took up most of the first half hour of the episode. Her booking marked a significant accomplishment for SNCC, because her interview was one of the few times a current member of "National" SNCC appeared on national television to talk about the organization.

Moreover, this episode featured one of the few sympathetic portrayals of Rap Brown in mainstream media. The show displayed pictures of Brown's younger years as the host provided a brief biographical sketch of the activist. After a discussion about SNCC, Doswell spoke about how she met her husband. Wedding photographs appeared on the screen as she talked about the day she married him. She and Haizlip then talked about Brown's book *Die Nigger Die!*, his antidrug work in prison, and the anti-dope movement named after him. She discussed several recent hardships such as the deaths of her father and Brown's mother and life under house arrest. Haizlip concluded the segment by asking Doswell to "give Rap our love." The telecast was SNCC's finest half hour on television in recent years.[17]

Although former SNCC members were busier with organizing than current members were, the federal government did not slacken its surveillance of SNCC. As long as the group existed, it remained a major social threat, and Congress reported about the organization as if it had never lost any influence. In 1972, the Senate Appropriations Committee reported that Muhammad Hunt was leading efforts to revive branches nationwide, and that he called for programs aimed toward African American revolutionaries, students, and youth groups. Edward "Saint X" McClendon tried and failed to restart SNCC–Chicago. The group had not been present in Chicago for years, and in the interim the BPP and gangs like the Blackstone Rangers had made inroads there among young African American men. As a result, by the beginning of 1972, all local SNCC activity took place in McClendon's house.

The group made further inroads in Texas, partially by carrying on Rap Brown's legacy of fostering relationships among minority groups. On January 25 SNCC–San Antonio met with La Raza Unida party, and both groups created a coalition for the 1972 campaign year. SNCC member Tommy "T. C." Calvert minimized the importance of the forming of the alliance, calling the coalition "informal." Mario Salas was realistic in expectations, saying, "It's going to be hard to change the generally hostile attitude the two minorities have toward political cooperation." Still, at least local African Americans and Mexican Americans were trying, and SNCC was virtually alone in the movement in doing so.[18]

SNCC–San Antonio also drew tactically from former member James Forman by targeting churches. The Texas-based activists did not present a manifesto of demands but instead peacefully reached out to Christian institutions to serve as allies. "We have to relate to the church," Salas said in February. "To totally alienate ourselves from the church would be to alienate ourselves from our people to a large extent." He claimed that local churches "have been very helpful." While not embracing nonviolence once again, SNCC's San Antonio residents were at least willing to work with churches instead of merely interrupting their services.[19]

Outside of San Antonio, former members of SNCC won much more press attention than current ones did, and Angela Davis was arguably the most popular alumnus at the time. A book supporting her case arrived in bookstores in early 1972. *If They Come in the Morning* received mixed reviews, especially because of its inconsistent content. Reviewers did not know what message the book tried to convey through the quotes from writings by Davis and various activists. The *New York Times* considered Davis's words among the best in the collection. The rest was just "padding."

Nevertheless, *If They Come in the Morning* marked an important watershed in the literature of the movement. On the one hand, the book was only the latest in a long series of tomes written by or about African American activists. On the other hand, it lacked the militant tone of *Die Nigger Die!* and *Soul on Ice* and the fatalism of *Beyond Racism*. *If They Come in the Morning* did not suggest that African Americans arm themselves or start a violent revolution against the United States. Rather, the book used writings from Davis and her allies to argue for her right to a fair trial and for her liberation. The literary fad of the book-length diatribe against "whitey" had run its course. Moreover, by pleading Davis's case, *If They Come in the Morning* implied that she had a chance to win. It was the first movement book in years to convey hope.

If They Come in the Morning was also one of very few books not to focus specifically on civil rights but still include several factions of the movement. As a result, it captured the philosophical diversity of the movement in 1972. Whereas King's books argued for nonviolence and Brown's book supported violence, Davis's book presented both the conservative and militant sides of the movement. The ex-SNCC member naturally dominated the book, but it also contained statements of support from SCLC leaders Ralph Abernathy and Coretta Scott King and a message from the BPP.

Indeed, the movement had infiltrated popular culture so deeply that pop musicians now crafted songs about the injustices that specific individuals like Davis suffered. "Message music" had evolved beyond generic calls for brotherhood and peace. In the middle of 1972, new albums by the Rolling Stones and John Lennon included songs that paid homage to Davis. The former's "Sweet Black Angel" and the latter's "Angela" were timely, because they were published while she remained under intense media scrutiny. However, with her now out of prison, their musical pleas for her release were outdated.[20]

Unity without uniformity—it could have been the motto of the movement in 1972. It happened to be the slogan of an African American coalition that met in Gary, Indiana, in March. The National Black Political Convention boasted a politically diverse collection of participants—Pan-Africanists, separatists, integrationist civil rights activists, an African American adviser to the White House, and various Democratic and Republican politicians. The gathering had more political diversity than the meetings of CAP and the African-American Institute. Moreover, the participation of the nation's most prominent African American elected officials guaranteed press coverage to a greater degree than the coverage of the previous Pan-African conferences. Representative Charles Diggs was on hand to moderate the proceedings, and both he and Delegate Walter Fauntroy had helped to organize the event with Imamu Amiri Baraka. The clothing of the participants reflected the political diversity at the convention, ranging from "establishment" suits to "movement" denim and African dashikis.[21]

The participants acknowledged their collective involvement in a common struggle because of their skin color and African heritage. By this time Jesse Jackson was fully supportive of Baraka's concept of black nationhood, leading the delegates in a call-and-response chant for "Nation Time" during his speech. His closing remarks broke from the political integrationism of civil rights organizations because he called for the attendees to "form our own political party."[22] Now that he led his own civil rights group and no longer had to align his views with those of SCLC or Abernathy, Jackson felt free to publicly embrace electoral separatism. He was virtually alone in the movement in doing so, and his stance did not help him get along with the leaders of the other organizations.

Aside from Jackson's address, civil rights leaders played a minimal role in the convention. The gathering attracted some people because it chartered a new direction away from civil disobedience. Representative John Conyers of Michigan, for example, considered the movement "almost flat on its rear end" by the time he attended the convention.[23] CORE leader Roy Innis's presence reflected his long-term commitment to separatism. Ralph Abernathy and Coretta Scott King represented SCLC there, and SNCC's Fran Beal promoted the cause of African American feminism at the convention. Vernon Jordan of the NUL said very little during the proceedings, but participants appreciated his attendance.

The NUL director's praise for the convention was significant because of the organization's history of disparaging separatism. Jordan saw the convention's existence as a victory in and of itself because it "brought together the disparate elements of the black community in common cause." It was quite a leap from the "exclusion from the very idea of politics" that African Americans rampantly faced only a few years earlier. It had its flaws, but it had no more disorganization than any other convention. Suggesting the end of the era of the prominent ethnic speaker, Jordan saw the convention as a signal that "people no longer see political power as a function of charismatic personality." He focused on the potential for African Americans collectively to attain power, celebrating that "there is far more that unites black people than divides, and that the will to unity is strong and vital."[24]

Wilkins was less enthusiastic than Jordan, but still gave the convention a positive review in his newspaper column. He could not resist criticism of "forbidding manning of the floor microphones, the separatist demands for parity, delayed credential treatment for certain groups" and so on. He lamented "the repetitive and often ridiculous rhetoric about blackness." Echoing Jordan, he acknowledged that "the convention, just by holding together for the scheduled time, was an event of significance." Still, he mostly offered backhanded compliments, as when he admitted that addressing grievances as a separate political entity was still "better than with violence widening the gap between citizens, with bitter outrage drawing thousands of blacks to a dead-end of separatist philosophy." He noted, however, that if the government addresses the convention's concerns, "the nation is better off." Thus, with Wilkins's reserved approval, civil rights leaders were in agreement as to the usefulness of the convention and—by extension—of gatherings of African Americans by virtue of their ethnic identity.[25]

The National Black Political Agenda, as stipulated by the convention attendees, was written with primarily African American readers in mind. It was peppered with the pronouns "we," "us," and "our." The agenda challenged African Americans to become "harbingers of true justice and humanity, leaders in the struggle for liberation." It argued that neither the Democrats nor the Republicans would help African Americans but that fundamental systemic changes in the country would. It warned that if African Americans did not create an independent "Black life," then they would "slip back into the decadent white politics of American life."[26]

The delegates had a point. The first day of the gathering—March 10—was in the midst of Wallace's anti-busing campaigning in Florida. As his rhetoric gained traction from his Democratic supporters, other candidates in the party shied away from the topic. President Nixon's opposition to busing that same month showed where the Republican Party stood. The convention needed to develop an independent alternative because the established parties criticized busing more than they affirmed desegregation. The alternative would have to be so formidable that it would force the established parties to take the "Black Agenda" more seriously than it currently did.

On the other hand, being independent did not mean being strident. Since the late 1960s, the federal government had taken violent threats from activists seriously, but it merely responded by developing the "law and order" culture. African American concerns that had been the context for the violent threats remained ignored. As a result, the convention's agenda called for African Americans to move past "loud-talking, 'militant' pawns." It was an indirect admission that the time of the revolutionary speaker had passed.[27]

In contrast to the qualified compliments to the convention, Wilkins publicly declared the agenda "impossible for the NAACP to endorse." He was disappointed that the proceedings did not focus on issues on which the attendees had a large consensus. More importantly, he decried the agenda's vision of "a separate black nation, a separate black politics, and the establishment (with the help, ironically, of the rejected 'white nation') of separate black institutions." He had hoped for a call for African Americans to have "an equitable black share of control in institutions and agencies now controlled and dominated by whites." The movement's brief period of unity through skin-color exclusivity was over.[28]

Shortly after the convention, Abernathy gave minors a turn at activism for the Children's March for Survival in Washington, D.C., on March 25. The organization was no stranger to casting children in marches; nine years earlier, SCLC had led children in demonstrations in Birmingham, Alabama. Now, in the nation's capital, the event went smoothly, with the children free from attacks by police with dogs and firehoses, as in Birmingham. As a result, the press ignored the march.

SCLC tried to make the demonstration newsworthy, using Abernathy's daughter Donzaleigh as a speaker. She was an unusual choice because civil rights groups did not rely on children for the responsibility of delivering speeches at protests. Any speaker at any political event was in a vulnerable position because, alone at a lectern, that person became a prime target for assassination, not unlike Malcolm X's death by gunfire in 1965. Also, the speech was a central part of a protest; the orator used the remarks to state the rationale and goals concerning the event. A clearly stated rationale and reasonable objectives, in turn, motivated people to support the demonstration, but adults in SCLC with years of experience in public speaking were having trouble attracting people to the organization's programs.

An inexperienced speaker, Donzaleigh merely followed her father's example of blaming the White House for perpetuating poverty. "We are marching for survival today because the men who run our country have failed—flunked out," she stated. "We are marching to say to the adults of America, give us new leadership." Through the demonstration, SCLC succeeded in putting a young face to the issue of poverty and showed that the group could still attract younger generations to its events. Nevertheless, the March for Survival amounted to children imitating how SCLC members marched and how SCLC leaders spoke, and, as such, it was a novelty act and another example of the group's descent into self-parody.[29]

Despite SCLC's current problems, the group continued to inspire people, even in the least likely places. Helen Seaman, a close acquaintance of John Lennon, alerted Abernathy by letter of the impending deportation of the ex-Beatle and his wife on an old marijuana charge. She wrote on behalf of her group—the Justice for John and Yoko Committee. According to Seaman, "the government's action arises more from John and Yoko's public stand against the war, and their humanitarian work in this country." She asked him to sign her organization's petition of support for the couple, coaxing him with flattery about his reputation as an activist. "The use of your name will add a new dimension of moral integrity to our efforts on behalf of John and Yoko," she reasoned.[30] Although Lennon and Abernathy did not work in the struggle together, both of them not only opposed the fighting in Southeast Asia but also advocated for Angela Davis's freedom. In that sense, Seaman's request was not without context.

Also, some militant African Americans toned down their militancy. After charges against BPP leader Huey Newton were dropped in late 1971, he took full control of the organization and revamped it. Although he did not embrace SCLC's nonviolence, he made a strong effort to steer the BPP away from its violent reputation. The Panthers were not going to publicly arm themselves anymore. To Newton, firearms were irrelevant to revolution. "The gun itself does not symbolize a revolutionary," he said in late January 1972. "Fascists also carry guns."[31] He had a point; only two years earlier, police had killed Fred Hampton as part of the federal government's attempt to suppress a specific group of people.

He envisioned changing the BPP's structure in ways that also resembled SCLC. Just as King had run SCLC to implement his vision, Newton guided the BPP alone and wanted the Panthers to put his ideas into practice. He pressured businesses in the BPP's home base of Oakland to either financially support his organization or face a boycott. Although the NAACP conducted boycotts to end businesses' segregationist practices, Roy Wilkins was unimpressed by Newton's implementation of the tactic. To Wilkins, it amounted to little more than "extortion."

Still, by choosing nonviolent tactics, the BPP was coming around to the movement's style of activism. Not unlike SNCC's Freedom Summer and SCLC's Resurrection City, the Panthers provided free services for people in Oakland such as tests for sickle cell anemia and bags of groceries. Also, like SCLC's members who had gravitated to politics, the BPP wanted to be taken seriously as a political force. "I am not optimistic about a new system of things coming about through the electoral process," Newton admitted, "but I believe it some areas we can get some benefits." By the spring, he was stationing BPP members at voter registration desks inside the organization's community building in Oakland, and he hoped to extend his voter registration drive well beyond Oakland—through the Deep South. He had revamped the BPP so effectively that by the summer of 1972, *Ebony* listed him among the nation's six current civil rights leaders; Abernathy, Innis, Jackson, Jordan, and Wilkins were the others.[32]

SNCC was not represented in *Ebony*'s list, but it had no leader for the periodical to identify. However, some of its former members still maintained ties with civil rights groups. Angela Davis continued to affirm SCLC, agreeing to a joint interview with Abernathy on April 21. Abernathy complained about the nation's problems and assigned blame to various people, but Davis discussed people who labored to help solve the problems. When asked about the White House's management of the Vietnam War, the SCLC leader expressed skepticism. "I don't put anything past President Nixon," Abernathy sneered. "He might temporarily halt the American involvement just to get reelected." In contrast, Davis complimented her fellow interviewee in some of her answers. "I think the way in which Rev. Abernathy is a leading spokesman of the black liberation struggle in this country," she began, "is something which is very honest, very strong, and an extremely important desire in our communities."[33]

On May 1, the movement received some unexpected validation from the press. Columnist Jack Anderson reported some of the clandestine activities of the FBI against private U.S. citizens. Unlike other reports the longtime self-identified "muckraker" had written about it, this particular column referred to documents from the bureau itself. Most of the people he identified as targets were left-leaning celebrities like Harry Belafonte, but Anderson also named several civil rights activists, such as Roy Innis of CORE and SCLC's Ralph Abernathy. Moreover, the reporter made a point of revealing that while the FBI's monitoring of King was "no secret," the press had not previously disclosed that the bureau was currently "watching his widow." After all the years that movement officials had talked about the government being out to get them, now they had their proof.[34]

The FBI's secrecy was severely compromised. After FBI director Hoover had ended COINTELPRO in 1971, he still directed his agents to monitor civil rights activists and groups. In addition, merely drafting a memo to "officially" dissolve a program did not necessarily mean that Hoover prevented his agents from conducting the neutralization tactics in another capacity. COINTELPRO agents would have struggled to immediately develop new means of thwarting domestic enemies after 15 years of activity in the program. Indeed, some agents simply kept neutralizing, but not in the name of the program anymore.[35]

The FBI barely had time to recover from the revelations. Only one day after Anderson's column was published, J. Edgar Hoover died. He had been the bureau's only director and had headed it for 48 years, developing nearly five decades' worth of informants, agents, and files. With his longtime assistant Clyde Tolson retiring from the bureau days later, the bureau was in a state of flux. President Nixon would not be able to find anyone with as much experience in the agency as Hoover and Tolson. He could only hire someone who shared his—and Hoover's—intense animosity toward militant speakers and civil disobedience.

To find such a person, the president looked to his own Justice Department instead of the FBI and named L. Patrick Gray the interim director of the bureau. Gray had served as an assistant to former attorney general John Mitchell. Like Richard Kleindienst, Gray was also familiar with Mitchell's activities against civil rights activists. When he started at the FBI on May 3, he tried to maintain business as usual for the bureau's anti-movement machinations. He ordered no changes to the monitoring of civil rights organizations and their members. SNCC still had an active file, as did Coretta Scott King. Over 7,400 "ghetto informants" continued to roam the streets and collect information on possible "black extremist" threats. As with Kleindienst replacing Mitchell as attorney general, Gray's transition hardly disrupted the FBI's continued surveillance upon civil rights activists. In addition, with Nixon appointees now leading both the FBI and the Justice Department, the administration completely ran the federal government's campaign against the movement. Nixon had the last word on how the government would pursue—and punish—the "irresponsible militants."[36]

Elsewhere in the nation's capital, the TWWA helped organize African Liberation Day. On May 27, about 12,000 people of African descent marched on the city's streets to support African freedom fighters and protest U.S. policy in Africa. They walked through Embassy Row for nearly three hours, denouncing the leadership of the United States, Portugal, Rhodesia, and South Africa along the way. When they finished their march at the Washington Monument, they listened to a diverse array of speakers ranging from congressmen to activists. The TWWA's participation kept SNCC involved—albeit indirectly—in political activism, because some of the organization's members remained SNCC associates.

In addition, SNCC's history permeated the march. Former members Cleveland Sellers and Stokely Carmichael attended the march, but for the latter the event had less to do with the movement than with the Pan-Africanism he had helped to inject into it. "This is not a civil rights march," Carmichael insisted. "It is a Pan-Africanist demonstration. This must advocate a revolutionary posture." For one participant, the event marked a return to activism. The Pan-African theme inspired him to participate in a demonstration for the first time since the deaths of SNCC members Ralph Featherstone and Che Payne two years earlier. "Irish people identify with Northern Ireland; many Jewish people identify with Israel," he noted. "I'm hoping our physical concern (evidenced by Afro haircuts and African clothing) will move toward intellectual concern."[37]

Other civil rights groups expressed their solidarity, thus maintaining the momentum from March's convention for African American political gatherings. Walter Fauntroy and CORE chairman Roy Innis were among the civil rights leaders present, as was longtime activist Dick Gregory. Ralph Abernathy supported the gathering, having spoken to the UN General Assembly Committee on Apartheid and Racism to ask the organization to declare May 27, 1972, African Liberation Day. By championing Pan-Africanism, the SCLC leader showed that he was in solidarity with black nationalists. He also crushed Hosea Williams's hopes of fashioning African Americans like the Chinese. Abernathy did not appropriate Chairman Mao's leadership style or wear Mao jackets at demonstrations. Eventually, neither did Williams.

The festivities also affected SCLC in a superficial sense. That same month, SCLC–Atlanta/DeKalb started weekly People's Liberation Day rallies on Saturdays. Despite the language borrowed from African Liberation Day, the meetings had nothing to do with Pan-Africanism. Rather, SCLC saw People's Liberation Days as a means to end unemployment and start an African American community economic base. In the tradition of renaming "Black Power" as "Soul Power," the phrase "People's Liberation" marked the group's latest rewording of a popular separatist-sounding phrase in order to remain integrationist."[38]

After the Pan-African rallies of early 1972, civil rights organizations lacked another issue to bring them together. As a result, they immediately resumed their internal and movement-wide factions. New civil rights groups and leaders had emerged for the duration, and competition for political influence and media access among the organizations intensified during the election season. For late 1972, their best hope was that the threat of another four years for President Nixon and Vice President Agnew would unite the groups as well as the cause of African unity had.

CHAPTER 15

Groovin' on Democracy

Throughout the life of the movement, civil rights workers struggled to connect with adolescents and young adults. In the early 1960s, the elders of the NAACP and the SCLC had tried to convince the SNCC to conform to their traditional, nonconfrontational means of activism. SNCC's militant rhetoric and civil disobedience over the years exasperated the coalition's senior comrades, who preferred legal action, boycotts, and marches. Now, in the summer of 1972, the SNCC joined the movement establishment, suffering the same disconnection from young people that the NAACP and SCLC had first experienced over 10 years earlier.

The release of the movie *Superfly* on July 1 caused a cultural shift among young African Americans. It redefined the African American counterculture as glamorous, underground economizing instead of radical political activism. The era of the Afro'ed "Linc" from the television program *The Mod Squad* gave way to the era of the processed drug pusher named "Priest"—*Superfly*'s protagonist. Many young men, following Priest's lead, wore their hair long and straight and dressed in flashy suits. In addition, the film's soundtrack came from the same man who had written the movement's earlier unofficial anthem "We're a Winner," but the songs in the movie were decidedly less optimistic. They centered on the main character, who conducted his illegal business transactions in order to make a living and to reach for a quality of life someday that did not require selling drugs for income.

Superfly spoke to a new generation of African American youth. Older African Americans were able to remember years of segregation before the existence of SCLC and SNCC. People turning 18 years old in 1972, however, were born in 1954—the year of the Supreme Court's decision to declare segregated schools unconstitutional in *Brown v. Board of Education.* They had spent their childhood and adolescence amid constant reports of marches, demonstrations, angry speeches, and the desegregation of businesses and facilities. But as those children entered adulthood, many of them found themselves still poor and jobless after all those events. For some of them, *Superfly* offered an appealing alternative because the movie promoted the idea that selling drugs was a way to "get over" that did not require getting one's head crushed during a sit-in or burning down a city during an urban uprising. Young people responded enthusiastically to the film, prompting magazines, rhythm-and-blues artists, and television shows to popularize the "Superfly look."

The NAACP and the CORE joined other organizations to try to stop the movie's distribution and exhibition, arguing that Priest was a terrible role model for young African Americans. Roy Innis of CORE specifically called for Hollywood to send scripts of movies featuring African American characters to a review board for approval, stating that African American communities should have access to edit such movies not yet released. He also wanted European American producers of those films to provide opportunities for African Americans to learn how to make their own movies. If Hollywood refused these demands, he would resort to boycotts and legal action against the studios. But in a subtle repudiation of Brown's rhetoric, Innis noted that he did not want militant violence against them.

The coalition was conducting an old-fashioned protest. Decades earlier, the NAACP had tried to pressure the film industry through boycotts and letter-writing campaigns. The organization had wanted Hollywood to withdraw the pro–Ku Klux Klan movie *Birth of a Nation* and cancel the neo-minstrelsy television series *Amos 'n' Andy* and *Beulah.* In *Superfly,* the pimp and pusher replaced the childlike "sambo" and the sexless domestic "mammy" as stock characters. But to the pressure groups, any stereotype stood to harm African Americans, whether the caricature was grotesque or glamorous. Moreover, the NAACP had been successful in getting rid of some of the films it had targeted, and the anti-*Superfly* coalition had no reason to think that similar efforts would not be successful again.[1]

Although SNCC was not officially part of the coalition, it also decried *Superfly*'s influence on young African Americans. In a letter to its members, SNCC's governing body—the RPC—attacked the movie as useless in helping young African Americans attain political consciousness. In addition, the organization identified the movie as a tool used by oppressive forces against African Americans to keep young African Americans politically ignorant. "Why is the oppressor more successful in getting Black Youth to see

Superfly than we are in getting them to see the *Battle of Algiers?*" SNCC complained.[2]

African American outcry about *Superfly* paled in comparison to African American outrage over a shocking revelation. On July 25, the Associated Press publicized the Tuskegee Syphilis Study. Peter Buxtun, a disgruntled member of the U.S. Public Health Service (PHS), told reporter Jean Heller that for the past four decades, the government agency had conducted an experiment upon African American sharecroppers. The PHS had allowed the farm laborers to remain untreated for syphilis since 1932 in order for the agency to study the disease's effects on people. The doctors withheld the helpful drug penicillin from them to keep their bodies from improving in health, which would have ruined the experiment.

Some African Americans considered the study's revelation as proof that the federal government was against African Americans. After all, the government had willingly sought the deaths not of Spiro Agnew's "irresponsible militants" but rather of impoverished African Americans far removed from political activism. *Jet* magazine, when reporting the story, called the country a "hostile, white dominated society" and referred to the story as "just a drop in the bucket of oppression." Thus, in the summer of 1972, civil rights workers intensely confronted forces they considered oppressive. For some groups those forces were the leaders of national government, and the activists encamped and rallied to remove them from office. Other activists found their oppressors in their own organizations, accusing them of thwarting revolution through discriminatory behavior.[3]

Although African Americans increasingly expressed futility toward directing the federal government's attention to their concerns, the PPC still believed that "the system" was worth confronting. As the summer began, the coalition prepared to launch its political direct action drive. SCLC, the National Welfare Rights Organization, and the National Tenants Organization issued a collective call to the Democratic Party. This coalition—the PPC—requested specific policies such as a guaranteed annual income of $6,500 for a family of four, elimination of the flow of drugs into poor communities, and free, quality medical and dental care, as well as a program of productive jobs for the unemployed. Other requests were more general and centered on social justice. The PPC demanded total equality in employment and the administration of justice, quality education for all, representative control of schools, and decent housing for all families. The coalition referred to its statement as the "poor people's platform" to the DNC and intended to deliver it to the Democratic Party delegates in person.[4]

Once again, a civil rights group was facilitating a large-scale, nonviolent protest in the summer in the South, but the advent of Resurrection City II generated very little fuss among the locals. George Rodericks, special security consultant to Dade County, predicted that only 6,000 nondelegates would arrive at Miami Beach and that only 2,000 of them would actually need live-in campsites. On July 6, the PPC began to congregate at Flamingo Park in Miami in anticipation of the convention. SCLC immediately started work on establishing Resurrection City II, with Bernard Lafayette serving as the city manager. James Orange took on the role of security chief despite the makeshift city's lack of a jail and Orange's refusal to use guns. Among his first tasks was to stop an outbreak of nude sunbathing that day.

Meanwhile, Flamingo Park filled up with squatters. By the following day, the population of Resurrection City II had grown to about 500 hippies, Yippies, Zippies, Vietnam vets, and Jesus People. They had erected 100 tents, and SCLC expected still others—300 to 400 poor people from Alabama, Georgia, Mississippi, and Florida—to arrive shortly. As in the first Resurrection City, the sequel was divided into "city" sections for each group of people represented at Flamingo Park.

Two days later, the first rally of Resurrection City II gave the encampment an impressive launch. A demonstration that Abernathy had announced to the press was scheduled to take place in Miami's Manor Park. The venue was in Liberty City, the largest African American community in Miami. As a result, Abernathy had the potential to reach a large African American audience and attract a large number of people to his organization. A sizable African American gathering in the same city as the DNC also had potential for significant national media coverage. About 3,000 people gathered at the park for a rally sponsored by four African American groups and the VVAW. An African American band began playing a song. People raised their fists in response. As in the old days of the movement, this event also attracted celebrities. Prominent activists Dave Dellinger, Benjamin Spock, Imamu Amiri Baraka, and Gloria Steinem took turns addressing the crowd.

Then Abernathy spoke, claiming that the occupants at Flamingo Park had leverage with the Democratic Party. Implying that the impoverished could be bribed, he announced that "the price of poor people votes has gone up." He stated that unless Democrats helped address the concerns of the poor, they would not receive the votes of the poor and would, therefore, not be successful in November. "It's collection time in 1972," he bantered, "so the Democratic Party has to dig in deep if they want to get their votes to go higher." In addition, the party owed it to the poor because of all the work they had done for the party. "It is poor people who have delivered most of the votes in the Democratic Party for the past forty years," he noted. He concluded by borrowing from Rap Brown's July 1967 remarks about African Americans collecting dues, except this time the collectors were not just African American. "This year the poor people have come to collect the unpaid bills."[5]

The next day the PPC turned to confrontation. The DNC opened in Miami, and the activists corresponded with a demonstration outside of Resurrection City II. When the day started, people at the convention in the Fontainebleau Hotel could hear the noise from Flamingo Park two blocks away. Later that day, some of the occupants at the park gathered at a chain-link fence that separated them from the convention proceedings. They demanded that 750 seats at the convention be opened to them for observation of the proceedings. Leading the group, SCLC also publicly opposed President Nixon's campaign for reelection. "We are here to evict Richard Milhous Nixon from the White House," Abernathy declared from the far end of the fence, "but just because we are against the re-election of Nixon doesn't mean that we are for the Democratic Party."[6]

To prove his point about not necessarily supporting the Democrats, his organization led an effort to disrupt the convention proceedings. Demonstrators in the crowd, including members of both SCLC and SDS, tried to either destroy the fence or climb over it. Some of them proceeded to tear down part of the fence and attempt to enter the Fontainebleau. A chant began among them: "Open the door! Open the door!"

The security on the ground soon had backup to stop the bum's rush. Police officers rushed out of the convention hall to stop them. Although Hare Krishnas swooped into the fray and started chanting and dancing, the officers successfully prevented the protestors from storming the hotel. Only Abernathy was allowed inside the convention. The Krishnas continued their performance, and entertained onlookers tossed money at them in appreciation.

Overall, the unrest was minor. It was nowhere near the level of vandalism that Abernathy had facilitated at the Alabama swimming pool three years earlier, which itself was a small-scale rebellion. Still, for the second time since becoming the SCLC president, Abernathy had left his residency to travel out of state to lead a mass of people into destroying public property. No government officials pursued him for violating the H. Rap Brown Act, but the SCLC leader was once again personifying Brown's rhetoric more than Brown himself was.

Meanwhile, back at Flamingo Park, the campers struggled with the Miami summer heat. The muggy air at the encampment held an oppressive combination of marijuana, rank body odor, and suntan lotion. Although marijuana was illegal, the police chief decided not to have his policemen arrest anyone for smoking it during the occupation. After having camped for several balmy days without bathing, some of the Resurrection City II dwellers carried offensive scents that wafted into the nostrils of unappreciative bystanders. The heat had overpowered many sunblock-layered demonstrators, and some of them lay en masse inside the park's medical tent for treatment.

Nevertheless, the residents of Resurrection City II went about their business. A small coed group of people went skinny-dipping. Women bared their breasts to the public, and couples openly engaged in sexual intercourse. About 100 Gay Activist Alliance members sat cross-legged on Flamingo Park's lawn and burned candles. Twenty Jesus Freaks cavorted in front of them. Later in the day, they played Frisbee with Satanists. Saffron-robed Hare Krishnas paraded by the Young Socialists. Borrowing the language of the PPC, activists in favor of the legalization of marijuana organized a Pot People's Campaign, and Yippies and Zippies staged a smoke-in toward that end. Their crayoned "POT PEOPLE'S PARTY" sign attracted the largest crowd of onlookers and sightseers that day.

The occupants supported causes that were so politically radical that the movement had not yet endorsed them, such as amnesty for draft dodgers and abortion rights. One reporter at the scene referred to the atmosphere there as "more carnival than confrontation." Moreover, it was a *nonviolent* carnival. The activities at Resurrection City II earned attention only because journalists marveled at the lack of confrontation that took place there. It was a completely different outcome than the events at both the first Resurrection City and the 1968 DNC. Negotiations between SCLC's Stoney Cooks and Miami Beach Police chief Rocky Pomerance allowed for the encampment to take place at Flamingo Park without incident. As a result, according to one of the residents, "There aren't any real villains here." A young Democratic bystander likened the occupation of the park to a Boy Scout jamboree.[7]

Resurrection City II unwittingly highlighted some social changes that American society had experienced since 1968. "Law and order" had evolved from nightsticks to negotiations because police officers did not want to shame Miami with violent publicity. Whereas the 1968 PPC had been merely multiethnic, the 1972 PPC displayed diverse politics, sexual orientations, and religious faiths, as well as skin colors. Indeed, it was one of the first times that Christian ministers (in SCLC) sponsored gay rights activism in the United States. The press had fixated on the 1968 Resurrection City for weeks to see how SCLC would fare in its first major project without King's leadership. Four years later, journalists saw the Miami encampment as harmless and gave it very minimal coverage after the first two days.

With all the media attention focused on the circuslike environment of Flamingo Park and the restraint of the police, SCLC once again became lost in the shuffle. The organization had failed to draw the nation's attention to the problem of poverty. SCLC's act of occupying the park mattered less to the press and onlookers than what the other groups did while occupying. Also, Abernathy failed to make a memorable impression inside the DNC at the Fontainebleau Hotel. All one person could remember was the SCLC leader bringing 25 people inside to sing "We Shall Overcome." In addition, the frivolity at Flamingo Park diminished the PPC's sense of purpose in Miami. After all, none of SCLC's demonstrations under King were called "carnivals" or "jamborees." SCLC's descent into self-parody was now complete.

After the first day of the DNC, the PPC's occupation failed to gain momentum. When the convention center was empty, the National Welfare Rights Organization demonstrated there for two hours. Miami politician Tom Washington marched with the coalition. But early on the morning of July 11, vandals broke into the SCLC–Miami office and destroyed telephones, typewriters, and two days' worth of food for Resurrection City residents. They also left written death threats to SCLC's Ray Betts and Leroy Jackson. Also that week, Abernathy made his way through the PPC encampment at Flamingo Park, trying to persuade the squatters to go to a rally at Manor Park and hear him speak. It was going to be about "the politics of poor people," he told them. Celebrities were going to be there.[8] When the appointed time for the demonstration arrived, 500 African American locals and 500 NWRO members had gathered at Manor Park. However, Abernathy and the headliners he had promised were no-shows.

Resurrection City II was not yet a week old, yet it was already showing the same kind of disorganization that had plagued its Washington, D.C., predecessor. A significant number of people left Flamingo Park within the week, not wanting to stick around for the encampment's eventual funeral. As disappointed PPC campers retreated, only 100 antipoverty settlers bothered to show up to hold a prayer vigil at the southwest corner of the convention on July 13. Resurrection City II remained in operation for the entire the week of the DNC as a sideshow of politics and activism. When the permit expired, SCLC decided not to remain in Miami for the RNC later that summer.[9]

The encampment barely affected DNC proceedings, but the Democratic Party was heavily influenced by movement participants and allies that year.

The Voting Rights Act of 1965 and the Twenty-Sixth Amendment had opened the electoral process to African Americans and 18-year-olds, respectively, and they won their races for delegates where they had significant numbers. Senator George McGovern, a civil rights ally who had pushed for years for greater ethnic inclusion and an antiwar position in the party, won the convention's nomination for presidential candidate. Although Alabama's segregationist governor George Wallace—now paralyzed and wheelchair-bound after the assassination attempt—attended the convention, many African Americans from the South were now delegates, too. Jesse Jackson of the group PUSH joined Illinois's delegation. Yippie Leader Abbie Hoffman—one of the Chicago Eight, who was accused of violating the H. Rap Brown Act a second time in 1971—was also a delegate, and he was in shock. "I'm groovin' on democracy!" he beamed. "This thing really freaks me out!"[10]

The Democratic Party, meanwhile, was groovin' on the Vietnam veterans. As antiwar activists who had served in the conflict they now opposed, the VVAW strongly legitimized the Democrats' complaints about the Nixon administration's handling of the Vietnam War. The convention fawned over the 50 or so VVAW members whom the party had invited to attend the proceedings. The delegates treated the veterans like royalty all week long. The Democrats welcomed the VVAW with passes to the convention floor. Delegates arranged to have meals of pizza and fried chicken sent daily to the veterans, and the honored guests received 50 cases of beer a day to wash the food down. In addition, the DNC passed a resolution supporting the VVAW, as the White House sought to discredit it.

Civil rights organizations had yet to achieve such political legitimacy. The Democrats did not personally invite SCLC or any other part of the PPC to the convention. Civil rights activists had not successfully shown that President Nixon specifically was to blame for poverty and skin-color discrimination, whereas the veterans powerfully illustrated the president's shortcomings in his conduct of the Vietnam War. Moreover, the DNC prioritized attacking Nixon more on the war than on poverty and civil rights that election year. Ironically, Jesse Jackson and Ralph Abernathy entered the DNC by confrontation, but the veterans had taken the movement's model of nonviolent protest and become the convention's invited guests.[11]

Civil rights leaders put forth a show of almost movement-wide political unity, collectively hinting at supporting the Democrats that summer. On August 2, McGovern consulted in his senate office in Washington, D.C., with Julian Bond, Walter Fauntroy, Coretta Scott King, and a few other prominent African American figures. The senator sought their advice on whom he should nominate for his second running mate. His first running mate, Thomas Eagleton, had resigned from the position earlier that week after his disclosure of mental health problems had embarrassed the Democratic Party—especially McGovern. Abernathy, reinforcing his reputation for tardiness, showed up over an hour after the meeting had begun. The senator still received him, and the front pages of newspapers nationwide the next morning presented a photograph of the two seated and talking.

The conversation was a newsworthy event because Abernathy had not received an audience with a major national political figure since his White House meeting with the Nixon administration in May 1969. Now, three years later, Nixon's opponent established a relationship with SCLC. A victory for McGovern, therefore, had the potential to carry that relationship all the way to the White House and bring SCLC back to the good graces of the executive branch for the first time since King had opposed the Vietnam War in 1967. Moreover, McGovern and SCLC had similar political views. He had participated in the March against Repression in May 1970, and both he and the organization called for an immediate end to the Vietnam War.[12]

The following week, SCLC experienced major political setbacks. On August 8, Hosea Williams lost his bid for the Georgia senate. Because he had not resigned from SCLC while campaigning, he was able to return without fanfare to full-time concentration on group activities. Still, despite his busy schedule in the organization and his frequent media coverage in Georgia, he had failed to translate people's familiarity with him into votes. In contrast, that same day, Andrew Young won his district's Democratic primary election for the House of Representatives. Although out of SCLC for two years, he had managed to remain a strong political figure. He was now positioned to face the Republican incumbent Fletcher Thompson in a rematch.

One week later, SCLC regrouped at its annual convention in Dallas. The organization publicly aligned itself with radical individuals and groups to a greater degree than in previous conventions. Some of the members cried out the BPP's logan, "Power to the people!" Promoting Pan-Africanism three months after African Liberation Day, the conference declared its support for Rhodesia's indigenous Africans. In addition, the organization actively expressed solidarity with various ethnic groups for the first time in four years, facilitating its strongest associations with Latinos since Reies Tijerina and the SHLG had deserted Resurrection City in 1968. SCLC called for Puerto Rico's independence and African American and Mexican American unity. The group also announced its endorsement of the candidacy of Ramsey Muniz for governor of Texas. The gesture of goodwill to Mexican Americans was part of an overall movement strategy; SNCC–Texas had already expressed the need for African Americans and Mexican Americans to work together to overcome oppression. As a result, SCLC was once again following SNCC's lead. Regardless, Muniz stood to benefit from an endorsement by a major social organization because he was a third-party candidate competing against an establishment Republican and a millionaire Democrat.

Still, the radicalism had its limits—one of which was still nonviolence. In contrast to only a few years earlier, when SCLC had tried in vain to compete with urban insurrectionists for attention, the group now claimed the era of the urban disturbance as finished. "We can't waste our time burning and looting. You don't have to worry about that anymore," said local delegate Darlene Wise. "We are going to come to power politically with the SCLC as a guideline for blacks, poor people, minorities." Despite her confidence, her promise was difficult to fulfill. She offered no specifics on how the organization would allow the impoverished and ethnic minorities to ascend politically. Although reaffirming that violence was not the way, the group did not say what exactly was the way. Most importantly, SCLC was nowhere near the national convention of the political party that was currently in power. As the Republicans met in Miami, no one from SCLC confronted them or attempted to address the concerns of the poor there.[13]

Despite the group's lack of a consistent message, SCLC was able to garner significant press coverage for its convention because of the celebrities that the group still attracted as speakers. Andrew Young temporarily returned to the fold just to participate in the convention. The organization had a strong branch in Atlanta, where Young had just won the Democratic Party's primary in his district for a seat in Congress. His attendance at SCLC's proceedings demonstrated his continued commitment to African American uplift, and this commitment stood to attract African American potential voters in November. By telegram, Abernathy congratulated Young, telling him that despite not having visually and vocally supported the candidate as much as before, the SCLC president pledged to stand by him "not only through the general election but in all of your future endeavors."[14]

The recently freed Angela Davis was another major figure who spoke at the convention. In the weeks following her release from jail in February, she had become a popular, highly sought-after public speaker. SCLC scored a major accomplishment in securing her presence at the convention. Abernathy gave her a special award from SCLC for "her personal courage in supporting black liberation," as he put it. While delivering her address about prison reform, she again publicly declared her support for the SCLC leader. "One of the greatest highlights during the period of my imprisonment was Dr. Abernathy's visit to me in Marin County Jail," she admitted. In the conclusion of her speech, she rallied the audience to follow his leadership. "We are all with you, Dr. Abernathy," she cheered. "We are ready to go with you in that journey to freedom." Her remarks made headlines in newspapers nationwide the next day.[15]

For all the public tiffs the First Lady of the movement had with the organization, Coretta Scott King continued to support the group her late husband had founded. She was on hand at the convention to echo the organization's public calls for the eviction of Nixon from office on Election Day. She claimed that he did not deserve to win reelection because of his failure to end the Vietnam War, which he had promised to do. "At this moment I am convinced that the President is not sincere in attempting to meet his commitment," she lamented. She also claimed that the war's longevity validated her late husband's opinion of the conflict. She reminded her listeners of the harsh backlash he had received for calling the war "unjust" and "immoral." Now, in 1972, "more than 59 percent of the working people in America believe it to be a war that is unjust and immoral," she stated.[16]

The press also anticipated the convention because of SCLC's new relationship with McGovern, and Abernathy did not disappoint. "I made it clear we weren't going to endorse anyone in the Republican or Democratic Party," he reminded the convention attendees. "But the spirit of the Lord is upon me tonight," he declared, "and I am going to give an endorsement tonight." He then rallied his listeners: "We are going to go out there, and with your help we're going to elect George McGovern as the next president." His endorsement thus ended the group's 15-year commitment to refuse to endorse candidates. He significantly set himself apart from his predecessor.[17]

Abernathy's break from SCLC policy reflected his heightened self-esteem from the public support from Davis and McGovern, and his self-confidence peaked at the SCLC convention. The SCLC leader boasted that the movement was "just beginning"—a dubious claim because the oldest national civil rights group—the NAACP—turned 63 in 1972. However, Abernathy was not talking about the coalition of civil rights organizations but rather of an entirely different entity. "There is no way for the SCLC to grow old or no way to kill it," he bragged, "because we are not an organization. We are a movement."[18]

The notion of SCLC-as-movement was as vague as Black Power had been six years earlier. Abernathy did not clearly define the concept, nor did he differentiate the so-called SCLC movement from the civil rights movement. His announcement was part of his tendency to make unilateral, unfounded claims, not unlike his self-appointed role as the African American middleman to the government and his declaration of a King holiday. Nevertheless, as the head of an "SCLC movement," Abernathy could now identify himself as an omnipotent movement leader by his own logic, just as the media had portrayed King as the undisputed leader of the civil rights movement.

Moreover, SCLC-as-movement was just one of several prominent social movements—Chicano rights, Native American rights, women's liberation, antiwar, gay liberation—to have emerged since the 1960s. In recent years these new movements had taken some of the media spotlight away from civil rights groups. By setting itself apart from the increasingly unpopular civil rights movement, SCLC could potentially resurrect its relevance to news reporters again. With renewed media attention, Abernathy was poised that summer to reintroduce SCLC to the public as a powerful political force.

Jesse Jackson, meanwhile, parlayed his celebrity as an activist into the entertainment industry that summer. On August 20, he hosted Wattstax—an outdoor concert produced by the rhythm-and-blues music label Stax. He was a kindred spirit to the label's vice president Al Bell, an African American who frequently promoted social causes. Bell, who wore suits and ties, was more superficially conservative than Jackson. The PUSH leader's Afro was large as usual, and he wore a short-sleeved dashiki to Wattstax. It was only fitting for an activist in countercultural garb to appear at an event that some in the press called the "Black Woodstock." As some of the acts went onstage wearing such futuristic apparel as silver-colored Afro wigs, Jackson at times appeared to be the most conservatively dressed person on stage.

Very little of the concert related to the movement or Jackson's politics appeared in the concert. He led the crowd in a raised-fist salute as Kim Weston belted out the "Black National Anthem." Otherwise, the gathering was largely apolitical, for the concert's acts simply took their turns on stage to perform their songs. Rufus Thomas sang "Do the Funky Chicken"—hardly the music that fueled revolutions.

The following month, Jackson the emcee became Jackson the impresario. He hosted his own concert—Save the Children. It was a major event featuring several of the most popular contemporary rhythm-and-blues artists. Unlike Wattstax, Save the Children was developed around a central theme— the problem of poverty. The title of the concert came from a catchphrase that Jackson often used in his speeches. Jackson had become a celebrity, and as such, was able to attract other celebrities. Like Wattstax, however, Jackson's concert consisted largely of entertainers whose music lacked sociopolitical messages. Several of the acts came from the Motown music label, which had fostered a reputation for shunning "message music." Although Marvin Gaye delivered a performance there in the wake of his successful political album

What's Going On, the less controversial Temptations, the Jackson Five, and the Supremes were also on the bill.

Save the Children was a triumph for Jackson, but the concert could not have happened if he had not been in SCLC for the past few years. Although demonstrations made the headlines for movement organizations, concerts were the fundraisers that enabled the groups to facilitate the demonstrations. SCLC had hosted several concerts over the past 15 years of its existence. When Jackson had just joined SCLC in Chicago in the mid-1960s, the group organized a concert in the Windy City in 1966. Five years later he organized the Black Expo. If he and SCLC had not parted ways because of how he had put the event together, he would not have been free to develop Save the Children for his own organization and on his own terms.

While SCLC and PUSH experienced triumphs in the summer of 1972, SNCC faced significant struggles. The group's de facto leader, Muhammad Hunt, left New York for Cincinnati, Ohio, to work with the local SNCC branch in increasing membership. He faced an uphill battle in resurrecting the organization. SNCC New York's sole business venture—its official bookstore—had recently closed. In addition, nearly a year had passed since the media had paid significant attention to SNCC in the context of Rap Brown's arrest at the New York bar. The group had yet to generate its own publicity. As a result, the African American magazine *Ebony* mistakenly but understandably announced in its August 1972 issue, "SNCC is dead."[19]

Whenever the media contacted former members of SNCC to comment about current African American problems, the activists made remarks that validated *Ebony*'s assessment. Around this time James Forman's memoir—*The Making of Black Revolutionaries*—was published. In the book he discussed his lifetime of activism, including the entire period of his association with SNCC, but he referred to the organization in the past tense. As current SNCC members did not publicly deny claims of its demise, the perception stuck with the public. Soon, only *Jet* magazine continued to acknowledge SNCC as a current entity. It was also one of the few periodicals to still identify the group as the "Student National Coordinating Committee," for many reporters had returned to the old name upon Brown's 1971 arrest.

Several concurrent problems hampered SNCC's ability to conduct business. In Brown's absence, Muhammad Hunt struggled to effectively lead all of the members. On August 11, he wrote only to the "Brothers," although the group still had female members. The omission was glaring, considering the media attention that the women received as part of the TWWA. The oversight suggested tension between the male and female associates. Also, in the letter Hunt apologized for the cancellation of a meeting in Atlanta. He said that on June 11, his driver had been hurt in a "suspicious" car accident and needed 88 stitches on his face. Trying to sound encouraging, Hunt defiantly claimed that "every sacrifice moves us that much closer to final victory. Love . . . Struggle . . . victory!" Despite having relocated to Ohio, he closed the letter with "The East is Strong!"[20]

Meanwhile, SNCC began taking on one of SCLC's problematic qualities— becoming defined by the absence of the group's leader. Brown's persona still hovered over the organization despite his incarceration. Hunt concluded his letter by asking members to keep Brown informed about the outside world. He did not want Brown to think that people had deserted the former chairman. "It would be very good for the moral [sic] of Bro. Rap if you could drop him a periodic line of solidarity," Hunt suggested. "Include your name, address, and title or position & maybe some newsclippings from your area." For all of Hunt's concern, however, he considered Brown irrelevant to the current business of SNCC. He followed the media's lead in referring to Brown's participation in the group in the past tense: "You can also include books, and post greeting cards or whatever you think will let him know that we are still in the struggle he was so involved in."[21]

SNCC's efforts in the movement were also undermined by the return of bitter, divisive factionalism. Members and their allies accused Hunt of manipulative activities. They claimed that he had drafted a "Super Spy" list. He did not directly accuse people of being informants for the FBI, but he allegedly warned friends and coworkers that those listed were not to be trusted. The list also had a sexual dynamic. When the women Hunt allegedly propositioned refused him, they and their husbands and boyfriends and partners were supposedly put on the list. Names included people in SNCC and the TWWA.

Hunt appeared to have held a personal grudge against the TWWA on an organizational level as well. He and two other SNCC–New York members consistently opposed the faction. SNCC's male leadership disputed the TWWA's relevance to African American liberation, saying that the faction only served the interests of white women. The male leadership also attached sexual orientation to the TWWA's gender-based militancy, accusing the women of organizing independently in the first place because of lesbianism. The remarks suggested the men's jealousy of the TWWA's soaring popularity as SNCC spiraled in decline. Nevertheless, despite the barbs and hostility from the men, Fran Beal stayed in SNCC at least for the sake of convenience. The organization had a branch in New York, where she lived, so she remained involved.[22]

Some of the disgruntled allies and former members scheduled a meeting for September 8 to discuss the group's problems. SNCC members asked for three weeks to collect evidence for the meeting. The others refused. "A 'cadre' doesn't accuse people of being agents and then need three weeks to gather proof," the TWWA explained. "Evidence is gathered first, and then accusations are made."[23] The aggrieved coalition held the meeting without SNCC.

Some of the women in the TWWA spoke at the meeting of how much they disliked Hunt's leadership. They accused him primarily of sexual intimidation. They claimed that he had made sexual advances to most of the SNCC women despite living with a prominent TWWA member and fathering a now three-year-old child with her. They also alleged that Hunt had used physical violence at least twice against people criticizing him for making unsubstantiated allegations.

Later that month, an editorial in the TWWA's *Triple Jeopardy* newsletter outlined the group's grievances. "Ever since its inception, the movement has been plagued by three elements: Agents, Opportunists, and Fools," it began. "Within SNCC itself, many of the cadres have taken on the role of the fool." The editorial accused SNCC members of excusing or remaining silent about Hunt's alleged behavior. "The opportunist often focuses on people that have influence among other people and attempts to gain their confidence. Through the fool, the opportunist can then control and/or manipulate others in an organization," the editorial explained. To the writer, Hunt had played the "opportunist" role "with a certain amount of success."[24]

The editorial warned that civil rights activists could sabotage their own struggle, because "opportunists" and "fools" stunted movement progress. Their actions "can sometimes cause an entire organization to take erroneous positions," the writer declared. "Criticism and self-criticism" could make this development less likely.[25] According to the TWWA, SNCC needed to have members who felt as if they could constructively comment on Hunt's actions, and vice versa. Also, Hunt needed to honestly assess his leadership.

The TWWA was not going to idly allow Hunt to thwart the revolution with his behavior. The editorial concluded, "As members of revolutionary organizations, we repudiate the allegations made by Mohammad Hunt and continue to demand that either these charges be documented or repudiated." Then, not letting the "fools" go blameless, the newsletter continued, "We also repudiate anyone who spreads malicious rumors without backing them up and who deals in a sexist way with sisters, claiming they are agents after they refuse to go to bed with him." Returning to Hunt's alleged actions but not naming him, the journal stated, "We repudiate anyone who attempts to isolate people through physical and mental intimidation and resorts to violence against those who confront him with his contradictions." Finally, the TWWA offered an invitation to SNCC to speak on the matter: "The people's court is in session. We are still prepared to meet to resolve this serious situation."[26]

The dispute was largely among people formerly or currently affiliated with SNCC–New York. However, members of the organization outside of New York saw cause for concern for the group's well-being. Outside of New York, the only other branches existed in Ohio, Oklahoma, and Texas—a fact that testified to the group's success in revitalizing itself in the South. SNCC–Oklahoma member John Payne, who served as the coordinator of SNCC's Western Zone, addressed the rest of the organization about the internal conflict. He informed the "Brothers and Sisters" by letter that his branch was calling for an emergency national meeting in Tulsa for October 7 and 8, due to "very serious contridictions [sic] raised concerning the National Apparatus." Payne admitted that the local branches "have not been and are not able to resolve" the national SNCC's problem.[27]

The conflict did not end before SNCC suffered a significant change in membership. On September 29, TWWA members Fran Beal and Yemaya Rice resigned from SNCC. In a joint letter, they clarified that their dispute was with SNCC–New York and not with the national organization. Addressing the "Brothers & Sisters," they wrote, "The organization for some time now has not been respecting the concept of collective leadership. Decisions are made without consulting anyone not even people who are supposedly members of the Revolutionary Political Council." SNCC had started as a leaderless organization, in which each participant had equal power. Beal and Rice did not like that some people were assuming the power of others. The two had tried to keep the group collective, but "when criticisms were made on our method of work, the response that 'we no longer operate as we once did and we are a different type of group now,' was used as an excuse not to grapple with those criticisms."[28]

"Neither of us will be able to attend the meeting called in Tulsa for October 7th & 8th," the two women announced. Payne's invitation was too little, too late. "We feel that the situation has gotten completely out of control," they observed, "and that these are not minor contradictions, but rather so serious that it is no longer a question of us trying to resolve them, but a question of us resigning from SNCC." Finally, emphasizing their departures one last time, Beal signed off as "Ex-Member" of the RPC, and Rice signed off as "Ex-SNCC cadre."[29]

Predictably, SNCC disagreed with much of the content in the letter by Beal and Rice, and the group's RPC responded with a letter of its own. The response displayed little love lost for one of SNCC's former members and revealed that the organization did not agree with the TWWA's linking of gender inequality with skin-color inequality. However, the council mistakenly assumed that the TWWA aspired to the same goals that European American feminists sought. The SNCC men were woefully ignorant of fundamental differences between African American feminists and their European American counterparts. Even after Beal had distinguished the two groups while reading aloud her "Double Jeopardy" statement in a 1970 SNCC meeting, the attendees apparently had failed to understand what she had said. "Forget about Gloria Steinem and Betty Freidan," SNCC snidely advised Beal and Rice, "and stop subordinating the hard reality of a war of liberation to the conflicts between males and females."[30]

The damage caused by the SNCC-TWWA dispute had become tangible by October. SNCC–New York's membership had dropped to three people, and all of them were men. Even Hunt's wife Barbara Hunt had resigned from the organization due to differences with her husband. Only Texas and Oklahoma had branches of an equal if not greater number of members. The few remaining individuals claiming SNCC membership in the rest of the country were George Hughes in Cincinnati and William Coleman in Atlanta. The group tried to keep old connections intact; John Payne remained in communication with former member James Forman, for example. But SNCC had entered a period of free fall.

Meanwhile, President Nixon welcomed the prominence of the radicals during the election year to the extent that he could exploit them. His staffers entertained suggestions that saboteurs plant Viet Cong flags at rallies. Nixon himself suggested that publicizing left-wing extremist support from Abbie Hoffman and Angela Davis for McGovern could draw Democrats away from their party, and his White House paid African Americans to picket one of the Democratic presidential candidates. The next few months of activity from the politicians and their supporters determined whether the movement's candidate or the incumbent president would win the election.[31]

CHAPTER 16

Their Most Vulnerable, Hopeless Position

As the RNC gathered in the summer of 1972, President Nixon remained skeptical about nominating Agnew as his running mate again. If they were to win a second term, the vice president would be the likely Republican nominee for president in another four years. However, Agnew's performance in office had disappointed some Republicans so deeply that they called for the president to appoint a new running mate, and Nixon considered doing so. On the other hand, Agnew was a popular figure among the Silent Majority—especially among staunch conservatives. The president needed conservative support to win reelection, and many conservatives threatened to abandon him if he were to abandon Agnew. Nixon was miffed that the conservatives preferred Agnew to him. Four years ago he had only wanted Agnew to be a preferable alternative to Alabama governor George Wallace, but now that the conservatives had cast their ultimatum to the president, he had no choice but to comply.

Thus, at the RNC, Nixon dutifully announced that Agnew was back. He put on his game face, giving the announcement a humorous spin. "I thought he was the best man for the job four years ago," he recalled to the crowd. "I think he is the best man for the job today." Then, taking a jab at McGovern's replacing of Eagleton, Nixon joked, "And I'm not going to change my mind tomorrow." The audience laughed and cheered.[1]

For African American newspaper columnist Carl T. Rowan, the leadership of the Republican Party that year was not good news for African Americans. However, the problems extended beyond the re-endorsement of the Nixon-Agnew team. Rowan lamented that California governor Ronald Reagan,

Senator Barry Goldwater of Arizona, and movie star John Wayne had become "the darlings of the Republican Party."[2] Reagan had echoed the vice president's vitriol against dissent for the past five years and had blamed Martin Luther King's civil disobedience for his own death. Goldwater had similarly considered King a threat for taking similar political positions with the "lesser lights" of the movement, as he put it. Although Wayne had no problem with African Americans exercising their voting rights, he opposed the Civil Rights Act's desegregation of businesses.

Rowan blamed African American militants for creating a political climate that allowed African Americans to suffer "their most vulnerable, hopeless position in half a century." He expressed relief that Carmichael was in Africa and Brown was incarcerated, for those two and their imitators had "either proven themselves to be craven hustlers who sold out at the first opportunity" or had become "impaled upon their own rhetoric, their own stupidity." Rowan lamented, however, that their "irresponsible tactics" and "silly rhetoric" in the late 1960s had created the European American backlash that Reagan, Goldwater, and Wayne led. African Americans were unfortunately bearing the consequences of a backlash-fueled government, such as the reluctance of a Democrat-majority Congress to address the busing issue.[3]

Still, no reconciliation between Washington, D.C., and the movement was immediately forthcoming. Even the most conservative civil rights leaders expressed little optimism for the federal government, especially the White House. Ever the integrationist, Roy Wilkins saw Nixon's expression of anti-busing sentiment as support for separatism. The president seemed to speak on behalf of people nostalgic for 19th-century Jim Crow. "Now, just as [African Americans] are getting more youngsters finishing elementary and high schools and more are going to college, the white folks, led by the President, are getting all high and mighty about busing," Wilkins observed. To him, the anti-busing fuss really meant denying quality education to African Americans. "The short, ugly version is that black children must subsidize the comfort of white parents of children," he noted. "It fits into the pattern of 1896, the separate-but-equal constitutionality that was always separate but never equal."[4]

The NAACP joined its leader and officially attacked Nixon just as strongly, issuing an "emergency resolution" against him during its annual convention that summer. The group criticized the president for pushing for anti-busing legislation because of his position as an executive—not legislative—official, and the resolution blamed his rallying behind the issue for arousing "passions of hate and bitterness." Also at the convention, Stephen Spottswood repeated his identification of the Nixon White House as "anti-Negro."[5]

Unlike SNCC and SCLC, Wilkins tempered the NAACP's criticism of Nixon with a determination to focus on the issues and not meander into personal attacks. The resolution did not constitute an endorsement of the Democratic Party, and the NAACP never endorsed George McGovern or any other candidate that year. Moreover, Wilkins reassured the press, the organization was not anti-Nixon but merely against the president's exploiting of busing. Still, the NAACP remained critical of the president through the fall, saying in the *Crisis* that he "failed to bring the people together" but rather had encouraged "racial polarization." The group came close to endorsing the Democratic Party by cheekily noting that despite expressing neutrality concerning the presidential candidates, "no one needs wonder where the Association stands."[6]

None of the major national civil rights organizations supported Nixon's bid for reelection, but they did not form a strong collective effort to get out the vote against him. This shortcoming followed the movement's pattern of reactive solidarity—uniting in opposition to an issue like the Vietnam War or the spring 1970 killings, but failing to devise a unified alternative program on the issue. Thus far, the groups had failed to end the war or pressure the president to change his civil rights efforts merely by standing together in protest. Now, with civil rights leaders differing on how overtly to support McGovern, they waited to see how collective resistance to Nixon would affect the election's outcome.

The Nixon-Agnew ticket became an unlikely flashpoint for a disagreement among African Americans about ethnic loyalty. Most African Americans supported George McGovern in response to Nixon's problematic responses to their concerns, but some of them endorsed the incumbent. In 1972, however, an increasing number of African Americans saw political affiliation as an extension of skin-color solidarity, and they saw the Democratic Party as the party of their interests. Taking a page from the movement, they implemented boycotts and pickets of any performances by African American entertainers who supported Nixon.

Sammy Davis Jr.'s endorsement of the current president unwittingly symbolized the African American political divide. Davis still supported civil rights activism and had recently called for Angela Davis's release. However, he accepted Nixon's invitation to serve on the National Commission on Drug Abuse. At the president's request, Davis also entertained African American troops in South Vietnam in order to give them "somebody . . . who relates" and to provide a show that said, "Hey, man, this is from black folks at home." Then in August 1972, Davis welcomed a surprise visit from Nixon during a concert in Miami, and the singer hugged the president. The entertainer explained his political shift almost as if it happened by default. "JFK and Bobby Kennedy were great men, but they ain't here," he reasoned. Then, he noted that Nixon had increased funding for African American colleges and had abolished the quota system. "I dig Nixon because he doesn't do any front-running," he beamed. Davis interpreted the president's invisibility during the campaign year as a practical way to avoid criticism from his detractors. The singer concluded, "There's an honesty about the man I love."[7]

No one from the civil rights movement publicly agreed with Davis's assessment, but activists were split in their responses to it. Despite political differences, Jesse Jackson of PUSH invited him to the Expo that year, but several people booed the singer there. Davis's friend Charles Evers said, "Sammy did what he thought was right. He shouldn't be criticized for hugging the President." In contrast, an African American–owned music store borrowed a tactic from the movement by boycotting Davis's recordings. Also, ex-SNCC member Julian Bond openly disagreed with Davis and sharply noted, "He's a great entertainer, but that doesn't mean he knows anything about politics." Civil rights workers rarely publicly debated each other's differences concerning political affiliation, and Bond's comment highlighted the divisions within the civil rights coalition.[8]

Ironically, the movement had helped make this division possible by contributing to the struggle for voting rights only a few years earlier. Before 1965, an African American's attempt to register to vote often led to failure via resistant registrars and occasionally to death at the hands of segregationists. Any act of voting was a triumph for African Americans, and civil rights groups had conducted individual and collective efforts to register them. When legal barriers to the vote disappeared, so did the movement's unity in relation to voting.

Nixon never had the opportunity to win back Jackie Robinson's vote. The baseball legend admitted that he had no grave concerns about the president's reelection bid. On the other hand, Robinson remained concerned about Nixon's continued reliance upon Spiro Agnew and John Mitchell, because the former ballplayer did not consider either person a strong advocate for African Americans. Meanwhile, Robinson had slightly adapted to the African American counterculture's growing prominence, using the word "black" instead of "Negro" when calling for an African American manager in baseball. He started publicizing his upcoming autobiography *I Never Had It Made*, but weeks before its publication, he died suddenly of diabetes on October 24.

The president issued an official statement about Robinson's death. "This nation to which he gave so much in his lifetime will miss Jackie Robinson,"

Nixon said, "but his example will continue to inspire us for years to come." Specifically noting the ballplayer's contributions to interethnic relations, the president continued, "His courage, his sense of brotherhood and his brilliance on the playing field brought a new human dimension not only to the game of baseball but to every area of American life where black and white people worked side by side."[9] Nixon knew of what he had spoken, because he had worked with Robinson on a few occasions. As early as 1957, as vice president, he had sought Robinson's counsel on civil rights concerns, and the athlete had supported Nixon's presidential campaign three years later. Now, as Nixon's own vice president had helped distance the administration from African American leaders, one of the few that the president had most trusted was silenced.

For all the division that African Americans experienced among themselves that election season, Robinson's passing became an opportunity for social and political divisions to heal—at least temporarily. African Americans united to reflect upon the meaning of his life. People of Robinson's generation greatly outnumbered younger visitors to the funeral home that hosted his wake; after all, younger people had not been alive to watch him break baseball's color barrier. Nevertheless, they knew he had done something important, and some young African American men took off their hats to enter the funeral home and pay their respects to him.[10]

Jesse Jackson's eulogy represented this unification of the generations. He was not a likely choice to deliver the address because he had disagreed with Robinson on several issues. Jackson spoke out against the Vietnam War, but the former ballplayer—a veteran of World War II—had not done so. Whereas Robinson had spoken out against militant leaders like Brown, the PUSH leader had publicly supported the former SNCC chairman. Also, Robinson and Jackson had been visually different in recent years; the former's short "natural" hairstyle and suits contrasted sharply to the latter's fringe vests and ever-widening Afro.

On the other hand, the PUSH leader constantly reached out to Roy Wilkins and other elders in his perpetual quest to develop a strong civil rights network for the organization, and he did the same albeit posthumously— for Robinson. Jackson not only saw the commonalities they shared but also the inspiration the ball player had given to him. Speaking for 15 minutes, Jackson said that Robinson's desegregating of the Brooklyn Dodgers affected more than just the sport of baseball. "When Jackie took the field, something in us reminded us of our birthright to be free," he recalled. "All of us are better off because a man with a mission passed this way."[11]

The older generation, in turn, reached across to the younger shortly afterward, when the NAACP publicized part of its commission's report about BPP–Chicago leader Fred Hampton's death. Roy Wilkins and former Attorney General Ramsey Clark, who replaced Arthur Goldberg on the commission, held a press conference on November 2, acknowledging that they had completed the report the previous year but had to wait for judicial proceedings against municipal officers to end. The commission's "statement of conclusions" accused the police of "wanton disregard for human life and the legal rights of American citizens." The members referred to the killing as both "excessive use of gunfire" and "all more suited to a wartime military commando raid." The war analogy was ironic considering that four years earlier, Clark had appeared on television to say that nobody was putting African Americans into concentration camps. Now he was admitting that a military-style execution of people of a specific ethnic group had taken place—in a sense, reinforcing Rap Brown's Nazis-Jews catchphrase. The former attorney general called the matter "a total failure of the systems of criminal justice." Then, aware of the gravity of his words, he added, "I don't say that lightly. I'm a man of the law."[12]

Five days later, the president's "law and order" administration won reelection in a landslide. The election results validated Nixon's decision to keep Agnew as the running mate. He had reduced the vice president to making speeches against busing instead of speaking out against undesirable candidates, as he had done in the 1970 elections. Nixon trusted Agnew enough to allow him to travel without presidential staff this time. The vice president, for his part, deliberately adopted a more reserved speaking style. He reasoned that when he used less name-calling and moderated his tone, reporters had less of an opportunity to misconstrue his remarks. Two weeks before the election, the vice president had even told reporters "no comment" when asked a barrage of questions. *Time* magazine dubbed the reelection bid "Once More, with Feeling." The campaign did not impress everyone; one disgruntled journalist quipped about the toned-down vice president, "The trouble with the revised Agnew is that he remains Agnew."[13]

Many politically left organizers were extremely disappointed by McGovern's defeat. He had supported their causes, and although he was part of "the establishment" as a U.S. senator, some activists had embraced him as one of them. When Americans rejected him on Election Day, organizers felt as if the voters had rejected them, too. As "outside agitators" they had already felt estranged from political power. Nixon's reelection shut them off from it for the duration. Chicago Eight defendant Abbie Hoffman, who just four months earlier had "grooved on democracy" as a DNC delegate, now spent election night crying with friends over his candidate's drubbing.[14]

The NAACP felt the administration's shutoff from African Americans immediately after the contest. An editorial in *The Crisis* the following month groused that the "magic ingredient" of "racism" had caused European American Democrats who had voted against Nixon four years earlier to elect him in 1972. "They came to believe and were, in fact, encouraged by the White House to believe that Nixon would help them retain their lily-white exclusivity," the column observed, "and turn back the hordes of non-white peoples demanding their constitutional rights to equality of opportunity in education, employment, housing and politics." The editorial also professed that African Americans voted overwhelmingly for McGovern in order to prevent four more years of "benign neglect." Thus, the NAACP had moved beyond calling the Nixon administration "anti-Negro," now accusing the White House of catering to "white privilege."[15]

Among civil rights activists, Ralph Abernathy perhaps stood the most to lose from McGovern's loss. With Nixon remaining as president for another term, Abernathy lost the opportunity to regain any influence in the White House. In addition, even Abernathy's spirituality was repudiated when McGovern—the candidate God had told him to endorse—lost. Now the minister would have to explain to people whether he had heard God correctly or why God would tell him to endorse a candidate who was destined for defeat. Abernathy stopped talking about SCLC as its own movement, and the organization resumed work with other groups in the civil rights movement.

Voters may have rejected the movement's presidential candidate, but they did not agree with the administration's anti-movement stance as strongly as before. On that same day in Georgia, voters braved a heavy rainfall to elect ex-SCLC official Andrew Young to Congress. He was going to become the first African American Georgia representative since the end of Reconstruction. Throughout his campaign the press noted his former ties with SCLC and identified him as a former "top aide" to King. But unlike his failed campaign in 1970, his political views and former associations no longer worked against him. Also, his district had been remapped in a way that allowed him to reach more supporters. Meanwhile, SCLC was only too happy to mention its ties to the new representative-elect. In its *Soul Force* newsletter, the organization boasted of its alumnus in reflected glory, "It was a great victory for SCLC which Andy helped to fashion and for the legacy of Dr. King who lived and died that the disinherited might also share the power."[16]

SCLC's pride was natural, considering how many members had contributed to the new congressman's campaign. Longtime civil rights activists, including Young himself, also saw a link between his victory and his tenure in the movement. He called his election "the satisfying culmination of a decade's worth of hard work." Much of the work that took place in 1972 alone came from civil rights activists. Stoney Cooks had quit SCLC to manage Young's campaign. Former King aide Fred Bennett told Young to recruit Jesse Hill and speak more to neighborhood leaders than he had in 1970. When Representative-elect Young greeted his supporters in victory on election night, Mrs. King was among those sharing the platform with him.[17]

The winner marveled at his victory, sounding as if he could not believe he had won. "This is a district with a white voting majority in a Deep South city," he recalled, "and they picked a black man—from the civil rights movement yet—for Congress and with everything going for Richard Nixon." But after thinking about his obstacles, he talked about the meaning of his win. In contrast to the pessimistic speakers of the movement groups, Young sounded hopeful about the future of moderate European Americans voting in agreement with African Americans. "I think if blacks take the next two to four years to build this kind of coalition, they will be able to pull this off anywhere, North or South," he predicted.[18]

Young was part of a wave of victorious civil rights and antiwar congressional candidates from the 1972 elections. Despite all of the success of the Nixon administration and the FBI in weakening civil rights organizations, the federal government was unable to prevent the political ascension of dissenting individuals. William Clay handily won his reelection bid even after the previous year's comments about the vice president, as did VVAW ally Ron Dellums. Massachusetts voters sent Republican civil rights ally Edward Brooke back to the Senate, and an African American woman—Barbara Jordan of Texas—won a congressional race in the South for the first time ever. The NAACP expressed relief for these "notable gains" in *The Crisis*.[19]

Even scrappy Joseph Rhodes Jr. was now an elected official. After the folding of President Nixon's Commission on Campus Unrest in late 1970, the African American former Harvard student honed his public speaking skills. He lectured at events held by movement groups and other organizations. He occasionally took time to disprove Vice President Agnew's arguments about dissent by giving speeches and writing newspaper columns. Eventually, however, he saw his own political involvement as the best way to bring about the changes he had tried to convince the Nixon administration to perform since 1970. He ran for a seat in the Pennsylvania state legislature to serve the district that included his hometown of Pittsburgh. He won his electoral contest on November 7. Only four years after Agnew had risen to the vice presidency by denigrating African Americans, an African American successfully groomed himself for political office by denigrating the vice president. Agnew offered no comment on Rhodes's victory.

Exactly two weeks later, on November 21, the U.S. Court of Appeals for the Seventh Circuit reviewed the "American verdict," as the vice president had referred to the Chicago Eight outcome. A three-judge panel ruled 2–1 that Judge Julius Hoffman had made four major mistakes. He had asked potential jurors some questions that could have been prejudicial to the Chicago Eight and did not question them about how pretrial publicity would affect the proceedings. He had sent notes to the deadlocked jury without telling the attorneys. He had refused documents that stated, according to the defendants, why they had come to the convention in Chicago. He had prohibited testimony of the defense's expert witnesses. In addition, the panel did not like the "sarcasm" and "ridicule" he had given to the defense during the trial.

Therefore, the judges decided to reverse the convictions of February 18, 1970, which meant that the five guilty defendants were no longer guilty of violating the Rap Brown Act. The antiriot provision remained federal law, and the panel allowed the federal government to retry the defendants if it were willing to reveal the extent of the Justice Department's wiretaps and surveillance against them. Within days, however, the federal government announced that it would not retry the defendants. A representative for the newly freed activists called the panel's decision "a tremendous victory for the antiwar movement in this country and for the right of the people to dissent and demonstrate." The first men to be convicted of having violated the Rap Brown Act were free men, and Agnew's "American Verdict" was no more. Once again, the vice president gave no comment on this latest repudiation of his idea of "law and order."[20]

The freeing of those five of the Chicago Eight launched the federal government's revisiting of what constituted an "irresponsible militant." On November 30, the FBI ended its four-year surveillance of Coretta Scott King. She had not decreased any of her activism, but she now mostly gave speeches at political demonstrations. Ever since her husband's assassination, the FBI had tried to make "a determination as to any affiliation on her part with extremist or subversive individuals or organizations." The bureau failed to do so, and under Interim Director L. Patrick Gray, the FBI finally stopped spying upon her and closed her case. "No information has come to the attention of Atlanta which indicates a propensity for violence or affiliation with subversive elements," the bureau concluded.[21]

Although President Nixon rarely invited civil rights organizers to his house, his predecessor allowed many of them into his. On December 11 and 12, former President Lyndon Johnson hosted a civil rights conference in Texas. Civil rights leaders Roy Wilkins and Vernon Jordan were among the participants. Some of the attendees had publicly opposed the former president's handling of the Vietnam War, but his willingness to invite them suggested no hard feelings. Moreover, Johnson himself seemed to have co-opted the movement, at least on a superficial level, since his retirement to Texas three years earlier; eschewing his close haircut of his political days, he now sported long silver locks. In an ironic twist of fate, he was out of public office but now had the chance to see movement veterans who had entered it.

Some of the activists brought their organizational disputes and competitiveness with them to Texas. NAACP and CORE officials especially bickered at each other there. Their old arguments about effective African American leadership threatened to disrupt the gathering. CORE's leader Roy Innis and New York–based activist A. Kendall Smith demanded that the symposium continue in New York, in order to "expand and deal with a new definition of equality." They claimed that the gathering did not welcome viewpoints that differed from those of the movement's "establishment" figures. Longtime NAACP member Clarence Mitchell argued against their complaint, feeling that he had a need to "speak against black demagoguery."[22]

It was the last thing Wilkins needed. He had wanted to retire at the end of the month, on New Year's Eve. His wife Minnie was already retired, he was 71 years old, and his cancer had started to debilitate him. However, many of his NAACP staff had either taken ill or died during the year, and he did not want to leave the organization in such a vulnerable state. Therefore, he decided to postpone his retirement. He brightened when he saw his old friend Lyndon Johnson at the symposium, but the argument between Mitchell and Innis threatened to embarrass Wilkins and his organization.[23]

Johnson did his best to restore order to the proceedings. His ability to bring people to consensus on issues had contributed to his civil rights victories during his presidency. He had been a master at bringing factions of Congress together to pass the Civil Rights Act of 1964 and the Voting Rights Act of the following year. He had failed to convince Congress to pass the Civil Rights Bill of 1966, and only the urban rebellions of the King assassination and the compromise of the antiriot provision motivated Congress to pass the Civil Rights Act of 1968. Nevertheless, Johnson hoped that he could work his old magic to the movement's factions at his symposium. Still, the movement had been difficult for King to bring to consensus, and just before his assassination he had failed to do so. What more could Johnson do with an even more fractured civil rights coalition?

Much of Johnson's speech suggested solidarity with the movement. He first introduced the topic of the "special plight of the Black man," but then had a caveat: "And let me make it plain that when I say 'Black,' I also mean 'brown' and 'yellow' and 'red' and all other people who suffer discrimination because of their color and heritage. Every group meets its own special problems, of course—but in a broad sense, the problem of equal justice applies to us all." His inclusion of several minority groups as "black" echoed the multiculturalism Brown had endorsed in SNCC, and the concern for "equal justice" for "us all" reflected the integrationism of the NAACP, NUL, and SCLC. Johnson's reference to African Americans as "black" showed how Stokely Carmichael's promotion of Black Power had led even the former commander in chief to replace the word "Negro." Johnson also affirmed African American ethnic self-pride in the face of social inequality: "To be black—to one who is black—is to be proud, is to be worthy, is to be honorable. But to be black in a white society is not to stand on level ground. While the races may stand side by side, whites stand on history's mountain and blacks stand in history's hollow. Until we overcome unequal history, we cannot overcome unequal opportunity."[24]

Johnson's remarks diverged from current movement rhetoric when he suggested new approaches of activism for civil rights workers. In recent years, SCLC had started to refer to "poor people" collectively, and both SNCC and the BPP had called for power to "the people." In contrast, the former president wanted the country to move past helping "groups as groups" and to shift to assisting "individuals as individuals." He noted, "As we have lifted from groups the burdens of unequal law and custom, the next thrust of our efforts must be to lift from individuals those burdens of unequal history." Johnson also expressed great optimism that countered the pessimism that African Americans like Carl Rowan had expressed earlier in the year. Despite intolerance, discrimination, hate, and suspicion among all people, Johnson professed that "great progress is possible." His proof was in the "progress which has been won this past ten years." He made multiple references to African Americans currently doing things "where they were not ten years ago," such as "eating now, shopping now, going to the bathroom now, riding now, spending nights now, obtaining credit now, giving now, [and] attending classes now."[25] The civil rights leaders in attendance favorably received his balancing of items of progress and problems that remained, and they applauded that portion of his speech.

The former president returned to movement language for his rousing conclusion. "And if our efforts continue, if our will is strong, if our hearts are right and if courage remains our constant companion," he promised as he raised his voice, "then my fellow Americans, I am confident that we shall overcome."[26] He had used the movement's signature song before, when he had told Congress to pass the Voting Rights Act seven years earlier. Activists watching that speech on live television rejoiced, in shock that the president embraced the movement's point of view. Now in 1972, in the three years since Nixon had taken office, the federal government had not only refrained from civil rights catchphrases but also gone to great lengths to distance itself from the movement. Johnson's reference to "We Shall Overcome" let the symposium audience know that at least one nationally powerful person still cared about the movement's point of view.

A grateful audience gave the former president rapturous applause and hearty compliments when he finished his address. Reporting for the *CBS Evening News*, Hal Walker noted that through the symposium, Johnson had suddenly become identified with the civil rights movement of the 1960s. Out of office, he was not as politically powerful as he had been as president. He was not even as physically powerful as before. He suffered poor health and had taken nitroglycerin pills while delivering his address. Still, he was willing to do what he could to help America overcome, and the warm, positive response from the activists motivated him to lend his assistance.[27]

Three of the nation's most prominent ongoing developments of the 1960s—space exploration, the Vietnam War, and the civil rights struggle—showed signs of slowing that December. When NASA blasted Apollo 17 off to the moon, the agency announced that no further lunar missions would take place. President Nixon started a new bombing campaign over North Vietnam, but the administration also promised impending peace. Meanwhile, Nixon whittled the number of U.S. servicemen in Indochina down to 24,000—a dramatic reduction from the 500,000 troops at the end of his predecessor's term. Civil rights organizations had long protested space exploration and the war, but that month they refrained from demonstrating against Apollo 17 and the "Christmas Bombing." Civil rights workers were exhausted from their ill-fated work to unseat Nixon, and many of the groups suffered from low funds and shrinking membership. On the other hand, other issues concerning each event contributed to the silence of the activists.

The absence of SCLC's mule train from Cape Kennedy in December reflected the nation's fatigue with the space race. With the United States having beaten the Soviet Union to the moon, critics considered the succeeding trips there at best anticlimactic and at worst both unnecessary and expensive. Also, television viewers were not interested in live coverage of Apollo 17. In contrast to the hours of coverage of Apollo 11, networks opted to show more of their regularly scheduled programming. Some of the occasions on which the networks interrupted shows to broadcast the lunar mission drew complaints from disgruntled viewers. Thus, if anyone in the movement had attended Apollo 17's launch to protest the government's failure toward the poor, many fewer reporters and viewers were around to care.[28]

The impassioned verbal protests against the "Christmas Bombing" contrasted with the tepid demonstrations against it. The war's opponents were
angry at the new round of bombing for several reasons. The bombing was
not in response to new North Vietnamese military aggression, and Nixon
had withdrawn troops without resorting to air power over the country for
most of his first term. In addition, Nixon conducted the bombing without
public explanation, offering no speeches or press conferences on the new
campaign. His critics responded to his silence with bitter invective. Ohio
senator William Saxbe said that the president had "left his senses," and the
Milwaukee Journal newspaper called the raids a "new reign of terror."[29] On
the other hand, few marches took place against the December bombings, and
civil rights leaders refrained from joining the small numbers at the rallies. The
freezing rain that fell over much of the country that month restricted rally
attendance to only the most dedicated demonstrators, and the raids failed
to distract people from preparing for the upcoming Christmas holiday. Also,
after having tried and failed several times over four years to persuade Nixon
to end the war, protesters did not know what else to do after his reelection.
They seemed to be "nodding at the wheel," as columnist Jonathan Schell of
the *New Yorker* put it.[30]

Critics of the dissenters were also at a loss. Without any public statements
from civil rights leaders against the bombing, Nixon's supporters could only
take earlier statements of protest and present them as preemptive criticism
of the "Christmas Bombing." In his newspaper column, William F. Buckley
lamented that the media censored statements of approval of Nixon's war policy. "The outburst against the renewal of the bombing of North Vietnam was,
of course, to be expected," Buckley sighed. He identified Abernathy as part of
the "Communist propaganda machine," which allowed the American public
to hear and read "only denunciations of American policy." However, instead
of proving that the SCLC leader had contributed specifically to the media
coverage of the new aerial campaign, Buckley cited the minister's recent trip
to East Germany as evidence of his influence in the "machine." The columnist claimed that Abernathy's compliments to "the Soviet Colony in Germany"
during his two-day visit diminished his standing as "an apostle of justice and
freedom." On the other hand, Buckley's strained attempt to equate support
for East Germany with opposition to the "Christmas Bombing" signaled that
the war's old debate between the "hawks" and the "doves" had devolved
into farce.[31]

Even political prisoners had begun lying low. Unlike the celebrity Angela
Davis and Huey Newton had generated behind bars, Rap Brown avoided
media attention as he awaited trial for the October 1971 holdup. If he had

any possibility of mobilizing people for violent revolution at that point, he forfeited the opportunity through his isolationism. His activism now largely was confined to the prison itself, where he participated in antidrug campaigns on behalf of his fellow inmates. He offered no statements for SNCC to publicize, letters from jail, or hunger fasts.[32]

To the outside world, it was just as well. The public remained fascinated by Brown—not in his capacity as a militant speaker but rather as a caught fugitive whose fate the courts had yet to completely settle. In October 1972, *New York* magazine published an eight-page article by Robert Daley, a former deputy police commissioner in New York. The author gave an account of how one of the city's patrolmen apprehended Brown, telling the story from the viewpoint of the officer. Daley reported that the officer had no idea whom he was pursuing, and the writer correspondingly depicted the militant speaker merely as an anonymous figure running away from the policeman. Daley did not identify the culprit by name until the last page, when the author wrote of the officer finally learning his detainee's identity. The article reduced Brown to a common criminal, just as Vice President Agnew had done four years earlier. Moreover, the unflattering depiction of the movement leader through an officer's eyes in a major commercial magazine was a triumph for the "law and order" culture of the Nixon administration.[33]

The SNCC women Brown had supported carried on without him. By the end of November, the TWWA had started meeting in the SNCC office every Saturday morning under Fran Beal's leadership. Some of the members of St. Peter's Church had heard that the women of SNCC had formed a separate group because they had felt that the male members did not respect them. The church folk also heard that the men of SNCC were discriminating against the women. Women's liberation remained a point of contention between the gendered factions. The SNCC women considered women's liberation an important focus for the cause, but the men disagreed. They wanted to concentrate only on the issue of skin-color discrimination. Nevertheless, with Hunt often absent from New York throughout the year, the TWWA was actively using the office space more often than SNCC was. On any given Saturday, a church member dropping by the office was likely to see several African American women "milling about and busy," as one witness put it, and sporting large Afros.[34] One of the church members remembered seeing Angela Davis at SNCC's headquarters at one point.

Brown's withdrawal from his SNCC subordinates and Hunt's relocation away from the national office in New York threw the organization into a state of flux. The internal strife that had plagued SNCC since the summer came to a head at the end of the year. On December 23 and 24, SNCC held its annual national meeting in Cincinnati, where Hunt had been trying to strengthen the local branch. During the proceedings Hunt resigned from SNCC's Eastern Zone and, therefore, from his unofficial chairmanship. George "Fidel" Love, John Payne, Charles Broadnax, and Donald Payne also attended the meeting. SNCC discussed relocating the dormant organization newsletter *National SNCC* to the San Antonio branch, although no one from SNCC–San Antonio was present to discuss the transition.

With Hunt's resignation, SNCC effectively returned to its original status as a series of local organizations united in name if not in philosophy. Each branch became more individualized. Instead of a de jure or de facto national chairman, SNCC now had several local coordinators running their own branches—Carlos Richardson and Mario Salas in San Antonio, John Payne in Tulsa, George Hughes in Cincinnati, and William Coleman in Atlanta. The cadres were now smaller and more individually autonomous than ever before, but they still decided to continue publishing the *National SNCC* newsletter and hold more national meetings. SNCC was not yet dead, but it was slowly but surely killing itself.

The group began the year 1973 by reducing and isolating itself further. On January 9, SNCC circulated a document called "A New Level of Struggle." In the letter, the group announced its separation from the TWWA. SNCC's statement declared that any agreements between the two organizations no longer had validity and that no chance of a future resumption of their partnership existed. The TWWA had been the last tie that SNCC had kept from the days when the "N" in SNCC had meant "Nonviolent." It was the lone surviving program influenced by ex-member James Forman, who had left SNCC when the "N" became "National." The severing of SNCC from the TWWA showed how much support the former group's female members had lost from the male members after Forman's resignation. The TWWA was also the only remaining access SNCC had with the press. Now SNCC would have to compete with all the other activist organizations for media coverage without Beal's unique ability to draw reporters through African American feminism.[35]

Meanwhile, gender-based conflict resurfaced in SCLC, too. That same month, the group suffered its most public internal blowup since King's assassination. The old dispute between the organization and Mrs. King's center to honor her late husband came to a head in the press. She announced a benefit concert to be held at the Omni in Atlanta on King's birthday (January 15), the proceeds of which would go to the Martin Luther King Jr. Center for Social Change. "The center is entrusted with the continuation of my husband's work and teachings and to the construction of a permanent memorial here in his home city," she explained.[36] None of the money raised at the event was to go to SCLC. Members of the group took issue, because they considered *their* activities a continuation of King's work.

SCLC's Hosea Williams was especially miffed about the proceeds issue and recited his grievances to reporters. His chief complaint was that Mrs. King's project confused people. If both her center and SCLC carried King's torch, then people did not understand both entities as separate from each other. Williams noted that although Mrs. King's center and SCLC were indeed their own institutions, people donated to the King foundation under the impression that they were helping SCLC, too. Her concert, therefore, "forces us to break our silence on what is truly happening to the works of Dr. King."[37] In other words, if SCLC went without funds, how could the work to make King's dream come true get done?

Mrs. King made no apologies for the concert, however. As far as she was concerned, SCLC did not have a monopoly on doing "the works of Dr. King." Mrs. King called Williams's remarks "full of misconceptions" and publicly addressed them "for the sake of the nonviolent cause." She noted that she remained affiliated with SCLC while working on the center, and she pointed out that she had already labored substantially for the group's financial well-being. "In Mr. Williams's apparent preoccupation with money, he seems to have forgotten that I have had the honor of helping to raise millions of dollars exclusively for the Southern Christian Leadership Conference," she observed. Moreover, as with TWWA members overshadowing SNCC, Mrs. King still generated as much press as SCLC, if not more, just because she was King's widow. She remained a highly sought speaker at events sponsored by various activist groups. SCLC was fortunate because its opposition to the success of her independent project did not cause her to leave the organization, unlike the recent decisions of Beal and Rice to leave SNCC for full-time work in the TWWA.[38]

The conflict could not have come at a worse time for SCLC. One of its former members had just dealt another blow to the relevance of the organization's traditional form of activism. On January 3 in Washington, D.C., Andrew Young took his oath of office at his inauguration and officially became a congressman. He was now on a par with President Nixon and Vice President Agnew as an elected official serving in the federal government, and as such, no longer as easy for the Nixon administration to ignore as when Young was in the civil rights movement. Agnew could not simply dismiss Representative Young as a "radic-lib," because he was now a "radic-lib" whom the people of Georgia had elected to represent them. Whereas SCLC still struggled to achieve political legitimacy with the Nixon White House, Young had won it by leaving SCLC and the movement altogether.

By January 1973, little had changed in the long-term problems of the United States over the past year. African Americans won more political representation at local levels but struggled to gain a foothold into national politics. Civil rights leaders stayed shut out from the White House, and the electorate's dismissal of the movement's preferred presidential candidate vividly demonstrated its disconnection from the Silent Majority. Poverty and the Vietnam War remained, despite the best efforts of civil rights groups toward eliminating them. Most importantly, the movement's most powerful opponents—President Nixon and Vice President Agnew—retained their offices. Unless a major collective civil rights offensive emerged, the year 1973—and the next four years as well—prepared to offer more of the same as 1972.

CHAPTER 17

Kicking the Blacks Around

In January 1973, the nation was awash in a cultural fad of nostalgia. Theater patrons and television audiences wanted entertainment that illustrated life from before the late 1960s, and they gravitated away from dramatizations of current domestic unrest. *The Waltons*—a new television series set during the Great Depression—won high ratings, and *Grease* was a popular Broadway show about the 1950s. These shows ignored the social problems that preceded the late 1960s—especially segregation—and suggested that life in the United States was better and happier in earlier times. Also, as "message music" garnered lower and lower positions on pop music charts throughout the early 1970s, longtime rock-and-roll singers Elvis Presley and Chuck Berry, whose careers had begun nearly two decades earlier, had new hit songs by successfully introducing their old music style to a new generation of listeners.

Upon his inauguration on January 20, President Nixon selectively referred to the recent past as a means to tout his accomplishments while in office. "When we met here four years ago, America was bleak in spirit, depressed by the prospect of seemingly endless war abroad and of destructive conflict at home," he reminded his fellow Americans. But then he beamed, "As we meet here today, we stand on the threshold of a new era of peace in the world." He neglected to mention how the nation arrived at that "new era." America's "Christmas Bombing"—a relentless 12-day bombing campaign over North Vietnam the previous month—convinced the war's negotiators to resume peace negotiations, and the FBI's sabotaging of the movement for the past five years had crushed potential for "destructive conflict at home."[1]

On the surface, the president seemed to want the same things that the movement wanted. "We have the chance today to do more than ever before in our history to make life better in America," he boasted. He saw opportunity for improvements in education, health, housing, transportation, and "the God-given right of every American to full and equal opportunity." However, he wanted America to achieve these improvements his way. As a result, he called for "respect for law" to improve, too. He also let the movement leaders know that their confrontational demands to the federal government for attention and financial assistance to the poor would continue to fall on deaf ears. "Let us remember," he declared, "that America was built not by government but by people, not by welfare but by work, not by shirking responsibility but by seeking responsibility."[2]

On the other hand, the president began his second term by shirking African Americans. He was overhauling his cabinet and extracting American troops from Southeast Asia at the time, but African Americans—especially civil rights activists—remained lost in the shuffle after January. Nixon no longer received notes from staffers about quotes in the press from movement leaders, now that he was constantly firing or repositioning his employees as the Watergate scandal started to unravel. With the FBI still headed by an interim director, the agency slackened in sending the president memoranda about the activities of the civil rights groups or any other African American "militant" organization. Moreover, the president stopped welcoming "responsible militant" Roy Wilkins to the White House, which almost completely closed off the movement's access to the Nixon administration.

Wilkins, meanwhile, had lost no love for the president. Shortly before the start of Nixon's second term, the NAACP leader visited the Senate Committee on Labor and Public Welfare to call for the rejection of the president's choice for secretary of Labor. While there, he repeated a federal judge's claim that nominee Peter Brennan, the main spokesman for the AFL-CIO's construction unions and the head of the Building and Construction Trades Council, practiced "a broad and pervasive pattern of racial discrimination." Wilkins's rhetoric still took on the more dramatic elements of the militant "youngsters" he criticized, lamenting that the Nixon administration had placed African Americans in a collective "state of siege."[3]

Vernon Jordan was not as fatalistic as Wilkins, but then again Jordan could still play tennis with John Ehrlichman. The NUL leader sadly admitted to *Newsweek*, "Once again the nation seems weary of the struggle." Nixon's inaction on civil rights convinced Jordan that "[t]here is persuasive evidence that the Second Reconstruction is coming to an end." He believed, as Young had in *Beyond Racism*, that the civil rights laws and desegregation court decisions of recent years had significantly equipped African Americans for struggle if not accomplishment. Jordan, however, considered the future very bright for African Americans. "There is a new brother about," Jordan boasted. "He's tasted the sweet fruit of victory. He's got resources and allies, and his mind is free."[4]

Nixon's estrangement from the movement and the sense of a new era among civil rights leaders suggested the winding down of civil rights protest as it had existed for years. The media immediately took note of this development. As the television series *Rowan & Martin's Laugh-In* ended its five-year run, an episode from January 1973 parodied the movement's past instead of predicting its future. In one brief sketch, Sammy Davis Jr. and Willie Tyler played African American students planning a sit-in at a diner but changing their minds when the eatery's clumsy waitress dropped food all over her European American customer. The sketch was part of the episode's theme of nostalgia for the 1950s and early 1960s, suggesting that nonviolent sit-ins were part of days gone by instead of current activism. For the sketch, Davis and Tyler wore conservative attire that replicated the clothing of the sit-in students of the early 1960s.

In early 1973, civil rights groups took their own turn at nostalgia, moving to familiar turf in order to reverse their dwindling funds, personnel, and public stature. As a result, they better positioned themselves to help African Americans attain those new "resources and allies" that Jordan had mentioned. They toned down some of the countercultural elements they had adopted and instead based more of their new programs on their successful campaigns of the previous decade. Demonstrators organized in locations that they had recently neglected, and activists who had become estranged from each other resolved their differences. They even began reaching out to the federal government and local governments, seeking political offices and making amends with political foes.

On January 22, one of those former foes—former president Lyndon Johnson—spent his morning the way that he had normally spent his mornings in Texas since January 1969. He spoke on the telephone with several associates. Next, he toured his massive ranch for daily inspection. By the early afternoon, he was ready for his nap. He broke from his routine when he awakened shortly before 4:00 p.m. with chest pains. Suffering his second heart attack in less than one year, he picked up the telephone in his bedroom and called for the Secret Service to see him immediately.

Nearly two hours later, over 1,000 miles away in New York, Walter Cronkite delivered the evening news on CBS. He mentioned a few of the same topics that he had covered during the Johnson administration. He briefed his viewers on the latest developments of the Vietnam War. He talked about the activities of antiwar activists. After a report about peace negotiations, he picked up the telephone at his desk to receive some breaking news. He conversed with the other party while still on camera. When he hung up the telephone, he informed his viewers that Johnson had just died.

The press barely stopped to mourn the former president's passing. As fate would have it, his death preceded President Nixon's televised announcement of a peace settlement for the Vietnam War by only one day. Just as the war had overrun Johnson's presidency, the end of the war overshadowed his death. Although the television networks broadcasted his funeral live a few days later, national weekly mainstream news magazines *Time* and *Newsweek* chose the cease-fire, not Johnson's death, as their cover stories.

In contrast, African American reporters and activists mourned Johnson's death as a setback in the civil rights struggle. They were virtually alone in the media in asserting that his passing affected the current status of the movement. That week's issue of the African American magazine *Jet* put the late president on the cover alongside a photo of Dr. King. The split image affirmed the assessment given by CBS News last month—that Johnson had become associated with the movement. After Robert Kennedy's assassination in June 1968, four years had passed before activists had considered trusting anyone to lead the movement nearly as much as they had trusted the late senator. Just as they began to embrace Johnson in that role after his civil rights symposium of December 1972, now he too was gone. In Wilkins's statement on the former president's death, the NAACP leader announced "the end of an era" of "unprecedented progress . . . towards elimination of racial bias, providing for the basic needs of the nation's poor, and lifting the horizons of disadvantaged groups within American society." In addition, Wilkins eulogized Johnson with rhetoric that hinted at a positive social disruption instead of adherence to American tradition, declaring that the late president "wrought a revolution of national conscience in regard to race and poverty."[5]

Outside of the African American press and civil rights groups, few people in the media publicly discussed President Nixon's handling of civil rights at the time. However, at the president's press conference of March 2, a reporter broke the silence. He began his inquiry with cautious remorse: "I apologize for this question before I ask it."

Nixon quipped, "Nobody else does." The journalists roared with laughter.

The reporter resumed, "The only reason I do so is because I think you should have a chance to answer it, but I was in Richmond shortly after your re-election and a State Senator, who was a Negro, got up and asked me, 'When is President Nixon going to stop kicking the blacks around?'"[6]

Nixon initially responded by denying the allegation in the question. "Well, I could not stop unless I started it, and I have not, I believe," he said. The president then very verbosely acknowledged that, although African Americans had indeed been "kicked around" over the years, he himself had not done the kicking. Specifically addressing "the people who happen to be black Americans in this country," as he redundantly put it, he wanted them to "understand that the President of this nation is one who first would not, of course, ever say that he would ever admit, and I trust there would be nothing in the record to indicate that he had kicked any group in the population around and particularly one that deserved far better than that because of what they have been exposed to through the years." He recognized that some journalists—especially African American ones—would skeptically think of him, that "because I did not get a substantial number of black votes, although greater than in 1968, that therefore now we don't owe anything to them."[7]

He tried to reassure African Americans that he indeed cared about them as fellow citizens. "Let me say that is not the issue at all," he said about owing African Americans nothing. "The issue is doing what is right. This nation owes something to all of its people, and it owes something particularly to those who have been disadvantaged." These remarks were some of the most supportive that Nixon had publicly made to African Americans during his presidency. His answer slightly resembled SCLC's claims that the federal government owed certain provisions to its poorest citizens. Then again, he could afford to be generous with his words, because he had already won reelection and was starting his final four-year term. He did not have to worry anymore about appeasing Southerners, "hardhats," or the Silent Majority with carefully chosen words about civil rights.

He concluded his reply in the traditional Nixon-Agnew administration style. He vowed to continue giving the disadvantaged what the government owed them, but he would do it his way. "We, I believe, have done a very effective job in that respect in terms of what we have done, maybe not in terms of what we have said so well, and we are going to continue to do well," he declared, "and we hope eventually that our citizens will recognize that we have done so."[8] He saw no problem in how he was helping the poor. Moreover, he did not seek any advice from people outside the government concerning his assistance of the impoverished. African Americans would just have to settle for what Nixon was doing, just as they had during his previous four-year term.

The president moved on to another reporter, who proceeded to change topics. The brief exchange about African Americans was complete. From that moment onward, the press never asked the Nixon administration any more questions specifically about African American issues. The media had now joined the Nixon administration in exercising "benign neglect" of African Americans.

Some civil rights leaders helped to form a new coalition to attract the federal government's attention on the issue of economic inequality. The activists appeared ready to move beyond the visual gimmickry of the immediate post-King period and return to less dramatic protest. On February 20, thousands of antipoverty demonstrators rallied for three hours in Washington, D.C., to protest slashing of funds for a government agency—the Office of Economic Opportunity (OEO). The event's main speakers had given addresses at antiwar or antipoverty demonstrations before, but now they were in the same rally together for the first time. The movement's congressional allies Bella Abzug and Shirley Chisholm spoke, and Jesse Jackson, Coretta Scott King, and Ralph Abernathy represented civil rights organizations there.

Jackson gave an inconsistent speech. As with the other leaders of the movement since King's death, Jackson had yet to master the skill of using violent speech to promote nonviolence. He referred to an early tactic of SCLC by calling on his listeners to fill the jails to capacity in order to force the president to pay attention to poverty. On the other hand, he portrayed the idea as a suicide mission. Evoking former SNCC chairman H. Rap Brown's combination of determination and fatalism from the Orangeburg shootings, the PUSH leader intoned, "We're going to be shot in the back anyway. We might as well be shot in the chest."[9]

This time SCLC behaved much differently than before. The group did not erect a tent city, nor did it announce Resurrection City III. There was not even a mule train. Rather, the group used nostalgic rhetoric to goad the federal government into helping the poor. Evoking Dr. King, his widow claimed that Nixon's funding cuts were a retreat from her late husband's dream. Abernathy took a different line than Mrs. King with that kind of rhetoric by focusing on the violence associated with SCLC's past. He made minor headlines by saying that with Nixon's OEO cutbacks, "this nation will experience the hot summers of the 1960s all over again."[10] He was clever in vaguely mentioning violence without saying who exactly would cause it. On the other hand, his threat completely contradicted SCLC's claim from the previous August that African Americans were now beyond urban uprisings. Moreover, with Nixon's "law and order" administration effectively cracking down on rioters, Abernathy was overestimating the power of African Americans to create a new hot summer in the first place.

Civil rights leaders were unified in their disappointment with the president's budget cuts. On March 16, Vernon Jordan, the newest of the leaders, made national television news for the first time as NUL director with his anti-Nixon statement. For nearly two years, he had deviated from his predecessor's constant television coverage by keeping a low profile; even Roy

Innis of CORE publicized his group on the television news more than Jordan exposed the NUL. However, Nixon's civil rights slashes inspired Jordan to break his television shutout and publicly reprimand the president, and Walter Cronkite reported the criticism.[11]

SCLC applied King's ideas to other causes besides poverty. On March 7, Abernathy traveled to South Dakota to speak to indigenous activists. The violent, militant vigilante American Indian Movement (AIM) had occupied the infamous battle site since February 27, at the request of the Oglala Sioux. They used the media's attention on the occupation to call attention to the federal government's indifference to their poverty and its continued oppression of the indigenous. Abernathy's visit to the protest was his latest attempt to latch onto an already popular campaign from another group. Moreover, the occupants' success in publicizing American poverty to a global audience validated SCLC's idea of encamping impoverished masses. Still continuing King's antipoverty work as an advocate for poor people, Abernathy saw his support for the Wounded Knee demonstrators as the latest stage of the PPC. Further evoking King, Abernathy deliberately paraphrased the "free at last" closing of the "I Have a Dream" speech to encourage the occupants. "As I look into your faces," he beamed, "I know that you will be free! You *will* be free!"[12]

On the other hand, several parts of Abernathy's address deviated from traditional movement rhetoric. Whenever SCLC supported militant groups like the Black Panthers in recent years, it made a point of reassuring people of its continued commitment to nonviolence. At Wounded Knee, however, Abernathy did not publicly disagree with AIM's armed self-defense, nor did he mention SCLC's willingness to stay nonviolent. By not talking about nonviolence, he was showing that he could not draw people to SCLC with it. People did not want to hear about it anymore. He wisely chose to express empathy with the anti-government sentiment of the protesters instead of discussing how they expressed that sentiment. After four years of bitterness toward the Nixon administration, Abernathy could relate to AIM's anger.

Indeed, the SCLC leader was as reactionary as ever, hurling several insults at the federal government. He sounded like Rap Brown that day, using clever puns and rhymes to present his complaints. He said that the Bureau of Indian Affairs, or BIA, was "MIA" because of its neglect of indigenous people's poverty. He called the Department of the Interior "the Department of the Inferior." He told the demonstrators that they were already victorious, because they "taught the white man what he would rather forget" and "dramatized what he has refused to remember." He praised them for challenging authority. "No longer can the government of the United States treat Indians as they did before," he bantered. "You have changed that!"[13]

Meanwhile, the federal government learned a different lesson from the occupation. Through Wounded Knee the FBI found a new way to use the H. Rap Brown Act. The occupants attracted indigenous people of various tribes in a show of pan-Indian solidarity. However, the militants of AIM were armed, and they were taking a stand against the federal government. Ironically, some of them had formerly fought for the government in the Korean and Vietnam Wars. The agency worried once again that outside agitators like Abernathy would cause a violent uprising—this time among the rural and impoverished indigenous instead of urban, impoverished African Americans. In addition, as the occupation lasted into the spring season, the government considered it likely that college and university students soon to be dismissed for the summer would flock to Wounded Knee. Consequently, before the end of March, federal officials at the site started turning away people who had driven from out of state to meet with the occupants. If the travelers crossed the state line into South Dakota, the officers had the authority of the FBI to arrest them. The agency invoked the H. Rap Brown Act while doing so.

The FBI treated the Wounded Knee detainees as it had treated the movement demonstrators and antiwar activists of recent years. Interim Director L. Patrick Gray ordered 24-hour surveillance for the incarcerated AIM supporters. He also set their bail extremely high in order to send a message to potential travelers. As a result, Abernathy and other activists were discouraged from returning to Wounded Knee. Although supporters continued to pour into the area well into mid-April, no one from SCLC or SNCC was among them.[14]

SCLC did not completely abandon its efforts at helping the indigenous poor, however. In April members of the organization visited the Tuscarora people of North Carolina and printed their demands in the organization newsletter. SCLC photographer Elaine Tomlin gave a Black Power salute while riding on horseback with the Tuscarora. In a further move away from the mule trains and PPC marches of the past five years, Abernathy was now meeting the impoverished where they lived and allowing them to speak on their own behalf instead of parading them in major cities and speaking as their "leader."[15]

Meanwhile, national foreign policy returned to the past in a way that significantly affected the movement. In accordance with the cease-fire agreement of late January, the North Vietnamese released U.S. prisoners of war, and the United States accelerated the withdrawal of all of its troops from South Vietnam. On March 29, President Nixon announced on television that all of America's troops were out of Vietnam and that all of the POWs were released. The United States returned to the advisory role it had played before starting active combat in 1965. After eight years of antiwar rhetoric and demonstrations, antiwar activists and their civil rights allies now had the challenge of revising their language and programming in order to establish relevance in a postwar climate. They responded to the dilemma by demonstrating against the country's daily bombing of Cambodia between February and August, and they called for amnesty for "draft-dodgers." But these causes failed to mobilize people who had become fatigued by the Vietnam War.

March 29 concluded not only an era of U.S. militarism abroad but also of militant rhetoric at home. As the last U.S. troops departed South Vietnam, Rap Brown's trial for the robbery of October 1971 came to an end thousands of miles away in New York. It had begun on February 1, with the former SNCC leader addressing the court. He opened with a prayer from the Koran. The judge immediately instructed him to stop, but Brown kept praying anyway. He then spoke to the jury, but his trademark wordplay sometimes drifted into incoherence. He told the jurors that he knew they were not his peers. He let them know that he knew that they did not presume him to be innocent. Then he concluded, "Truth is the eye of the storm, and I myself no more than a raindrop looking for a fertile place to fall; a poet who speaks to the deaf; a scribe whose ledger is the wind; a rainbow in the mind of the blind."[16] And then he fell silent. There were no musings on cultural violence, no threat for revolution. It was an unspoken admission that his earlier rhetorical style had no place in a holdup trial.

Brown then returned to his seat. His codefendants, all of whom had been in SNCC during his tenure, decided to let his remarks represent them, too. However, it would be the last time that Brown spoke for them or for anyone in SNCC. On March 19, he chose not to testify in court. Ten days later a jury found him and his codefendants guilty of armed robbery and assault with a deadly weapon.

For the first time, the former SNCC leader was now convicted of charges that had not directly stemmed from his controversial rhetoric. Brown's earlier trials had centered on his violations of the government's attempts to detain him in New York. The attempts at detention, in turn, had related to Agnew's pursuit of Brown's incarceration for the activist's remarks of July 1967. In contrast, after the holdup trial no one launched any new "Let Rap Rap" campaigns or organized further "Free Rap" rallies. Later that spring a court sentenced Brown to between 5 and 15 years in prison. His brother Ed and nationalist poet Imamu Amiri Baraka pleaded to the judge on the defendant's behalf, but their cries fell on deaf ears. The war abroad was over for Americans, and the man who had most vociferously called for war at home was now locked away for a robbery instead of a revolution.[17]

Ironically, Brown's conviction dovetailed with the decline of the SNCC–New York branch he had run for so many years. The TWWA continued to grow without its association to SNCC, and Fran Beal no longer suffered distractions from her former male comrades. The TWWA simply did not need the SNCC name anymore to attract and organize masses of people. On the other hand, the separation between the groups was primarily SNCC's loss, because the activities of the TWWA had helped keep its parent organization in the press by extension. Without dedicated and active members like Beal, SNCC–New York's members struggled to keep the cadre alive.

Nevertheless, they put forth some effort. On April 29, it issued the statement "Hard Work, Education, Organization, Equals Power." The organization echoed the TWWA in calling for criticism of others and itself in order for African Americans to achieve "revolutionary political power." In contrast to SCLC members entering politics, SNCC pushed for people to continue to struggle from outside the government. "The educational system of U.S. imperialism and the consistent anti-communist hysteria prevailing in the U.S. do not foster, but seek to destroy the study of revolutionary thought and the development of political education," the statement declared.[18]

SNCC, therefore, called for African Americans to ready themselves for revolution through a "political education program." The proposal was a return to the concept of the "liberation school" idea of the late 1960s and the "freedom schools" in Mississippi during "Freedom Summer" in 1964. "Throughout the history of SNCC, there have been various discussions about an education program for the members of the organization," the statement read. "There must be a systematic attempt to educate ourselves; to train new members; to instill a sense of history of the organization, its objectives, successes and failures; and to discuss and analyze many events occurring in the world." Suggesting mandatory political indoctrination, SNCC warned, "Without a doubt, every time we allow a new member to join our cadre without undergoing some political education, we are contributing to misunderstanding, suspicion ill-will, wasted effort and lost time." All members had to give similar answers to "basic questions" about the organization. "If there can be no agreement on certain fundamentals, or at least continuous discussion while one worked, then SNCC as a political unit cannot survive."[19]

By the next day, however, SNCC no longer had a national office. The Episcopal Diocese of New York was terminating its subsidy to St. Peter's Church. At the time all of the groups that used space at the church had been welcomed by the full-time priest there to do so. Those organizations, including SNCC, may have paid a token amount of rent, or they may not have paid rent at all. With the subsidy discontinued in the spring of 1973, the church could no longer afford to pay for a full-time priest. As the priest departed, the church began renting out space at market rates. All of the groups that had been using space at St. Peter's for free or a token rent were subsequently evicted. SNCC was among the evicted because the church had decided to charge $50 per month for rent of the office space.

The closing of the SNCC–New York office effectively killed that branch of the organization. Although the TWWA stopped using St. Peter's for meetings and as a New York headquarters in the spring of 1973, it immediately found new office space on the same street. On the other hand, SNCC–New York never successfully relocated. When SNCC left St. Peter's church, the New York branch simply stopped gathering together. The local members also stopped conducting activities in the name of SNCC. The branch that Rap Brown had developed and led only survived for one month and one day after his robbery conviction.[20]

As spring led into summer, the other branches of SNCC failed to make national headlines beyond the legal problems and obituaries of former members, and local newspaper coverage of individual branches was rare. With the New York office gone, the Texas branch became the most productive that summer. It was an isolated cadre, not unlike the one that Angela Davis had coordinated in Los Angeles. It continued to function as a hybrid of SNCC and the BPP, and, like the Panthers, the branch facilitated free services for local minority communities. On the other hand, SNCC–Texas members followed in the footsteps of former national chairman Stokely Carmichael by promoting Pan-Africanism. "Schools make Africans in America believe our brothers and sisters in Africa are against us," said Salas. "This prevails in our society and should be eradicated."[21]

SNCC–Texas routinely attracted press attention in San Antonio because of its programs and demonstrations in San Antonio. On July 20, members of black student union groups in the city picketed outside of the city's federal building. They protested the Byrd Amendment of the Military Procurement Act of 1971, named after Senator Robert Byrd of West Virginia. Salas was among those in attendance, trying to stop "cultural genocide" and to "make more people aware of the problem blacks face and the inconsistencies in the policies of the federal government."[22] He complained that the law allowed U.S. corporations to purchase and import chrome from Rhodesia and that the legislation marked an attempt to bypass international law and preserve British colonialism in Africa. With Salas's participation in the protest, SNCC–Texas indirectly validated the NAACP. Although four years had passed since

Roy Wilkins had suggested that the militant "youngsters" look to Rhodesia as a true example of segregation, Salas was now taking his advice.

Despite its isolation from other branches, SNCC–Texas tried to foster an identity as a part of the national organization. In addition to keeping Carmichael's Pan-Africanism, the branch showed deference to other recent national luminaries of the group. Two weeks before SNCC–New York lost its office, Salas had written a letter on behalf of the Texas branch with a "cc" to H. Rap Brown at SNCC's New York address. Ironically, with the former chairman's incarceration, he was no longer reachable by mail at the office. By the time of the Byrd Amendment protest, Salas had started using Muhammad Hunt's closing for SNCC correspondence: "Love and Revolution." Still, SNCC–Texas remained concerned mostly about local matters and barely communicated with its fellow cadres in Tulsa and Atlanta. It hardly addressed national concerns.[23]

The rest of the movement groups picked up SNCC's slack, however. During the last week of March, SCLC, PUSH, and the National Welfare Rights Organization testified before the Treasury Department, alerting the nation to unequal distribution of revenue sharing money to the poor. The movement was at its most unified since the National Black Political Convention. By securing an opportunity together to speak directly to the federal government, the three organizations found that there was strength in numbers. Then again, the coalition had scored a major victory just by securing an audience with the cabinet.

It was Abernathy's first time before a cabinet official since his ill-fated May 1969 meeting with the Nixon administration. This time, his remarks were unusually brief and restrained. He avoided the ad hominem attacks, repetitious phrases, and clichéd platitudes from the previous meeting. In his address he advocated for the poor, but he also used his time before the Treasury to argue that the movement was still relevant. "The long dark night of discrimination is not yet over in our country," he lectured.[24]

Then, taking a coded swipe at the White House, he added that "there are those in high places who wish to increase and prolong the darkness." Even during this moment of triumph for SCLC, he could not resist nursing his grudge against Nixon. Nor could he stay consistent in his message. He couched the rights of the poor to revenue sharing in the history of African Americans, saying that "our movement to secure these rights is in no mood to put up with the kind of trickery and cruel deception which was the experience of our people when Reconstruction was brutally ended one hundred years ago." On the other hand, he also defined the poor as African Americans, Puerto Ricans, Mexican Americans, and "millions of whites."[25]

Still, Abernathy's former colleague, Representative Andrew Young of Georgia, could not have been prouder. The freshman congressman paid tribute to the SCLC president on the House floor. Young entered Abernathy's testimony into the *Congressional Record*. The representative also called attention to the activist's most important remarks. He suggested that his fellow legislators "take note of Dr. Abernathy's reminder that the victims of poverty and discrimination are taxpayers, too, and have a right to their full share of the funds disbursed under revenue sharing." With Young supporting Abernathy and discussing poverty on the SCLC leader's terms, the movement had effectively infiltrated "the system."[26]

Indeed, in the spring of 1973, several journalists sensed a new era in civil rights activism. Ever since Spiro Agnew had first attacked Rap Brown in July 1967, reporters had looked at the early years of the movement with wistfulness, wondering whatever had happened to the nonviolent sentiment. Now, however, the media portrayed the movement as if it were poised for a nostalgic comeback. On the fifth anniversary of King's death, Abernathy gave a public address at the slain leader's coffin, talking as if he were speaking directly to King. The audience around him sang the movement's longtime anthem, "We Shall Overcome." At least one television reporter was confident that the splintering of the movement that had taken place over the past few years was reversing itself, because other groups liked the NWRO and PUSH expressed willingness to work with SCLC.

PUSH leader Jesse Jackson, in fact, agreed to have his organization cosponsor the King assassination observance. He sat with Abernathy, gave him a "soul" handshake, and played with Abernathy's son Kwame. It was the first time that Jackson and Abernathy had cosponsored an event since Jackson had left SCLC to start PUSH. Both men insisted that they had no hard feelings toward each other and had never felt any. In fact, later in the year, they made plans for another reunion based on activism. Jackson was working with labor leaders and asked Abernathy—on their behalf—to come to their luncheon.[27]

However, SCLC soon squandered whatever momentum it may have generated from the press after the coverage of the assassination anniversary. On May 12 in Atlanta, Abernathy and Rev. Joe Boone were arrested at the home of Harold Brockey, board chairman of Rich's department store. They had been organizing some striking workers who complained of discrimination by skin color. Abernathy led about 150 people to the front of Brockey's house, where they sang hymns. When he tried to walk up to the driveway, Atlanta Police captain Charles Forrester told him to leave. When Abernathy refused, Forrester arrested him. "This was part of the harassment and strike that's been going on for a month," Forrester said later. "But I don't think there were more than ten Rich's employees in the group." The next day Abernathy was freed on $1,000 bond.[28]

SCLC's demonstration offered many of the tried-and-true elements of its recent protests. By championing another group of strikers, the organization was attempting to have the same high-profile victories it had won in Memphis in 1968 and in Charleston in 1969. The Brockey protest also implemented the group's tactic of taking oppressed people directly to those with the most power to alleviate their conditions. SCLC tried something new in leading the strikers in a residential area instead of the street outside the offending place of business, and the group made the protest more personal than others by taking marchers to Brockey's house.

Another, more damaging new dynamic of this protest for SCLC was the absence of media coverage of Abernathy's arrest. The arrest of an SCLC official, especially its president, had been a key part of the organization's negotiation of the media narrative about the movement. Whenever King had announced a city in which he would demonstrate, that community immediately became apprehensive. The city had feared negative publicity from the national press if King were to have been arrested. Coverage of an arrest had led the community to resolve the issue King had attacked in order to take the media spotlight off the city. In Albany in 1962, its police chief simply paid King's bail. In Chicago in 1966, Mayor Richard Daley addressed urban problems to undermine King's complaints about the city's slums. Now, however, Abernathy's arrest in Atlanta barely made the back pages of newspapers beyond that city, and it did not generate any national television news coverage at all.

Soon afterward Abernathy decided to take SCLC into a new direction. On July 9, he gave a press conference at the organization's national headquarters in Atlanta. Sitting below a picture of himself and his predecessor, he began his remarks by giving a brief history of his work with King. He then noted the accomplishments of his presidency—the PPC, Charleston, the first march at Cape Kennedy, the March against Repression, the 1971 march in Washington, and even Resurrection City II. He estimated that he had been jailed 36 times during his 18 years in SCLC. He complained, however, that after 5 years as the leader, he did not have the resources to continue his work in that position. Thus, he announced his resignation from the SCLC presidency.

Abernathy then outlined his three reasons for quitting. African Americans had ascended to higher levels of employment and income due to SCLC's work but stopped contributing to the group as they rose from poverty. Also, fewer donations meant severe cuts in staffing, which made the day-to-day operations of the group more difficult. Finally, he stated that he needed more time at his church as he and his flock arranged to move into a new house of worship that fall. He did not name a replacement but stated that his resignation would not go into effect until the group's convention the following month.

He concluded his remarks and took questions from reporters. As usual, one of them asked about his feud with Mrs. King. This time, however, Abernathy gave the press something to exploit by blaming her in part for the group's troubles, especially the financial woes. In his view, her successful fundraising for a memorial to her late husband came at the expense of her late husband's organization. He claimed that she could have saved SCLC by giving some of that money to the group. His comments marked a definitive break from the group's tradition of keeping internal conflicts private—a break that had begun when Abernathy publicly suspended Jesse Jackson nearly two years earlier. Although she had committed no violations and had not been suspended, Abernathy was less gracious to her than to Jackson in the presence of the reporters.

After the press conference, Abernathy led reporters on one final march. They walked for a block to his predecessor's grave. He couched his remarks there as a monologue to King. In Abernathy's mind, he was not supposed to have been left behind, without King. He had always thought that he and King would die together. Perhaps someone would put a bomb in the car they would drive, and the bomb would explode with them in the car together. Instead, King had died without his lieutenant. By becoming the leader of SCLC, Abernathy had tried to do what he had not prepared to do and had not thought he would have to do. Yet on the day he resigned, he was at peace with his presidency. "Martin, my record is clear," he said to the crypt. "It is well with my soul. I did what you asked me to do. I tried to keep the team together." Still, sensing that he had let his friend down by stepping down, he requested, "I hope that you can find it in your heart to forgive me for resigning this day." Finally, after promising, "I'll see you in the morning," he lowered his head to kiss the crypt, stood erect, turned his back on the press, and walked away.[29]

He did not totally abandon the press, however. He made himself accessible to *Jet* magazine for an interview shortly after his resignation. In turn the periodical placed him on the cover of the issue for the first time in months. He assured the reporter that the resignation did not mean that SCLC would soon disband. "I will continue to work through and for SCLC," he promised before adding the condition, "that is, unless it gets into the hands of some egotistical leaders who are concerned only in promoting their welfare and getting their pockets filthy rich, rather than looking out for the welfare of the poor."[30]

As much as Abernathy disliked the vice president, he borrowed Agnew's tactic of dividing the movement. Instead of responsible and irresponsible militants, the ex-SCLC president distinguished honest leaders from dishonest ones. Moreover, he put only himself in the former category. And just as Agnew had decided against bringing the irresponsible ones to the discussion table, Abernathy refused to consider dishonest leaders as capable of filling his shoes. After stating that his successor had to believe in "honesty and integrity," he observed that no such person existed. "I would put no one as leader of the Southern Christian Leadership Conference, frankly," he announced, "because I do not see an individual on the horizon at this point who is dedicated enough to the welfare of poor people like Martin Luther King Jr. started and wanted us to be about." Repeating his assessment of himself as the only person capable of leading the group, he concluded, "I don't see another leader with enough honesty and integrity for me to put my stamp of approval on him." He was content to leave the choice up to SCLC and to God, especially because of the pool of talent from which the SCLC and God had to choose for president. "Every leader that I see is trying to get rich himself," Abernathy lamented, "and they are so full of trickery, and they are all schemers, trying to make the headlines."[31]

He tried to make his presidency look good, letting the public know what they would miss after his departure. But his assertion that no one could replace him also suggested that he had echoed King's mistake in failing to adequately groom a successor. More importantly, his valedictory remarks implied that for five years he had led a group full of either self-enriching schemers or of passive sheep. Concerning the schemers, Abernathy did not elaborate on whether they were his colleagues in the movement at large or former SCLC members who had defected for various reasons. In the case of the sheep, Abernathy may have been unable to train SCLC members to become potential leaders, or he may have wanted them so dependent on him that he made them into followers.[32]

Despite the lack of preparation King had given Abernathy for the presidency, King had at least named his best friend as the successor years before the assassination. Abernathy's resignation, on the other hand, left SCLC in a state of confusion. His abrupt departure caught the organization off guard because it did not happen during a more natural point of transition such as the annual convention. He had not named a successor before leaving the presidency, as King had done. Although King had trusted his lieutenant to take over the group, Abernathy did not outwardly express the same confidence in his own second-in-command,

Bernard Lee. Still, Abernathy had not vacated the presidency through death, like his predecessor. He had merely resigned, which meant that the panicked SCLC had a chance to convince him to change his mind.

Ironically, as much as people had blamed Abernathy for failing to keep King's team together, SCLC underwent further discord upon Abernathy's resignation. Williams joined Abernathy in condemning Mrs. King for not giving more of her foundation funds to save SCLC. Lee did not chastise her but instead cited her feud with the resigned president as a significant contributing factor to his resignation. He publicly called on both of them to settle their differences. In usual SCLC hyperbole, Lee overstated the importance of the disagreement. "The division between Dr. Abernathy and Mrs. King is only symptomatic of a deeper division in the country," he exaggerated. "In order to heal, I recommend that a meeting occur immediately between Dr. Abernathy and Mrs. King."[33]

Mrs. King, meanwhile, tried to stay above the fray. She issued a press statement on the same day of his press conference, expressing surprise at his decision to quit the presidency. She acknowledged, "I regret that Reverend Abernathy felt it necessary to resign." She chose not to respond to any of his charges against her but rather to focus on his strengths. More importantly, her example of one of his admirable qualities came from one of his first activities upon succeeding her husband as SCLC president. "I personally will cherish the memories of Rev. Abernathy's support in my most trying circumstances following my husband's assassination," she revealed. She then offered him her best wishes for his future endeavors and said no more.[34]

Although she felt no need to defend herself, Walter Fauntroy took on that task. By this time he had joined her at the King Center and knew something about the finances of her project. Therefore, he gave his own press release to set her record straight. By his estimation, she had actually given $1 million to SCLC over the past five years. He noted that "more than $750,000 from the proceeds of the exhibition of the King Film in its movie house and television presentations was given to the Southern Christian Leadership Conference." He added that Mrs. King had hosted an art sale, a concert, and a fundraising dinner—all of which collectively earned $250,000—and donated the entire amount to her husband's organization.[35]

The public was not as concerned about SCLC's internal squabbling as about the suddenness of Abernathy's announcement. People's responses nationwide were immediate and overwhelmingly positive. Very few people wrote to him to criticize him for resigning or to complain about how he resigned. Those who did were upset at his characterization of African Americans as apathetic and miserly. On the other hand, most of the letters he received contained messages of support and prayer. One person even offered himself to replace Abernathy as president. Some people empathized with the difficulty of the SCLC leader's decision. Large, childlike scrawling filled one postcard that addressed Abernathy's concerns about funding; it simply read:

SIR
DON'T GIVE UP
MONEY WILL FOLLOW.[36]

The press was not as kind to the outgoing SCLC president. Newspaper columnist Carl T. Rowan used the occasion of Abernathy's resignation to compose a blistering assessment of him and of the movement in general. Indeed, in Rowan's opinion, the organization had suffered after King's death. "SCLC dwindled to inconsequence under Abernathy," he remarked. "If it faded from existence tomorrow, not many blacks would know or care." Rowan lambasted Abernathy for his "less-than-brilliant, not-so-inspiring leadership" and cited as examples his motel stay during Resurrection City I and the parading with mules to end hunger (although this idea was King's).[37] The author also did not like that Abernathy blamed SCLC's problems on both comfortable African Americans who did not donate to the group and Coretta Scott King for her fundraising efforts for a memorial to her late husband. The former SCLC leader's unwillingness to at least partially blame himself for the organization's decline especially irked the columnist. Rowan apparently shared movement participant Fran Beal's notion that an effective activist organization needed both critics and self-critics.

On the other hand, not every problem in SCLC was the outgoing leader's fault. Rowan argued that Abernathy's greatest shortcoming was shared by the movement at large. The activists had become victims of their own success. African Americans were now able to sit anywhere on buses, purchase a soda at any drugstore fountain, and receive lodging at any motel. The movement, however, had failed to adapt to these advancements and develop strategies for other problems, according to the writer. Beyond SCLC, "CORE and SNCC are almost unheard of these days—and just as well. The NAACP and National Urban League are not giving the same kind of leadership they once did," he critiqued. "The truth is that most of the current civil rights groups have no mass following. None of the groups is motivating and directing the mass of blacks to take bold, meaningful steps in the interest of their own freedom." These problems were certainly too daunting for Abernathy to solve by himself, but the civil rights organizations collectively kept trying to overcome them throughout the rest of 1973.[38]

CHAPTER 18

The Movement of the Seventies

Through the first half of 1973, movement activists said very little against Vice President Agnew. Then again, he made very few inflammatory public statements during that period. The president spent the two months between his reelection and his second inauguration rearranging his cabinet, shuffling officials to different departments or calling for their dismissals. Agnew retained his office because of the previous November's election, but he had less to do in it. With the end of the Vietnam War and the protests it had sparked, Nixon did not need Agnew to do what he did best—"attack-dog" speeches against demonstrators. The president reassigned many of Agnew's duties to other employees and gave him less glamorous assignments, which the vice president considered a waste of his time. In addition, Nixon terminated many of Agnew's staffers. The president's actions against the vice president suggested that Nixon did not want his former running mate to become the next president.[1]

However, by the end of April, the president had to fire some of his own employees, too. The Senate Watergate Committee began hearings about administration officials involved in the June 1972 break-in at the Watergate Hotel, and polls revealed a drop in support for President Nixon. Many of the officials involved in the scandal were part of Nixon's inner circle. One member of his circle had been one of the few people in the Nixon administration who worked on the concerns of the movement. Domestic Affairs assistant John Ehrlichman had helped bring Joseph Rhodes Jr. onto the Commission on Campus Unrest three years earlier, and he had regularly met with Vernon Jordan of the NUL to play tennis. Jordan, in fact, was the only civil rights activist who regularly met with a member of Nixon's inner circle. When the president demanded Ehrlichman's resignation on April 30, the movement effectively lost its access to the White House.[2]

Attorney General Richard Kleindienst, who had helped his predecessor John Mitchell pursue activists under the auspices of the H. Rap Brown Act, resigned on the same day. Nixon's replacement of Kleindienst in May with Elliot Richardson brought an end to the Justice Department's role in the federal government's pursuit of militant speakers. Unlike his predecessor, Richardson had no previous ties to John Mitchell's various campaigns against agitators. Moreover, the new attorney general gave time and attention to the Watergate scandal, supervising the work of Special Prosecutor Archibald Cox, whom he had recently appointed to investigate the matter. The Justice Department's dogged pursuit of criminal officials in the Nixon administration distracted the White House from its domestic surveillance activities of the previous four years. Under Richardson's direction, the department did not indict any more people for having violated the H. Rap Brown Act.

Similarly, the removal of L. Patrick Gray from the FBI caused another dramatic shift in the government's antiriot crusade. He resigned in April, because he revealed to the White House that he had destroyed documents pertaining to Watergate. Three months later, Clarence Kelley became the new permanent director of the FBI, and he took the agency into a less invasive direction. Only three weeks into the job, on July 31, he ended the FBI's "Ghetto Informant Program," which Hoover had started six years earlier in order for the agency to learn from informants about the potential for uprisings in urban areas. Thanks to Kelley, the agency no longer considered urban militant speakers relevant to internal security. In addition, as the unraveling Watergate scandal led reporters to start investigating the domestic spying the agency had performed over the past few years, Kelley became increasingly occupied with combating negative press coverage.

During the spring and summer months, the press reported much of the extent to which President Nixon had tried to crush dissent. The public learned that the federal government had broken into the office of antiwar activist Daniel Ellsberg and had conducted illegal wiretapping on him. Also, periodicals revealed a list of over 200 domestic, liberal-leaning "enemies," compiled by the Nixon administration in 1972. Civil rights activists on the list included Joseph Lowery and Ralph Abernathy of SCLC, George Wiley of the NWRO, and Bayard Rustin of the NAACP. Twelve more African American "enemies" served in the House of Representatives. One of them—William Clay—had called Agnew a "buffoon" in 1971, and another—Charles Diggs—had thanked him for doing so. Other African American "enemies,"

however, included less inflammatory politicians, entertainers, and columnists who may have publicly criticized Nixon or supported the movement.
Columnist Carl Rowan, one of the listed, wrote a damning response: "This
list proves that President Nixon was surrounded by a bunch of neo-fascists
who by their very nature considered anybody black or reasonably literate to
be their natural enemies." It also underscored why the president had not
welcomed many civil rights leaders to the White House since 1969. If African
Americans who served in government were "enemies," what chance would
African American radicals have to enter his good graces?[3]

Listings of civil rights demonstrators revealed the impact of their activism
on the Nixon administration as late as 1972. In his official response to the
list, Abernathy called his inclusion among other freedom fighters a "distinct
honor and privilege." Referring to himself as an enemy not of the White
House but of "the practices and programs of the Nixon Administration," he
professed to "love the White House with such deep and abiding affection
that I will do all within my power to see to it that President Nixon is removed
from this place."[4] Abernathy's inclusion reflected Nixon's personal animosity
toward the SCLC leader, because members of civil rights organizations that
Nixon favored—the NAACP and the NUL—escaped mention. Meanwhile,
owing more to the decline in prominence of both SNCC and CORE than to
their politics, no one from those organizations appeared on the list, either.

Although Wilkins was not on the list, he now regularly issued statements
that were as anti-Nixon as any remarks from Abernathy and other "enemies."
On July 3, the NAACP leader gave an address that criticized the president
but failed to mention Watergate. The exclusion implied that Nixon's treatment of civil rights issues caused more damage to African Americans than
the political scandal did. In essence, the civil rights figure accused the White
House of practicing fascism. "A rallying cry of the Nixon Administration has
been for 'law and order,' by which it meant 'law and order for Negro criminals,'" Wilkins quipped. "We shall not comment on the irony of a 'law and
order' Administration punishing penny ante Negro crime while plotting in
the highest echelons of government the theft of the liberties and freedoms of
a whole people."[5]

On the other hand, the NAACP's response to the Watergate scandal revealed dissention among the civil rights organizations on the matter.
SNCC and SCLC had demanded Nixon's removal from office long before
Watergate, and the "enemies list" reports merely gave Abernathy an excuse
to renew his call. In contrast, the NAACP made no such call and did not
even mention Watergate in any resolutions at its annual convention that summer. *The Crisis* described the break-in as illegal and foolish, and the editors

rhetorically asked how the president could not have known about the act. The NAACP was disheartened that the country's "law and order" culture remained strong, noting that Nixon's reelection showed that the nation's voters valued corruption in politics more than radicalism.

Watergate became a mixed blessing to the movement. The scandal's fallout damaged the federal government's efforts at neutralizing civil rights activism, but the press's constant coverage of the affair left civil rights leaders struggling to redirect the nation's attention to the problems of hunger and economic inequality. The stronger organizations like the NAACP and the NUL elected to stay focused on the administration's treatment of African Americans. The weaker groups like SCLC, SNCC, and CORE were in turmoil and lacked the massive numbers they had once enjoyed for major protests. Meanwhile, more African Americans entered electoral contests to capitalize on the previous year's victories. In the absence of major marches or sit-ins during late 1973, electoral campaigns were the most visible African American political activities, and the outcomes of the contests helped determine the future relevance of the movement.

For most of the year, the mainstream press covered Agnew favorably. Columnists began to look ahead to the 1976 presidential election and considered him a very likely winner of the Republican presidential nomination. He deplored his prohibition from White House meetings, but his distance from Nixon's group of confidantes left him untouched by Watergate. As a result, in comparison to the deposed White House staffers and cabinet officials under investigation, Agnew looked very good. He no longer gave tough, blunt speeches about alleged activist criminals, but he came to epitomize "law and order" more as Nixon's stature began to diminish. His supporters urged him to start securing delegates for the next RNC.[6]

Then on August 6, the press reported that the vice president was being investigated by the Justice Department for bribery charges. Agnew had allegedly taken kickbacks during his tenure as Maryland's governor and for the first three years of his vice presidency. The report was a long time in coming. Agnew himself had known about the investigation for six months, and President Nixon had also known about it before August. One businessman who had told Maryland officials that he was paying off Agnew had informed them back in January.[7]

August 8 was the fifth anniversary of Agnew's nomination by Nixon to serve as his running mate for the 1968 election. Instead of celebrating, however, the vice president held an emotionally tense news conference to address the bribery allegations. He had not wanted to speak on the matter. On the other hand, he could not remain silent as people leaked statements to the press about him that were "false and scurrilous and malicious," as he put it. "I have no intention to be skewered in this fashion," he glowered. The anger that he usually reserved for the press or for dissenters now went directly to the Maryland businessmen implicating him. He had often reprimanded political demonstrators for their crude language as well as their references to violence. Now Agnew himself used profane language when he referred to the charges against him as "damned lies."[8]

While the Nixon administration grappled with Watergate and with Agnew's problems that August, SCLC struggled with its own crisis of leadership. Over a month had passed since Abernathy's resignation without the group having settled the problem of its vacant presidency. The organization's members spent that time in intense and frank self-reflection, trying to figure out what went wrong with their group. Noah Robinson of Operation Breadbasket admitted, "SCLC today is not the viable organization it once was." He claimed that the movement had evolved "from the era of protest . . . to the era of program" and stated that Abernathy needed to learn about effectively "mobilizing masses to secure economic gains." By doing this, "he can still serve a vital role in SCLC's future," Robinson predicted.[9]

Tyrone Brooks, the executive director of SCLC–Atlanta, was just as blunt as Robinson but directed his overview to Abernathy. Brooks empathized with Abernathy's hardships—the 36 arrests since 1955 and, more recently, "the deadness of your staff and the lack of support they give you." Those difficulties "must be a terrible thing to have to live with from day to day," he said. Although Brooks did not excuse the people who treated Abernathy disrespectfully, he criticized the outgoing SCLC president for allowing them to do so. "Some of this is your fault due to your kindness, a lack of firmness, and your failure to put your foot down and say, 'This is it and that's the way it's going to be,'" Brooks observed.[10] If Abernathy were to receive the funding SCLC so badly needed, then Brooks suggested the SCLC leader should rescind his resignation. Otherwise, every official of the group—including Brooks—should resign along with Abernathy.

The SCLC staff collectively agreed with Brooks. They sent a letter to the organization's board that month, asking its members to "join with us in refusing to allow Dr. Abernathy to resign and to re-elect him to another term as President."[11] The group had not named a successor. Then again, the vacant presidency left much to be desired, because anyone replacing Abernathy stood to inherit a mess. Someone needed to know how to supervise several projects simultaneously with few personnel and low funds. The new leader also needed to help bring together those who supported Mrs. King with those who criticized her.

SCLC announced its choice for president on August 15, during the group's annual convention. The board followed the staff's advice and rejected Abernathy's resignation. As with Abernathy's ascendancy upon King's death, the group sent a solid—yet anticlimactic—collective message that it wanted no one else but Abernathy to be in charge. Moreover, with no rising stars like Andrew Young and Jesse Jackson remaining in the organization, the board's announcement was SCLC's strongest and least divisive public validation of Abernathy's leadership.

Unlike his initial arrival into the office, his return to the presidency was not publicly announced by Mrs. King. It was a sign of how estranged she had become from some of the people in the organization. In 1968, SCLC had accepted her as the face of the group and the best-suited person to frame SCLC's decisions in the context of what her husband would have wanted. But now the organization felt confident enough to represent itself collectively when announcing how it would continue King's work. The group's gamble of refusing Abernathy's resignation worked, and he decided not to leave the presidency. However, he left the conflict with Mrs. King unresolved.

Abernathy's victory was bittersweet because the media almost completely ignored it. Once again, the movement shared news coverage with violence in Southeast Asia, for the SCLC board's decision to keep Abernathy was on the same day that all U.S. combat operations in Indochina ended. Months earlier, in June, Congress and Nixon had agreed to cease funding after August 15 for the bombing of Cambodia—the last daily U.S. military campaign in Indochina. When that day finally arrived, the end of U.S. military action there after 12 consecutive years dominated front-page headlines and television news reports. Civil rights and antiwar activism converged one last time, as Dick Gregory participated in a "kneel-in" on the White House grounds during the bombing's final week. He and three others were arrested while praying for the country.

Otherwise, civil rights was history to the press. Except for 10-year retrospectives on the March on Washington, the news ignored the issue that month and concentrated instead on Watergate, Agnew, and the end of the war. No television network newscast even mentioned Abernathy's return to the presidency, and newspaper articles about his new term at the helm appeared in the back pages of periodicals. With or without Abernathy in charge, the media agreed with Nixon that SCLC was irrelevant.[12]

The vice president was slipping into irrelevance as well. The longer his controversy lasted, the more his public stature diminished. Agnew's scandal had no connection to Watergate, but it was still a scandal in the Nixon administration. Journalists increasingly began to tie the two scandals together, considering them both as indicators of a rapidly deteriorating presidency. "Just as the televised Senate hearings into the Watergate scandal were winding up for the summer recess and the White House and President Nixon's embattled supporters were beginning to breathe a shade more easily," wrote columnist Michael Davie, "the Agnew scandal broke."[13]

Agnew even began to look more criminal. On September 22, news reports told of the establishment of a defense fund for Agnew. With this development, he now borrowed the same tactic as many of the radicals he had previously denounced—an irony not lost on people like editorial cartoonist Herbert Block. The artist drew the vice president in his office, which was partly adorned with a "Free Spiro" poster. The Agnew caricature sat at his desk and talked on the phone. "Hello, Angela Davis," he greeted, "You may be a little surprised to be hearing from me."[14]

The vice president also came very close to portraying himself as a radical. Speaking at the Republican Women's Convention on September 28, he claimed that the Justice Department had faltered the Watergate investigation so badly that it wanted to bring him down in order to redeem itself. "I'm a big trophy," he bantered.[15] Like the movement leaders, the vice president was now talking about how the federal government was out to get him. The only difference was that Agnew *was* part of the federal government.

Agnew made a dramatic show of his side of the story. He declared his innocence to the women, repeatedly vowing in a raised voice not to resign if indicted. He couched his will to politically survive as a patriotic act. "I would forsake the principles of the Founding Fathers if I abandoned this fight," he reasoned to the crowd, "and I do not intend to abandon it." He stepped off the stage to rapturous applause, having once again won over his supporters.[16]

The vice president did not, however, win over the White House. For the second time in three years, he had publicly criticized a government official appointed by the president. By attacking the Justice Department's investigation of Agnew, the vice president was—by extension—attacking Henry Peterson, whom Nixon had chosen to study the allegations against Agnew. The vice president's remarks strained his relationship with Nixon even further than his critique of Joseph Rhodes had. More importantly, just as Nixon had not dumped Rhodes from the commission, nor did he remove Petersen from the investigation.

President Nixon's refusal to intervene in the case left Agnew at the mercy of whatever evidence the investigators would find. In an early October press conference, Nixon publicly supported Agnew's right to contest the charges but acknowledged the seriousness of the allegations. Despite the vice president's pledge not to resign, he did exactly that on October 10. He then pleaded nolo contendere to the bribery charges in a Maryland courtroom. Upon leaving the court, he vowed to give an address to the nation in a few days.

On October 15, Agnew fulfilled that promise and gave a 15-minute farewell address on network television, informing viewers that his plea of nolo contendere was not an admission of guilt. He portrayed himself as a martyr, saying that he had resigned, despite his innocence, in order to keep the nation from being distracted and hampered by his troubles. He did, however, admit to two flaws. He stated that for the past two months, the country had not had "a Vice President in whom they can have unimpaired confidence and trust." Also, after defining for the audience his case as "allegations that I permitted my fund raising activities and my contract dispensing activities to overlap in an unethical and unlawful manner," he revealed, "Perhaps, judged by the new post-Watergate political morality, I did."[17]

The speech contained several of Agnew's trademarks. It included some multisyllabic phrases, as when he promised not to leave the public in a "paroxysm of bitterness." He offered kind remarks to the president and celebrated their accomplishments together. He jabbed at the media one last time as well. Even his reference to "post-Watergate political morality" was standard, because he said it to rationalize his nolo contendere plea.[18] It was no different than his rationalizing of his Japanese slur in 1968 by identifying himself as a fellow ethnic minority.

Ironically, the former vice president had contributed greatly to this new "morality" that he now credited for his downfall. By publicly calling with Nixon for a heavier emphasis on preserving "law and order" in 1968, Agnew had initially succeeded in stifling only African American dissent. By 1970, his new criminals were antiwar demonstrators. Three years later, the Watergate hearings constituted part of the same desire the country had for "law and order." Now that the Nixon administration had crushed the movement through COINTELPRO and had curtailed antiwar protest by removing U.S. troops from Indochina, the attention of the Justice Department turned increasingly to the political corruption of high-ranking officials.

Agnew's conviction and his couching of it as a change in the public's moral standards ended his credibility as a defender of law and order. Five years earlier, as a candidate for vice president, he had publicly declared that no person had the right to determine which laws were right or wrong. No one had the right to assess the correctness of a law. Now, he implied that his bribery had only become illegal because Watergate brought Nixon administration officials under more legal scrutiny. Then again, because he was now out of office, he no longer had the responsibility of defending "law and order." Instead, he was merely defending himself.

Still, Agnew reversed the position that had made him a "Silent Majority" icon. Thus, most Americans reacted unfavorably to his speech. Although a few diehard supporters thought someone had framed Agnew, the majority of Americans simply did not believe him anymore. At the annual meeting of the Conservative Party of New York, which had just featured Agnew as the keynote speaker the previous year, more than half the members walked out of the former vice president's address as it blared on a television set in one of the gathering rooms. One of the people who had watched the speech perfectly summed up the conflicting feelings of many Americans that night. "I've never seen him so humble, and I doubted he had it in him," the person acknowledged. "But I don't believe a word of it."[19]

For many African Americans, the former vice president's conviction was irrelevant because they had dismissed him long ago. Agnew had cultivated very few African American fans over the years and had instead repulsed several of them with his hard line against civil rights activism. As a result, the African American press expressed extremely minimal sorrow concerning his resignation. For the *Chicago Defender*, Frank Stanley penned the editorial "Pity Spiro Agnew Not," and Louis Martin more bluntly titled his *Pittsburgh Courier* commentary, "There Are No Tears for Vice President Agnew."[20]

Although the movement's old adversary was gone, civil rights workers disagreed on how to mark the occasion—yet another sign of the movement's unraveling. Some activists were less charitable toward the disgraced ex-official than others. Spoken-word artist Gil Scott-Heron recorded the song "H2O-Gate Blues" on the night of the former vice president's farewell address, calling him "Spearhead X—the ex-second in command." Dick Gregory, speaking at an event in Chicago that fall, provided a humorous coda to the movement's acrimonious relationship with the former vice president. "I don't think Agnew was guilty," Gregory began before chiding that "you've got to be smart to deal with kickback." He also tied Agnew's downfall to both the "law and order" culture and Watergate. "You can't say Nixon lied to us. He told us if he ever got to be President, he was going to take all the crime out of the streets," Gregory observed. "It's your fault for not asking where he was gonna put it."[21] Ex-SNCC associate Lynne Doswell also was not sorry to see Agnew go; he had made life miserable for her and her husband.

Rap Brown himself was philosophical of his former pursuer's political demise. The former SNCC chairman expressed neither pity nor humor but rather considered Agnew's political fate a natural inevitability. He noted that either downfall or death removed a public official from office. To Brown, the former vice president unwittingly became a national historical footnote because of his own actions. He accelerated his decline by taking bribes and then publicly denying his criminality, and the bribery diminished the legacy of his tenure as second-in-command after his departure.[22]

In contrast, the NAACP grieved for the country. Its official statement on the resignation called the event a national "sad time" because it tragically revealed "the deep malaise which envelopes this country." The group bitterly described Agnew's tenure as "touring the country castigating civil rights leaders," but it expressed neither sadness nor glee at his political demise.[23] Then again, the NAACP had always criticized the administration without personally attacking it—even as Watergate began—in order to preserve its ties to federal officials. Thus, the group's response to the Agnew ordeal was par for the course.

Moreover, the scandal distracted the country from important civil rights work. The NAACP hoped that Nixon would choose the "astute and able" African American senator Edward Brooke to replace Agnew, but the president picked House Minority Leader Gerald Ford, who to the NAACP had a "mixed record" of votes on civil rights legislation. The organization reserved judgment on Ford but printed his civil rights voting record in its entirety in *The Crisis* to allow readers to judge him for themselves.[24]

The decline of the White House's "law and order" culture throughout 1973 resulted in progress for African Americans in the South without demonstrations from national civil rights organizations. Some of the last remnants of institutionalized Jim Crow disappeared, and these holdovers included vehicles that state governments had implemented to curb or punish activists of nonviolent civil disobedience. The "New South" governors removed many of the remnants, tacitly acknowledging the new political reality that politicians could no longer win elections by advocating segregation. In April, Mississippi governor William Waller vetoed funding for the State Sovereignty Commission after June 30, thus fulfilling one of his major campaign promises from two years earlier. Members were stunned, and they bitterly complained that the veto had taken place after the state legislature had adjourned for the year. Unwilling to go quietly, the defunded commission defiantly held one last meeting on November 9. In contrast, Alabama governor George Wallace asked the state legislature to continue funding a similar commission, but the legislators cut off the money after September 30. Wallace's office handled the program's residual expenses until its account completely ran out of funds in December.[25]

Southern correctional facilities made news in the summer and fall for desegregating their living quarters for inmates. They were among the final government institutions to defy the Civil Rights Act. Their desegregation was significant, because they represented the fear and terror that state governments had fostered to discourage African Americans from seeking their civil rights. Going to jail was "not the thing to do" for an African American in the South, as one activist put it. A person's arrest brought embarrassment to the family. In addition, many African Americans who went off to jail never came back, because they were killed while in custody. However, federal district courts began reviewing grievances of inmates and calling for drastic changes, and new wardens started to update prison conditions. Missouri State Penitentiary integrated its cellblocks in November 1973. The following month, Mississippi's infamous "Parchman Farm" penitentiary, which the state's executive branch had used to incarcerate SNCC members during the Freedom Rides in 1961, desegregated the convicts' housing facilities and ended its long practice of arming convicts to serve as prison guards. The state had just hired a "Yankee" penologist as the prison's superintendent, and he implemented the changes.[26]

Atlanta, Georgia, seemed poised for major civil rights changes, too. Maynard Jackson, the city's African American vice mayor, ran for mayor that year against the incumbent—a Jewish man named Sam Massell. Jackson had success in attracting voters without having to rely on the movement. Part of his popularity came from the efforts of college and university students, but the students were not part of any movement organization. SNCC, whose national headquarters had formerly been in the city, no longer had office space for whatever remained of its local branch. Atlanta had left the organization behind.

On October 14, Mayor Massell warned against a Maynard Jackson–Hosea Williams administration, saying that "Atlanta's too young to die."[27] They were all involved in runoff election campaigns, and before now ethnic tensions concerning Jackson and Williams had not been a subject discussed by Massell. The incumbent insisted that he did not believe that Atlanta would die solely if Jackson were elected. Rather, he did not want Williams to win the election for city council president—formerly known as the position of vice mayor. Still, Massell was running against Jackson, not Williams, and the mayor's distraction from his own opponent rankled even Jackson himself.

By continuing his line of attack on Williams, Massell tried the same tactics that had launched Agnew's national political career. The mayor tried to use an African American's militant words to exercise political power. Massell harped on the vice mayor's endorsement of Williams's 1972 run for the state senate. During that campaign, the SCLC member had said that the hopes of African Americans rested in "bucks, ballots, and bullets." Massell did not think that such rhetoric was appropriate for a potential city council president, and he said so. "I just have the guts to say a black man can be bad, just like the whites can," he declared.[28] The mayor's proclamation was not unlike Agnew's challenge to Maryland's African American activists in April 1968. Just as the former governor had said that African Americans should condemn their own incendiary speakers, Massell was calling on Jackson to repudiate a fellow African American's inflammatory speech. The major difference was that Agnew had spoken in a state that had a mostly European American population. Massell, on the other hand, took a major risk in borrowing from Agnew's color-baiting in a mostly African American city.

Atlanta's election season presented a dynamic in the movement that had not existed since before King's death. The local and national press fed into the Massell campaign's fearmongering by identifying Williams solely as either an "activist" or a "militant"; reporters did not mention Williams's leadership of Atlanta's branch of the nonviolent SCLC organization. After years of SCLC being promoted in the media as the positive alternative to black militants, SCLC was now depicted as militant and the less desirable choice for a European American liberal. Not only was the movement narrative approach localized to Atlanta, but SCLC was the antagonist. The depiction greatly resembled how politicians and reporters had talked about King's increasing militancy and his intent to "destroy America from within" in 1967 and 1968. Ultimately, the propaganda against Williams worked, because he lost the city council presidential election on October 16.

On the other hand, Jackson won the mayoral contest that same day. The South now had an African American elected to mayor of a large city in the region. Many veterans of the movement claimed his accomplishment as theirs, too. Jesse Jackson traveled to Atlanta to be with Maynard Jackson on election night and stood beside him as the new mayor-elect gave his victory speech. More poignantly, Coretta Scott King tied the history of SCLC with Jackson's win. "This is a very significant victory, not only for Atlanta but for the rest of the South and the nation," she began. "I believe it represents the fulfillment of part of my husband's dream when he spoke of black and white people sitting down together to work their problems out in peace." Her connection of the election to her husband's dream was ironic, considering that King had not believed in effecting change by entering politics. Her remarks validated not only the campaigns of SCLC veterans Andrew Young, Walter Fauntroy, Hosea Williams, and Jesse Jackson, but also Maynard Jackson's claim that politics was "the Civil Rights Movement of the Seventies."[29]

Atlanta's mayoral election also precipitated the movement's final split. Many civil rights leaders agreed that Jackson's victory meant that it was now time to retire marches and sit-ins as tactics. In November, Hosea Williams devised a think tank of advisers for the mayor-elect. Williams said his first method of attack against incidents of racism and discrimination would not be marches but rather negotiations. He vowed to meet with Atlanta industry board members and try to settle with them first. "If we can't come to an agreement, I'll go back into the streets—picketing, marching and demonstrating." On the other hand, he did admit that by moving SCLC–Atlanta from the streets to the negotiating tables, "The SCLC here has been brought as far as one man can take it."[30]

Later that fall, ex-CORE director James Farmer proposed another think tank: the Public Policy Training Institute at Howard University. He hoped that the institute would steer African Americans into a more progressive direction, because protests from civil rights groups had not alleviated major socioeconomic problems. He criticized SCLC's antipoverty demonstrations such as the mule trains and "Resurrection City" encampments of the past five years without mentioning anyone specifically by name. "Income gaps do not respond to sit-ins," he concluded, "and reading levels are not improved by freedom marches."[31]

On the other hand, the NAACP saw no reason to discontinue any of its current activities or rethink its positions on skin-color exclusivity. On November 6, two more cities elected their first African American mayors. Coleman Young won the election in the major midwestern city of Detroit, and L. E. Lightner captured the contest in Raleigh, North Carolina. To win these contests the candidates needed both African American and European American votes, and the NAACP saw the outcomes as validation of its integrationist approach. The mayoral victories merely constituted "the end of the separatist movement" that the other groups had embraced, as far as the NAACP was concerned.[32]

The elections of Young and Lightner took place on the same day that Rap Brown finally stood trial for his incitement charge from his Cambridge remarks. Six years had passed since the State of Maryland had originally charged him, and in the interim Brown's other court cases, his time as a fugitive, and a dispute over the legality of the charge delayed his incitement trial. Now he was transported from Attica Prison to an Ellicott City, Maryland, courtroom. He had not changed much physically over the past few years. The familiar wire-rim glasses lay on his nose, and a toothpick rested in his mouth, as usual. He wore blue dungarees, a blue turtleneck sweater, and a red bandanna. On the other hand, he lacked his usual bravado in the courtroom. Spending time either in courtrooms or prison cells for the previous two years seemed to have sapped his strength, and one observer noted that the defendant did not appear to know what was happening, nor did he care to find out. Reporter John Jasper was stunned by how "zombie-like" Brown looked. "Any resemblance of Rap Brown in 1973 and the Rap Brown I knew at the height of the black struggle for survival in the '60s was purely accidental," Jasper quipped.[33]

The drama in the trial peaked at the very start. The judge ordered Brown to stand and raise his right hand. Brown, ever defiant, said very softly, "It's not necessary."[34] Journalists in the front row of the jury box had to strain to hear Brown because he spoke very quietly.

The judge insisted that the defendant swear an oath. "It's customary, Mr. Brown," the judge argued. "It's not necessary," Brown whispered. "All right," the judge answered.[35]

The rest of the trial then proceeded without incident. The state's attorney for Dorchester County requested that the court drop the charges. The lawyer argued that too much time had passed, and "we have nothing to gain by it anymore."[36] Also, he claimed, most of the key witnesses had either become senile or died. The judge agreed and dropped the charges. Although he sentenced the activist to one year in prison for having been absent on his March 1970 trial date, the judge allowed Brown's time in prison since June 1972 to count as time served for the absentee conviction. Brown remained incarcerated, however, for his previous convictions.

The court decision was the latest reflection of Agnew's waning public stature. The clearing of the incitement charge repudiated the means by which the former governor of Maryland rose to the nation's vice presidency. On the occasion of the trial's conclusion, two reporters from the *Baltimore Afro-American* bitterly chronicled Agnew's rise and fall in the context of how he treated local activism. Troy Bailey claimed that the ex-governor's harangue at Baltimore's civil rights workers in April 1968 "took him all the way to the White House," and he then snidely asked, "Where is Agnew now?" Nathaniel Knight, meanwhile, mocked Agnew as a politically irrelevant hypocrite who reaped what he had sown by pursuing the former SNCC chairman on bogus charges. He also rhetorically inquired, "What has become of Brown's chief oppressor in this state?"[37]

The former vice president offered no comment on Brown's victory to the press.

One day after a Maryland court suggested Brown's right to African American militant speech, the NAACP did the same for the Black Panthers. Roy Wilkins and Ramsey Clark finally published their commission's study, calling it *Search and Destroy*. Wilkins and Clark held a press conference to announce the publication, and they called upon the Justice Department to reopen slain BPP–Chicago leader Fred Hampton's case "so that people can have some confidence that the laws will be faithfully executed," as Clark put it. The commission claimed it was probable that authorities had drugged Hampton at the time of the killing, the police—not Hampton—were the first to fire any shots, and only 1 of the nearly 100 shots came from the Panther. Clark considered Hampton "murdered in the legal sense of the word." Once again, the former attorney general used strong language about the case, but it suggested his agreement with the NAACP that "law and order" under Nixon was "anti-Negro." Now that separatism seemed on the wane, government officials and integrationists were belatedly ready to defend the ideology's imprisoned or dead advocates.[38]

This development mattered little to one of the most separatist civil rights organizations, however. At the time SNCC was in a precarious condition; almost half of its branches—the New York and Cincinnati cadres—had closed over the past few months. On the other hand, their disappearances allowed the group to accomplish by default one of Muhammad Hunt's goals, for the organization had not only returned to the South but had become completely Southern. Its strongest chapters that fall were in Oklahoma and Texas, and the most prominent members were coordinators William Coleman of Atlanta, Donald Payne of Tulsa, and Mario Salas of San Antonio.

SNCC held a national meeting in Tulsa on November 24, but members of the Texas branch did not go. Those in attendance changed the organization's name from the Student National Coordinating Committee to the Revolutionary Democratic Party. The new name resembled the name Rap Brown had originally chosen for the group four years earlier—the Revolutionary Action Party. The change reflected, however, that the "SNCC" acronym was a misnomer. The organization no longer consisted largely of students, and its decline to three Southern branches made it less national than regional. The name change merely made the demise of SNCC—as people had known it since its founding in 1960—a formality.[39]

The movement itself was over, too. After having come to a consensus on Black Power, Pan-Africanism, and Vietnam, civil rights groups split yet again on feminism, separate African American political organizing, and federal political corruption. In addition, they lost followers as they adopted new causes and as COINTELPRO sabotaged their programs. Maynard Jackson's mayoral victory gave weary civil rights leaders an excuse to announce that they would stop marching and withdraw into boardrooms and think tanks. The NAACP, the NUL, CORE, SCLC, the NWRO, the TWWA, and PUSH continued to work in their individual ways to end poverty and inequality.

Between 1967 and 1973, the civil rights organizations yielded significant short-term fruit as they struggled to keep the movement alive. They redefined nonviolent protest to keep it relevant after King's assassination. They bridged the movement's internal generation gap when expressing ethnic pride and advocating for young, oppressed militants like Rap Brown or Fred Hampton. In 1972, the groups collectively were powerful enough for Democratic presidential candidates to curry their favor, and they remained major political players until that November.

Civil rights groups also produced a long-term legacy by extending African American political influence beyond the movement. The organizations provided some of the first public forums for veterans in opposition to war and for gay rights advocates. The presence of conservative groups like the NAACP and the NUL at Black Power and Pan-African gatherings helped widen the appeal of both causes beyond the young, radical sects that had originally championed them; and more people accepted those causes as legitimate outgrowths of ethnic identity instead of calls for separatist revolution. Mrs. King and members of the TWWA blazed new trails of struggle for their rights as both African Americans and women, exposing the hypocrisy of militant "liberation" rhetoric from sexist male colleagues. The movement disintegrated after diversifying its personnel and issues so broadly, but it empowered masses of people to lead themselves.

Epilogue: Leaders without a Movement

In the fall of 1974, Tracy Amalfitano watched the city of Boston, Massachusetts, descend into chaos over the issue of busing. Judge Arthur Garrity had ordered the Irish Americans of South Boston—Amalfitano's neighborhood—and the African Americans of Roxbury to bus their children to each other's schools. Amalfitano defied her neighbors by complying with the order, and some of them vandalized her house and car because she placed her son on the bus each morning. As she faced this violence in the North, she wistfully remembered the movement of the early 1960s—"all the liberals that got on the buses and went south for sit-ins and boycotts." She wondered about those liberals, "Where were they *now?*"[1]

In a sense, the civil rights activists had never left. Many of them sharply rebuked President Gerald Ford that October when, barely one month after pardoning ex-president Nixon for Watergate, he publicly disagreed with Judge Garrity's decision. A few days later, the new president discontinued his predecessor's banning of civil rights leaders from the White House and welcomed them to discuss Boston and other issues concerning African Americans. Among the attendees were Dorothy Height of the NCNW, Clarence Mitchell of the NAACP, Jesse Jackson of PUSH, and Vernon Jordan of the NUL. SCLC, meanwhile, was still shut out of the White House.[2]

For this first crisis in ethnic relations since the dissolution of the movement, the national civil rights organizations addressed the crisis in Boston in different ways. The lack of cohesion among them showed that no collective movement existed anymore. The NAACP had taken its usual legal route in 1972, suing the Boston school board for its deliberate segregating of the public schools. During the violence associated with busing in 1974, SCLC participated in a march. On the other hand, Amalfitano's wish for integrated "freedom rides" to the North was unlikely to happen. CORE and SNCC had been integrated and pacifist when they facilitated the rides of May 1961, but in 1974, SNCC was gone and CORE preached separatism. As Bayard Rustin put it in the mid-1970s, "It is pointless to talk of unity between Roy Wilkins, who advocates integration, and Roy Innis, who wants to resegregate black schools."[3]

With the movement dead, people immediately offered different interpretations as to its ultimate meaning. In Boston, some European American opponents to busing implemented tactics from previous civil rights campaigns. Just as African Americans had boycotted the buses in Montgomery two decades earlier, South Bostonians arranged for their children to boycott the public schools. The volunteer-run, makeshift independent schools they established for the boycotting students echoed the schools that student activists had started in rural Mississippi for segregated African American students. In speeches, South Bostonians connected their plight to Reconstruction. At one rally a woman reminded the audience that the Fourteenth Amendment applied to her, too. "I am white, and I want *my* rights!" she bellowed.[4]

South Boston's anti-busing activists considered themselves inheritors of the movement's legacy. They grew frustrated that others did not see them that way, but they failed to consider what African American civil rights activists knew all too well by 1974. Just as the urban riots of the late 1960s turned people away from the civil rights struggle, the violence associated with anti-busing feelings damaged the reputation of the opponents' cause. To Vernon Jordan of the NUL, there was one major difference. "If blacks had engaged in some of the practices seen in Boston, they would have been labeled 'rioters,'" he observed, "but instead, we just hear about 'protesters' or demonstrators.'" Still, the city's anti-busing activists were puzzled by their poor reputation. "If Martin Luther King was a hero for sitting on the street, or, blocking traffic, or picketing or demonstrating, how come we're not heroes?" they would sincerely ask. "How come the media are treating us differently than it did the white college students who opposed Vietnam, or the blacks who had sit-ins?"[5]

The activism of the South Bostonians and the relative inactivity of national civil rights groups showed how localized the civil rights struggle had become. Former SNCC associate Julian Bond did not even acknowledge national organizations when discussing the civil rights coalition that had evolved after the early 1970s. He saw the movement as "a lot of miniscule, separate local groups that don't know their right arm from the left," and concluded, "It's fragmented, torn apart." Some veterans of the movement tried to reclaim it for themselves. As early as July 1974, activists expressed hope that a march against the death penalty in North Carolina would launch "a rebirth of the civil rights movement." It never restarted, however.[6]

Some civil rights leaders accepted the end of the movement and were able to evolve as civil rights activists more easily than others. The more adaptable ones focused on their strengths. Ella Baker remained an activist gadfly, offering her wisdom to new organizations and causes until her death in 1986. Meanwhile, Fran Beal kept organizing African American feminists, and Angela Davis still advocated for political prisoners. Vernon Jordan's networking skills restored the NUL's closeness to the White House after President Nixon's resignation in 1974.

Coretta Scott King remained as much of an activist after the movement's demise as during its existence. On the other hand, after the early 1970s, SCLC's feud with her dissipated. The press's assessments of Abernathy's leadership of the group validated Mrs. King's claim that her work for the King Center did not influence SCLC's financial troubles. Meanwhile, her political stock rose to the point where she seconded former Georgia governor Jimmy Carter's nomination for president at the 1976 DNC, and she advised him on civil rights issues after he defeated President Gerald Ford's reelection bid that November. She remained a powerful, popular figure until her death 30 years later.[7]

Ralph Abernathy, on the other hand, struggled without the movement. He led SCLC for four more years after rescinding his resignation in 1973. The group still offered little more than marches and speeches, and it went further into the red. The press ignored the organization, offering more articles on SCLC's financial woes than on its demonstrations. SCLC's board of directors finally asked for his resignation, and in 1977, he complied. He privately complained of the group's ingratitude for his return to the helm at *their* insistence, but he publicly expressed his resignation as an opportunity to enter politics.

He tried yet again to recapture ties to the White House by supporting Ronald Reagan's presidential candidacy in October 1980. With Mrs. King advising President Jimmy Carter on civil rights issues, Abernathy had failed to attract Carter's attention over the previous four years. In contrast, Reagan conversed with Abernathy and promised him more African Americans in the private sector, and the minister believed in the candidate's plans to initiate job programs for the poor. Likening the presidency to a medical doctor,

Abernathy explained that "we as the patient are getting sicker, and we need to change doctors." Because of unemployment, inflation, and interest rates, he "just couldn't support Carter for another term." However, after Reagan won the election, the new president shut Abernathy out—just as other presidents had done.[8]

Meanwhile, his relationship with Mrs. King remained strained. She dismissed the gravity of Abernathy's support for Reagan, noting that "there's no rationale for it, really." After President Reagan signed the King Holiday into law in November 1983, he named her to head the commission to plan the holiday's first scheduled observance. Her omission of Abernathy from the commission greatly offended him. "Certainly, nobody was more qualified than me to serve on the commission," he complained. Hardly helping matters, a commission staffer noted that the members that received invitations had "clout and constituencies," implying that Abernathy had neither.[9]

The former SCLC leader was conflicted about his legacy by the late 1980s, but his steps to secure it isolated him from his fellow movement veterans. Whenever his family complained about his former colleagues' slights against him, he reassured them that historians would someday correctly tell his story. However, he wanted to tell the public his own story, too. In 1989, Harper & Row published his autobiography, *And the Walls Came Tumbling Down*, in which he resurrected old beefs with former comrades and detailed King's extramarital affairs. He reasoned that other writers had discussed King's dalliances without exploring the context of his life in those moments, and Abernathy merely wanted to justly and more fully explain King's affairs. Current and former civil rights leaders roundly condemned the book, and even former SCLC colleague Hosea Williams called Abernathy a "Judas." Abernathy died a civil rights pariah the following year.[10]

Roy Wilkins retired from the NAACP presidency in 1977—the same year that Abernathy stepped down from SCLC leadership. Whereas Abernathy continued seeking a major role for himself in the civil rights struggle, Wilkins withdrew from the media spotlight. He wrote in his autobiography, *Standing Fast*, that the civil rights struggle had not ended. "Unemployment, faulty education, poor housing—the stewing of the ghettos still mocks our claim to equality for all," he reasoned. By retiring, however, he demonstrated that he did not see himself as indispensable to the struggle. He noted that others shared his faith in the country and predicted that their shared faith "will last and guide us long after I am gone." He died in 1981, shortly before his autobiography's publication.[11]

Rap Brown's post-movement life started with promise. In 1974, as he served the prison sentence that Judge Lansing Mitchell had handed down,

Washington Post reporter Bob Woodward informed him and his wife about the judge's private threat to "get that nigger." The disclosure soon made the newspapers, and the former SNCC chairman became a free man in 1976. He then stayed out of the public eye for nearly a quarter century, living in Atlanta as an imam. He and his wife—now a lawyer—renamed themselves Jamil and Karima Al-Amin. He rarely granted interviews, but he attended funerals of fallen colleagues in the civil rights struggle.

Suddenly, as the new millennium began, his life fell apart. In 2000, he was accused of murdering a sheriff's deputy in Fulton County, Georgia. The defense attorney reminded the jury of Brown's work in ending segregation, and Andrew Young asked the jury to have mercy upon him. Also, Brown's fingerprints did not appear on any weapons associated with the incident, and another man confessed to having committed the crime shortly after it had taken place. Nevertheless, Brown was convicted in March 2002 and sentenced to life in prison without parole. One of his supporters called him a "political prisoner" who was merely "guilty of fighting for the rights of African Americans and fighting for the rights of Muslims."[12]

As the Voting Rights Act enfranchised African American voters, civil rights veterans who sought public office won many African American votes. Activists turned politicians tended to trumpet their participation in activities with King, which meant that they celebrated the earlier years of civil rights struggle. Jesse Jackson of SCLC and PUSH was one of the few prominent figures of the movement's later years to gain traction, running for president twice and winning South Carolina's Democratic primary in 1984. Then again, he also had marched alongside King. On the other hand, even the country's continued nostalgia for only the pre-1967 movement was part of the legacy of the post-1967 movement. King's image became SCLC's permanent icon immediately after his death, and SNCC tried to connect the sit-ins of 1960 with its calls for revolution in 1968.

The romanticizing of the early struggle resulted from the later movement's unhappiness with how the struggle had evolved. Between 1967 and 1973, civil rights leaders failed to develop a new, long-term, offensive collective strategy and instead reacted to the country's violence. They quoted old slogans and catchphrases from the "irresponsible militants" and adopted countercultural fashions and gestures. Into the 2010s, the movement's self-distancing from the 1970s remained part of the legacy of the later struggle. When SNCC veterans facilitated a conference to observe the group's fiftieth anniversary in 2010, nearly all of the panels focused on events from before 1967.

The movement of the late 1960s and early 1970s helped bring the nation out of the segregation that had shaped the country for almost a century. The activists defied state-level efforts at preserving Jim Crow, and they organized masses to protest federal policies that had perpetuated their repression. As more African Americans voted out their old oppressors, they voted in candidates who shared their political concerns. After breaking from the past, however, the later movement had no collective idea on how to shape the future. As a result, civil rights groups remained disunited by the time politics had become the "new" movement. Nevertheless, if civil rights workers before the late 1960s planted the seeds of desegregation, the workers of the late 1960s and early 1970s watered the seeds. The generations since then have begun to harvest the fruits of that labor.

Notes

INTRODUCTION

1. Schwartz, "Between the Lines of the Voting Rights Act"; "Excerpts from Supreme Court Ruling That Voids Key Part of the Voting Rights Act."
2. John Lewis, interview.
3. "Black America Now."

CHAPTER ONE

1. Roy Wilkins, quoted in "Awakenings," *Eyes on the Prize.*
2. Wilkins and Mathews, *Standing Fast,* 265, 269; "Whatever Happened to Robert F. Williams," 202; Wilkins, "The Meaning of the Sit-Ins," 16 April 1960, in *In Search of Democracy,* 404–5.
3. Wilkins, "The Meaning of the Sit-Ins," 16 April 1960, in *In Search of Democracy,* 404–5; Wilkins and Mathews, *Standing Fast,* 265, 269.
4. Carmichael, *Ready for Revolution,* 142–43; Forman, *The Making of Black Revolutionaries,* 216–17; Ransby, *Ella Baker & the Black Freedom Movement,* 242–44, 259.
5. Branch, *At Canaan's Edge,* 539; "King Refuses to Take Slap at 'Black Power'"; Weiss, *Whitney M. Young, Jr. and the Struggle for Civil Rights,* 177–78.
6. Roy Wilkins, "Sail Our NAACP Ship 'Steady as She Goes,'" 5 July 1966, in *In Search of Democracy,* 424; "Editorial," *The Crisis,* June July 1966, 299; "Freedom News," *The Crisis,* December 1966, 549.
7. "Integration: Military Style," 526.

8. "Editorial," *The Crisis*, April 1967, 127; Weiss, *Whitney M. Young, Jr. and the Struggle for Civil Rights*, 158–59.

9. Bob Zellner and Constance Curry, *The Wrong Side of Murder Creek*, 296–98; Dorothy M. Zellner, "My Real Vocation," 325.

10. "Cambridge Negroes Resume Protests," 2; "Employment Programs Begin in Cambridge," 4.

11. Gloria Richardson Dandridge, "The Energy of People Passing through Me," 277–86; Pearson, "German Claims DeGaulle Not Hero"; Carson, *In Struggle*, 252.

12. H. Rap Brown, *Die Nigger Die!*, 33–34; Payton, "Where's Rap Brown Gone?"

13. Arnold, "Newark Meeting on Black Power Attended by 400," 8.

14. David Boesel and Louis C. Goldberg, "Crisis in Cambridge," in *Cities under Siege: An Anatomy of the Ghetto Riots, 1964–1968*, 110–11.

15. Carson, *In Struggle*, 253; Carmichael, *Ready for Revolution*, 565.

16. Boesel and Goldberg, "Crisis in Cambridge," 111.

17. Franklin, "SNCC Chief Shot in Cambridge, Md.," 1, 20.

18. Carson, *In Struggle*, 239–41.

19. Franklin, "SNCC Chief Shot in Cambridge, Md.," 1, 20.

20. Ibid.

21. Boesel and Goldberg, "Crisis in Cambridge," 111, 116.

22. Brown, *Die Nigger Die!*, 100–101; Marsh, *Agnew the Unexamined Man*, 69.

23. Marsh, *Agnew the Unexamined Man*, 69; Collins, "They're Bitter, Fearful, Bewildered"; Boesel and Goldberg, "Crisis in Cambridge," 111–12.

24. Marsh, *Agnew the Unexamined Man*, 69; Collins, "They're Bitter, Fearful, Bewildered"; Boesel and Goldberg, "Crisis in Cambridge," 124.

25. Witcover, *Very Strange Bedfellows*, 11–12; Albright, *What Makes Spiro Run*, 182–83; Lippman, *Spiro Agnew's America*, 106–7.

26. "Gwynn Oak Park to Admit Negroes."

27. Seppy, "Negro Leader Brown Free on $10,000 Bail"; Albright, *What Makes Spiro Run*, 173–74.

28. "Goodbye to Wing-Tips," *Time*, 19 November 1973; Ransby, *Ella Baker and the Black Freedom Movement*, 259; Abel, *Signs of the Times*, 264–65.

29. Marsh, *Agnew the Unexamined Man*, 69.

30. "News Conference, July 26, 1967," *Executive Records of Governor Spiro T. Agnew, 1967–1969*.

31. Ibid.

32. "Brown Freed to Fulminate."

33. Ibid.

34. Ibid.; Karima Al-Amin, interview.

35. Albright, *What Makes Spiro Run*, 175–76.

36. Ibid.

37. Ibid.

38. Lyndon B. Johnson, "The President's Address to the Nation on Civil Disorders," 27 July 1967, in *Public Papers of the Presidents: Lyndon B. Johnson, 1967*, Book II, 721–24.

39. Ibid.

40. Lyndon B. Johnson, "The President's News Conference of 31 July 1967," 31 July 1967, in *Public Papers of the Presidents: Lyndon B. Johnson, 1967*, Book II, 728–29.

41. Nick Kotz, *Judgment Days: Lyndon Baines Johnson, Martin Luther King, Jr., and the Laws that Changed America*, 394; "The Promised Land," *Eyes on the Prize II*.

42. Director, FBI, letter to SAC, Albany, 4 March 1968, *COINTELPRO: The Counter-Intelligence Program of the FBI: Black Nationalist Hate Groups*, reel 1; Director, FBI, letter to SAC, New York, 25 July 1968, *COINTELPRO: The Counter-Intelligence Program of the FBI: Black Nationalist Hate Groups*, reel 1; David Cunningham, *There's Something Happening Here*, 32–33.

43. Elmer Holland, 15 August 1967, *Congressional Record: 90th Congress, Session One* (Washington: United States Government Printing Office), 22686; William Cramer and Roman Pucinski, 16 August 1967, *Congressional Record: 90th Congress, Session One*, 22775.

44. "Black People Make Fool of Kirk," *Ghetto Voice*, 15 August 1967, the Student Nonviolent Coordinating Committee Papers, Lamont Library, Harvard University.

45. Ibid.

46. "Florida Governor Snubbed by Black Power Advocate," *Press-Courier*, 10 August 1967; "Newspapers Back Kirk's Action," *Sarasota Herald-Tribune*, 13 August 1967; Harold Rummel, "Kirk Grandstand Plays Frustrate His Opponents," *St. Petersburg Times*, 15 August 1967.

CHAPTER TWO

1. Martin Luther King Jr. et al., "Joint Statement on Violence in the Cities," 26 July 1967, 1–2, the Martin Luther King, Jr. Center for Nonviolent Social Change.

2. Austin Scott, "Riot-Torn Cities Feel the New Mood of Young Negroes."

3. Columbia SDS, telegram, 27 July 1967, the Student Nonviolent Coordinating Committee Papers.

4. "Wilkins Tops Rights Leadership Poll," 457.

5. "The Urban Coalition," 134.

6. Whitney M. Young, *Beyond Racism*, 1969, 86; Bond, letter, 20 July 2013.

7. Gertsel, "Young: Liberate or Exterminate."

8. Marlow, "Civil Rights Protests Are Going Far Afield."

9. Martin Luther King Jr., telegram to H. Rap Brown, 9 January 1968, the Martin Luther King, Jr. Center for Nonviolent Social Change; Carmichael, *Ready for Revolution*, 646, 658.

10. Central Committee Meeting minutes, 22 September 1967, the Student Nonviolent Coordinating Committee Papers, reel 3, box 1; Karima Al-Amin, interview.

11. Central Committee Meeting minutes, 22 September 1967, the Student Nonviolent Coordinating Committee Papers, reel 3, box 1.

12. Ibid.

13. Forman, *The Making of Black Revolutionaries*, 502.

14. Lester, *Look Out, Whitey! Black Power's Gon' Get Your Mama!*, 132–33; Payne, *I've Got the Light of Freedom*, 372.

15. Carson, *In Struggle*, 289.

16. Lester, *Look Out, Whitey! Black Power's Gon' Get Your Mama!*, 53–54.

17. Ibid.

18. Ibid.

19. Payne, *I've Got the Light of Freedom*, 372; Ransby, *Ella Baker & the Black Freedom Movement*, 346; Dorothy M. Zellner, "My Real Vocation," 324–25.

20. Varela, "Time to Get Ready," 569–70; Atlanta, Georgia, memo, "Student Nonviolent Coordinating Committee (SNCC)," 18 December 1967, FBI Files on the Student Nonviolent Coordinating Committee, *FBI Reading Room*. www.fbi.gov; Forman, *The Making of Black Revolutionaries*, 502–3.

21. Reies Lopes Tijerina, letter to Srita. Maria Varela, 14 September 1967, FBI Files on the Student Nonviolent Coordinating Committee.

22. Varela, "Time to Get Ready," 569–70; Atlanta, Georgia, memo, "Student Nonviolent Coordinating Committee (SNCC)," 18 December 1967, FBI Files on the Student Nonviolent Coordinating Committee.

23. Seale, *Seize the Time*, 217–21.

24. Angela Davis, *Angela Davis: An Autobiography*, 165–66.

25. Carson, *In Struggle*, 281–82; Davis, *Angela Davis: An Autobiography*, 167–68.

26. Carson, *In Struggle*, 289–90; Brown, *Die Nigger Die!*, 113; Karima Al-Amin, interview.

27. Davis, *Angela Davis: An Autobiography*, 169–70.

28. Brown, *Die Nigger Die!*, 114–15.

29. Branch, *At Canaan's Edge*, 640–41; Heppermann and Oehler, "This Weekend in 1968: The Legacy of Resurrection City."

30. Carson, *In Struggle*, 254; "The Promised Land."

31. Carmichael, *Ready for Revolution*, 646, 658; Honey, *Going Down Jericho Road*, 184.

32. SA, Atlanta, Georgia, memo, "Student Nonviolent Coordinating Committee (SNCC)," 14 May 1968, FBI Files on the Student Nonviolent Coordinating Committee.

33. Daniel Schorr, quoted in *Voices of Freedom*, 457.

34. Ibid.

35. Ibid.; Ralph D. Abernathy, *And the Walls Came Tumbling Down*, 229, 497; "The Promised Land."

36. Mike Davis, "Eyewitness Report from Mike Davis."

37. McKee, "Peace Returns to Orangeburg"; "Revenge for Deaths Threatened by SNCC"; Nelson and Bass, *The Orangeburg Massacre*, 108

38. McKee, "Peace Returns to Orangeburg"; "Revenge for Deaths Threatened by SNCC."

39. "Justice Department Files Suit"; "U.S. Files New Orangeburg Suit."

40. "King Renews Appeal for Non-Violent Action."

41. National Advisory Commission on Civil Disorders, *Report of the National Advisory Commission on Civil Disorders*, 91, 93.

42. Leifermann, "Middle-Class Negroes Scrambling to Lead Own Race in New Revolution"; "Hot Camp-In Ahead."

43. SAC, Baltimore to Director, FBI, 8 March 1968, *COINTELPRO: The Counter-Intelligence Program of the FBI: Black Nationalist Hate Groups*; Director, FBI, to SACs Atlanta, Baltimore, Chicago, 14 March 1968, *COINTELPRO: The Counter-Intelligence Program of the FBI: Black Nationalist Hate Groups*.

44. Honey, *Going Down Jericho Road*, 200, 209, 210, 259, 344–45, 378; "Hot Camp-In Ahead"; Cotton, *If Your Back's Not Bent*, 256–57; Federal Bureau of Investigation, "Freedom of Information and Privacy Acts: Martin Luther King, Jr.," 31 January 1977, 17–18, FBI Reading Room.

45. Honey, *Going Down Jericho Road*, 368; Branch, "The Last Wish of Martin Luther King."

46. "President Vows Violence Won't Take Over Nation."

47. Abernathy, *And the Walls Came Tumbling Down*, 497; Cotton, *If Your Back's Not Bent*, 251

48. Abernathy, *And the Walls Came Tumbling Down*, 497; Branch, *At Canaan's Edge*, 734.

CHAPTER THREE

1. West, "Pop Artists Prove 'Winner' in Ghetto"; Guralnick, *Sweet Soul Music*, 268.

2. SAC-New York, memorandum to Director-FBI, 4 April 1968, *COINTELPRO: The Counter-Intelligence Program of the FBI: Black Nationalist Hate Groups*, reel 1.

3. Andrew Young, *An Easy Burden*, 466; Schulke and McPhee, *King Remembered*, 245–46; Ralph Abernathy, interview, "The Promised Land."

4. Statement by the President on the Assassination of Dr. Martin Luther King, Jr.," in *Public Papers of the Presidents: Lyndon B. Johnson, 1968–69*, 493.

5. Ibid.

6. "Nation 'Died a Little' with King's Death, Reagan Says."

7. "Editorial," *The Citizen*, May 1968.

8. Ibid.; Burns, *Burial for a King*, 27.

9. Carmichael, *Ready for Revolution*, 656–57.

10. Okoh, "'White America Killed Our Hopes'"; "We're Not Afraid . . . We're Gonna Die for Our People."

11. Ibid.

12. Ibid.

13. Ibid.

14. Ibid.

15. Ibid.

16. Ibid.

17. Fairclough, *Martin Luther King, Jr.*, 124; Carmichael, *Ready for Revolution*, 657–59.

18. Wilkins and Mathews, *Standing Fast*, 327.

19. Weiss, *Whitney M. Young, Jr. and the Struggle for Civil Rights*, 179.

20. Burns, *Burial for a King*, 86–87; Southern Christian Leadership Conference papers, Emory University, box 12, folder 8 contains Ray Hartsough's April 5, 1968 letter to Ralph Abernathy and Charles S. Spivey's April 5, 1968 letter to Ralph Abernathy.

21. Douglas, "Ralph Abernathy," 44; Belafonte, *My Song*, 336.

22. Abernathy, *And the Walls Came Tumbling Down*, 439.

23. Young, *An Easy Burden*, 469.

24. 7 April 1968, *Meet the Press*, v. 12, 212–13, 217.

25. Abernathy, *And the Walls Came Tumbling Down*, 458–60.

26. Ibid., 450; Clarke, *The Last Campaign*, 113–14; Ambrose, *Nixon*, vol. 2, 151; "Thousands See King's Body in Spelman Chapel"; Nixon, *RN: The Memoirs of Richard Nixon*, 301; Aitken, *Nixon*, 281–82.

27. Carmichael, *Ready for Revolution*, 657–59; Clarke, *The Last Campaign*, 122; "Students Stage Sympathy Marches across Alabama."

28. Clarke, *The Last Campaign*, 125–26, 129, 131–33; Andrew Young, interview, "The Promised Land."

29. J. Edgar Hoover, letter to Lyndon Johnson, 6 April 1968, The Confidential File of the Johnson White House, Part 1: Confidential Name and Subject Files, reel 40.

30. SAC–New York, memorandum to Director-FBI, 11 April 1968, *COINTELPRO: The Counter-Intelligence Program of the FBI: Black Nationalist Hate Groups*, reel 1.

31. Albright, *What Makes Spiro Run*, 186–90; Lippman, *Spiro Agnew's America*, 112; Marsh, *Agnew the Unexamined Man*, 91.

32. Albright, *What Makes Spiro Run*, 186–90; Lippman, *Spiro Agnew's America*, 112; Marsh, *Agnew the Unexamined Man*, 91.

33. Albright, *What Makes Spiro Run*, 186–90; Lippman, *Spiro Agnew's America*, 112; Marsh, *Agnew the Unexamined Man*, 91.

34. Albright, *What Makes Spiro Run*, 186–90; Lippman, *Spiro Agnew's America*, 112; Marsh, *Agnew the Unexamined Man*, 91.

35. Marsh, *Agnew the Unexamined Man*, 101; "Relative Peace Prevails but Techniques Are Argued Over."

36. Lucas, *Agnew*, 61.

37. Witcover, *Very Strange Bedfellows*, 14.

38. "Trial: Back to Chicago."

39. Ibid.

40. "Remarks upon Signing the Civil Rights Act," in *Public Papers of the Presidents: Lyndon B. Johnson, 1968–69*, 509.

CHAPTER FOUR

1. Abernathy, *And the Walls Came Tumbling Down*, 499.

2. Good, "'No Man Can Fill Dr. King's Shoes'—But Abernathy Tries."

3. *Jet*, 30 May 1968.

4. Fager, *Uncertain Resurrection*, 54–55.

5. Clarke, *The Last Campaign*, 146, 246–47, 252–54.

6. "The Promised Land."

7. Fager, *Uncertain Resurrection*, 58; Hepperman and Oehler, "This Weekend in 1968: The Legacy of Resurrection City."

8. Hepperman and Oehler, "This Weekend in 1968: The Legacy of Resurrection City."

9. *COINTELPRO: The Counter-Intelligence Program of the FBI: Black Nationalist Hate Groups*, reel 1, contains Mr. W. C. Sullivan, letter to G. C. Moore, 20 May 1968; Witcover, *White Knight*, 175, 211–12.

10. June 16, 1968, *Meet the Press*, v. 12, 346, 354, 356.

11. Southern Christian Leadership Conference papers, Emory University, box 16, folder 1, contains the postcards.

12. Fager, *Uncertain Resurrection*, 67.

13. Southern Christian Leadership Conference papers, Emory University, box 64, folder 5, contains the cabinet officials' responses to the PPC; Southern Christian Leadership Conference papers, Emory University, box 64, folder 6, contains the PPC's responses to the cabinet departments.

14. *Jet*, 4 July 1968.

15. Fager, *Uncertain Resurrection*, 78–80.

16. Ibid.

17. *Jet*, 4 July 1968; Fager, *Uncertain Resurrection*, 81, 83.

18. *Jet*, 4 July 1968; Fager, *Uncertain Resurrection*, 81, 83.

19. Peake, *Keeping the Dream Alive*, 240; Young, *An Easy Burden*, 488.

20. *Jet*, 11 July 1968.

21. Fager, *Uncertain Resurrection*, 115–17.

22. Ibid.

23. Roger Wilkins, quoted in *Voices of Freedom*, 482.

24. Fager, *Uncertain Resurrection*, 118.

25. Southern Christian Leadership Conference papers, Emory University, box 16, folder 1, contains Joseph Lowery's July 1, 1968 telegrams; Southern Christian Leadership Conference papers, Emory University, box 16, folder 2, contains Esau Jenkins's July 5, 1968, letter; Nettie D. Boddie's July 5, 1968, letter referring to *The Merv Griffin Show*; and Gwen Cotton's July 7, 1968, letter referring to the radio broadcast.

26. Southern Christian Leadership Conference papers, Emory University, box 16, folder 1, contains Lillie Hunter's July 1, 1968, letter to Ralph Abernathy; Southern Christian Leadership Conference papers, Emory University, box 16, folder 2 contains Esau Jenkins's July 5, 1968 letter.

27. Southern Christian Leadership Conference papers, Emory University, box 16, folder 1, contains L. D. Reddick's July 3, 1968, letter to Ralph Abernathy.

28. Fager, *Uncertain Resurrection*, 138–39; Southern Christian Leadership Conference papers, Emory University, box 16, folder 1, contains Dagmar Wilson and Hosea Williams, telegrams, 5 July 1968.

29. Charles Evers, 7 July 1968, *Face the Nation: 1968*, 186.

30. Cohen, "View Violence in America as Product of History, Materialism, Gun Fetish."

31. *Jet*, 4 July 1968.

32. SNCC–New York, letter, 24 May 1968, the Student Nonviolent Coordinating Committee Papers.

33. Ibid.

34. Karima Al-Amin, interview.

35. "Stokely Carmichael Expelled by SNCC"; Carson, *In Struggle*, 292.

36. "Statement of Objectives Adopted by the Student Nonviolent Coordinating Committee at Its Annual Meeting of June, 1968," the Student Nonviolent Coordinating Committee Papers.

37. Ibid.

38. Ibid.

39. Carson, *In Struggle*, 291; J. Edgar Hoover, letter to Lyndon Johnson, 21 June 1968, The Confidential File of the Johnson White House, Part 1: Confidential Name and Subject Files, reel 40.

40. Carmichael, *Ready for Revolution*, 676.

41. Forman, *The Making of Black Revolutionaries*, 534, 538–39; Director, FBI, letter to SAC, New York, 8 August 1968, *COINTELPRO: The Counter-Intelligence Program of the FBI: Black Nationalist Hate Groups*, reel 1; J. Edgar Hoover, letter to Lyndon Johnson, 26 July 1968, The Confidential File of the Johnson White House, Part 1: Confidential Name and Subject Files, reel 40.

42. SAC, New York, letter to Director, FBI, 8 August 1968, *COINTELPRO: The Counter-Intelligence Program of the FBI: Black Nationalist Hate Groups*, reel 1; Director, SAC, New York, letter to Director, FBI, 25 July 1968, *COINTELPRO: The Counter-Intelligence Program of the FBI: Black Nationalist Hate Groups*, reel 1.

43. Davis, *Angela Davis: An Autobiography*, 170, 180–86.

44. SAC, Atlanta, letter to Director, FBI, 19 June 1968, *COINTELPRO: The Counter-Intelligence Program of the FBI: Black Nationalist Hate Groups*, reel 1; SAC, Atlanta, letter to Director, FBI, 29 July 1968, *COINTELPRO: The Counter-Intelligence Program of the FBI: Black Nationalist Hate Groups*, reel 1.

45. Records of the Southern Christian Leadership Conference, Part 3, contains David C. Burns, letter to Andrew Young, 10 July 1968; Records of the Southern Christian Leadership Conference, Part 3, contains Robert Wheat, letter to Andrew Young, 11 July 1968; Records of the Southern Christian Leadership Conference, Part 3, contains Mrs. Jay B. Davis, letter to Andrew Young, 9 July 1968.

46. Young, *An Easy Burden*, 508.

CHAPTER FIVE

1. Spiro Agnew, "Statement to Executive Session, National Governors' Conference," 23 July 1968, Maryland State Archives.

2. Flyer, FBI File on the Student Nonviolent Coordinating Committee.

3. Witcover, *The Year the Dream Died*, 300–301.

4. Witcover, *Very Strange Bedfellows*, 28; Ambrose, *Nixon*, vol. 1, 338; Witcover, *The Year the Dream Died*, 304–5.

5. "Jackie Robinson Bolts Republicans."

6. September 8, 1968, *Meet the Press*, vol. 12, 549, 554–55, 557.

7. Witcover, *The Year the Dream Died*, 368–70.

8. Ibid.

9. Ibid.

10. *New York Times*, 29 August 1968.

11. Spiro Agnew, 13 October 1968, *Face the Nation: 1968*, 298.

12. Ibid.

13. "Smith, Carlos Raise Black Power Issue at Games"; "Tommie Smith Carols Return in Grim and Silent Mood."

14. Ibid.

15. Christopulos, "U.S. Justified in Expelling Duo."

16. Fraser, "SNCC in Decline after 8 Years in Lead."

17. SAC-Atlanta, letter to Director-FBI, 6 November 1968, *COINTELPRO: The Counter-Intelligence Program of the FBI: Black Nationalist Hate Groups*.

18. Mae Jackson, letter to author, 20 October 2010.

19. Mae Jackson, interview, 4 November 2010.

20. The Confidential File of the Johnson White House, Part 1: Confidential Name and Subject Files, reel 40.

21. UPI, "Negro Brass Feel Nixon on Probation."

22. Ibid.

23. Nixon, *RN*, 435.

24. "Trial: Back to Chicago."

25. Ibid.

26. Wilkins and Mathews, *Standing Fast*, 333.

27. Ambrose, *Nixon*, vol. 1, 338.

28. Nixon, *RN*, 436; Daniel Moynihan, letter to Ralph Abernathy, 1 May 1969, Southern Christian Leadership Conference papers, Emory University, box 20, folder 2.

29. R. K. Price, Memorandum to the President, 13 May 1969, Personal Files of President Richard M. Nixon.

30. Price, Memorandum to the President, 13 May 1969; Peake, *Keeping the Dream Alive*, 262.

31. Price, Memorandum to the President, 13 May 1969.

32. Ibid.

33. Ibid.

34. Ibid.

35. Ibid.

36. Ibid.; Haldeman, *The Haldeman Diaries*, 55.

37. Price, Memorandum to the President, 13 May 1969.

38. Abernathy, *And the Walls Came Tumbling Down*, 554.

39. Osbourne, *The Third Year of the Nixon Watch*, 39; Haldeman, *The Haldeman Diaries*, 55.

40. Nixon, *RN*, 436; Daniel Moynihan, Memorandum, 19 May 1969, Papers of the Nixon White House, Part 6, Series B: Daily News Summaries Annotated by the President, 6B-7-27.

41. Nixon, *RN*, 436; Ambrose, *Nixon*, vol. 2, 247–48.

42. Franklin, "The Poor."

43. Southern Christian Leadership Conference papers, Emory University, box 20, folder 3, contains George McGovern's May 8, 1969, invitation to Ralph Abernathy and Ralph Abernathy's May 20, 1969, letter of thanks to George McGovern.

CHAPTER SIX

1. "CORE Constitution Rejected; Members Set August Meet"; "CORE Leaders Pledge New Militancy"; Weiss, *Whitney M. Young, Jr. and the Struggle for Civil Rights*, 183; Wilkins and Mathews, *Standing Fast*, 330.

2. Gent, "TV: Racial Attitudes Poll"; *Jet*, 8 August 1968.

3. Fairclough, *To Redeem the Soul of America*, 388.

4. Rieder, *The Word of the Lord Is upon Me*, 38.

5. *The Huntley-Brinkley Report*, 15 August 1968.

6. Ibid.

7. "Coretta King: In Her Husband's Footsteps."

8. "Jesse Jackson: Heir to Dr. King?"

9. Young, *An Easy Burden*, 490; Belafonte, *My Song*, 336, 338; Douglas, "Ralph Abernathy," 45; Cotton, *If Your Back's Not Bent*, 202–4, 274.

10. Central Committee Meeting Minutes, 28–30 October 1968, Student Nonviolent Coordinating Committee Papers, reel 3.

11. Ibid.

12. Ibid.

13. *Movement*, January 1969.

14. Beal, interview.

15. Ibid.

16. Carson, *In Struggle*, 251, 293–94.

17. Mae Jackson, letter, 20 October 2010; Gwen Patton, letter to author, 13 January 2011.

18. Mae Jackson, letter to author, 4 November 2010.

19. Beal, interview.

20. Patton, 13 January 2011.

21. "The Third Conrad Kent Rivers Memorial Award."

22. Mae Jackson, letter, 22 October 2010.

23. Brown, *Die Nigger Die!*, 26.

24. Ibid., 142.

25. Forman, *The Making of Black Revolutionaries*, 543–45, 547–48; Carson, *In Struggle*, 160.

26. "Black Manifesto," 183–87.

27. Ibid.

28. "Nixon Administration Target of Attack," 276–77.

29. Douglas, "Ralph Abernathy," 50; "Cautious Optimism Prevails in Racially Tense Area."

30. McGrath, "Brave Woman Stands behind Ralph Abernathy."

31. Ibid.

32. Ralph Abernathy, speech at Charleston, 1969, Southern Christian Leadership Conference papers, Emory University, box 603, folder 21.

33. Ibid.

34. Ibid.

35. *Lodi News-Sentinel*, 3 May 1969.

36. Ralph Abernathy, "To Preach the Gospel to the Poor," 29 April 1969, Hosea Williams Collection, series 10, subseries A, box 2, folder 4.

37. Ibid.

38. Abernathy, *And the Walls Came Tumbling Down*, 552–53, 555.

39. Citizens' Council et al., letter to Ralph Abernathy, 11 June 1969, Southern Christian Leadership Conference papers, Emory University, box 20, folder 4; Roach, "GOP Chairman Attacks SCLC."

40. Whitney Young, *Beyond Racism*, 249–52.

41. Ibid.

42. Ibid.

43. Ibid., 22–23, 254.

44. Ibid., 3, 13, 53, 69.

45. Ibid.; King, *Where Do We Go from Here*, 10–12, 178, 191.

CHAPTER SEVEN

1. Fulton Tutor, "Memorandum," 7 May 1969, Mississippi State Sovereignty Commission.

2. "Charles Evers Has a Dream for His Town."

3. Buresh, "NAACP Raps Decision on Schools"; "Observance by Negroes Included Honoring of Civil Rights Victims"; Pearson, "Fayette—Where History Is Made."

4. "Mitchell Plans Task Force on Dissidents"; Scott, "Education Official to Get Facts on Campus Revolution."

5. Transcript of press conference of H. Rap Brown and Muhammad Hunt, 22 July 1969, FBI Files of the Student Nonviolent Coordinating Committee.

6. Jamil Al-Amin, letter to author.

7. Transcript of press conference of H. Rap Brown and Muhammad Hunt, 22 July 1969, FBI Files of the Student Nonviolent Coordinating Committee.

8. Ibid.

9. "Stokely No Longer Panther."

10. Roy Wilkins, "Voluntary Segregation—A Disaster," March 1969, in *In Search of Democracy*, 430.

11. Beal, interview; Karima Al-Amin, interview; Mae Jackson, letter, 20 October 2010; Br. Christopher Jenks, letter, 2010; Bishop Donegan, letter to Rector Weeks, 23 July 1969.

12. Varela, "Time to Get Ready," 571; Patton, "Born Freedom Fighter," 586; Belafonte, *My Song*, 237, 338.

13. Ransby, *Ella Baker and the Black Freedom Movement*, 352.

14. "SNCC's Agrarian Reform Program," FBI Files of the Student Nonviolent Coordinating Committee.

15. Martinez, "Neither Black Nor White," 538.

16. "Charleston Strike Won!" *1199 Drug & Hospital News*, July 1969, Records of the Southern Christian Leadership Conference, part 3, reel 7.

17. Southern Christian Leadership Conference papers, Emory University, box 20, folder 5, contains Ralph Abernathy's July 2, 1969 letter to his staff.

18. Southern Christian Leadership Conference papers, Emory University, box 20, folder 4, contains George Shultz's June 17, 1969, letter to Ralph Abernathy, and Leon Panetta's June 13, 1969, letter to Abernathy; Southern Christian Leadership Conference papers, Emory University, box 20, folder 5, contains Patsy Mink's July 9, 1969, letter to Ralph Abernathy, and Columbia

Pictures' 9 July 1969 letter to Ralph Abernathy; William Clay, letter to Ralph Abernathy, Southern Christian Leadership Conference papers, Emory University, box 20, folder 6.

19. Southern Christian Leadership Conference papers, Emory University, box 20, folder 5 contains publicity about *Operation Breadbasket*.

20. "Demonstrators Pray for End to Hunger, Successful Flight."

21. Ibid.; De Groot, *Dark Side of the Moon*, 234–35.

22. *Soul Force*, 13 August 1969.

23. Ralph Abernathy, speech in Eutaw, 29 July 1969, Southern Christian Leadership Conference papers, box 608, folder 10; Ralph Abernathy and Hosea Williams, telegrams, 3 July 1969, Southern Christian Leadership Conference papers, Emory University, box 20, folder 5.

24. *The Huntley-Brinkley Report*, 12 August 1969.

25. Ibid.; *Soul Force*, 13 August 1969.

26. Franklin, "Mourning for Dr. King Ended."

27. Ibid.

28. Fairclough, *To Redeem the Soul of America*, 395.

29. Coretta Scott King, 28 September 1969, *Face the Nation: 1969*, 262–64, 266.

30. Ibid.

31. Records of the Southern Christian Leadership Conference, Part 2.

32. Ralph Abernathy, speech at the New Mobilization to End the War in Vietnam, 15 November 1969, Southern Christian Leadership Conference papers, Emory University, box 69, folder 34.

33. Ibid.

34. Current, "The Hot Sixtieth—A Memorable Convention," 293; Weiss, *Whitney M. Young, Jr. and the Struggle for Civil Rights*, 195.

35. Hayden, *Trial*, 77; *New York Times*, 17 August 1969.

36. Ibid.

37. Hayden, *Trial*, 89–90; Perlstein, *Nixonland*, 451.

38. "A Nation of Law," *Eyes on the Prize II*.

39. Evans and Novak, *Nixon in the White House*, 236; "Nixon Poverty Speech Draws Bitter Criticism."

40. Ibid.

41. *The Huntley-Brinkley Report*, 10 December 1969; "$5 Million Cast Sings with Mitch for Racial Harmony and Love," 8–9.

42. Tully, "King and the Panthers."

43. "The Police vs. the Black Panthers," 24–25.

44. Ibid., 24; Papers of the Nixon White House, Part 4, the John Ehrlichman Alphabetical Subject File, 1969–1973.

45. Papers of the Nixon White House, Part 4, the John Ehrlichman Alphabetical Subject File, 1969–1973.

46. Nixon, *RN*, 435–36.

47. *Soul Force*, November–December 1971.

48. John J. Resnick, House of Representatives, 26 January 1970, *Congressional Record: 91st Congress, Session Two*, 1230.

49. Tully, "King and the Panthers;" Ambrose, *Nixon*, vol. 2, 331.

50. Panetta and Gall, *Bring Us Together*, 350–62, 365.

51. Young, *An Easy Burden*, 502–3, 508; "Rev. Young Declares Candidacy for Congress."

CHAPTER EIGHT

1. Spiro Agnew, quoted in Hayden, "The Trial."

2. James M. Mohead, "Weekly Report: 5-5-69 thru 5-10-69," Sovereignty Commission Online, Mississippi Department of Archives and History.

3. Bigart, "Kunstler Sees 'Fear' at Site of Rap Brown Trial," 34.

4. Ibid.

5. Karima Al-Amin, interview.

6. Ibid.; "Bombing: A Way of Protest and Death"; Bernstein, "2d Bel Air Car-Bomb Victim Identified as SNCC Worker"; *The Huntley-Brinkley Report*, 10 March 1970.

7. "Bombing: A Way of Protest and Death"; Lewis, *Walking with the Wind*, 427.

8. Jay, "Woman Sought in Bombing at Cambridge"; "Bombing: A Way of Protest and Death."

9. Ibid.

10. "2 Policemen Hurt in Clash at School," 32.

11. Manns, "Ashes Spread Over Africa"; Ridley, "'Feather' Was Bridegroom of Three Weeks."

12. "Che Buried in Hometown."

13. Mann, "No Sign of Rap Brown on Bel Air Trial Eve"; "Statement to the Black Communities in the United States from the Student National Coordinating Committee," FBI Files of the Student Nonviolent Coordinating Committee.

14. Ibid.

15. "Official Statement from the Student National Coordinating Committee," 16 March 1970, FBI Files of the Student Nonviolent Coordinating Committee.

16. "Hasty FBI Report on Car Blast Irks Civic Leaders."

17. George Allott, Senate, 16 March 1970, *Congressional Record: 91st Congress, Session Two*, 7480–81.

18. *The Huntley-Brinkley Report*, 18 March 1970; Manns, "Rap's Trial Delayed."

19. *The Ed Sullivan Show.*

20. Ibid.

21. Ralph D. Abernathy, 29 March 1970, *Face the Nation: 1970*, 99–104.

22. Ibid.

23. Ibid.

24. Ibid.

25. Ibid.

26. Ibid.

27. "Yale Strike Urged to Black Panthers."

28. Ibid.

29. George Allott, Senate, 23 April 1970, *Congressional Record: 91st Congress, Session Two*, 12730.

30. "Agnew Asks Scalp of Yale President."

31. *The President's Commission on Campus Unrest*, 96–97.

32. Bell, "6 Dead as Racial Violence Breaks Out in Augusta."

33. *The Huntley-Brinkley Report*, 15 May 1970.

34. *The President's Commission on Campus Unrest*, 417–36.

35. Ibid.; *The Huntley-Brinkley Report*, 15 May 1970.

CHAPTER NINE

1. "Maddox Warns against March"; "Delay Start of Georgia SCLC March."

2. "Maddox Warns Against March"; "Delay Start of Georgia SCLC March."

3. "Maddox Warns Against March"; "Delay Start of Georgia SCLC March."

4. "Mule Power Takes Protest Just 12 Miles."

5. Ibid.

6. "Police Protect March."

7. Ibid.

8. *The Huntley-Brinkley Report*, 22 May 1970.

9. Peake, *Keeping the Dream Alive*, 274; *Jet*, 11 June 1970.

10. *Jet*, 11 June 1970; "SCLC Names 'Bottom' Ten."

11. *Jet*, 11 June 1970; "SCLC Names 'Bottom' Ten."

12. "SCLC Turns to Politics."

13. Southern Christian Leadership Conference papers, Emory University, box 24, folder 4, contained the May 1970 letter from Diahann Carroll to Abernathy; the May 24, 1970, letter from the Women's International League for Peace and Freedom of Fairfield, Connecticut, to Abernathy; and Eldon H. Cuppett's May 24, 1970, letter to Abernathy.

14. Johnson, "5-Day March in Georgia Ends with Massive Rally."

15. Roy Wilkins, "Toward a Single Society," 30 June 1970, in *In Search of Democracy*, 431–35.

16. Ibid.

17. Ibid.

18. *ABC Evening News*, 19 May 1970; *The Huntley-Brinkley Report*, 19 May 1970.

19. "Freedom of Information and Privacy Acts: Martin Luther King, Jr.," 31 January 1977, 137, FBI Reading Room.

20. Reinhold, "Negro on Campus Panel Feels 'Solemn' Duty to Stop Killings."

21. Ibid.

22. *The Huntley-Brinkley Report*, 16 June 1970.

23. Ibid.

24. Ibid.

25. Ehrlichman, *Witness to Power*, 154.

26. "Agnew Retorts to President of A.B.A. Who Called for Restraint."

27. "Campus Panelist Upset That Nixon Lets Agnew Speak."

28. Richard Nixon, "Statement upon Signing the Voting Rights Act Amendments of 1970," 22 June 1970, *Public Papers of the Presidents: Richard Nixon, 1970*, 513.

29. "Supplemental Correlation Summary," 7 June 1971, FBI File on Coretta Scott King, Federal Bureau of Investigation.

30. Thimmesch, "Leftward Ho with Whitney Young?"

31. Current, "The 61st Annual Convention—Arousing a National Storm," 255–56.

32. "In the Nation's Press," 276–82; "Whitney Young Denies He Is Anti-Negro."

33. Joseph Rhodes Jr., 27 September 1970, *Meet the Press*, v. 14, 544, 548.

34. Ibid.

35. "Agnew Assails Report on Campuses."

36. Ehrlichman, *Witness to Power*, 155.

37. "Agnew Says Nixon Wants Cramer, Kirk to Win in November."

38. "Campus Unrest Panelist Says 'Real' Issues Are Being Ignored."

39. Witcover, *Very Strange Bedfellows*, 129.

40. Papers of the Nixon White House, Part 6, Series B: Daily News Summaries Annotated by the President, 6B-31-3.

41. Young, *An Easy Burden*, 503; Halberstam, *The Children*, 679–81.

42. Director-FBI, letter to SAC-Chicago, 21 August 1970, *COINTELPRO: The Counter-Intelligence Program of the FBI: Black Nationalist Hate Groups*.

43. Taraborrelli, *Michael Jackson*, 81; Posner, *Motown*, 64, 168, 237.

44. Sanders, "Finally I've Begun to Live Again," 172.

45. Young, *An Easy Burden*, 510–11; Roy Wilkins, "A Letdown in Atlanta."

46. "Words of the Week," 30.

47. Weiss, *Whitney M. Young, Jr. and the Struggle for Civil Rights*, 202.

CHAPTER TEN

1. Pearson, *The Shadow of the Panther*, 221–22, 226–27.

2. George Jackson, *Soledad Brother*, 128.

3. Ibid., 237.

4. Lester, "Blacks Rage to Live."

5. FBI–New York, "Student National Coordinating Committee," 25 May 1970, FBI Files on the Student Nonviolent Coordinating Committee; FBI–New York, "Student National Coordinating Committee," 10 May 1971, FBI Files on the Student Nonviolent Coordinating Committee.

6. Mae Jackson, interview, 4 November 2010.

7. Beal, "Double Jeopardy."

8. Ibid.

9. Ibid.

10. Ibid.

11. SAC–New York, letter to Director-FBI, 17 July 1970, *COINTELPRO: The Counter-Intelligence Program of the FBI: Black Nationalist Hate Groups*; Director-FBI, letter to SACs–New York and Atlanta, 26 July 1970, *COINTELPRO: The Counter-Intelligence Program of the FBI: Black Nationalist Hate Groups*.

12. SAC–New York, letter to Director-FBI, 23 July 1970, *COINTELPRO: The Counter-Intelligence Program of the FBI: Black Nationalist Hate Groups*; SAC–New York, letter to Director-FBI, 28 July 1970, *COINTELPRO: The Counter-Intelligence Program of the FBI: Black Nationalist Hate Groups*.

13. Mae Jackson, interview, 4 November 2010.

14. Giddings, *When and Where I Enter*, 304–5, 309.

15. Ibid.

16. G. C. Moore, memorandum to C. D. Brennan, 3 September 1970, *COINTELPRO: The Counter-Intelligence Program of the FBI: Black Nationalist Hate Groups*.

17. Mario Salas, letter, 20 April 2010; Mae Jackson, interview, 4 November 2010; Beal, interview, 6 January 2011; Karima Al-Amin, interview.

18. Mae Jackson, letter, 20 October 2010.

19. Beal, interview; Hunter, "Black Women's Lib Groups Think 'Sexism' Irrelevant."

20. Beal, interview.

21. "Words of the Week," 30.

22. *ABC Evening News*, 3 September 1970; "It's Nation Time"; Weiss, *Whitney M. Young, Jr. and the Struggle for Civil Rights*, 187–89.

23. Amiri Baraka, "Speech to the Congress of African Peoples," September 1970, in *Modern Black Nationalism*, 145–57.

24. Ibid.

25. "Official: Rap Brown Charge Phony."

26. Richard Nixon, "Statement upon Signing the Organized Crime Control Act," 15 October 1970, *Public Papers of the Presidents: Richard Nixon, 1970*, 847; Richard Nixon, "Presidential News Conference," 10 December 1970, *Public Papers of the Presidents: Richard Nixon, 1970*, 1106–7.

27. "Americans Pause to Honor Memory of King."

28. Ibid.

29. "Blacks Protest Apollo 14 Shot."

30. Ibid.; Brown, *Die Nigger Die!*, 140.

31. Abernathy, "I Bring an Indictment against the American System," 2 February 1971, 276–78; Abernathy, speech for the Angela Davis Defense Committee, 2 February 1971, Papers of the Southern Christian Leadership Conference, Emory University, box 71, folder 20.

32. Ralph Abernathy, "I Bring an Indictment Against the American System," 2 February 1971, in Angela Davis, ed., *If They Come in the Morning*, 276–78; Ralph Abernathy, speech for the Angela Davis Defense Committee, 2 February 1971, Papers of the Southern Christian Leadership Conference, Emory University, box 71, folder 20.

33. Ralph Abernathy, "I Bring an Indictment Against the American System," 2 February 1971, in Angela Davis, *If They Come in the Morning*, 276–78; Ralph Abernathy, speech for the Angela Davis Defense Committee, 2 February 1971, Papers of the Southern Christian Leadership Conference, Emory University, box 71, folder 20.

34. Ralph Abernathy, "I Bring an Indictment Against the American System," 2 February 1971, in Angela Davis, *If They Come in the Morning*, 276–78; Ralph Abernathy, speech for the Angela Davis Defense Committee, 2 February 1971, Papers of the Southern Christian Leadership Conference, Emory University, box 71, folder 20.

35. SAC–New York, letter to Director-FBI, 10 December 1970, *COINTELPRO: The Counter-Intelligence Program of the FBI: Black Nationalist Hate Groups.*

36. SAC–Atlanta, letter to Director-FBI, 10 February 1971, *COINTELPRO: The Counter-Intelligence Program of the FBI: Black Nationalist Hate Groups.*

37. FBI–New York, March 1971, FBI Files on the Student Nonviolent Coordinating Committee.

CHAPTER ELEVEN

1. Roy Wilkins, "Report of the Executive Director for the Board Meeting of January–March 1971," March 1971, in *In Search of Brotherhood*, 356–57; Spark Matsumaga, House of Representatives, 26 February 1971, *Congressional Record: 92nd Congress, Session One*, 4146–47.

2. Glick, *War at Home*, 7, 20.

3. President Richard Nixon, memorandum to John Ehrlichman, 8 February 1971, quoted in Oudes, *From the President*, 214.

4. Weiss, *Whitney M. Young, Jr. and the Struggle for Civil Rights*, 214–15.

5. Roy Wilkins, "Death of Whitney M. Young, Jr.," March 1971, in *In Search of Brotherhood*, 358; Bond, letter, 20 July 2013.

6. Weiss, *Whitney M. Young, Jr. and the Struggle for Civil Rights*, 228; *ABC Evening News*, 16 March 1971.

7. "Minister Is Threat to Daley."

8. Herrington, "Fauntroy Wins D.C. Election"; "Clergyman Winner in D.C. Voting."

9. "SCLC Promotes Williams, Makes Other Staff Changes"; "Daley Foe Says He's 'About Even.'"

10. George McGovern, letter to Hosea Williams, 14 January 1971, Hosea Williams Collection, Auburn Avenue Research Library, series 5, subseries F, box 1, folder 18; Hosea Williams, letter to George McGovern, 1 March 1971, Hosea Williams Collection, Auburn Avenue Research Library, series 5, subseries F, box 1, folder 18.

11. Coretta Scott King, letter to Ruth Gage-Colby, 26 March 1971, FBI Files of Coretta Scott King.

12. Stacewicz, *Winter Soldiers*, 244–49; "Viet Veterans Fling Medals on Capitol Steps"; "Homefront, USA."

13. Stacewicz, *Winter Soldiers*, 244–49; "Viet Veterans Fling Medals on Capitol Steps"; "Homefront, USA."

14. *Washington Post*, 25 April 1971; Kidd, "Peace March Was Just That."

15. *Washington Post*, 25 April 1971; Kidd, "Peace March Was Just That."

16. *Washington Post*, 25 April 1971; Kidd, "Peace March Was Just That."

17. Stacewicz, *Winter Soldiers*, 246.

18. D'Arazien, "Spring Offensive: Scenario for Peace"; "War Foes Shift Focus of Protest"; "Pro Victory Rally Follows Disobedience"; "Capitol Hill Rally Ends 17-Day Drive."

19. Webb Burke, report, 23 April 1971, Sovereignty Commission Online; Webb Burke, report, 20 July 1971, Sovereignty Commission Online; W. Webb Burke, "Statement of W. Webb Burke," 18 November 1971, Sovereignty Commission Online.

20. Katagiri, *The Mississippi Sovereignty Commission*, 218.

21. James M. Mohead, "Weekly Report: May 24, 1971–May 30, 1971," Sovereignty Commission Online; "A Senseless Killing."

22. James M. Mohead, "Weekly Report: May 24, 1971–May 30, 1971," Sovereignty Commission Online; "A Senseless Killing."

23. W. Webb Burke, letter to Honorable A. F. Sumner, 13 May 1971, Sovereignty Commission Online.

24. LeMaistre, "Miss Collier's Funeral May Be at School"; "Police Chief Leads Quiet Drew March."

25. LeMaistre, "Miss Collier's Funeral May Be at School"; "Police Chief Leads Quiet Drew March."

26. Harrist, "Negroes Mourn Slain Girl as Drew Tension Dissipates"; "A Senseless Killing."

27. *NBC Nightly News*, 30 May 1971.

28. "Same Old Thing, Same Old Place."

29. LeMaistre, "Abernathy: Love, Not Hate."

30. "A Senseless Killing."

31. LeMaistre, "Abernathy: Love, Not Hate"; Mills, *This Little Light of Mine*, 282.

32. *Soul Force*, July–August 1971.

33. Washington, *Afro-American*, 21 September 1971.

34. *Soul Force*, September 1971.

35. Ibid.; "Civil Rights Victory Follows Death of Alabama Girl," 12.

36. *Soul Force*, September 1971; "Civil Rights Victory Follows Death of Alabama Girl," 12.

37. *Soul Force*, September 1971; "Civil Rights Victory Follows Death of Alabama Girl," 12.

38. *Soul Force*, September 1971; "Civil Rights Victory Follows Death of Alabama Girl," 12.

CHAPTER TWELVE

1. Jordan, *Vernon Can Read!*, 232–33.

2. Semple, "Agnew Praises Africans, Chides Some U.S. Blacks"; Witcover, *Very Strange Bedfellows*, 182.

3. Semple, "Agnew Praises Africans, Chides Some U.S. Blacks"; Witcover, *Very Strange Bedfellows*, 182.

4. House of Representatives, 21 July 1971, *Congressional Record: 92nd Congress, Session One*, 26513–20.

5. Ibid.

6. Ibid.

7. Ibid.

8. Ibid.; Clay, interview.

9. House of Representatives, 22 July 1971, *Congressional Record: 92nd Congress, Session One*, 26615; Clay, interview, 13 July 2012.

10. "No Apology Made by Agnew, His Critics"; Clay, interview, 13 July 2012; Clay, *Just Permanent Interests*, 184.

11. "Abernathy Responds."

12. Witcover, *Very Strange Bedfellows*, 188–89.

13. Agnew, "The 'Root Causes' of Attica."

14. Ibid.

15. Reston, *The Lone Star*, 443.

16. Rhodes, "The Administration's Vision of the World."

17. Novak, "Jesse Jackson: Martin Luther King's Heir Apparent."

18. Higgins, "Meet the Man Behind 'Sweetback' Movie"; Bennett, "The Emancipation Orgasm," 90.

19. Higgins, "Meet the Man Behind 'Sweetback' Movie"; Bennett, "The Emancipation Orgasm," 90.

20. "NAACP 62nd Annual Convention Resolutions," 95.

21. Coretta Scott King, "Statement by Coretta Scott King," 4 June 1971, in Angela Davis, *If They Come in the Morning*, 282–83.

22. *Soul Force*, July–August 1971.

23. FBI, 16 May 1971, FBI Files on the Student Nonviolent Coordinating Committee.

24. Ransby, *Ella Baker and the Black Freedom Movement*, 244.

25. *Village Voice*, 23 September 1971.

26. "Prison Conditions Lead to Protests."

27. Clarity, "Rap Brown Wounded Here in Shootout after Holdup"; Daley, "The Man Who Shot Rap Brown," 39, 41–42.

28. Clarity, "Rap Brown Wounded Here in Shootout after Holdup"; Daley, "The Man Who Shot Rap Brown," 39, 41–42; Karima Al-Amin, interview.

29. Burks, "Brown Is Arraigned in Hospital in Robbery and Murder Attempt."

30. "Rap Brown Makes Court Appearance."

31. Chisholm, *The Good Fight*, 31–33.

32. "Black Expo '71 Brings Biggest Cadre of Businessmen, Politicians, Entertainers," 56.

33. "The Promised Land."

34. Ralph Abernathy, letter to Mao Tse-Tung, 24 June 1971, Hosea Williams Collection, series 7, subseries D, box 2, folder 2; "Williams Takes SCLC Greetings on Visit to Mao."

35. "Occasion Called a Party."

36. "Williams to Model Strategy on Mao's."

37. L. D. Reddick, letter to Hosea Williams, 29 November 1971, Hosea Williams Collection, series 7, subseries D, letter 2, folder 2.

38. "Blacks Want China Briefing."

39. *Rome News-Tribune*, 7 December 1971.

40. "Rights Leaders Upset over Child Bill Veto."

CHAPTER THIRTEEN

1. Rustin, "Coming of Age Politically," 298.

2. Abernathy Says Third Party May Be Formed," 17.

3. "Quinlan, "Shirley Chisholm: 98-Pound Dynamo."

4. Chisholm, *The Good Fight*, 33, 67, 68.

5. Philipps, lecture, Harvard University, July 2011.

6. Nixon, *RN*, 443–44.

7. Roy Wilkins, "Ego and Race," June 1971, in *In Search of Brotherhood*, 437–38.

8. Post Wire Services, "Busing Amendment Called Wrong Method of Attack."

9. "Nixon's Busing Stand Wallace Talk Target"; Thimmesch, "Wallace Pours It on in Florida."

10. Ibid.

11. "Agnew Says Unfair Innuendos Aimed at Wallace."

12. Ambrose, *Nixon*, vol. 2, 522–23.

13. "Agnew Backs Police Action."

14. *Soul Force*, April–May 1972.

15. Dave Clarke, letter to Ralph Abernathy, 5 April 1972, Southern Christian Leadership Conference papers, Emory University, box 61, folder 1.

16. John Conyers, letter to Ralph Abernathy, 28 April 1972, Southern Christian Leadership Conference papers, Emory University, box 37, folder 3.

17. *Soul Force*, September–October 1972.

18. "Rev. King's Widow Backs McGovern"; Coretta Scott King, letter of campaign endorsement, 18 May 1972, Southern Christian Leadership Conference papers, Emory University, box 37, folder 4.

19. George Wallace, quoted in Curt Smith, *Long Time Gone*, 141; Lesher, *George Wallace*, 480–81.

20. "Assassins Shake Faith in Politics."

21. Carson, *In Struggle*, 289–90.

22. "Brown Sentenced for Gun Carrying."

23. Ibid.

24. Ibid.

25. *NBC Nightly News*, 2 June 1972.

26. Beal, "The U.S. vs. H. Rap Brown."

27. Angela Davis, *Angela Davis*, 393.

28. Ibid.

29. Joe Waggonner, House of Representatives, 5 June 1972, in *Congressional Record: 92nd Congress, Session Two*, 19625.

30. Thomas, "Methodists Okay Controversial Legal Assistance Fund."

31. "Benefit Concert to Aid 'Anemia.'"

32. "Abernathy Attacks American System."

33. Ibid.

34. "'Poor' to Meet at Demo Confab."

35. "Poor City Mapped for Dem Convention."

36. Ibid.

37. Ibid.

38. Ralph Abernathy, address to the Tiger Bay Club Forum, 27 June 1972, Southern Christian Leadership Conference papers, Emory University, box 208, folder 28.

39. "Strict Delegate Proportion Not Required, U.S. Court Rules"; White, *The Making of the President, 1972*, 164–66; Perlstein, *Nixonland*, 692–94.

40. "Strict Delegate Proportion Not Required, U.S. Court Rules"; White, *The Making of the President, 1972*, 164–66; Perlstein, *Nixonland*, 692–94.

CHAPTER FOURTEEN

1. Harris, "Little Change in Esteem for Blacks."

2. Ibid.

3. Southern Christian Leadership Conference papers, Emory University, box 60, folder 7, contains Tony Brown's January 6, 1972, letter to Ralph Abernathy and the NET press release for "Is It Too Late?"; Reed, "Dr. King's Followers Modify His Approach in Their Continuing Pursuit of Social Change."

4. Reed, "Dr. King's Followers Modify His Approach in Their Continuing Pursuit of Social Change."

5. *Afro-American*, 18 December 1971.

6. Southern Christian Leadership Conference papers, Emory University, box 34, folder 6, contains Ralph Abernathy's December 13, 1971, press statement.

7. Southern Christian Leadership Conference papers, Emory University, box 34, folder 6 contains Daisy Marshall's December 11, 1971, letter, Ollie M. Smith's December 12, 1971, letter, and Geraldine Riley's December 1971 letter.

8. Landess and Quinn, *Jesse Jackson & the Politics of Race*, 65–66.

9. Abernathy, *And the Walls Came Tumbling Down*, 408, 476, 478; *Citizen*, December 1971.

10. "Black Leaders Eye Coalition Proposal," 12–14; *Jet*, 3 February 1972.

11. Ibid.

12. Ibid.

13. DeLeon, "A Look at Angela Davis from Another Angle: Her Jail Cell," 12–13.

13. *Jet*, 20 January 1972.

14. Reed, "Dr. King's Followers Modify His Approach in Their Continuing Pursuit of Social Change."

15. Beal, "The U.S. vs. H. Rap Brown"; Raspberry, "Vigilante Action Seen against Heroin Pushers"; "People Must Punish Pushers, Bond Declares."

16. Mae Jackson, interview, 5 August 2012; "Dope Is Death," 5.

17. Karima Al-Amin, interview; Bailey, "Black Excellence in the 'Wasteland,'" 44–46.

18. Bunting, "Black San Antonio V: Political Inroads."

19. Ken Bunting, "Black San Antonio IV: Liberation."

20. Book Review, *New York Times*, 12 March 1972; Doggett, *There's a Riot Going On*, 478–79.

21. Clay, *Just Permanent Interests*, 203–4.

22. Joseph, *Waiting 'til the Midnight Hour*, 279; *Voices of Freedom*, 570–71, 580.

23. *Voices of Freedom*, 570–71, 580.

24. Jordan, "To Be Equal."

25. Roy Wilkins, "Gary's Errors, Successes."

26. "National Black Political Agenda," 494–500.

27. Ibid.

28. Roy Wilkins, "The NAACP and the Black Political Convention," 229–30.

29. *Soul Force*, March 1972.

30. Southern Christian Leadership Conference papers, Emory University, box 37, folder 1, contains Helen Seaman's letter to Ralph Abernathy, 17 April 1972.

31. Clifford, "Newton: Panthers Shifting Strategy"; "New Panther Image: Church and Chickens."

32. Clifford, "Newton: Panthers Shifting Strategy"; Wilkins, "Panthers and Gun Rhetoric"; "New Panther Image: Church and Chickens"; "Speaking of People," 6–7.

33. Southern Christian Leadership Conference papers, Emory University, box 608, folder 2, contains Ralph Abernathy and Angela Davis, interview, 21 April 1972.

34. Gentry, *J. Edgar Hoover*, 718–19.

35. Ibid., 682.

36. Ibid., 602.

37. Prince, "12,000 Blacks March to Support Africa."

38. *Soul Force*, September–October 1972.

CHAPTER FIFTEEN

1. "Black Raps 'Exploitation' in Movies."

2. Revolutionary Political Council, letter, October 1972, Mario Marcel Salas Papers.

3. Brown, "Just a Drop in the Bucket of Oppression," 26–31.

4. "Convention Demonstrations Planned by 3 Black Groups."

5. Ibid., "Price Has Gone Up"; *Soul Force*, July–August 1972.

6. Police Line Cuts Momentum of Protest"; *Soul Force*, July–August 1972; "Resurrection City Set Up"; "Fence Section Torn Down Near Hall."

7. "Police Line Cuts Momentum of Protest"; *Soul Force*, July–August 1972; "Resurrection City Set Up"; "Fence Section Torn Down Near Hall"; "Radicals: Flamingo Park Jamboree"; White, *The Making of the President, 1972*, 168; "The Zippie-Hippie Miami Freak Show," 5.

8. *Soul Force*, July–August 1972; "Radicals: Flamingo Park Jamboree"; "Vandals Destroy SCLC Food"; Perlstein, *Nixonland*, 686; "The Zippie-Hippie Miami Freak Show," 5; Ryan, "Abernathy Marches on Convention."

9. *Soul Force*, July–August 1972; "Radicals: Flamingo Park Jamboree"; Perlstein, *Nixonland*, 686; "The Zippie-Hippie Miami Freak Show," 5.

10. "Radicals: Flamingo Park Jamboree."

11. Stacewicz, *Winter Soldiers*, 306–7; Moser, *The New Winter Soldiers*, 122.

12. "Choice at Hand for McGovern."

13. "Poor People's Power Pushed"; "SCLC Breaks 15-Year Tradition; Endorses McGovern Campaign."

14. Ralph Abernathy, telegram to Andrew Young, 11 August 1972, Southern Christian Leadership Conference papers, Emory University, box 37, folder 7.

15. *Soul Force*, September–October 1972; "Angela Pleads for Abolition of U.S. Prisons"; Angela Davis, speech at SCLC convention, Sheraton Hotel, Dallas, TX, 16 August 1972, Papers of the Southern Christian Leadership Conference, Emory University, box 607, folder 26.

16. "SCLC Breaks 15-Year Tradition; Endorses McGovern Campaign."

17. Ibid.

18. "Angela Pleads for Abolition of U.S. Prisons."

19. Anderson, "The Young Black Man," 132.

20. Muhammad Hunt, letter, 11 August 1972, Mario Marcel Salas Papers.

21. Ibid.

22. Beal, interview.

23. "Editorial," *Triple Jeopardy*, September–October 1972, 4.

24. Ibid.

25. Ibid.

26. Ibid.

27. John Payne, letter, 7 September 1972, Mario Marcel Salas Papers.

28. Frances Beal and Yemaya Rice, letter, 29 September 1972, Mario Marcel Salas Papers.

29. Ibid.

30. Revolutionary Political Council, letter, October 1972, Mario Marcel Salas Papers.

31. Doggett, *There's a Riot Going On*, 498; Perlstein, *Nixonland*, 629.

CHAPTER SIXTEEN

1. Osbourne, *The Fourth Year of the Nixon Watch*, 118; White, *The Making of the President, 1972*, 243; Rather and Gates, *The Palace Guard*, 256.

2. Rowan, "Violence Is Not Way Blacks Gain Stature."

3. Ibid.

4. Roy Wilkins, "In Back of the Busing Issue," August 1972, in *In Search of Democracy*, 442.

5. "NAACP Soft Pedals Controversial Issues," 46–47.

6. "The Nixon Phenomenon," 293–95.

7. Conaway, "Sammy Davis, Jr. Has Bought the Bus"; Sammy Davis, Jr., "Why I Went to the Troops," 141.

8. Delaney, "Black Supporters of President under Fire"; Haygood, *In Black and White*, 435–36.

9. Rampersad, *Jackie Robinson*, 454; Cady, "A Day for Harlem to Pay Its Respect."

10. Rampersad, *Jackie Robinson*, 454; Cady, "A Day for Harlem to Pay Its Respect."

11. "2,500 Attend Robinson's Funeral."

12. Darnton, "Citizens' Panel Assails Law Enforcement Officials Who Carried Out Chicago Panther Raid."

13. Kupcinet, "Kup's Column"; Osbourne, *The Fourth Year of the Nixon Watch*, 146–52.

14. Doggett, *There's a Riot Going On*, 512; "Radicals: Flamingo Park Jamboree."

15. "Four More Years of the Same," 29.

16. *Soul Force*, November–December 1972; Young, *An Easy Burden*, 518.

17. Young, *An Easy Burden*, 513, 519, 520.

18. "Black Owes Victory to Coalition."

19. Clay, interview; "Four More Years of the Same," 329.

20. Kifner, "Court Voids 5 Convictions in 1968 Convention Case."

21. SAC, Atlanta, memorandum to Acting Director, FBI, 30 November 1972, FBI Files of Coretta Scott King.

22. Herbers, "Johnson Mediates a Rights Dispute"; "LBJ Urges Blacks to Reason with Nixon on Civil Rights."

23. Wilkins and Mathews, *Standing Fast*, 337–38.

24. "Johnson Advised Blacks at Symposium in Texas."

25. Ibid.

26. Ibid.

27. *CBS Evening News*, 12 December 1972.

28. De Groot, *Dark Side of the Moon*, 252, 266.

29. Ripley, "More in Congress Decry the Raids," 1; "New Bombing Revives Antiwar Protests," 7.

30. Schell, *New Yorker*, 6 January 1973, in *Observing the Nixon Years*, 152.

31. Buckley, "Abernathy Used by Reds to Promote Propaganda."

32. "The Young Black Man," 130.

33. Daley, "The Man Who Shot Rap Brown," 35–42.

34. FBI, memorandum, 30 November 1972, FBI Files of the Student Nonviolent Coordinating Committee; Aiken, letter to author.

35. SNCC, "A New Level of Struggle," 9 January 1973, FBI Files on the Student Nonviolent Coordinating Committee.

36. "SCLC President Clashed with Mrs. King over Money Crisis."

37. Ibid.

38. Ibid.

CHAPTER SEVENTEEN

1. Richard Nixon, "Oath of Office and Second Inaugural Address," 20 January 1973, *Public Papers of the Presidents: Richard Nixon, 1973*, 12–14.

2. Ibid.

3. Roy Wilkins, "NAACP Urges Senate to Reject Nomination of Peter Brennan for Secretary of Labor," 18 January 1973, in *In Search of Brotherhood*, 360; *Jet*, 25 January 1973.

4. "Black America Now," 29, 34.

5. Roy Wilkins, "Death of Lyndon Johnson," January 1973, in *In Search of Brotherhood*, 361.

6. President Richard Nixon's press conference, 2 March 1973, in *Nixon: The Fifth Year of His Presidency*, 154A–55A.

7. Ibid.

8. Ibid.

9. "Welfare Militants Threaten 'Long, Hot Summer.'"

10. United Press International, "SCLC Leader Angry."

11. *CBS Evening News*, 16 March 1973.

12. Ralph Abernathy, speech at Wounded Knee, 7 March 1973, Southern Christian Leadership Conference papers, Emory University, box 72, folder 25.

14. D'Arcus, "Protest, Scale, and Publicity," 730–1; "Part 5: Wounded Knee," *We Shall Remain*.

15. *Soul Force*, March–April 1973.

16. Sibley, "Rap Brown Lectures His Jury on 'Peers.'"

17. Sibley, "Rap Brown Won't Testify; 'Final Witness Contested'"; Sibley, "Rap Brown and 3 Convicted of Robbery and Assault."

18. SNCC, "Hard Work, Education, Organization Equals Power," 29 April 1973, Mario M. Salas Papers.

19. Ibid.

20. Jenks, letter; FBI-New York, report, 11 December 1973, FBI Files on the Student Nonviolent Coordinating Committee.

21. "Federal Building Picketed."

22. Ibid.

23. Mario Salas, letter to Sickle Cell Anemia Foundation, 19 April 1973, Mario M. Salas Papers; Mario Salas, letter to ALSC, 22 July 1973, Mario M. Salas Papers.

24. Andrew Young, House of Representatives, 26 March 1973, *Congressional Record: 93rd Congress, Session One*, 9509–10.

25. Ibid.

26. Ibid.

27. *Soul Force*, March–April 1973; Jesse Jackson, telegram to Ralph Abernathy, 5 July 1973, Southern Christian Leadership Conference papers, Emory University, box 42, folder 1.

28. "Abernathy Free after Arrest"; "Abernathy Free on $1,000 Bond."

29. *NBC Evening News,* 9 July 1973; Jahn, "Abernathy Resigns as Leader of SCLC"; Ralph Abernathy, statement of resignation, 9 July 1973, Southern Christian Leadership Conference papers, Emory University, box 64, folder 16; Schulke and McPhee, *King Remembered,* 246.

30. Robert E. Johnson, "Is There a Future for SCLC without Ralph Abernathy?"

31. Ibid.

32. Ibid.

33. "Abernathy, Mrs. King Urged to Bury Hatchet"; "Mrs. King Draws Criticism."

34. Southern Christian Leadership Conference papers, Emory University, box 64, folder 16, contains Coretta Scott King's July 9, 1973, press statement.

35. Southern Christian Leadership Conference papers, Emory University, box 64, folder 16, contains Walter Fauntroy's July 10, 1973, press statement.

36. Southern Christian Leadership Conference papers, Emory University, box 42, folder 2, contains Charles Robert Gordon's July 13, 1973, letter to Ralph Abernathy and the postcard to Abernathy.

37. Rowan, "Is SCLC Irrelevant in New Era?"

38. Ibid.

CHAPTER EIGHTEEN

1. Witcover, *Very Strange Bedfellows,* 249–53.

2. Jordan, *Vernon Can Read!,* 233.

3. "23 Blacks on White House 'Screw' List."

4. Ibid.

5. Roy Wilkins, "The Task Ahead," 3 July 1973, in *In Search of Democracy,* 449–50.

6. Van Der Linden, "Agnew Showing Little Concern about 1976."

7. Witcover, *Very Strange Bedfellows,* 263–66.

8. Witcover, *A Heartbeat Away,* 161.

9. Neal Robinson, letter, July 1973, Southern Christian Leadership Conference papers, Emory University, box 42, folder 2.

10. Tyrone Brooks, letter, 20 July 1973, Southern Christian Leadership Conference papers, Emory University, box 42, folder 3.

11. Southern Christian Leadership Conference staff, letter to board, 11 July 1973, Southern Christian Leadership Conference papers, Emory University, box 64, folder 16.

12. "Gregory Jailed after Protest."

13. Davie, "Agnew's Crisis: A Tangled Web or 'Damn Lies.'"

14. Herblock, editorial cartoon.

15. Witcover, *A Heartbeat Away*, 265–68.

16. Ibid.

17. Spiro Agnew's resignation address, 15 October 1973, in *Nixon: The Fifth Year of His Presidency*, 25.

18. Ibid.

19. Carroll, "Buckley Scores Agnew Position"; "Public Reaction to Agnew Talk Is Found to Be Mostly Negative."

20. Stanley, "Pity Spiro Agnew Not"; Martin, "There Are No Black Tears for Vice President Agnew."

21. *Jet*, 20 December 1973.

22. Karima Al-Amin, interview; Jamil Al-Amin, letter to author.

23. "Morsell Says Agnew Resignation Reveals Nation's Malaise," 351.

24. Mitchell, "Mr. Ford and Civil Rights: A Mixed Record," 7.

25. Katagiri, *The Mississippi State Sovereignty Commission*, 224–26; "Minutes: Mississippi State Sovereignty Commission," 9 November 1973, Papers of the Attorney General, Mississippi Department of Archives and History; "Minutes: Alabama State Sovereignty Commission," 30 September 1973, Papers of the Alabama State Sovereignty Commission; Ledger, 1971–1973, Papers of the Alabama State Sovereignty Commission.

26. John Lewis, quoted in *Voices of Freedom*, 58; William G. Anderson, quoted in *Voices of Freedom*, 102.

27. Associated Press, "Atlantans Voted Issues, Says Winner."

28. Ibid.

29. Ibid.; "Black America Now."

30. "Williams Outlines New SCLC Plan"; "SCLC Chapter Reorganized."

31. "Farmer: Freedom Marches Won't Close Income Gaps, Boost Reading."

32. "Towards Political Sophistication," 6.

33. Jasper, "How Md. 'Fraud' Led to Rap Brown's Legal Genocide."

34. "Drop Riot Charges against Rap Brown."

35. Ibid.

36. "H. Rap Brown Finally Tried in Maryland."

37. Del. Troy Bailey, "When Agnew Was Governor"; Knight, "Rap Hunted and Hounded."

38. Kifner, "New Study Asked in Blacks' Deaths"; "The Police and the Panthers," 27.

39. FBI–New York, 11 December 1973, FBI File of the Student Nonviolent Coordinating Committee.

EPILOGUE

1. "The Keys to the Kingdom."

2. Carlson, "Ford Leadership Questioned by 8."

3. "The Keys to the Kingdom"; Bayard Rustin, *Strategies for Freedom*, 65.

4. "The Keys to the Kingdom."

5. Alan Lupo, quoted in *Voices of Freedom*, 611; Jordan, "Boston Riots a Step Backward."

6. "March Organizers' Goal Rights Movement Rebirth"; Julian Bond, quoted in Smith, *Long Time Gone*, 114.

7. Daniel, "Abernathy Defends Support of Reagan."

8. Abernathy, *And the Walls Came Tumbling Down*, 584, 590–91, 596, 598; "Ralph Abernathy Endorses Reagan"; Donalson, "Abernathy: Reagan Broke Jobs Promise."

9. "Backing Criticized"; Douthat, "Abernathy Feels Frozen Out of King Holiday Observances."

10. Ralph Abernathy, III, interview, May 2011; Abernathy, *And the Walls Came Tumbling Down*, 470–71; *Jet*, 6 November 1989.

11. Wilkins and Mathews, *Standing Fast*, 342–43.

12. Karima Al-Amin, interview; "Rap Brown Conviction Reversed"; Firestone, "Ex-Black Militant Gets Life for Murdering Deputy"; Muhammad, "End the Persecution of Imam Jamil Al-Amin."

Bibliography

BOOKS AND ARTICLES

Abel, Elizabeth. *Signs of the Times: The Visual Politics of Jim Crow.* Berkeley: University of California Press, 2010.

Abernathy, Ralph D. *And the Walls Came Tumbling Down: An Autobiography.* New York: Harper & Row, 1989.

Abernathy, Ralph D. "I Bring an Indictment against the American System," 2 February 1971. In *If They Come in the Morning,* edited by Angela Davis, 265–67. New York: Third, 1971.

"Abernathy Attacks American System." *Telegraph,* 3 March 1972.

"Abernathy Free after Arrest." *Pittsburgh Press,* 14 May 1973.

"Abernathy Free on $1,000 Bond." *Atlanta Daily World,* 15 May 1973.

"Abernathy, Mrs. King Urged to Bury Hatchet." *Rock Hill Herald,* 11 July 1973.

"Abernathy Responds." *New York Times,* 18 July 1971.

"Abernathy Says Third Party May Be Formed." *Jet,* 20 July 1972.

Afro-American. 18 December 1971.

"Agnew Asks Scalp of Yale President." *Milwaukee Journal,* 29 April 1970.

"Agnew Assails Report on Campuses." *Deseret News,* 29 September 1970.

"Agnew Backs Police Action." *Spokesman-Review,* 20 March 1972.

"Agnew Retorts to President of A.B.A. Who Called for Restraint." *New York Times,* 5 July 1970.

"Agnew Says Nixon Wants Cramer, Kirk to Win in November." *Sarasota Herald-Tribune,* 16 October 1970.

"Agnew Says Unfair Innuendos Aimed at Wallace." *The Day,* 16 March 1972.

Agnew, Spiro T. "The 'Root Causes' of Attica." *New York Times,* 17 September 1971.

Aitken, Jonathan. *Nixon: A Life*. Washington, DC: Regnery, 1993.

Albright, Joseph. *What Makes Spiro Run*. New York: Dodd, Mead, 1972.

Ambrose, Stephen E. *Nixon*. Vol. 1. New York: Simon & Schuster, 1991.

Ambrose, Stephen E. *Nixon*. Vol. 2. New York: Simon & Schuster, 1991.

"Americans Pause to Honor Memory of King." *Washington Afro-American*, 19 January 1971.

Anderson, Maurice. "The Young Black Man." *Ebony*, August 1972, 132.

"Angela Pleads for Abolition of U.S. Prisons." *Modesto Bee*, 17 August 1972.

Arnold, Martin. "Newark Meeting on Black Power Attended by 400." *New York Times*, 20 July 1967, 8.

"Assassins Shake Faith in Politics." *Milwaukee Journal*, 16 May 1972.

Associated Press. "Atlantans Voted Issues, Says Winner." *Tri City Herald*, 17 October 1973.

"Backing Criticized." *Press-Courier*, 18 October 1980.

Bailey, Del. Troy. "When Agnew Was Governor." *Baltimore Afro-American*, 6 November 1973.

Bailey, Peter. "Black Excellence in the 'Wasteland.'" *Ebony*, March 1972, 44–46.

Baraka, Amiri. "Speech to the Congress of African Peoples," September 1970. In *Modern Black Nationalism*, edited by Molefi K. Asante, 145–57. New York: New York University Press, 1997.

Beal, Frances. "Double Jeopardy." In *The Black Woman: An Anthology*, edited by Toni Cade, 109–22. New York: New American Library, 1970.

Beal, Frances. "The U.S. vs. H. Rap Brown." *Amsterdam News*, 1 April 1972.

Belafonte, Harry. *My Song: A Memoir*. New York: Knopf, 2011.

Bell, Ray. "6 Dead as Racial Violence Breaks Out in Augusta." Harlan *Daily Enterprise*, 12 May 1970.

"Benefit Concert to Aid 'Anemia.'" *San Antonio Express*, 15 June 1972.

Bennett, Lerone. "The Emancipation Orgasm." *Ebony*, September 1971.

Bernstein, Carl. "2d Bel Air Car-Bomb Victim Identified as SNCC Worker." *Washington Post*, 12 March 1970.

Bigart, Homer. "Kunstler Sees 'Fear' at Site of Rap Brown Trial." *New York Times*, 10 March 1970, 34.

"Black America Now." *Newsweek*, 19 February 1973, 29, 34.

"Black Expo '71 Brings Biggest Cadre of Businessmen, Politicians, Entertainers." *Jet*, 21 October 1971, 56.

"Black Leaders Eye Coalition Proposal." *Jet*, 20 January 1972, 12–14.

"Black Manifesto." In *Modern Black Nationalism: from Marcus Garvey to Louis Farrakhan*, edited by William L. Van Deburg, 182–87. New York: New York University Press, 1997.

"Black Owes Victory to Coalition." *Lakeland Ledger*, 10 November 1972.

"Black People Make Fool of Kirk." *Ghetto Voice*, 15 August 1967.

"Black Raps 'Exploitation' in Movies." *Eugene Register-Guard*, 21 September 1972.

"Blacks Protest Apollo 14 Shot." *Rome News-Tribune*, 2 February 1971.

"Blacks Want China Briefing." *Reading Eagle*, 14 December 1971.

"Bombing: A Way of Protest and Death." *Time*, 23 March 1970.

Boesel, David, and Peter H. Rossi, eds. *Cities under Siege: An Anatomy of the Ghetto Riots, 1964–1968*. New York: Basic, 1971.

Book Review. *New York Times*, 12 March 1972.

Branch, Taylor. *At Canaan's Edge: America in the King Years, 1965–68*. New York: Simon & Schuster, 2006.

Branch, Taylor. "The Last Wish of Martin Luther King." *New York Times*, 6 April 2008.

"Brown Freed to Fulminate." *Star-News*, 28 July 1967.

Brown, H. Rap. *Die Nigger Die!* Chicago: Chicago Review, 1969.

"Brown Sentenced for Gun Carrying." *Pittsburgh Courier*, 10 June 1972.

Brown, Warren. "Just a Drop in the Bucket of Oppression," *Jet*, 23 November 1972, 26–31.

Buckley, William F., Jr. "Abernathy Used by Reds to Promote Propaganda." *Beaver County Times*, 30 December 1972.

Bunting, Ken. "Black San Antonio IV: Liberation." *San Antonio Express*, 16 February 1972.

Bunting, Ken. "Black San Antonio V: Political Inroads." *San Antonio Express*, 17 February 1972.

Buresh, Bernice. "NAACP Raps Decision on Schools." *Milwaukee Sentinel*, 4 July 1969.

Burks, Edward C. "Brown Is Arraigned in Hospital in Robbery and Murder Attempt." *New York Times*, 21 October 1971.

Burns, Rebecca. *Burial for a King: Martin Luther King's Funeral and the Week that Transformed Atlanta and Rocked the Nation*. New York: Scribner, 2011.

Cady, Steve. "A Day for Harlem to Pay Its Respect." *New York Times*, 26 October 1972.

"Cambridge Negroes Resume Protests." *Student Voice*, 3 March 1964, 2.

"Campus Panelist Upset That Nixon Lets Agnew Speak." *New York Times*, 6 July 1970.

"Campus Unrest Panelist Says 'Real' Issues Are Being Ignored." *New York Times*, 2 November 1970.

"Capitol Hill Rally Ends 17-Day Drive." *Pittsburgh Press*, 5 May 1971.

Carlson, Gene. "Ford Leadership Questioned by 8." *Washington Afro-American*, 2 November 1974.

Carmichael, Stokely. *Ready for Revolution: The Life and Struggles of Stokely Carmichael (Kwame Ture)*. New York: Scribner, 2003.

Carroll, Maurice. "Buckley Scores Agnew Position." *New York Times*, 16 October 1973.

Carson, Clayborne. *In Struggle: SNCC and the Black Awakening of the 1960s*. Cambridge, MA: Harvard University Press, 1981.

"Cautious Optimism Prevails in Racially Tense Area." *Rome News-Tribune,* 5 January 1970.

"Charles Evers Has a Dream for His Town." *Spartanburg Herald,* 15 May 1969.

"Che Buried in Hometown." *Baltimore Afro-American,* 21 March 1970.

Chisholm, Shirley. *The Good Fight.* New York: Harper and Row, 1973.

"Choice at Hand for McGovern." *Spokesman-Review,* 3 August 1972.

Christopulos, Mike. "U.S. Justified in Expelling Duo." *Milwaukee Sentinel,* 30 October 1968.

Citizen. December 1971.

"Civil Rights Victory Follows Death of Alabama Girl." *Jet,* 7 October 1971, 12.

Clarity, James F. "Rap Brown Wounded Here in Shootout after Holdup." *New York Times,* 17 October 1971.

Clarke, Thurston. *The Last Campaign: Robert F. Kennedy and 82 Days That Inspired America.* New York: Holt, 2009.

Clay, William L. *Just Permanent Interests: Black Americans in Congress, 1870– 1991.* New York: Amistad, 1992.

"Clergyman Winner in D.C. Voting." *Toledo Blade,* 24 March 1971.

Clifford, James O. "Newton: Panthers Shifting Strategy." *St. Petersburg Times,* 31 January 1972.

Cohen, Ronald G. "View Violence in America as Product of History, Materialism, Gun Fetish." *Youngstown Vindicator,* 7 June 1968.

Collins, George W. "They're Bitter, Fearful, Bewildered." *Baltimore Afro-American,* 5 August 1967.

Conaway, James. "Sammy Davis, Jr. Has Bought the Bus." *New York Times,* 15 October 1972.

Congressional Record: 90th Congress, Session One. Washington, DC: United States Government Printing Office, 1967.

Congressional Record: 91st Congress, Session Two. Washington, DC: United States Government Printing Office, 1970.

Congressional Record: 92nd Congress, Session One. Washington, DC: United States Government Printing Office, 1971.

Congressional Record: 92nd Congress, Session Two. Washington, DC: United States Government Printing Office, 1972.

Congressional Record: 93rd Congress, Session One. Washington, DC: United States Government Printing Office, 1973.

"Convention Demonstrations Planned by 3 Black Groups." *Toledo Blade,* 1 July 1972.

"CORE Constitution Rejected; Members Set August Meet." *Washington Afro-American,* 9 July 1968.

"CORE Leaders Pledge New Militancy." *Milwaukee Journal,* 17 September 1968.

"Coretta King: In Her Husband's Footsteps." *Ebony,* September 1968.

Cotton, Dorothy F. *If Your Back's Not Bent*. New York: Atria, 2012.

Cunningham, David. *There's Something Happening Here: The New Left, the Klan, and FBI Counterintelligence*. Berkeley: University of California Press, 2005.

Current, Gloster B. "The Hot Sixtieth—A Memorable Convention." *The Crisis*, August–September 1969, 293.

Current, Gloster B. "The 61st Annual Convention—Arousing a National Storm." *The Crisis*, August–September 1970, 255–56.

"Daley Foe Says He's 'About Even.'" *Rock Hill Herald*, 1 April 1971.

Daley, Robert. "The Man Who Shot Rap Brown." *New York*, 23 October 1972, 39, 41–42.

Dandridge, Gloria Richardson. "The Energy of People Passing through Me." In *Hands on the Freedom Plow: Personal Accounts by Women in SNCC*, edited by Faith S. Holsaert et al., 273–97. Urbana: University of Illinois Press, 2010.

Daniel, Leon. "Abernathy Defends Support of Reagan." *Youngstown Vindicator*, 20 November 1980.

D'Arazien, Steven. "Spring Offensive: Scenario for Peace." *Village Voice*, 15 April 1971.

D'Arcus, Bruce. "Protest, Scale, and Publicity." *Antipode*, 730–31.

Darnton, John. "Citizens' Panel Assails Law Enforcement Officials Who Carried Out Chicago Panther Raid." *New York Times*, 3 November 1972.

Davie, Michael. "Agnew's Crisis: A Tangled Web or 'Damn Lies.'" *The Age*, 13 August 1973.

Davis, Angela. *Angela Davis: An Autobiography*. New York: Random House, 1974.

Davis, Mike. "Eyewitness Report from Mike Davis." *Baltimore Afro-American*, 13 February 1968.

Davis, Sammy, Jr., "Why I Went to the Troops." *Ebony*, June 1972, 141.

De Groot, Gerard J. *Dark Side of the Moon: The Magnificent Madness of the American Lunar Quest*. New York: New York University Press, 2006.

Delaney, Paul. "Black Supporters of President Under Fire." *New York Times*, 17 October 1972.

"Delay Start of Georgia SCLC March." *Lewiston Evening Journal*, 19 May 1970.

DeLeon, Robert A. "A Look at Angela Davis from Another Angle: Her Jail Cell." *Jet*, 24 February 1972, 12–13.

"Demonstrators Pray for End to Hunger, Successful Flight." *Eugene Register-Guard*, 16 July 1969.

Doggett, Peter. *There's a Riot Going On: Revolutionaries, Rock Stars, and the Rise and Fall of the '60s*. Edinburgh, UK: Canongate, 2007.

Donalson, Al. "Abernathy: Reagan Broke Jobs Promise." *Pittsburgh Press*, 8 January 1982.

"Dope Is Death." *Albany Student Union*, 3 December 1971, 5.

Douglas, Carlyle C. "Ralph Abernathy." *Ebony*, January 1970.

Douthat, Strat. "Abernathy Feels Frozen Out of King Holiday Observances." *Fredericksburg Free Lance-Star*, 16 January 1986.

"Drop Riot Charges against Rap Brown." *Jet*, 22 November 1973. "Editorial." *The Citizen*, May 1968.

"Editorial." *The Crisis*, April 1967, 127.

"Editorial." *The Crisis*, June–July 1966, 299.

"Editorial." *Triple Jeopardy*, September–October 1972, 4.

Ehrlichman, John. *Witness to Power: The Nixon Years*. New York: Simon & Schuster, 1982.

"Employment Programs Begin in Cambridge." *Student Voice*, 9 June 1964, 4.

Evans, Rowland, and Ralph Novak. *Nixon in the White House: The Frustration of Power*. New York: Random House, 1971.

"Excerpts from Supreme Court Ruling That Voids Key Part of the Voting Rights Act." *Washington Post*, 26 June 2013.

Face the Nation: The Collected Transcripts from the CBS Radio and Television Broadcasts. New York: Holt Information Systems.

Fager, Charles. *Uncertain Resurrection*. Grand Rapids, MI: Eerdmans, 1969.

Fairclough, Adam. *Martin Luther King, Jr.* Athens: University of Georgia Press, 1995.

Fairclough, Adam. *To Redeem the Soul of America: the Southern Christian Leadership Conference and Martin Luther King, Jr.* Athens: University of Georgia Press, 1987.

"Farmer: Freedom Marches Won't Close Income Gaps, Boost Reading." *Afro-American*, December 1973, 18–22.

"Federal Building Picketed." *San Antonio Light*, 21 July 1973.

"Fence Section Torn Down Near Hall." *Bangor Daily News*, 11 July 1972.

Firestone, David. "Ex-Black Militant Gets Life for Murdering Deputy." *New York Times*, 14 March 2002.

"$5 Million Cast Sings with Mitch for Racial Harmony and Love." *Jet*, 25 December 1969, 8–9.

"Florida Governor Snubbed by Black Power Advocate." *Press-Courier*, 10 August 1967.

Forman, James. *The Making of Black Revolutionaries: A Personal Account*. New York: Macmillan, 1972.

"Four More Years of the Same." *The Crisis*, December 1972, 329.

Franklin, Ben A. "Mourning for Dr. King Ended." *New York Times*, 17 August 1969.

Franklin, Ben A. "The Poor." *New York Times*, 18 May 1969.

Franklin, Ben A. "S.N.C.C. Chief Shot in Cambridge, Md." *New York Times*, 25 June 1967, 1, 20.

Fraser, C. Gerald. "SNCC in Decline after 8 Years in Lead." *New York Times*, 7 October 1968.

"Freedom News." *The Crisis*, December 1966, 549.

Gent, George. "TV: Racial Attitudes Poll." *New York Times*, 3 September 1968.

Gentry, Curt. *J. Edgar Hoover*. New York: W. W. Norton, 1991.

Gertsel, Steven. "Young: Liberate or Exterminate." *Star-News*, 28 July 1967.

Giddings, Paula. *When and Where I Enter: The Impact of Black Women on Race and Sex in America*. New York: Morrow, 1984.

Glick, Brian. *War at Home: Covert Action against U.S. Activists and What We Can Do about It*. Cambridge, MA: South End, 1999.

Good, Paul. "'No Man Can Fill Dr. King's Shoes'—But Abernathy Tries." *New York Times Magazine*, 25 May 1968.

"Goodbye to Wing-Tips." *Time*, 19 November 1973.

"Gregory Jailed after Protest." *Washington Afro-American*, 14 August 1973.

Guerrero, Ed. *Framing Blackness: The African American Image in Film*. Philadelphia: Temple University Press, 1993.

Guralnick, Peter. *Sweet Soul Music: Rhythm and Blues and the Southern Dream of Freedom*. New York: Little, Brown, 1999.

"Gwynn Oak Park to Admit Negroes." *New York Times*, 20 July 1963.

Halberstam, David. *The Children*. New York: Random House, 1998.

Haldeman, H. R. *The Haldeman Diaries*. New York: Berkley, 1995.

Hampton, Henry, and Steve Fayer, eds. *Voices of Freedom: An Oral History of the Civil Rights Movement from the 1950s through the 1980s*. New York: Bantam, 1990.

Harris, Louis. "Little Change in Esteem for Blacks." *St. Petersburg Times*, 13 January 1972.

Harrist, Ron. "Negroes Mourn Slain Girl as Drew Tension Dissipates." *Jackson Clarion-Ledger*, 30 May 1971.

"Hasty FBI Report on Car Blast Irks Civic Leaders." *Baltimore Afro-American*, 17 March 1970.

Hayden, Tom. *Trial*. New York: Holt, Rinehart, and Winston, 1970.

Hayden, Tom. "The Trial." *Ramparts*, July 1970.

Haygood, Wil. *In Black and White: The Life of Sammy Davis, Jr.* New York: Alfred A. Knopf, 2003.

Heppermann, Ann, and Kara Oehler. "This Weekend in 1968: The Legacy of Resurrection City." *Weekend America*. National Public Radio, 8 May 2008.

Herbers, John. "Johnson Mediates a Rights Dispute." *New York Times*, 13 December 1972.

Herblock. Editorial cartoon. *Washington Post*, 2 October 1973.

Herrington, Gregg. "Fauntroy Wins D.C. Election." *Fredericksburg Free Lance-Star*, 13 January 1971.

Higgins, Chester. "Meet the Man Behind 'Sweetback' Movie." *Jet*, 1 July 1971.

Honey, Michael K. *Going Down Jericho Road*. New York: W. W. Norton, 2007.

"Hot Camp-In Ahead." *Spokesman-Review*, 24 March 1968.

"H. Rap Brown Finally Tried in Maryland." *New Journal and Guide*, 17 November 1973.

Hunter, Charlayne. "Black Women's Lib Groups Think 'Sexism' Irrelevant." *The Day*, 18 November 1970.

"Integration: Military Style." *The Crisis*, December 1966, 526.

"In the Nation's Press." *The Crisis*, August–September 1970, 276–82.

"It's Nation Time." *Ebony*, December 1970.

"Jackie Robinson Bolts Republicans." *Windsor Star*, 10 August 1968.

Jackson, George. *Soledad Brother*. New York: Bantam, 1970.

Jahn, Ed. "Abernathy Resigns as Leader of SCLC." *Atlanta Journal*, 9 July 1973.

Jasper, John. "How Md. 'Fraud' Led to Rap Brown's Legal Genocide." *Baltimore Afro-American*, 13 November 1973.

Jay, Peter A. "Woman Sought in Bombing at Cambridge." *Washington Post*, 12 March 1970.

"Jesse Jackson: Heir to Dr. King?" *Harper's Magazine*, March 1969.

"Johnson Advised Blacks at Symposium in Texas." *Jet*, 8 February 1973.

Johnson, Robert E. "Is There a Future for SCLC without Ralph Abernathy?" *Jet*, 16 August 1973.

Johnson, Thomas A. "5-Day March in Georgia Ends with Massive Rally." *New York Times*, 24 May 1970.

Jordan, Vernon E., Jr. "Boston Riots a Step Backward." *Evening Independent*, 4 October 1974.

Jordan, Vernon E., Jr. "To Be Equal." *The Afro-American*, 8 April 1972.

Jordan, Vernon E., Jr. *Vernon Can Read!: A Memoir*. New York: Public Affairs, 2001.

Joseph, Peniel. *Waiting 'til the Midnight Hour*. New York: Henry Holt, 2006.

"Justice Department Files Suit." *Sumter Daily Item*, 14 February 1968.

Katagiri, Yasuhiro. *The Mississippi Sovereignty Commission*. Jackson: University Press of Mississippi, 2001.

Kidd, Paul. "Peace March Was Just That." *Calgary Herald*, 26 April 1971.

Kifner, John. "Court Voids 5 Convictions in 1968 Convention Case." *New York Times*, 22 November 1972.

Kifner, John. "New Study Asked in Blacks' Deaths." *New York Times*, 8 November 1973.

King, Coretta Scott. "Statement by Coretta Scott King." 4 June 1971. In *If They Come in the Morning*, edited by Angela Davis, 282–83. New York: Third, 1971.

King, Martin Luther, Jr. *Where Do We Go from Here: Chaos or Community?* New York: Harper & Row, 1967.

"King Refuses to Take Slap at 'Black Power.'" *Tuscaloosa News*, 17 October 1966.

"King Renews Appeal for Non-Violent Action." *Lexington Dispatch*, 20 October 1966.

"Kirk Grandstand Plays Frustrate His Opponents." *St. Petersburg Times*, 15 August 1967.

Knight, Nathaniel. "Rap Hunted and Hounded." *Baltimore Afro-American*, 6 November 1973.

Kotz, Nick. *Judgment Days: Lyndon Baines Johnson, Martin Luther King, Jr., and the Laws That Changed America*. New York: Houghton Mifflin, 2005.

Kupcinet, Irv. "Kup's Column." *Anchorage Daily News*, 28 October 1972.

Landess, Thomas H., and Richard M. Quinn. *Jesse Jackson & the Politics of Race*. Ottawa, IL: Jameson, 1985.

"LBJ Urges Blacks to Reason with Nixon on Civil Rights." *Jet*, 28 December 1972.

Leifermann, Henry P. "Middle-Class Negroes Scrambling to Lead Own Race in New Revolution." *Bryan Times*, 16 January 1968.

LeMaistre, George, Jr. "Abernathy: Love, Not Hate." *Jackson Clarion-Ledger*, 31 May 1971.

LeMaistre, George, Jr. "Miss Collier's Funeral May Be at School." *Delta Democrat-Times*, 28 May 1971.

Lesher, Stephan. *George Wallace: American Populist*. Reading, MA: Addison-Wesley, 1994.

Lester, Julius. *Look Out, Whitey! Black Power's Gon' Get Your Mama!* New York: Dial, 1968.

Lewis, John. Interview. *Andrea Mitchell Reports*, MSNBC, 25 June 2013.

Lewis, John. *Walking with the Wind*. New York: Simon & Schuster, 1998.

Lippman, Theo, Jr. *Spiro Agnew's America*. New York: W. W. Norton, 1972.

Lodi News-Sentinel. 3 May 1969.

Lucas, Jim G. *Agnew: Profile in Conflict*. New York: Award, 1970.

"Maddox Warns against March." *Reading Eagle*, 19 May 1970.

Mann, Jim. "No Sign of Rap Brown on Bel Air Trial Eve." *Washington Post*, 16 March 1970.

Manns, Adrienne. "Ashes Spread Over Africa." *Baltimore Afro-American*, 17 March 1970.

Manns, Adrienne. "Rap's Trial Delayed." *Baltimore Afro-American*, 17 March 1970.

"March Organizers' Goal Rights Movement Rebirth." *Rock Hill Herald*, 4 July 1974.

Marlow, James. "Civil Rights Protests Are Going Far Afield." *Kentucky New Era*, 9 August 1967.

Marsh, Robert. *Agnew the Unexamined Man: A Political Profile*. New York: M. Evans, 1971.

Martin, Louis. "There Are No Black Tears for Vice President Agnew." *Pittsburgh Courier*, 27 October 1973.

Martinez, Elizabeth Sutherland. "Neither Black Nor White." In *Hands on the Freedom Plow: Personal Accounts by Women in SNCC*, edited by Faith S. Holsaert et al., 531–40. Urbana: University of Illinois Press, 2010.

McGrath, Kathy. "Brave Woman Stands behind Ralph Abernathy." *Calgary Herald*, 17 January 1970.

McKee, Don. "Peace Returns to Orangeburg." *Sumter Daily Item*, 10 February 1968.

Meet the Press: America's Press Conference of the Air. Vols. 12 & 14. Washington, DC: Kelly.

Mills, Kay. *This Little Light of Mine: The Life of Fannie Lou Hamer.* New York: Dutton, 1993.

"Minister Is Threat to Daley." *Palm Beach Post*, 15 February 1971.

Mitchell, Clarence. "Mr. Ford and Civil Rights: A Mixed Record." *The Crisis*, January 1974, 7.

"Mitchell Plans Task Force on Dissidents." *Toledo Blade*, 14 June 1969.

"Morsell Says Agnew Resignation Reveals Nation's Malaise." *The Crisis*, December 1973, 351.

Moser, Richard. *The New Winter Soldiers: GI and Veteran Dissent during the Vietnam Era.* New Brunswick, NJ: Rutgers University, 1996.

Movement. January 1969.

"Mrs. King Draws Criticism." *Rome News-Tribune*, 13 July 1973.

Muhammad, Askia. "End the Persecution of Imam Jamil Al-Amin." *Final Call*, 14 August 2007.

"Mule Power Takes Protest Just 12 Miles." *Windsor Star*, 20 May 1970.

"NAACP 62nd Annual Convention Resolutions," 4–9 July 1971. *The Crisis*, March 1972, 95.

"NAACP Soft Pedals Controversial Issues." *Jet*, 27 July 1972, 46–47.

"Nation 'Died a Little' with King's Death, Reagan Says." *Bulletin*, 6 April 1968.

National Advisory Commission on Civil Disorders. *Report of the National Advisory Commission on Civil Disorders.* Washington, DC: Government Printing Office, 1968.

"National Black Political Agenda." In *The Eyes on the Prize Civil Rights Reader: Documents, Speeches, and Firsthand Accounts from the Black Freedom Struggle*, edited by Clayborne Carson et al., 493–99. New York: Penguin, 1991.

"Negro Brass Feel Nixon on Probation." *Beaver Country Times*, 14 January 1969.

Nelson, Jack, and Jack Bass. *The Orangeburg Massacre.* New York: World Publishing, 1970.

"New Bombing Revives Antiwar Protests." *New York Times*, 23 December 1972.

"New Panther Image: Church and Chickens." *The Age*, 3 April 1972.

"Newspapers Back Kirk's Action." *Sarasota Herald-Tribune*, 13 August 1967.

New York Times. 17 August 1969.

New York Times. 29 August 1968.

"Nixon Administration Target of Attack." *The Crisis*, August–September 1969, 276–77.

"The Nixon Phenomenon." *The Crisis*, November 1972, 293–95.

"Nixon Poverty Speech Draws Bitter Criticism." *Leader-Post*, 3 December 1969.

Nixon, Richard M. *RN: The Memoirs of Richard Nixon.* New York: Grosset and Dunlap, 1978.

Nixon: The Fifth Year of His Presidency. Washington, DC: Congressional Quarterly, 1974.

"Nixon's Busing Stand Wallace Talk Target." *Evening Independent*, 7 March 1972.

"No Apology Made by Agnew, His Critics." *Daytona Beach Morning Journal*, 22 July 1971.

Novak, Ralph. "Jesse Jackson: Martin Luther King's Heir Apparent." *Southeast Missourian*, 7 June 1971.

"Observance by Negroes Included Honoring of Civil Rights Victims." *Palm Beach Post*, 5 July 1969.

"Occasion Called a Party." *New York Times*, 6 October 1971.

"Official: Rap Brown Charge Phony." *Palm Beach Post*, 16 January 1971.

Okoh, Gim. "'White America Killed Our Hopes.'" *Baltimore Afro-American*, 9 April 1968.

Osbourne, John. *The Fourth Year of the Nixon Watch.* New York: Liveright, 1973.

Osbourne, John. *The Third Year of the Nixon Watch.* New York: Liveright, 1972.

Oudes, Bruce, ed. *From the President: Richard Nixon's Secret Files.* New York: Harper and Row, 1989.

Panetta, Leon E., and Peter Gall. *Bring Us Together: The Nixon Team and the Civil Rights Retreat.* Philadelphia: J. B. Lippincott, 1971.

Patton, Gwen. "Born Freedom Fighter." In *Hands on the Freedom Plow: Personal Accounts by Women in SNCC*, edited by Faith S. Holsaert et al., 572–86. Urbana: University of Illinois Press, 2010.

Payne, Charles. *I've Got the Light of Freedom: The Organizing Tradition and the Mississippi Freedom Struggle.* Berkeley: University of California Press, 1995.

Payton, Jack R. "Where's Rap Brown Gone?" *Sun*, 9 November 1970.

Peake, Thomas R. *Keeping the Dream Alive: A History of the Southern Christian Leadership Conference from King to the Nineteen-Eighties.* New York: P. Lang, 1987.

Pearson, Drew. "Fayette—Where History Is Made." *St. Petersburg Times*, 7 July 1969.

Pearson, Drew. "German Claims DeGaulle Not Hero." *Toledo Blade*, 1 August 1967.

Pearson, Hugh. *The Shadow of the Panther*. Reading, MA: Addison-Wesley, 1994.

"People Must Punish Pushers, Bond Declares." *Spartanburg Herald-Journal*, 5 February 1972.

Perlstein, Rick. *Nixonland: The Rise of a President and the Fracturing of America*. New York: Scribner, 2008.

"Police Chief Leads Quiet Drew March." *Jackson Clarion-Ledger*, 28 May 1971.

"Police Line Cuts Momentum of Protest." *Milwaukee Journal*, 11 July 1972.

"The Police and the Panthers." *The Crisis*, January 1974, 27.

"Police Protect March." *Leader-Post*, 22 May 1970.

"The Police vs. the Black Panthers." *The Crisis*, January 1970.

"Poor City Mapped for Dem Convention." *Pittsburgh Press*, 8 June 1972.

"Poor People's Power Pushed." *St. Petersburg Times*, 21 August 1972.

"'Poor' to Meet at Demo Confab." *Evening Independent*, 9 March 1972.

Posner, Gerald. *Motown: Music, Money, Sex and Power*. New York: Random House, 2005.

Post Wire Services. "Busing Amendment Called Wrong Method of Attack." *Palm Beach Post*, 16 February 1972.

"President Vows Violence Won't Take Over Nation." *Spartanburg Herald-Journal*, 29 March 1968.

The President's Commission on Campus Unrest. Washington, DC: Government Printing Office, 1970.

"Price Has Gone Up." *Anchorage Daily News*, 8 July 1972.

Prince, Richard E. "12,000 Blacks March to Support Africa." *Washington Post*, 29 May 1972.

"Prison Conditions Lead to Protests." *Sarasota Herald-Tribune*, 3 October 1971.

"Pro Victory Rally Follows Disobedience." *San Antonio Times*, 7 May 1971.

Public Papers of the Presidents: Lyndon B. Johnson, 1968–69. Book I. Washington, DC: United States Government Printing Office, 1970.

Public Papers of the Presidents: Lyndon B. Johnson, 1967. Book II. Washington, DC: United States Government Printing Office, 1968.

Public Papers of the Presidents: Richard Nixon, 1970. Washington, DC: Government Printing Office, 1971.

Public Papers of the Presidents: Richard Nixon, 1973. Washington, DC: Government Printing Office, 1974.

"Public Reaction to Agnew Talk Is Found to Be Mostly Negative." *New York Times*, 17 October 1973.

Quinlan, James. "Shirley Chisholm: 98-Pound Dynamo." *Palm Beach Post*, 5 March 1972.

"Radicals: Flamingo Park Jamboree." *Time*, 24 July 1972.

"Ralph Abernathy Endorses Reagan." *Fort Scott Tribune*, 17 October 1980.

Rampersad, Arnold. *Jackie Robinson*. New York: Ballantine, 1997.

Ransby, Barbara. *Ella Baker & the Black Freedom Movement: A Radical Democratic Vision*. Chapel Hill: University of North Carolina Press, 2003.

"Rap Brown Conviction Reversed." *Pittsburgh Press*, 25 September 1976.

"Rap Brown Makes Court Appearance." *New York Times*, 14 December 1971.

Raspberry, William. "Vigilante Action Seen against Heroin Pushers." *Spokesman-Review*, 12 February 1972.

Rather, Dan, and Gary Paul Gates. *The Palace Guard*. New York: Harper and Row, 1974.

Reed, Roy. "Dr. King's Followers Modify His Approach in Their Continuing Pursuit of Social Change." *New York Times*, 7 January 1972.

Reinhold, Robert. "Negro on Campus Panel Feels 'Solemn' Duty to Stop Killings." *New York Times*, 15 June 1970.

"Relative Peace Prevails but Techniques Are Argued Over." Bryan *Times*, 13 April 1968.

Reston, James. *The Lone Star: The Life of John Connally*. New York: Harper and Row, 1989.

"Resurrection City Set Up." *Bangor Daily News*, 10 July 1972.

"Revenge for Deaths Threatened by SNCC." *Toledo Blade*, 9 February 1968.

"Rev. King's Widow Backs McGovern." *Milwaukee Sentinel*, 19 May 1972.

"Rev. Young Declares Candidacy for Congress." *Atlanta Daily World*, 6 March 1970.

Rhodes, Joseph, Jr. "The Administration's Vision of the World." *New York Times*, 22 September 1971.

Ridley, Ike. "'Feather' Was Bridegroom of Three Weeks." *Baltimore Afro-American*, 17 March 1970.

Rieder, Jonathan. *The Word of the Lord Is upon Me: The Righteous Performance of Martin Luther King, Jr.* Cambridge, MA: Belknap, 2008.

"Rights Leaders Upset over Child Bill Veto." *Jet*, 30 December 1971.

Ripley, Anthony. "More in Congress Decry the Raids." *New York Times*, 30 December 1972, 1.

Roach, Jack. "GOP Chairman Attacks SCLC." *Charleston News and Courier*, 11 June 1969.

Rome News-Tribune. 7 December 1971.

Rowan, Carl T. "Is SCLC Irrelevant in New Era?" *Bangor Daily News*, 16 July 1973.

Rowan, Carl T. "Violence Is Not Way Blacks Gain Stature." *Spokane Daily Chronicle*, 30 August 1972.

Rummel, Harold. "Kirk Grandstand Plays Frustrate His Opponents." *St. Petersburg Times*, 15 August 1967.

Rustin, Bayard. "Coming of Age Politically." *The Crisis*, November 1972, 298.

Rustin, Bayard. *Strategies for Freedom*. New York: Columbia University Press, 1976.

Ryan, Terry. "Abernathy Marches on Convention." *Pittsburgh Post-Gazette*, 11 July 1972.

"Same Old Thing, Same Old Place." *Jet*, 17 June 1971.

Sanders, Charles L. "Finally I've Begun to Live Again." *Ebony*, November 1970, 172.

Schell, Jonathan. *New Yorker*, 6 January 1973. In *Observing the Nixon Years*, edited by Jonathan Schell, 150–51. New York: Vintage, 1989.

Schulke, Flip, and Penelope McPhee. *King Remembered*. New York: Pocket, 1986.

Schwartz, John. "Between the Lines of the Voting Rights Act." *New York Times*, 25 June 2013.

"SCLC Breaks 15-Year Tradition; Endorses McGovern Campaign." *Washington Afro-American*, 20 August 1972.

"SCLC Chapter Reorganized." *Waycross Journal-Herald*, 3 November 1973.

"SCLC Names 'Bottom' Ten." *Ellensburg Daily Record*, 25 May 1970.

"SCLC President Clashed with Mrs. King over Money Crisis." *Atlanta Daily World*, 7 January 1973.

"SCLC Promotes Williams, Makes Other Staff Changes." *Afro-American*, 20 March 1971.

"SCLC Turns to Politics." *Atlanta Daily World*, 26 May 1970.

Scott, Austin. "Riot-Torn Cities Feel the New Mood of Young Negroes." *Owosso Argus-Press*, 22 August 1967.

Scott, Paul. "Education Official to Get Facts on Campus Revolution." *Rome News-Tribune*, 17 June 1969.

Seale, Bobby. *Seize the Time*. New York: Random House, 1968.

Semple, Robert B., Jr., "Agnew Praises Africans, Chides Some U.S. Blacks." *New York Times*, 18 July 1971.

"A Senseless Killing." *Time*, 7 June 1971.

Seppy, Tom. "Negro Leader Brown Free on $10,000 Bail." *Owosso Argus-Press*, 26 July 1967.

Sibley, John. "Rap Brown Lectures His Jury on 'Peers." *New York Times*, 2 February 1973.

Sibley, John. "Rap Brown and 3 Convicted of Robbery and Assault." *New York Times*, 30 March 1973.

Sibley, John. "Rap Brown Won't Testify; 'Final Witness Contested.'" *New York Times*, 20 March 1973.

"Smith, Carlos Raise Black Power Issue at Games." *Bryan Times*, 17 October 1968.

Smith, Curt. *Long Time Gone*. South Bend, IN: Icraus, 1982.

"Speaking of People." *Ebony*, August 1972, 6–7.

Stacewicz, Richard. *Winter Soldiers: An Oral History of the Vietnam Veterans against the War*. New York: Twayne, 1997.

Stanley, Frank L. "Pity Spiro Agnew Not." *Chicago Defender*, 27 October 1973.

"Stokely Carmichael Expelled by SNCC." *Tuscaloosa News*, 22 August 1968.

"Stokely No Longer Panther." *St. Petersburg Times*, 4 July 1969.

"Strict Delegate Proportion Not Required, U.S. Court Rules." *Lewiston Morning Tribune*, 20 June 1972.

"Students Stage Sympathy Marches across Alabama." *Gadsden Times*, 4 April 1968.

Taraborrelli, J. Randy. *Michael Jackson: The Magic, the Madness, the Whole Story*. New York: Grand Central, 2010.

Thimmesch, Nick. "Leftward Ho with Whitney Young?" *Post-Dispatch*, 20 July 1970.

Thimmesch, Nick. "Wallace Pours It On in Florida." *Sarasota Herald-Tribune*, 9 March 1972.

"The Third Conrad Kent Rivers Memorial Award." *Negro Digest*, January 1970.

Thomas, Sylvia. "Methodists Okay Controversial Legal Assistance Fund." *San Antonio Express*, 31 May 1972.

"Thousands See King's Body in Spelman Chapel." *Rome News-Tribune*, 8 April 1968.

"Tommie Smith Carols Return in Grim and Silent Mood." *Miami News*, 22 October 1968.

"Towards Political Sophistication." *The Crisis*, January 1974, 6.

"Trial: Back to Chicago." *Time*, 26 September 1969.

Tully, Andrew. "King and the Panthers." *Lodi News-Sentinel*, 19 January 1970.

"23 Blacks on White House 'Screw' List." *Baltimore Afro-American*, 30 June 1973.

"2 Policemen Hurt in Clash at School." *New York Times*, 17 March 1970, 32.

"2,500 Attend Robinson's Funeral." *Bulletin*, 28 October 1972.

United Press International. "SCLC Leader Angry." *Rome News Tribune*, 5 March 1973.

"The Urban Coalition." *Ebony*, November 1967, 134.

"U.S. Files New Orangeburg Suit." *Milwaukee Journal*, 14 February 1968.

"Vandals Destroy SCLC Food." *Sarasota Herald-Tribune*, 12 July 1972.

Van Der Linden, Frank. "Agnew Showing Little Concern about 1976." *Lexington Dispatch*, 30 April 1973.

Varela, Maria. "Time to Get Ready." In *Hands on the Freedom Plow. Personal Accounts by Women in SNCC*, edited by Faith S. Holsaert et al., 552–72. Urbana: University of Illinois Press, 2010.

"Viet Veterans Fling Medals on Capitol Steps." *Montreal Gazette*, 24 April 1971.

Village Voice. 23 September 1971.

"War Foes Shift Focus of Protest." *Boca Raton News*, 29 April 1971.

Washington Afro-American. 21 September 1971.

Washington Post. 25 April 1971.

Washington Post. 16 October 1973, 1.

Weiss, Nancy J. *Whitney M. Young, Jr. and the Struggle for Civil Rights.* Princeton, NJ: Princeton University Press, 1989.

"Welfare Militants Threaten 'Long, Hot Summer.'" *Human Events*, 3 March 1973.

"We're Not Afraid. . . . We're Gonna Die for Our People." *Washington Post*, 6 April 1968.

West, Hollie I. "Pop Artists Prove 'Winner' in Ghetto." *Washington Post*, 21 April 1968.

"Whatever Happened to Robert F. Williams." *Ebony*, December 1972, 202.

White, Theodore H. *The Making of the President, 1972.* New York: Atheneum, 1973.

"Whitney Young Denies He Is Anti-Negro." *Palm Beach Post*, 20 July 1970.

Wilkins, Roy. "The NAACP and the Black Political Convention." *The Crisis*, August–September 1972, 229–30.

Wilkins, Roy. "Gary's Errors, Successes." *The Afro-American*, 8 April 1972.

Wilkins, Roy. "A Letdown in Atlanta." *Baltimore Afro-American*, 24 November 1970.

Wilkins, Roy. "Panthers and Gun Rhetoric." *Baltimore Afro-American*, 7 March 1972.

Wilkins, Roy, and Tom Mathews. *Standing Fast: The Autobiography of Roy Wilkins.* New York: Viking, 1982.

"Wilkins Tops Rights Leadership Poll." *The Crisis*, November 1967, 457.

"Williams Outlines New SCLC Plan." *Afro-American*, 1 December 1973.

"Williams Takes SCLC Greetings on Visit to Mao." *Palm Beach Post*, 20 September 1971.

"Williams to Model Strategy on Mao's." *New York Times*, 29 October 1971.

Wilson, Sondra Kathryn, ed. *In Search of Democracy: The NAACP Writings of James Weldon Johnson, Walter White, and Roy Wilkins.* New York: Oxford University Press, 1999.

Witcover, Jules. *A Heartbeat Away.* New York: Viking, 1974.

Witcover, Jules. *Very Strange Bedfellows: The Short and Unhappy Marriage of Richard Nixon and Spiro Agnew.* New York: Public Affairs, 2008.

Witcover, Jules. *White Knight: The Rise of Spiro Agnew.* New York: Random House, 1972.

Witcover, Jules. *The Year the Dream Died: Revisiting 1968 in America.* New York: Warner, 1997.

"Words of the Week." *Jet*, 3 December 1970, 30.

"Yale Strike Urged to Black Panthers." *New York Times*, 21 April 1970.

Young, Andrew. *An Easy Burden: The Civil Rights Movement and the Transformation of America*. Waco, TX: Baylor University Press, 2008.

"The Young Black Man." *Ebony*, August 1972, 130.

Young, Whitney M. *Beyond Racism: Building an Open Society*. New York: McGraw-Hill, 1969.

Zellner, Bob, and Constance Curry. *The Wrong Side of Murder Creek: A White Southerner in the Freedom Movement*. Montgomery, AL: New South, 2008.

Zellner, Dorothy M. "My Real Vocation." In *Hands on the Freedom Plow: Personal Accounts by Women in SNCC*, edited by Faith S. Holsaert et al., 311–26. Urbana: University of Illinois Press, 2010.

"The Zippie-Hippie Miami Freak Show." *Human Events*, 22 July 1972, 5.

PERIODICALS

Jet. Issues of 30 May 1968, 4 July 1968, 11 July 1968, 8 August 1968, 11 June 1970, 20 January 1972, 3 February 1972, 25 January 1973, 20 December 1973, 6 November 1989.

Soul Force. Issues of 13 August 1969, July–August 1971, September 1971, November–December 1971, March 1972, April–May 1972, July–August 1972, September–October 1972, November–December 1972, March–April 1973.

FILMS

"Awakenings." *Eyes on the Prize*. Documentary film. Produced by Judith Veccione. Blackside, 1986.

The Ed Sullivan Show. 22 March 1970. Television series episode. Produced by Robert Precht. Sullivan Productions, 1970.

"Homefront, USA." *Vietnam: A Television History*. Documentary film. Produced by Richard Ellison and Elizabeth Deane. WGBH Boston, 1983.

"The Keys to the Kingdom." *Eyes on the Prize II*. Produced by Jacqueline Shearer. Documentary film. Blackside, 1989.

"A Nation of Law." *Eyes on the Prize II*. Documentary film. Produced by Sam Pollard and Sheila Bernard. Blackside, 1989.

"Part 5: Wounded Knee." *We Shall Remain*. Documentary film. Produced by Mark Samels and Sharon Grimberg. American Experience, 2009.

"The Promised Land." *Eyes on the Prize II*. Documentary film. Produced by Paul Stekkler and Jacqueline Shearer. Blackside, 1989.

TELEVISION NEWS SERIES

ABC Evening News
CBS Evening News
The Huntley-Brinkley Report
NBC Nightly News

LECTURES

Phillips, Kimberley. Harvard University, Cambridge, MA, July 2011.

ARCHIVAL SOURCES

COINTELPRO: The Counter-Intelligence Program of the FBI: Black Nationalist Hate Groups. Microfilm reels. Lamont Library, Harvard University.

The Confidential File of the Johnson White House, Part 1: Confidential Name and Subject Files, Lamont Library, Harvard University.

Executive Records of Governor Spiro T. Agnew, 1967–1969. Maryland State Archives.

FBI File on Coretta Scott King. *FBI Reading Room.* www.fbi.gov.

FBI Files on the Student Nonviolent Coordinating Committee. *FBI Reading Room.* www.fbi.gov.

"Freedom of Information and Privacy Acts: Martin Luther King, Jr." 31 January 1977. *FBI Reading Room.* www.fbi.gov.

Hosea Williams Collection. Auburn Avenue Research Library.

Mario Marcel Salas Papers. The University of Texas at San Antonio.

The Martin Luther King Jr. Center for Nonviolent Social Change.

Mississippi State Sovereignty Commission. Mississippi Department of Archives and History.

Papers of the Alabama State Sovereignty Commission. Alabama Department of Archives and History.

Papers of the Attorney General. Mississippi Department of Archives and History.

Papers of the Nixon White House. Harvard University.

Personal Files of President Richard M. Nixon. Lamont Library, Harvard University.

Records of the Southern Christian Leadership Conference. Lamont Library, Harvard University.

Southern Christian Leadership Conference papers. Emory University.

Student Nonviolent Coordinating Committee Papers. Microfilm reels. Lamont Library, Harvard University.

PERSONAL INTERVIEWS AND LETTERS

Abernathy, Ralph, III. May 2011.
Aiken, Beckie. 2010.
Al-Amin, Jamil. 20 October 2012.
Al-Amin, Karima. 3 October 2012.
Beal, Fran. 6 January 2011.
Bond, Julian. 20 July 2013.
Clay, Bill. 13 July 2012.
Donegan, Bishop. Letter to Rector Weeks, 23 July 1969.
Jackson, Mae. 20 October 2010, 22 October 2010, 4 November 2010, 5 August 2012.
Jenks, Br. Christopher. 2010.
Patton, Gwen. 13 January 2011.
Salas, Mario. 20 April 2010.

Index

 403

About the Author

Christopher P. Lehman is a professor of ethnic studies at Saint Cloud State University in Saint Cloud, Minnesota. His honors include a *Choice* Outstanding Academic Title award for his book *The Colored Cartoon* and a visiting fellowship at the W. E. B. Du Bois Institute at Harvard University.

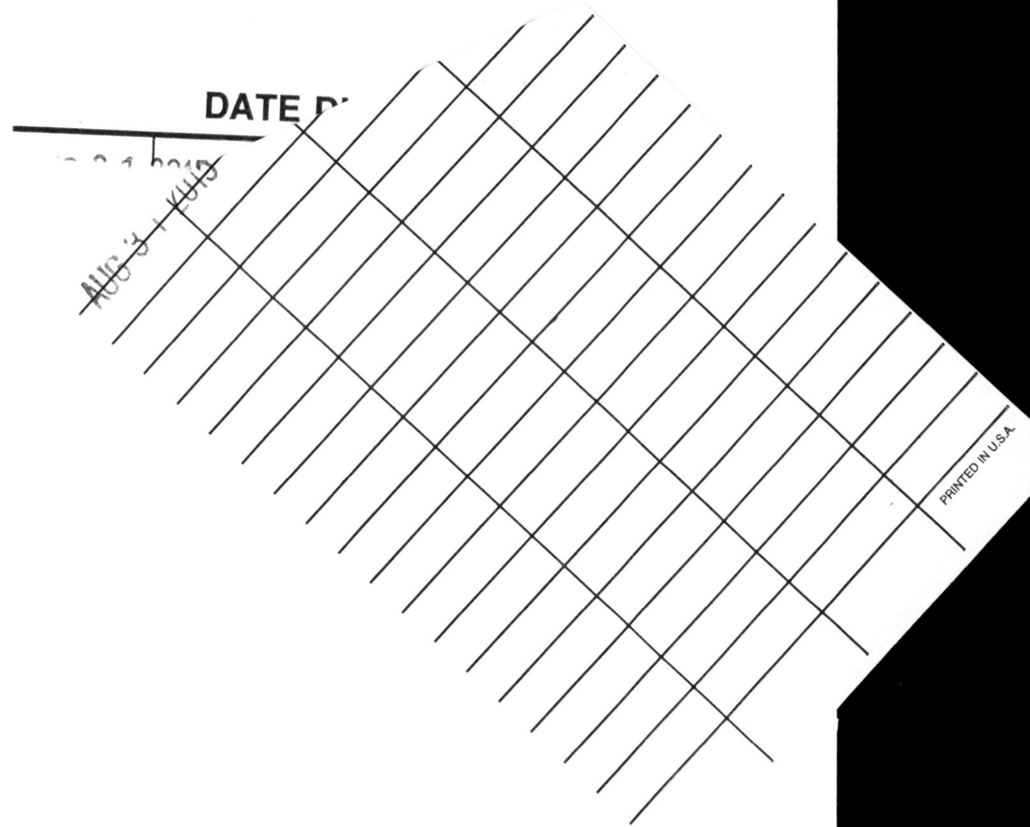
DATE DUE
AUG 3 1 2015
PRINTED IN U.S.A.